Stephen Dowell

A Sketch of the History of Taxes

in England from the Earliest Times to the Present Day - Vol. 1

Stephen Dowell

A Sketch of the History of Taxes
in England from the Earliest Times to the Present Day - Vol. 1

ISBN/EAN: 9783337096748

Printed in Europe, USA, Canada, Australia, Japan

Cover: Foto ©ninafisch / pixelio.de

More available books at **www.hansebooks.com**

A SKETCH

OF THE

HISTORY OF TAXES

IN ENGLAND

FROM THE EARLIEST TIMES TO THE PRESENT DAY

BY

STEPHEN DOWELL

VOL. I.—TO THE CIVIL WAR, 1642

'The revenue of the State is the State. In effect all depends upon it, whether for support or for reformation'—BURKE, *Reflections on the Revolution in France*

LONDON
LONGMANS, GREEN, AND CO.
1876

All rights reserved

TO

SIR WILLIAM HENRY STEPHENSON, K.C.B.

THE CHAIRMAN OF THE
BOARD OF 'COMMISSIONERS OF INLAND REVENUE,'

THIS VOLUME

IS,

WITH HIS PERMISSION,

RESPECTFULLY INSCRIBED

BY

THE AUTHOR.

PREFACE.

THIS volume forms the first Part of a work having for object to render easier the path of fiscal inquiry by giving something between a history and the sketch of a history of the various taxes imposed in this country from the earliest times to the present day. The style of writing used is lighter than that usually adopted in treating a fiscal subject; but the reader should not infer from that attempt in his service any want of care in regard to accuracy: the text may be tested in this point by means of the references to the Parliamentary Rolls, the Statute-book and other authorities given in the Notes. Some General Remarks embodied in the volume should be taken as little more than memoranda of certain points of contemporaneous national history, inserted with a view to recall to mind the altered circumstances of the country during the different periods into which the narrative is divided; to prevent, by effective separation of those periods, too continuous a strain on the reader's attention; and to enable the introduction of several points of minor importance, interesting nevertheless as having a certain bearing upon or connexion with the main subject of the volume.

Originally, the work was cast in one volume, in two parts; but in progress, it has been found expedient to change the original plan and publish the parts in separate volumes.

INLAND REVENUE OFFICE, SOMERSET HOUSE:
March 1876.

CONTENTS.

A SKETCH OF THE HISTORY OF TAXES IN THIS COUNTRY.

PART I.

FROM THE EARLIEST TIMES TO THE CIVIL WAR.

CHAPTER I.

	PAGE
Preliminary observations	1

CHAPTER II.

ANCIENT BRITAIN.

Probable sources of revenue	6
A precedent for the match tax	8

CHAPTER III.

FROM THE ROMAN CONQUEST OF BRITAIN TO THE NORMAN CONQUEST OF ENGLAND.

Character of Roman taxation generally	10
Roman taxation in Britain	10
Direct taxes:—1. Tithe of produce of lands. 2. The scriptura, or tax on cattle. 3. Capitation taxes. 4. Tax on the bodies of the dead	11

	PAGE
Indirect taxes	13
A few remarks on the subject of Roman taxation generally	14
Direct taxes:—1. Tribute from lands. 2. Taxes on houses. 3. Succession taxes. 4. Taxes on animals. 5. Income taxes on tradesmen, &c. 6. Tax on senators. 7. Taxes on persons	14
Indirect taxes:—The portoria. Auction and sale duties	16
Other means of revenue	17
State of the country after the departure of the Romans	17
The English conquest	19
Foundation of the Kingdom of England	20
Principal sources of revenue in the Heptarchic kingdoms and England before the Norman conquest	20
Taxes:—Fumage. The Dangeld. Shipgeld	21

CHAPTER IV.

FROM THE NORMAN CONQUEST TO THE COMMENCEMENT OF TAXATION OF MOVEABLES, A.D. 1066-1188.

Introduction of the feudal system	24
The royal revenue under the feudal system	27
The demesne. Purveyance and pre-emption. The feudal aids. Knight service	27
The feudal incidents:—1. Relief. 2. Primer seisin. 3. Wardship. 4. Escheat. 5. Forfeiture. 6. Fines on alienation of lands	29
Other casual revenue:—1. Waifs. 2. Estrays. 3. Wreck. 4. Bona vacantia. 5. Treasure trove. 6. Lands of idiots	32
Revenue from oblations, fines, penalties, amerciaments, and miscellaneous exactions	33
The land tax or danegeld	37
The foregoing are the principal sources of revenue during the Norman period:—The reigns of William the Conqueror, William Rufus, Henry I., Stephen	38
Collection of revenue—In the counties; in the towns	41
The Exchequer. Officers of the Court. The Treasurer. The upper and the lower exchequer. Easter and Michaelmas terms. The Rolls of the Exchequer	42
England under the Angevin kings	44

	PAGE
Introduction of scutage by Henry II.	44
The scutages of 1156; of Toulouse; of Ireland, 1172; and of Galloway, 1186	48
Commencement of taxation of moveables. The Assize of Arms a step in that direction	51
The Saladin tithe, 1188. The Ordinance for the Saladin tithe. The Saladin tithe as imposed in France	56

CHAPTER V.

FROM THE COMMENCEMENT OF THE TAXATION OF MOVEABLES, A.D. 1188, TO THE TERMINATION OF THE REIGN OF EDWARD III., A.D. 1377.

Order of the narrative during this period	60
Table of the principal taxes imposed 1189–1377	61

Taxes relating to Land.

1. SCUTAGE.

Scutage during the reigns of Richard I. and John. Constant taxation of the barons. Refusal of the northern barons to pay scutage	65
The Great Charter, 1215. The 12th and 14th articles	67
Scutage during the reigns of Henry. III. and Edward I.	68
Assessment and collection of scutage. Cartae baronum. The incidence of scutage. The lord's scutage	69
Later methods of assessment and collection	72
Form of writ appointing commissioners for assessment and collection	73

2. CARUCAGE.

Date of cessation of the Danegeld. A similar tax imposed under the name of carucage, in 1194 and in 1198	74
Method of assessment and collection. Penalties for evasion	75
A similar tax taken by John and by Henry III.	76
The last carucage	77
Tax on parishes, 1371. Miscalculation of the number of parishes. The tax altered by a great council	77

Tallage, or the arbitrary taxation of royal demesne.

	PAGE
The era of tallage, 1163–1304	80
Subdivisions of royal demesne:—1. Forest. 2. Demesne in hands of rural tenants. Rent at first paid in kind. The ferm of the county. Dona or auxilia. Tallage	80
3. Demesne in hands of urban tenants	83
History of towns in England. The early township. The burgh. Most of the towns situated on royal demesne. The rent of towns. The towns obtain special compositions. The firma burgi. The auxilium burgi	83
The auxilium burgi is extended, on disappearance of the danegeld, to the rural tenants, and becomes tallage	86
Principal occasions for exaction of tallage. The practice in collection	87
The principal tallages in the reigns of Henry II., Richard I., and John	88
No mention of tallage in Magna Carta	89
Tallages in the reign of Henry III., 1216–72	90
London acknowledged to be talliable	91
Tallages in the reign of Edward I. Ruddlan. General grant of a thirtieth	92
The last of the tallages	94
Statute de Tallagio non concedendo	95
Writ for collection of tallage in 1304	95
Ordinary form of writ	96

The Exchequer of the Jews.

The king's treatment of 'the Judaism.' Exactions from them. Fines and amerciaments. Expulsion of the Jews in 1290	97

The Taxation of Moveables, 1189–1377.

Difference between moveables in present and past times	100
Moveables in present times:—Money; household and personal moveables; farm moveables; investments of various descriptions; stock in trade; shipping, &c.	100
Moveables in the 13th and 14th centuries:—No national debt existed. 'Usury' was prohibited. No money was invested	

	PAGE
or deposited with others. Scarcity of money. No manufactures existed. Modern origin of our greatest branches of industry. Commerce of England at this date. The internal trade of the country—retarded by bad roads, defective police, and the 'men in armour.' The dread of tallage prevents accumulation of wealth in towns	101–12
Moveables in the castle of the period	113
In manor and other houses—in camera; in coquina; in cellario; in larderio; in grangia	114
Taxes on moveables fell mainly on the landowners	116
History of taxes on moveables: the earlier grants vary in amount	116
Those in the reigns of Richard I., John, Henry III., and Edward I.	117
Severe taxation from 1290 to 1297; and the complaints to which it gave rise	119
Reign of Edward II.	121
Cessation of this system of taxation in the reign of Edward III.:— Severe assessment in 1332; composition for the fifteenth and tenth, 1334; establishment of fixed sums to be levied on counties and towns	122
Total of the sums charged for a fifteenth and tenth in 1373	124
The incidence, assessment, and collection of the earlier grants	125
Writ for the thirteenth, 1207	125
Writ for the fifteenth, 1225	126
Writ for the fortieth, 1232	128
Writ for the thirtieth, 1237	129
The probable practice in assessment	130
Writ for the fifth and eighth, 1297; when the practice had become settled. Taxors appointed in each county	131
The Roll or Ordinance for assessment. Assessment by selected men of the township. Chief taxors to be surveyors; and make surcharges. Collection of the tax	132
Exemptions—(1) as regards knights and gentlemen; (2) as regards citizens and burgesses	134
The minimum taxable	135
Schedule of assessment	135
Oath of chief taxors and others	136
Writs of assistance sent to the sheriffs	136
Specimen of a Property Tax Act, viz. the Ordinance for assessment of the tenth and sixth of 1322, original text	138

Specimens of Schedules of Assessment:—1. Schedule of Assessment for the seventh of 1295, Burgus Colchester.—The goods of the prior; a vicar; a sea-coal dealer; a tanner. Small assessments. Number of tanners. The most striking features of the schedule 142
2. Schedule of assessment for Colchester for the fifteenth, 1301: Improvement in the art of assessment. Particulars of assessment:—in pecunia nummata; in thesauro; in camera . 146
Comparison of the two schedules 148
Personal review of the tax payers 149
Small assessments. Principal assessments. Wine. Total assessment for the borough 151

Customs and Port Duties.

Explanation of the term 'customs' 152
Origin of taxation by toll 152
Its origin in England 153
Customary tolls legalized by Magna Carta in 1215 . . 154
Prisage of wine 155
Custom of wool 155
Legislative commencement of port duties 156
The maletoute of wool 156
Antiqua custuma—the ancient customs 157
Commutation of prisage, in 1302 158
Nova custuma—the new customs 158
Butlerage—The king attempts to extend it to native merchants . 159
Improved yield of the customs in the reign of Edward III. The Crusades. Sugar. Cinnamon and other spices. First impulse to commerce. The sack of wool in its passage across the sea 160
Subsidies of port duties granted to Edward III. . . . 162
Chaucer a comptroller of the customs 168

Poll Taxes.

The Poll Tax of 1377 168
The amount of yield 169

General Remarks.

	PAGE
The reign of Richard I. The ransom of the king, how raised. The tournament tax	170
The reign of John	172
The reign of Henry III. His fiscal difficulties. His foreign proclivities	173
The reign of Edward I. His expedients for raising money	175
The new articles in Confirmatio Cartarum, 1297. Original text and translation	177
The reign of Edward II. Suppression of the Knights Templars. Ballad regarding unjust assessment of taxes	180
The reign of Edward III. Strange intermixture of feudalism and commerce. Edward as 'Greatest Knight'; as 'the father of English commerce'. Popularity of his policy. Edward as 'King of the seas'	181
The Black Death. The Statutes of Labourers	188
'Home farms' of the middle ages	190
Rise of the tenant farmer	191

CHAPTER VI.

FROM THE COMMENCEMENT OF THE REIGN OF RICHARD II. TO THE COMMENCEMENT OF THE CIVIL WAR, 1377–1642.

Chart of the period. 1. Reigns of kings during the period. 2. Wars—The Hundred Years' War. The Wars of the Roses. Flodden. Armada times	192
During this period gunpowder, the printing press, the mariner's compass, and the telescope changed the world	194
But there was little change in taxation in England	195
Order of the narrative	196

Poll Taxes.

Advantage of this form of taxation in rapidity of collection	196
In 1380, a large sum is required immediately. The lords suggest three kinds of taxes; but incline to advise a poll tax. Imposition of the poll tax	197
Provisions for mitigating the incidence of the tax	198
Difficulties in collection of direct taxes from the poor	199

xvi   TABLE OF CONTENTS.

	PAGE
This tax of 4d. not sufficient to account for the Peasant Revolt. The real cause	199
The Statutes of Labourers. Cancellation of charters of freedom. Diminished respect for 'men in armour'. Rapacity and insolence of the farmers of the tax	202
Brief history of the revolt, from a political poem of the period. The king's charters of freedom declared invalid	204
Comparison of the results of the peasant revolt and the 'Jacquerie'	206
Disappearance of villeinage and poll taxes in England; except poll taxes on aliens	206
List of merchant strangers in 1453	207

Taxes imposed in relation to Property.

'Fifteenths and tenths' continue in use. Subsequent introduction of subsidies	208
Two fifteenths and tenths granted in 1377	208
Tax by reference to rank, condition of life and substance, in 1379	209
Schedule of charge :—Earls, barons, knights, and esquires. The Knights Hospitallers. Lawyers. Trade and commerce. The franklin and the farmer. Advocates, proctors, &c. Hostelers. 'The general.' Merchant strangers	210
Small yield of the tax	212
Grant of a fifteenth and tenth in the usual manner	213
The landowners defray the tax of 1382; after the peasant revolt. This tax not to be considered a precedent	213
Fifteenths and tenths continued	214
Assessment of fifteenths and tenths. Instance of dispute as to proper assessment	214
Exemption granted in certain cases	215
First symptoms of a tendency to revert to ad valorem taxation. Grant of 5 per cent. on land and rent in 1404	216
Another tax on land and rent in 1411	216
The clergy and the House of Lancaster. Recommencement of the war with France	217
The victory of Azincourt in 1415; and subsequent grant of taxes	219
Ye batayle of Vernule, 1424	219
Tax, in 1427, on inhabitant householders in rural parishes and in urban parishes, and on knights' fees	219

	PAGE
The siege of Orleans raised	221

A tax, in 1430, on knights' fees and on other lands not held by knight service, and rents-seck and rent-charges. Commissioners to make inquisitions 221
Difficulties in the levy of these taxes. The inquisitions are 'entirely cancelled' 223
Another instance of total exemption from tenth . . . 224
General provision for relief of decayed towns. The usual practice 224
Tax on land, rent, annuities, and offices of freehold, in 1435. Commissioners to make inquisitions 225
The collectors of fifteenths and tenths, how appointed. Qualification for collectors for shires 226
A tax, in 1450, on—1. land, rent, annuities, offices, fees and profits of freehold; 2. other life annuities; 3. copyholds; and 4. certain offices, wages and fees less than freehold. Commissioners to be appointed. The tax not to be a precedent 227
Additional provisions required for enforcement of the tax . 229
Taxation during the Wars of the Roses 231
The old form of levy continued. Attempted alteration, in 1463, unsuccessful 231
Tax of the tenth part, for payment of 13,000 archers, in 1472. Inadequate yield. The residue charged in a novel manner. Collapse of the new tax 233
The commons revert to the old fifteenths and tenths . . 236
Coke's observations on old and new taxes . . . 236
The last 'fifteenth and tenth' 237
Introduction of the subsidy in the reign of Henry VIII. . 238
Practice of granting fifteenths and subsidies at the same time . 239
The Subsidy Acts. Connexion between them and the present Income Tax Act. 'Avi numerantur avorum' . . 239
Review of the Subsidy Acts. 1. Nature of the 'Subsidy.' 2. The usual amount of charge. 3. Incidence of the tax (*a*) As regards moveables, exemption of apparel, (*b*) As regards land. None are to be doubly charged, *i.e.* in respect of moveables and of land. Higher charge on aliens. The minimum taxable. Exemption of the inhabitants of the northern counties. 4. Provisions for management, assessment, and collection. Commissioners. Assessors appointed by the

Commissioners. The high collectors and the sub-collectors. Schedules of assessment. Precepts to collectors	240
Reasons for the small yield of a subsidy, and its decrease. The average yield	244
A practice commences of granting several subsidies at once	245
The capitation tax of 1641	246
The ship writs—drawn by Noy, attorney-general. First issue, in 1634. Reasons for charging only maritime places	246
A second issue intended, to extend to inland places. Second issue, in 1635. Form of writ for Dorsetshire. Similar writs for the other counties, &c. Commission for ships in aid, Nov. 16. Opposition to the tax	248
Case submitted to the judges. Their opinion	251
Third and subsequent issues	252
Produce of the tax	252
Distribution of ships to the several counties, &c.	252
Attempts to test the legality of the ship writs. Hampden's case, May 22, 1637	254
The Act against ship-money, 1640	254
The raising of the standard, Aug. 23, 1642	257
Specimen of an Italian tax on moveables in the sixteenth century	257

Customs and Port Duties.

Comprising (1) duties on wool and leather, (2) tunnage, and (3) poundage on goods	259
Duties on wool and leather granted to Richard II. for life	259
And to Henry V., after Azincourt; with tunnage and poundage	260
Grants of the port duties, for life, to Henry VI., Edward IV., Henry VII., Henry VIII., Edward VI., Mary and Elizabeth	261
Particulars of the 'Act of a subsidy of tunnage and poundage,' 1603	261
Reasons for the grant of the duties to Charles I. for a year only	265
Yield of the port duties—in 1421, 1431-3, 1590, 1604, 1613, 1617, 1622, and 1641	266
Method of valuation for poundage	269
Queen Mary's orders in council	270
Queen Elizabeth's Book of Rates	270
The rates are 'rectified' by James I., and a new book of rates is issued	271

	PAGE
Duty on tobacco	271
Charles I.'s new Book of Rates	272
The ancient port officers of the customs. Documents in use—the warrant and the cocket. Form of a cocket. The surveyor. Legal disabilities of officers. The tide waiters	272
Proposal, in 1420, to tax all strangers passing along the Channel	275

Loans and Benevolences.

Nature of loans to the king	276
Benevolences. Benevolences during the reign of Edward IV. Edward IV. and the widow	277
The statute against benevolences	279
Revival of benevolences by Henry VII. 'Morton's fork'	279
The 'amiable graunte' to Henry VIII.	280
End of benevolences. The Petition of Right	281

General Remarks.

Reign of Richard II. His enormous household. England let to farm	282
The Hundred Years' War. Azincourt. 'The Battle of the Herrings'	283
The Wars of the Roses. Destruction of the feudal nobility in the struggle for land	283
The reign of Henry VII. Strict enforcement of the Statutes of Liveries and the feudal rights of the crown. Empson and Dudley	284
The reign of Henry VIII. Rapid dissipation of the treasure accumulated by Henry VII.	285
The Wolsey period. Despotism in all but the power of the purse. Fall of Wolsey	285
The Cromwell period. The Statute of Appeals. The intolerable exactions of the Pope prohibited. The king 'Head of the Church'. Dissolution of the monasteries. 'The Terror.' Fall of Cromwell	286
Personal character of the reign of Henry VIII. Rupture of the Roman bonds. The river of blood—of queens, nobles, and illustrious men	289

TABLE OF CONTENTS.

	PAGE
What became of the lands of the monasteries and abbeys and knights of St. John	290
The reign of Elizabeth. Establishment of Protestantism. Popularity of the Queen. Animated recital to the first subsidy Act	291
Elizabeth's rule of conduct towards her people. Reasons for her popularity. The muster at Tilbury, 1588. Elizabeth's words to her soldiers. The struggle with Spain	294
Elizabeth's fiscal policy—to make the rich pay for splendour, and to spare the people	296
Agriculture, trade and commerce during the Tudor period	297
1. Agriculture, 1485 to 1602. Inclosures and conversion of tilled lands into pasture. Annexation of the smaller holdings to domains	298
Creation of enormous sheep farms. State of the Isle of Wight in 1487. Statutes of Tillage	298
Principal reasons for this conversion of tilled lands into pasture, as stated in an Act of 1533, viz. the rise of a monied trader class; increased demand for farms; and 'the great profit that cometh of sheep.' 'The several enormities that do ensue by the greedy desire of having many sheep.' Attempt to diminish the evil—1. by limitation of the number of sheep to be kept by any one farmer; 2. by prohibition of holding more than two farms, and enforcement of the Statutes of Tillage	299
Tax imposed on wool and sheep, in 1548	302
The decay of towns. Exodus of traders	303
Agriculture of the period in certain other particulars: wheat, barley, and oats. Treatises on agriculture. Buckwheat, beans, and peas; saffron; hemp and flax; hops	306
The kitchen garden: carrots, cabbages and turnips, and the potato; fruit trees—cherry, gooseberry, pippin and apricot	308
Honey. 'Turkeys' introduced from Mexico	309
Increase in the vagrant and pauper classes	310
Origin of local taxation	310
Original provision for the local poor out of the tithes of parishes	311
Maintenance of the local poor during the Middle Ages	312
First movement in the agricultural poor. Statutes of labourers	313
Aged and impotent vagrants, are to be returned to their own parishes	313

	PAGE
Origin of licensed begging within a certain precinct. Breakdown of the old system	314
After the dissolution of the monasteries, first the minister and the bishop, and afterwards the justices, are required to enforce the 'voluntary' system. A system of assessments is introduced	315
The Act for the relief of the poor, 1601	316
Compulsory work for the idle able-bodied . . .	316
The enactments against vagabonds. After the first outpoor on break-up of the military establishments. After the second outpour on dissolution of the monasteries . . .	316
Extreme severity. The Slave Act of 1547 . . .	318
Return to the old system of whipping and the stocks . .	319
Legislation during the reign of Elizabeth. The Act of 1597. The Rogue Roll of the Act	319
General hatred of idleness at this date	321
2. Internal trade and industry. Rise of the trader class .	321
The woollen manufacture. Principal seats of the manufacture. Greatness of Norwich. Woollen card making and card wire drawing	322
Hat and cap manufacture. Stockings; invention of the stocking-frame	326
Leather. Soap. Maltster and brewer. Introduction of the manufacture of sail cloth. Cables and cordage. Ordnance .	328
Knives. Glass. Plate. The standard for gold and silver wares	331
3. Commerce. Change in the known world during this period .	
The map of the Christian Topography . .	333
Discoveries of the Portuguese along the coast of Africa. Discovery of the sea route to India	334
Discovery of the New World by Columbus. The Bahamas discovered, Oct. 12, 1492. Magellan and his companions put a girdle round about the earth	335
Cabot's discoveries	336
Conquest of Mexico and of Peru. The New Crusade. War with Spain. Drake's raid on Chili and Peru . .	337
The new map 'with the augmentation of the Indies' . .	338
Discoveries of Sir H. Willoughby and Chancellor. Commencement of our commerce with Muscovy . . .	338
The Mediterranean. Decline of Genoa. Decline of Venice on discovery of the new sea route to India. Greatness	

	PAGE
of Lisbon. Commencement of our Turkey and Levant trade	339
Greatness of Spain and the Low Countries united	340
Consolidation of the kingdom of France	341
The Netherlands. Bruges, the great emporium of commerce, yields to Antwerp. Greatness of Antwerp. Ruin of the trade of the Netherlands. Sack of Antwerp. The Eastland towns superseded as carriers by Amsterdam	342
The first Charter of the East India Company	343
London not yet a city of the first rank	344
Abolition of the privileges of the Hanseatic merchants and the Steel Yard	344
Shipbuilding. Rise of the navy. Increase of merchant shipping. Practice of sea insurance	344
The New Building in Tudor times. Tudor development of Gothic architecture. Elizabethan manor houses. Elizabethan Halls	345
The Renascence in England as compared with the Renaissance in Italy and France	349
The Stuart period. Union of the crowns of England and Scotland	349
The decision in Bates' case	350
Purveyance and pre-emption. Monopolies. Compulsory loans and benevolences. Fines on political offenders	350
Sale of honours. Scale of charge	351
The first public lottery	351
Origin of the laws in restraint of 'drinking.' The inn or hostel of former times. The ale-house and victualling-house. The statutes against unlawful games. First licenses for ale and tippling-houses. The tavern	351
Revival of the habit of drinking during the wars in the Netherlands. The first Act against tippling in inns, alehouses and victualling-houses. The second Act. Subsequent enactments. The Acts are extended to tavern-keepers	355
Amount of the Revenue in 1617	358
The Reign of Charles I. Brief summary of events	358
Introduction of private coaches and hackney carriages Sedan chairs	361
Clocks and watches	362
Cards and dice taxed	363
Remarks of Michiel and Lord Bacon on taxation in England	364
A glance into the future. List of taxes subsequently imposed	365

A SKETCH

OF THE

HISTORY OF TAXES

IN THIS COUNTRY.

PART I.

FROM THE EARLIEST TIMES TO THE COMMONWEALTH.

CHAPTER I.

PRELIMINARY OBSERVATIONS.

In these utilitarian days the reader may, possibly, regard a reference back to the early date fixed for commencement of the present investigation of the history of taxes in this country with somewhat of the feeling expressed by the judge in 'Les Plaideurs,' when L'Intimé begins a peroration—'Avant la naissance du monde,' and he says, 'Avocat, ah! passons au déluge.' And, in fairness, let him know at once that he must not expect to discover in the annals of a nation in its infancy and earlier days much fiscal information of direct practical utility under the total different conditions of a nation arrived at full maturity. For taxation, in our modern sense of the word, does not exist in barbarous countries. It is a *late* product of civilization, very tardy in development,

> Delaying as the tender ash delays
> To clothe herself, when all the woods are green,

and its commencement in this country dates in effect from the times of the Commonwealth. If, therefore, the reader has a mind to deal only with immediately practical points, he may skip over the earlier part— Part I. of this volume, pass on, and cut in with the narrative at the commencement of Part II. He will thus avoid what may appear to him a rummaging with archæologists amongst useless antiquities.

On the other hand, for encouragement of the reader willing to go with the author from the commencement, it may be observed that the golden rule, 'begin at the beginning,' the only method for real mastery of any branch of learning, avoiding all unsatisfactory feeling of incomplete accomplishment and the dangers attending defective information, applies with peculiar force to the subject under present consideration, which is one emphatically within the maxim embodied in the well-known lines,

> A little learning is a dangerous thing;
> Drink deep, or taste not the Pierian spring.

Moreover, as Rousseau, with reference to the history

of nations, says that 'generally speaking, the most instructive part of the annals of nations is the history of their establishment;' so, in relation to the taxes that have been imposed in this country, may it be stated that many of them possess peculiar interest in their origin and earlier history. Much therefore is lost by a late commencement: as by launching on a river in full stream you may miss much of the scenery for which it is renowned. To take up the subject of the income tax at the date of its re-imposition by Sir R. Peel, is to embark at Cologne and sail down the broad river in expectation of seeing "the Rhine."

Again, it may be observed that the history of taxation, throughout its whole length, possesses considerable interest from the remarkable manner in which it is intertwined with the thread of contemporaneous national history. The well-informed in the annals of his country, reading the history of any tax, by his general knowledge of the pages of Hume, Lingard, or whoever may be his favourite historian, easily connects it with the history of a time. He will find in the earlier 'Dane-geld,' 'Scutage,' 'Saladin tithe', 'Poll-tax,' and 'Ship-money,' subjects no less pregnant with general interest than are in later times 'The General Excise Scheme,' 'The Stamp Act for America,' the 'Land tax,' and the 'Income tax.' And nothing will enable him more fully to realize the advance this country has made in civilization, and the extraordinary development in our national resources, than tracing our revenue from taxation all the way down its history, comparing its former diminutive proportions with the magnitude it has attained,[1] and contrasting the methods by which money was squeezed out of the people in days of yore with the present sources gushing in abundant supply.

Then, as regards the antiquarian point. If antiquities in arms, in coins, in ornaments, in pottery, in bathing appliances et hoc genus omne, have attractions and a certain importance for some persons, in short, as there exist antiquaries of divers kinds, is it unreasonable to infer, from the increasing interest in questions of taxation which distinguishes the times, the existence of a considerable class of persons to whom antiquities in taxes may, as such, prove not wholly devoid of interest? Particularly when they are presented ready to hand, available without the toil of excavation, so to put it, incident to a search through old parliamentary rolls and statute books, not less than to the process of bringing to light the hidden treasures of barrows and tumuli.

In conclusion of these preliminary observations, which amount, perhaps, to little more than an apology for an early commencement, is added an invitation to the reader to divest himself of any idea that the subject under consideration is forbidding, the path of travel steep, hard, and thorny. Let him accept the hand of a guide devoted to the service of rendering his progress easy, and in progress let him only show what Sterne terms a 'pleasurable ductility,' the journey will not be difficult. The first step takes him to ancient

---

[1] Of our revenue it may justly be said in the words of Eutropius regarding the Roman Empire: Neque ab exordio ullum fere minus, neque incrementis toto orbe amplius.

Britain, and we are at once in the Treasury, at any rate in the opinion of those who, according to Camden, derive the name from πρυτανεῖον.[1]

[1] On the correctness of this derivation of 'Britain' from the Athenian treasury I do not, of course, insist. It is only mentioned as interesting in a volume treating of fiscal subjects. Camden eventually dismisses it as untenable; but with fond delay, and only in favour of that more generally received, which has reference to Brutus, descendant of Æneas.

CHAPTER II.

ANCIENT BRITAIN.

In ancient Britain, a country the inhabitants of which were in a semi-nomad state, and where the first foundations of property were not securely laid, civilization can hardly be said to have existed previously to the arrival of the Roman conqueror. Indeed, the island was considered as practically separate [1] from the rest of the world—'penitus toto divisos orbe Britannos,' a Roman poet writes; no mere Hellespont intervening or Rhine to be bridged over by boats, but a stormy strip of ocean,—

> Beluosus qui remotis
> Obstrepit oceanus Britannis.[2]

In a word, the country was barbarous.

Our information of any kind regarding the ancient Britons is extremely limited and unsatisfactory, for the Druidical laws, customs, and history were unwritten and perpetuated by oral tradition only, and little

---

[1] Long after this, and far down the stream of time, we find people speaking of this island as a world of itself.

[2] Compare with the above—
> 'This precious stone set in the silver sea,
> Which serves it in the office of a wall,
> Or as a moat defensive to a house,
> Against the envy of less happy lands;'

Or the—'our streak of silver sea'—of the modern orator.

trustworthy on the subject is to be found in the Roman writers who have touched it—Cæsar and Tacitus.

As regards the manner in which the princes and chiefs of the inhabitants maintained themselves and their followers, the probability is that, as has been the case in most barbarous countries of which we find record, their main resources were—their own immediate possessions in land; occasional assistance from their subjects in the form of voluntary contributions in cattle and grain; and, doubtless, the usual incoming of robber revenue, viz., any plunder they could gather from their enemies in war. *(Probable sources of revenue)*

It is not improbable, however, that there may have existed in this island at the time of which we are treating some defined customs similar to those which prevailed in Ireland at a later date among a population of similar origin and under circumstances not very unlike those of ancient Britain; customs which consisted in exactions levied by the petty princes of the country under the barbarous names of bonaught, coshery, cuddy, cuttings, dowgello, kernetty, cess, reflection, and sorchin.[1]

'Bonaught' being free quarters on the subject for the chief's soldiers or gallowglasses; 'coshery,' free quarters on the subject for the chief for a limited time; 'cuddy,' a supper and lodging for a night for the chief; 'cuttings,' contributions to pay the chief's debts; 'dowgello,' a tax for the maintenance of the chief's dogs

---

[1] See *An Account of Ireland in* 1773, drawn up by Mr. (afterwards Lord) Macartney, Chief Secretary of Ireland, referred to in a *Return :—Pub. Inc. and Expend.* (1869.) Part II., p. 389.

and huntsmen; 'kernetty,' a tax per plough-land for the maintenance of the chief's mansion house; 'cess,' food for man and horse at a stipulated price; 'reflection,' the privilege of claiming for the chief a meal of cheese, curds, &c.; and 'sorchin,' meat and drink for a soldier or gallowglass one day in a fortnight.

<small>A precedent for the Match tax.</small>

The existence of such customs in this island at the date in question is, however, conjectural; and the single tradition of anything in the nature of a tax, as we understand the word, has relation to an annual payment exacted by the Druids from every family for the benefit of the priest of the temple of that district in which the family dwelt.

After the commencement of the use of houses and fire, according to Lucretius,

Tum genus humanum primum mollescere coepit.

This was probably the case in Britain, and the Druids appear to have availed themselves of the incipient softness by an ingenious provision for enforcing payment of this tax. Not only was it enforced by penalty of ecclesiastical anathema, as in later times were the subscriptions for the Crusades, but the consequences of evasion were brought home, so to speak, to the offender as follows:—

'The families were obliged, under penalty of excommunication, to extinguish their fires on the last evening of October, and attend at the temple with their usual payment, and on the first day of November to receive some of the sacred fire from the altar (or Carn)

to rekindle those of their houses,'[1]—and their neighbours were forbidden (under a similar penalty) to assist them. The result being that defaulters found themselves not only interdicted from the society of their fellow-men and from justice, the usual consequences of ecclesiastical excommunication, but also without that 'vital spark of heavenly flame' necessary for the fire so much needed at the approach of winter.

Here then, for a 'comparative' mind, as Shakespeare puts it—a mind quick at comparisons, is a fair precedent for one of the very latest attempts at taxation. The resemblance may not be perfect, but the principle is the same :—'Les anciens sont les anciens; nous sommes les gens de maintenant.' The lucifer match, as unknown in those days, could not be taxed. But at any rate this is the first recorded attempt in this island to obtain for fiscal purposes 'ex luce lucellum.'[2]

---

[1] Henry, *Hist. Great Brit.*, Lib. i. c. 2, s. 1.; who quotes Toland, *Hist. of the Druids.* See pp. 105, 106. Toland adds :—If he would brew, therefore, or roast, or boil, or warm himself and family, in a word if he would live the winter out, the Druid's dues must be paid by the last of October; so that this trick alone was more effectual than all the Acts of Parliament made for recovering our present clergy's dues: which Acts are so many and so frequent that the bare enumeration of them would make an indifferent volume.—Second Letter to Viscount Molesworth, July 1, 1718.

[2] We have thought it necessary to devise a motto for this novel species of taxation. On the match boxes which are sold at present we usually see a very odd and rather inappropriate device, one which suggests a rather watery idea—namely, Noah's Ark. But I propose to put this motto on our new match boxes—Ex luce lucellum. Speech of the Chancellor of the Exchequer. *The Times*, April 21, 1871.

CHAPTER III.

FROM THE ROMAN CONQUEST OF BRITAIN TO THE NORMAN CONQUEST OF ENGLAND.

Character of Roman taxation generally.

IN the whole history of taxation there is no record of a nation which has carried the fiscal art to a greater degree of perfection, certainly none of any which has more extensively developed it in practice, than the Romans under the empire.[1] Taxation was an essential part of that system of domination on which the Roman prided himself,

Tu regere imperio populos, Romane, memento,

and he excelled in that as in all the other arts of administration.

In taxing the different nations subject to their authority, the Romans do not appear to have followed any general rule, but varied the method of taxation according to the circumstances of each particular country at different times.

Roman taxation in Britain.

The taxation of Britain under the Romans (though we have no very clear information regarding it) appears to have been, in the aggregate, always heavy, and

---

[1] A cette époque (l'époque Romaine) l'impôt se présente sous des formes très-variées, très-ingénieuses, très-complexes, combinées avec art dans leur ensemble, organisées dans le détail avec un soin minutieux.—Clamageran, *L'Impôt en France*, i., 2.

occasionally oppressive, though probably never so crushing as their taxation of Gaul when at its culminating point.

In stating the different sorts of taxes exacted at various times, it will be well to observe the ordinary division of taxation into direct and indirect taxes— direct taxes being such as are imposed on persons or property directly; indirect, those imposed on articles of consumption.

1. First in the list of direct taxes comes a method of taxation obviously well adapted to a country not yet adequately supplied with money, viz., the levy in kind of a certain portion of the produce of lands; and this was generally a tenth. This mode of taxation has prevailed in almost every country of which we have fiscal record, at some period of its history. The remembrance of it was preserved to us in this country in the tithes payable to the clergy, till their determination in recent times by the operation of the Tithe Commutation Acts, and is still recalled by the existence in many places of enormous tithe barns. It exists in Turkey up to the present day.[1] But to go further abroad, Hernando Cortès found it in force in Mexico under the Aztec kings, and, for all we know, those magnificent tax-gatherers of Montezuma whom Prescott describes him as having captured on his way to the capital may have been on their rounds to collect the produce.

Direct taxes.
1. Tithe of produce of lands.

In collection of these taxes in kind the Roman tax-

---

[1] As to the baneful operation of this method of taxation in the Othoman Empire and elsewhere, see Finlay, *Hist. Greece*, v. 30. See also Mr. Horace Rumbold's *Report on Taxation in Turkey*. (1872.)

gatherer required delivery of the corn or other produce at the fiscal granary or barn; and it frequently happened that this was situated at a distance from the field of growth, and was accessible only by difficult roads. In such cases the cartage proved a tax more severe than the tribute itself: and the principal complaints against this species of taxation appear to have arisen from this inconvenience and difficulty of transport.

2. The scriptura, or tax on cattle.

2. The next direct tax to be mentioned was that imposed on cattle, which formed the principal part of the possessions of the inhabitants—' pecorum magnus numerus,' writes Cæsar; and again, 'lacte et carne vivunt.' This was imposed at so much a head, and was termed 'scriptura,' from the inscription in the tax-gatherer's roll of the number of head of cattle.[1]

This tax, no light and easy burden where the taxpayer had money at command, appears to have been peculiarly obnoxious from the fact that few of the inhabitants had the means of paying the sum required without recourse to the Roman usurer on his own exorbitant terms, or the sale of cattle and field produce at considerable loss.

[1] Very similar was the Roman 'vectigal alabarchiæ,' levied on flocks and herds on their passage from one place of pasturage to another, also occasionally termed 'scriptura' for the reason above given; a tax unsurpassed for ease and completeness of collection, as those will admit who have watched the arrival of the flocks and herds at their summer pastures on the Alps. A tax of this description was subsequently levied in several of the Italian republics, and Sismondi gives us some idea of its importance where he describes the two rival princes encamped at the foot of the mountain pass with their soldiers, and all ready for battle, but waiting the arrival on the bridge of war of the flocks and herds from which, in their passage, was to be levied payment practically of the expenses of the campaign.

3. A third kind of direct taxes, viz., capitation taxes, similar in principle to the hated poll taxes of later date, appear to have been occasionally exacted from the inhabitants; which, as direct payments of money, were liable, equally with the 'scriptura,' to the objection mentioned under that heading.

3. Capitation taxes.

4. And lastly, a tax was (it is stated) levied about the time of Boadicea on the bodies of the dead, enforced by prohibition of burial in case of non-payment. A tax of this description is obviously odious; and the burden of taxation in the aggregate had now become intolerable. It formed one of the principal causes of the revolt of the Iceni; and in the harangue which historians attribute to 'the British warrior queen,' when reviewing her forces previous to the battle with Suetonius, is ranked with the wrongs of her daughters and her beating with the Roman rods.

4. Tax on the bodies of the dead.

The indirect taxes levied by the Romans are of minor importance, for little, if any, revenue could have been derived from port duties during those times. The principal tolls exacted were probably levied on the internal conveyance of merchandise.

Indirect taxes.

Such, then, were the principal taxes levied by the Romans in Britain, and any endeavour further to investigate the subject lands us in conjecture. We need not, however, at once part company with the Roman taxgatherer. In the subsequent narrative we shall have to note the introduction and establishment in this country of a great variety of taxes; and—though few, if any, of such subsequent taxes can be regarded as revivals, even in a modified form, of Roman taxes formerly here in force, as M. Clamageran considers is the case in regard to France [1]—some acquaintance with Roman taxation generally will add considerably to the interest of the reader, who, thus informed, is enabled, as he notes the imposition of taxes in later times, to compare the ancient with the modern systems of taxation.

A few remarks on the subject of Roman taxation generally.

For this reason the reader is requested to run his eye over the following brief remarks regarding the principal taxes in use by the Romans. Some of them were provincial, some home taxes, but this distinction it is unnecessary for present purposes to observe. Let us take first the direct, afterwards the indirect taxes.

Direct taxes.
1. Tribute from lands.

On a comprehensive view of the Roman tribute from lands during its entire history, it would appear to have passed through three distinct phases. At first it was collected in the form of payments of a portion, usually the tenth, of the annual produce (decumæ, frumentum decumanum). Afterwards, it assumed the form of a charge on the net value of the annual produce estimated on the average of a term of years. And lastly, it became a charge on the estimated saleable value of the land ; when it was termed 'capitatio [2] terrena,' from caput, capital.

2. Taxes on houses.

2. Of house taxes there were various kinds. Some imposed directly in respect of the house itself,—as is the

---

[1] Il n'en est pas le même des institutions financières imposées à la Gaule par ses vainqueurs. . . . Peu à peu on les exhume sous des noms nouveaux, on les restaure tout en les modifiant; aujourd'hui même elles subsistent en partie au milieu de nous.—*L'Impôt en France.* i., 2.

[2] This should not be confounded with the 'capitatio humana' subsequently mentioned.

case with our existing house-duty; some by reference to the number of hearths in the house,—as was the hearth-money imposed, as we shall subsequently see, in the reign of Charles the Second; some by reference to the number of windows—wind-doors in the house (aericum), or its doors (ostiarium),—like our window duties repealed only a few years since, and the present portes et fenêtres tax in France; and some with respect to the columns of the house.

3. A tax on property on its devolution in consequence of death—(vicessima hereditatum et legatorum)—resembled in its principle our probate and legacy and succession duties. *3. Succession taxes.*

4. The 'scriptura' has already been mentioned, and, strictly speaking, that tax was a levy on cattle at grass in the public pastures. Besides this, other taxes were occasionally imposed in respect of cattle and other animals (capitatio animalium), which the reader will be able to compare with the tax on sheep imposed in the reign of Edward the Sixth, and the more modern taxes of this as well as other countries in respect of horses, dogs, &c. *4. Taxes on animals.*

5. A tax imposed on moveable property productive of income in the possession of tradesmen, merchants, and money scriveners was termed 'lustralis collatio,' from its collection every five years: and another species of property tax was the 'gleba senatoria,' which affected senators and the higher classes only; for the purposes of which the contributories were divided into different classes with reference to their dignity and their property. *5. Income taxes on tradesmen, &c.* *6. Tax on senators.*

7. Taxes on persons.

7. Such were the principal taxes imposed with relation to property: we may close the list of direct taxes with the 'capitatio humana,' a tax imposed on persons directly, at so much a head, resembling, as before stated, the subsequent poll taxes in this country.

Indirect taxes.

The portoria.

In indirect taxation the principal class of duties was that levied on merchandise at the ports, the portoria, or duties on exports and imports,—resembling our port duties or 'customs,' as we term them, when (as we shall hereafter see) they embraced articles exported as well as imports. 'Suetonius says that Julius Cæsar laid the first imposition upon foreign merchandise: Peregrinarum mercium portoria primus instituit; and that imposition was octava rerum pars.'[1] According to Cicero[2] the port duties in Syracuse amounted to the twentieth of the saleable value of the articles. But our information regarding this class of duties is by no means extensive or clear. Never, as far as we know, were they imposed at different rates with reference to the nature of the articles in transit, as—on raw materials and manufactured articles, or commodities of different sorts, or on exports and imports. In a word, this species of taxation was never fully developed under the Romans.

Auction and sale duties.

The duties imposed on commodities sold at auction or in the public market fell principally on eatables, and were always an unpopular tax; resembling, in that particular as well as in their incidence, the 'alcavala' of Spain in later times, but which our auction duties of

---

[1] Gilbert, *Treat. on the Exch.* App. p. 267.
[2] In Verrem, Act ii. Lib. 2, LXXV.

subsequent times can only be said to have resembled in a remote and limited degree.

Such were the principal taxes, direct and indirect, known to and used by the Romans at different times and in different countries; but the list of the sources from which that most tax-gathering nation derived revenue is by no means exhausted in the foregoing enumeration. The State lands; the rights of the State to a certain portion of the produce of mines, salt works, quarries, and chalk pits; a tax on slaves, in respect of the possession of them; a tax payable on the manumission of slaves (vicessima manumissionum); a tax on legal proceedings (quadrigessima litium), which had but a short duration—all these may be added to the lengthy roll; to which, in conclusion, may be appended a sweeping clause embracing 'duties on other articles too tedious to mention,' as Sinclair puts it,[1] and those revenues the State derived from 'les taxes perçues à propos des égouts, et celles que Vespasien imagina.'[2]

Other means of revenue.

Having thus acquired sufficient fiscal information for present purposes from the Romans generally, we may once more limit the horizon to Britain, and note the departure of the legions on their recall from this as from the other distant provinces of the empire in order to protect home quarters against barbaric invasion from the north. With the procurator, susceptores, exactores, et hoc genus omne—the staff of tax-gatherers —vanishes all fiscal ability. The arts of war and peace, of administration and government, soon disappear. Before long, hardly a trace of civilization in manners

State of the country after the departure of the Romans.

[1] *Hist. of the Revenue,* i. 17.
[2] See Clamageran, *L'Impôt en France,* i. 80.

C

and customs remains; and, eventually, darkness spreads, as it were, over the face of the land, a darkness to endure for ages, a darkness which may be felt.

Professor Stubbs in his *Select Charters* thus describes Britain in the fifth century—

'A land whose defenders had forsaken it, and had carried away with them most of the adventitious civilization which they had maintained for four hundred years; whose inhabitants were enervated and demoralized by long dependence, wasted by successive pestilences, worn out by the attacks of half savage neighbours and by their own suicidal wars; whose vast forests and unreclaimed marsh lands afforded to the new comers a comparatively easy conquest.'[1]

To follow the course of events. Hardly has the last of the receding triremes sunk below the verge, when attention is attracted by a cry of distress from the northern borders, where the Briton, unacquainted with arms in consequence of enforcement of the practice usual to the Romans in dealing with conquered countries, who, in abounding caution, always disarmed the natives and themselves engrossed the military part —used to the plough and not the sword, is wholly unable to stop the war path of his ferocious neighbours the Picts and Scots, against whom the border wall now proves no securer protection than a line of hurdles between sheep and wolves.

A few years pass, and we have to turn our eyes towards the eastern coast, and watch the arrival of the new comers to whom the passage before quoted

[1] *Select Charters*, p. 1.

from Professor Stubbs more particularly refers. They come from a land beyond the sea, and, according to some writers, by invitation to assist in repelling the Picts and Scots. But invitation is a phrase hardly applicable to intrusion not to be repelled. In this quarter we see, in the absence of the 'comes littoris Saxonici,'[1] the tragedy of the north re-enacted, though in a less ferocious manner. Angles, Jutes, and Saxons come pouring in, pressed onwards by wave upon wave of nations from further east sweeping against Germany; an overflow that the Briton can no more repel than could, in after years, Cnut the waters of the advancing tide.

As a cloud gathers shape, these visits from the mainland, after passing through preliminary phases of plunder and settlement, assume a definite form in the English conquest. This may be considered to have effectively commenced about the middle of the fifth century; and in process of time the Teutonic migration is completed in the practical expulsion into Wales and Ireland of the surviving Britons, and the occupation of the southern and eastern parts of the island by immigrants from the tribes of Lower Germany, the main stock of our forefathers, from whom are inherited our 'caerulei oculi, rutilae comae, magna corpora,' and our Teutonic institutions. *The English Conquest.*

Then follows the foundation or formation in different ways of various kingdoms, of which the seven principal are named the Heptarchy. The Danish invasions

---

[1] The shore infested by Saxon pirates. See Freeman, *Norm. Conq.*, i. 11.

commence, necessitating combination for resistance. In imitation of the acts of Charlemagne in Germany, Egbert of Wessex gradually subjects the other English kingdoms. The Bretwalda [1] develops into a permanent king. The government of the whole of the Anglo-Saxon territory and domains is centralized. And the result is the foundation of the kingdom of England, with one witenagemot imposing, when required, extraordinary taxation, and one king, leader of the national forces and supreme judge. Towards the close of the period under review, it may be added, there is observable a tendency to the development of institutions resembling, though in a remote degree, feudalism as established on the Continent.

Foundation of the Kingdom of England.

With the period comprising the fifth, sixth, seventh, eighth, ninth, and indeed the tenth centuries, and the first half of the eleventh century, we may deal compendiously, as presenting few features of fiscal interest.

Principal sources of revenue in the Heptarchic kingdoms and England before the Norman Conquest.

The principal source of revenue in the Heptarchic kingdoms was (as under the Franconian kings in Gaul)[2] the public land and estates of the king; and when these kingdoms became united under one king, the combined produce and rents of these domains enabled him with ease to maintain a considerable court. Some revenue accrued from fines freely inflicted on criminals of all sorts. The trinoda necessitas, the threefold

[1] Or Weilder of Britain.
[2] Dans la monarchie des Francs les revenus des rois consistaient alors dans leurs domaines. Montesquieu, *De l'esprit des lois*, Liv. 30. chap. 13. It may be observed, however, that in Gaul many of the Roman exactions did not totally lapse, but were continued by private individuals, the sub-kings of the feudal era, the lords of fiefs. Moreover, Montesquieu states 'Les rois levaient encore quelque droits sur les rivières lorsqu'il y avait un pont ou un passage.'—*Ibid.*

obligation from which no one was exempt, compelled the assistance of the subject for brig-bot (pontis reparatio), the repair of bridges; burh-bot (arcis reparatio), the construction and repair of forts; and fyrdung, going to the fyrd (expeditio contra hostem), military service in war. And, latterly, the military equipment of the king's forces was further secured by the introduction of the Danish custom of heriots, consisting of a tribute of arms and armour to the king on the death of a subject.

Of exactions from merchandise in transit some traces may be discovered; but, little indeed could have been derived from port duties during this period, and the tolls levied were principally in the nature of inland duties or octroi. It was not a time 'felix opportunitate' —a happy time for the merchant on the high seas when the Danish pirate was abroad, and the raven of Denmark clapped his wings.[1]

Mention has been made of extraordinary taxation—we may conclude the history of this period with a reference to the three taxes (in the ordinary sense of the word as we use it) which appear to have been levied during the concluding part of the period, of which the last two form the extraordinary taxation before mentioned as imposed by the witenagemot. *Taxes.*

The first was a house tax, termed 'Fumage, or Smoke-farthings;' of which we know little, except its subsequent mention in Doomsday Book. It was a customary payment to the king for every hearth in all *Fumage.*

---

[1] As to the Danish war flag, which by its different movements prognosticated, as the Danes believed, the good or bad success of any expedition, see *Chron. Sax.* A.D. 878; Hume, *Hist. of Engl.*, i. 67.

houses except those of the poor, and is interesting for two reasons: first, as the original of the 'Hearth-money' of Charles II., and its successor—the tax imposed in lieu of the hearth-money two years after its repeal by William of Orange on his accession to the throne—the well-known window tax, which continued in force up to the year 1853; and, secondly, as connected with the loss of Aquitaine to Edward the Black Prince, of which it was one of the principal causes when, in imitation, it is said, of the English custom, he attempted its introduction in that country.

<small>The Dane-geld.</small> The second was the famous Dane-geld, Dane-gild, or Dane-money, a land tax charged on all lands in the kingdom at so much a hide,[1] the rate varying from 1s. to 4s., as the emergency required. This appears to have been imposed originally, towards the close of the tenth century,[2] in order to bribe away the Scandinavian pirates, whose invasions have been before mentioned, known in France by the name of Northmen, in England by that of Danes, the ferocious followers of the Vikingr or Sea-kings, who hovered round the coast like birds of prey, intent to swoop down on any unprotected part; and having originated thus as a levy for tribute, was subsequently continued and collected as revenue by the king after the cessation of the Danish invasions,

---

[1] A hide consisted of about 100 acres. Hida a primitiva institutione ex centum acris constat.—*Dialogus de Scaccario*, i. 17.

[2] For the first time (on the advice of Archbishop Siric) in 991, when a sum of 10,000 pounds was levied and paid "for the great terror they (the Danes) occasioned on the coast." *Chron. Sax.* A.D. 991. Again, in 1002, 24,000 pounds. *Ibid.* A.D. 1102. In 1007, a tribute of 30,000 pounds is paid to the hostile army. *Ibid.* A.D. 1007. Again, in 1012, 48,000 pounds. And in 1018, 72,000 pounds.

sometimes, it may be added, under the specious pretext of resistance to future attacks.

The Dane-geld, as always unpopular, was difficult to collect.[1] Hence, probably, the employment, on the occasion of its levy, A.D. 1041, by Harthacnut, of the Housecarles[2] as collectors. Whose oppressive conduct in enforcing payment, leading to resistance and the slaughter of some of them, was followed by the memorable spoliation of Worcester by Royal command.

This tax, abolished about the middle of the eleventh century by Edward the Confessor, who imagined, according to Hoveden,[3] that he saw the devil astride of the money-bags in the treasury, was revived, as we shall subsequently see, under the kings of the Norman line.

The third was the Ship-geld, a tax imposed for the purpose of naval resistance to the enemy on special occasions of imminent peril, consisting in a contribution of a ship and its equipments levied on the shires in equal proportions.[4] This is the Ship-money so celebrated in after times in the attempt of Charles I. to revive it, and the refusal of Hampden to pay.

Ship-geld.

---

[1] *Dial. de Scacc.*, i. 11.

[2] As to the Housecarles or Thingmen—the paid military force—see Freeman, *Norm. Conq.*, i. 416, 440.

[3] Vol. i., p. 110. The King asks:—What are you doing here. The devil answers:—I guard my money. K.—I conjure you by Father, Son, and Holy Ghost to tell me why it is your money. The d.—Because it is unjustly taken from the substance of the poor. [Queen Eleanor and Earl Harold, who were present, had collected it unknown to the King.] K., to them:—Restore the money to those from whom it was taken.

[4] On this subject, see Freeman, *Norm. Conq.*, i. 336 et seq., and note LL.

CHAPTER IV.

FROM THE NORMAN CONQUEST TO THE COMMENCEMENT OF TAXATION OF MOVEABLES. A.D. 1066—1188.

Introduction of the feudal system. INDUBITABLY, the most important result of the Norman conquest, from our present point of view, was the introduction in this country of the feudal system.

The origin, growth, and nature of that military organization of a country termed the feudal system, it is not necessary on the present occasion deeply to investigate. The subject has occupied the attention of numerous writers, who have treated it in a variety of ways; and the reader is probably familiar with the leading features of the system, as well as the different opinions held by scholars regarding its origin and growth. At the risk, however, of what may appear to be unnecessary statement, it may be recalled to mind that, according to the inclination of modern opinion, the feudal system was the gradual development of the strong personality, the individual energy which was the marked characteristic of the Teutonic nations who occupied western Europe on the decline of the Roman empire—'Fille de la société Germaine,' M. Guizot terms 'la société feodale'—a development of the individual, which, shattered to pieces as was civilization in Europe in consequence of the barbaric invasions, was probably the only means by which the re-establishment of civilization could have been initiated.

It was a federation of great landowners, with sub-feudatories, and a king in chief, but only primus inter pares,[1] 'all bound together by obligation of service and defence,' as Professor Stubbs puts it,[2] having for its object the protection of the individual against private dangers, quite as much as security for the public safety. It prevailed so extensively in western Europe as to be termed by Spelman 'the law of nations in our western world;' and it was in force, in the eleventh century, in France, and, though in a more limited degree, in the country opposite our southern coast, where, about a century before, 'ces brigands du nord,' the Northmen, had at last resigned themselves to repose, renouncing brigandage and asking for lands, and their famous leader Rollo, after baptism and homage done by proxy,[3] had formed a settlement, closing the mouth of the Seine against new comers—a land held as a fief of France, and termed the Duchy of Normandy.

In England, previously to the Norman conquest, there existed, as before observed, in certain customs and obligations of the English, the germs of institutions resembling the continental feudal system; and this was especially observable in later years under Edgar and

[1] La royauté se cacha sous la suzeraineté. Guizot, *Civilisation en Europe*, p. 98.
[2] *Constit. Hist.*, i. 252.
[3] In rather a rough manner, by the way, for the proxy, stooping down to perform the act of homage, gave his lord's foot such a jerk that he upset the very man he was swearing to uphold.—See Michelet, *Hist. de France*, Ed. 1871, i. 254.

Cnut, when sub-infeudation and commendation—a practice by which the inferior put himself under the personal care of a lord, but without altering his title or divesting himself of his right to his estate,[1] extensively prevailed. 'From the end of the tenth century a change sets in which might ultimately by a slow and steady series of causes and consequences have produced something like continental feudalism.'[2] In a word, the seeds of feudalism were in the ground.

Their development in natural course was prevented by the Norman conquest. The campaign of Hastings, the battle of Senlac, the coronation of the Conqueror, and the grants of lands made to the immediate followers of the Conqueror—those 'participes et coadjutores' of the expedition, who, coming with William the Bastard, conquered their lands by the sword,[3] necessarily resulted in the introduction of considerable alterations all in the direction of feudalism. It would appear, however, to have been the design of the Conqueror to continue as far as possible to govern the kingdom as it had been governed under previous kings; but the revolt of the

---

[1] Stubbs, *Constit. Hist.*, i. 253. See also, as to commendation, Freeman, *Norm. Conq.*, i. 89 and note N.; Hallam, *Middle Ages*, Ed. 1868, i. 103 and 315, note xi.

[2] Stubbs, *Select Charters*, p. 13.

[3] The following is the well-known story of Earl Warren, in the words of W. de Hemingford, a chronicler whose descriptions have ever about them a ring of armed men:—Vocatusque est inter ceteros comes de Warenna coram justitiarios regis, et interrogatus quo warranto teneret, produxit in medium gladium antiquum et aeruginatum et ait, 'Ecce, domini mei, ecce warrantum meum. Antecessores enim mei cum Willelmo bastardo venientes conquaesti sunt terras suas gladio, et easdem gladio defendam a quocunque eas occupare volente. Non enim rex per se terram devicit et subjecit, sed progenitores nostri fuerunt cum eo participes et coadjutores.'

English landowners against Odo de Bayeux and William FitzOsbern, justices regent during his absence on the continent; followed as it was by wholesale confiscation of lands and the introduction and settlement in this country of a host of Norman nobles all willing upholders of the continental system of government; and the alarm of Danish invasions, which convinced English as well as Norman of the supreme necessity for putting the kingdom in a state of defence, forced on the current of change. Before the year 1086, ' all the landowners of the kingdom had become, somehow or other, vassals either of the king or of some tenant under him;'[1] and, in the event, feudalism was firmly established in this country.

Under the feudal system thus introduced in England, the royal revenue was principally derived from the demesne and the feudal aids and incidents; and, although it is the object of this volume to give a history of taxes rather than revenue of this description, a page or two may well be devoted to a brief statement of the nature and extent of the sources of revenue above indicated.

The royal revenue under the feudal system.

First, as regards the royal demesne. The demesne, including what was termed the ancient demesne, as having belonged to the Crown at the time of Edward the Confessor, and the large reservations from the lands confiscated in consequence of the recent rebellion, was of vast extent: and when, by order of the Conqueror, the limits were ascertained by a general survey recorded in Doomsday Book, it appears that to the Crown were appropriated no less

The demesne.

---

[1] Stubbs, *Constit. Hist.*, i. 267.

than 1,422 manors or lordships, besides farms and lands in Middlesex, Shropshire, and Rutland.[1] The produce of the demesne, including rents (still paid, it should be observed, during the reigns of William I. and William II. to a great extent in kind, owing to the scarcity of money), afforded abundant means of maintaining the king, his numerous personal retainers, and a splendid court, and of indulging at Christmas and other periods of the year in the most profuse hospitality. But in addition to this, with a special view to the maintenance of a magnificent court, there existed two important royal prerogatives—purveyance and pre-emption : the first of which consisted in the right of purchasing provisions and other necessaries for the royal household at an appraised value ;[2] the other, in the right of impressing carriages and horses for the service of the king in the conveyance of timber, baggage, and goods.

Purveyance and pre-emption.

The feudal aids.

On certain special occasions of expense the king received money subventions from his subjects, termed 'aids;' and though endeavours to multiply occasions for such assistance were frequent, the feudal 'aids,' properly so called, were threefold—that is, were limited to the three following occasions :—

1. Towards defraying the expenses incident to knighting the king's eldest son ;

2. To enable the king to marry his eldest daughter

---

[1] *Return:—Pub. Inc. and Expend.* (1869). Part II., p. 431.
[2] Compare with this the 'publica comparatio' of the Romans, a sort of forced sale of commodities for public purposes; bearing in mind, however, that under the Romans this obligation was rarely enforced but on the rich : moreover, the articles were purchased at market price.

with becoming magnificence, and give her a suitable dowry; and

3. To ransom his person if taken captive in war.

For the military exigencies of the kingdom provision was made by an arrangement which consisted in the compulsory service in arms of all the military tenants of the Crown for forty days in the year; and this was supplemented by certain incidents or casualties of tenure based on the admitted necessity of keeping up the warlike character and efficiency of the members of the military force, and a constant supply of arms for its equipment. *Knight-service.*

These incidents and casualties were principally as follows:—

1. Payments in arms, armour, and horses, due to the king on the death of a tenant, termed 'reliefs'; and the difference between the relief and the Danish 'heriot' was, that the heriot was payable out of the goods of the deceased, whereas the relief was due from his successor. For most probably in its origin when feuds were life estates only, the relief had been a kind of purchase-money for 'relieving' or taking up the estate; and having thus originated, continued to be paid after feuds became hereditary. At first arbitrary in amount, not long after its introduction in this country the relief was ascertained, *i.e.*, rendered certain, by William the Conqueror, and fixed at a certain quantity of arms and habiliments of war. Subsequently, after the Assize of Arms,[1] it was commuted for a money payment of 100s. for every *The feudal incidents. 1. Relief.*

---

[1] As to the Assize of Arms, see below, p. 55.

knight's fee; and as thus fixed it continued ever afterwards.

<small>2. Primer seisin.</small>

2. Primer seisin, the right of the king, on the death of a tenant in capite, to a year's profits of his lands—in the nature of a return for that protection which, according to the rule of feudal obligation, he was bound to afford by entering on the lands and warding off intruders till the heir appeared to claim the lands and do homage to him as lord.

<small>3. Wardship.</small>

3. The wardship of minors.—A provision as necessary, in those rough times, in the interest of the minor as of the lord. A minor under the age of twenty-one years was incapable legally of performing knight service to the king. He probably would be equally incapable of defending himself and his property from rapacious neighbours. The feudal provision for the case gave, therefore, to the king custody of his person and the full profits of his lands; and, on the other hand, the king was bound to maintain, educate, and train him to arms, providing out of the profits of the lands a person capable of supplying his services. In the case of females—a stronger one for protection—it obviously was necessary to provide also against marriage of the infant heiress to the king's enemy: for which reason the royal authority extended not only to custody of her person and lands, but also to the selection of a husband for her, the giving the heiress away in marriage to a person of suitable position and willing as well as able to perform knight service to the king. Theoretically these arrangements were admirable, but in practice the rights of wardship were much strained, if not abused,

by several of our kings, particularly the right of marriage. Heiresses were married to favourites of the king,[1] or disposed of to husbands in a manner, so to put it, favourable to the royal exchequer. The maritigium—or right of bestowal in marriage—came to be considered of direct money value, and if the infant declined a proffered marriage, or married without the king's consent, she or he (for the maritigium was subsequently extended to males—'sive sit masculus sive foemina,' as Bracton has it) forfeited to the king double the value of the marriage—duplicem valorem maritigii.

The Exchequer Rolls abound in records of fines paid for permission to marry, or to be excused from marriage. Thus:—Walter de Cancey gives xv*l*. for leave to marry when and whom he pleased. Wiverone of Ipswich gives iiij*l*. and a mark of silver, that she may not be married to any one except to her own good liking—ne capiat virum nisi quem voluerit: and so *upon the like occasion*, as Madox puts it,[2] Albreda Sansaver, Alice de Heriz, and many others, men and women. Not to accumulate instances, but conclude with our best, Geoffrey de Mandevill, that he might have to wife Isabell, Countess of Gloucester, with all her lands and knight's fees (this is temp. Hen. 3), gave to the king 20,000 marks.[3]

The royal profits derived from minors were completed by the fine of half a year's value of their lands, paid when, at the age of twenty-one for males, fourteen

---

[1] Against this abuse is directed the 6th article of the Petition of the Barons at the Parliament of Oxford (A.D. 1259); and the grievance is, that royal wards are married in disparagement 'hominibus qui non sunt de natione Angliae'—to foreigners.

[2] *Hist. Exch.*, p. 320. [3] *May. Rot.* 2 Hen. III. *R.t.* 7. *Ibid.*, p. 322.

at first and subsequently sixteen for females, they sued out their livery or ousterlemain, that is, obtained release from royal protection and control.

4. Escheat.

4. The escheat of lands to the king, that is, their reverter or return to him as paramount lord, in case of death of a tenant without heirs, or default of performance of due service to the king.

5. Forfeiture.

5. Forfeiture of lands on attainder for treason, and

6. Fines on alienation.

6. Fines on alienation of lands, *i.e.*, on their transfer on a change of tenancy otherwise than in consequence of death, as by sale or gift.

Other casual revenue.

Certain other advantages that accrued to the king as lord paramount, though comparatively of minor importance, may be mentioned briefly, viz. :—

The right to—

1. Waifs.

1. Waifs, bona waviata—goods stolen and thrown away by the thief in his flight:

2. Estrays.

2. Estrays—' valuable animals found wandering in a manor and no man knoweth the owner of them,'[1] after due proclamation made in the church and two market towns next adjoining to the place where they were found:

3. Wreck.

3. ' Wreck of the sea, whales, and great sturgeons :'[2]

4. Bona vacantia.

4. Bona vacantia—property for which there was no owner; and

[1] Blackstone, *Comm.*, lib. i. c. viii. s. xv.
[2] See 17 Edward II. Stat. 1, c. xi. It is for infraction of this prerogative that the men of Roger de Poles are amerced (tem. Henry II.), who wrongfully seized a royal fish—quia injuste saisiaverunt so de crasso pisce. See Madox, *Hist. Exch.*, p. 381, where the Great Roll is quoted. Thus also the town of Haltebarge pay two marks ' for a royal fish which they took without licence and concealed.' *Ibid.*, p. 349.

5. Treasure trove—'where any money, coin, gold, silver, plate, or bullion is found hidden in the earth or other private place, the owner thereof being unknown.'[1] *5. Treasure trove.*

The best reason for existence of such rights was, probably, the absence of any better claim; except, indeed, in the case of whales and great sturgeons, which were considered royal fish 'by reason of their superior excellence.'

6. The custody of lands of 'natural fools,' taking the profits without waste or destruction, and finding them their necessaries.[2] *6. Lands of idiots.*

Some revenue was also derived, during the Norman period and subsequently, from the following sources—

1. From oblations or gifts offered for the concession or continuance of liberties, franchises, and privileges of all sorts. As by burgesses and guilds for charters, confirmations of their liberties, &c., of which the following are instances taken, not indeed wholly at random, but without any peculiar care in selection, from those quoted by Madox from the Rolls:—In the fifth year of King Stephen, the Londoners fined in C marks of silver, that *Revenue from oblations.*

---

[1] Blackstone, Comm., lib. i. c. viii. s. xiii.

[2] The king's prerogative in the preservation of the lands of lunatics, described as:—'Where any, that beforetime hath had his wit and memory, happens to fail of his wit, and there are many perlucida intervalla,' was of a different nature. Their lands and tenements he was equally bound to preserve from waste and destruction, but the residue of the profits, after maintaining them and their household—' the residue besides their sustentation '—was to be 'kept to their use, to be delivered unto them when they come to right mind; the king was to take nothing to his own use'; and 'if the party died in such estate then the residue was to be distributed for his soul by the advice of the Ordinary.' See 17 Edward II. Stat. 1, cc. 9, 10.

D

they might have sheriffs of their own choosing. The burgesses of Bedford (13 Hen. II.) fined in XL marks, to have the same liberties as the burgesses of Oxford had. The burgesses of Bruges, in XX marks, to have their town at ferm, &c., &c. The citizens of Hereford fined in C marks and two palfreys, to have the king's charter that they might hold the city of Hereford at ferm, of the king and his heirs, to them and their heirs for ever, for 40*l*. to be yielded at the Exchequer ; and that they might for ever have a merchant guild, with a Hanse, and other liberties and customs thereto belonging, and that they might be quit throughout England of toll, and lastage, of passage, pontage, and stallage, and of leve, and danegeld, and gaywite, and all other customs and exactions. And in the same year, 2 Hen. III., the citizens of Lincoln fined in CC marks, that they might not be tallaged that time in the tallage [1] which was laid upon the king's demesnes, and that they might have their town in ferm that year as they had in the time of King John the father of the king, and that for the same year they might be quit of the XL increment of the ferm of their town (de cremento firmae villae suae). The fullers of Winchester gave 10 marks for the king's charter of confirmation of their liberties.[2] The burgesses of York CC marks for their liberties. The vintners of Hereford fined in 40*s*. to have the king's grant that a

---

[1] As to tallage, see below, cap. v.
[2] They also paid a yearly rent, as did the guilds in several towns. The weavers and the bakers of London. The weavers of Oxford, Nottingham, York, Huntingdon, and Lincoln, and others.

sextertium of wine might be sold for 10*d.* in Hereford for the space of a year. And by private persons for franchises, fairs, &c., of which the following are instances:—The Bishop of Salisbury and the Abbot of Burton gave palfreys that they might have respectively a market and a fair until the king's full age. Roger Bertram gave 10 marks that his fair at Mudford, which lasted four days, might last eight days. Peter de Goldington gave one hawk for leave to enclose certain land part of his wood of Stokes, to make a park of it. Peter de Perariis gave twenty marks for leave to salt fishes as Peter Chivalier used to do.

2. From fines in relation to law proceedings. For justice was sold, that is, fines were paid to the king to have, and for expedition of, right or justice; and writs were denied, and suits and proceedings were delayed, or were stayed, on payment of a counterfine, for the defendant sometimes out-bid the plaintiff. The Exchequer Rolls abound in records of payment of such fines: and against these evils was aimed the famous prohibitory clause in the Great Charter of our liberties: 'Nulli vendemus, nulli negabimus, aut differemus rectum aut justitiam.'—'To no one will we sell, to no one will we deny or delay right or justice.' Of these fines it is unnecessary to adduce instances: and the same may be stated with reference to the penalties recovered for crimes, trespasses, and offences of all sorts (under which we may include, for present purposes, infractions of the forest law); from which, however, a considerable revenue was derived during the

From fines.

From penalties.

Norman period, a time when 'justice was administered mainly on account of the profits'

From amerciaments.

3. Amerciaments—fines assessed on offenders who were in misericordia regis, at the mercy (merci) of the king, and compositions for offences real or supposed, formed a third source, resembling in character that last mentioned. It was from hence that William the Conqueror, on the eve of his departure from England, in 1086, drew largely, when, as the chronicler tells us, he 'gathered mickle scot of his men where he might have any charge to bring against them, whether with right or otherwise,' wringing money from men by false accusations.[1]

And from miscellaneous exactions.

Lastly, as an 'etcetera' to the foregoing, may be added extortions of a very miscellaneous character. In exaction the rule of the kings of the Norman line was—'Quocunque modo, rem'; and this accounts for many of the extraordinary items of receipt recorded in the Exchequer Rolls quoted in the pages of Madox. The wife of Hugo de Nevill gives to the king 200 hens, for permission to sleep with her husband, Hugo de Nevill, for one night: Thomas de Sandford being pledge for 100 hens. Ralph Bardolph fined in five marks, for leave to arise from his infirmity. Robert de Abrincis, so much, for pardon of the king's ill will in the matter of the daughter of Geldewin de Dol, &c., &c. The Bishop of Winchester owes a tonell of good wine, for not reminding the king about giving a girdle to the Countess of Albemarle.[2] And Robert de Vaux fines

---

[1] Freeman, Norm. Conq. iv. 696; Chron. Sax. A.D. 1086.
[2] Mag. Rot. 11 John, Rot. 14, *b.* Sudhant.

in five of the best palfreys—quinque optimos palefridos —'ut rex taceret de uxore Henrici Pinel'—that the king would hold his tongue about Henry Pinel's wife.[1] The foregoing are but instances of miscellaneous penalties inflicted for the benefit of the exchequer. To particularize every method of extortion employed would be impossible.

Thus much as regards revenue from demesne, feudal revenue, and miscellaneous revenue and exactions. The only real tax of the period was the land tax, termed Dane-geld, previously mentioned. This the Conqueror revived in 1084, in consequence of an apprehended attack of Sweyn, king of Denmark; demanding, however, 6s., in lieu of the previous rate which had usually been two shillings, a hyde.[2] A 'mycel gyld' especially severe as coming the year after the great famine or 'mycel hungor.' Henceforth the Danegeld was continued, at different rates varying with the exigencies of the crown, as a regular impost.[3]

The land tax or Danegeld.

The profits of demesne, the feudal profits, the oblations, fines, and amerciaments before mentioned, the Danegeld, and the auxilium burgi (which perhaps should be included in the profits of demesne, and of which more will be said hereafter under the head Tallage), formed, with voluntary gifts and all that could be ex-

---

[1] Mag. Rot. 12 John, Rot. 13, *a*. Cumbr.

[2] In the same year also, after midwinter, the king ordained a large and heavy contribution over all England; that was, upon each hide of land two and seventy pence.—Chron. Sax. A.D. 1083; Hoveden, i. 130.

[3] Vovit (rex Stephanus) quod Danegeldum, id est, duos solidos ad hidam, quos antecessores sui *accipere solebant singulis annis* in aeternum condonaret.—Hoveden, i. 190. See also Madox, Hist. Exch., p. 478.

38   HISTORY OF TAXES.

Sources of revenue during the Norman period.

torted from the subject as for voluntary gift, the principal sources of revenue of the kings of the Norman line.

By these means the necessities of the State were supplied—

1 William the Conqueror.

1. During the reign of the Conqueror, 'that king so very stark, who took of his subjects many marks of gold and more pounds of silver, that he took by right and with mickle unright of his land-folk for little need;'[1] who 'gave his land so dear to bargain as it might be dearest; then came some other and bade more than the other had given, and the king let it to the man that bade him more; then came the third and bade yet more, and the king let it to that man's hands that bade most of all; and he recked not how very sinfully the reeves got it of poor men, nor how many *unlaws* they did. And as man spake more of right law, so man did more *unlaw*.[2] They reared up unright tolls, and many other unright things they did that are hard to reckon;'—that king whose fiscal exactions 'grew with his growth,'[3] becoming at last almost intolerable, like that unwieldy person he endeavoured to reduce at Rouen by a course of waters, the size of which occasioned Philips' jest about churching,[4] which was followed by the fearful oath of vengeance,[5] the

---

[1] Freeman, Norm. Conq., iv. 620, 621; Chron. Sax. A.D. 1087; Michelet, Hist. de France, ii. 130, where the whole passage is quoted.

[2] 'Swa mann dyde mare unlaga'—committed more oppressions under cover of law.

[3] 'William's habits of exaction grew upon him in his later days.'—Freeman, Norm. Conq., iv. 620.

[4] 'Quand donc accouchera ce gros homme,' disait le roi de France.

[5] 'Per resurrectionem et splendorem Dei.' William was fearful in

desolation of the French Vexin, the total destruction of Mantes by fire, and the death of William in consequence either of fever occasioned by too near approach to the flames, or of the more usually accepted plunge of his horse on burning embers—'ignes suppositos cineri doloso.'

2. During the twelve long years of misery the nation endured under the tyranny of William Rufus.[1] *2 William Rufus.*

3. During the times of Henry I. Times of rigorous taxation,[2] principally for the expenses of foreign war; but times when strong rule and just though strict administration,[3] by the restoration of order, gave to the people such peace and confidence that they thought the king to be the 'Lion of Righteousness' of Merlin's prophecies. *3 Henry I.*

4. And during the twenty years of turbulence and anarchy that followed—a time of castle building and *4 Stephen.*

---

oaths; so indeed were many kings after him. Thus Henry II. in the Sheriff's fee-tax dispute with Becket—'Per oculos Dei dabuntur pro reditu;' and so on, through Plantagenets, Tudors, and indeed long after their days.

[1] Destructeur rapide de toute richesse; ennemi de l'humanité, de la loi, de la nature, l'outrageant à plaisir; sale dans les voluptés, meurtrier, ricaneur et terrible, &c. Michelet, Hist. de France, ii. 203.

[2] The year 1103 was 'a very calamitous year in this land, through manifold contributions.'—Chron. Sax. A.D. 1103. The year 1105 was also 'a very calamitous year through loss of fruits and through manifold contributions.'—Ibid. 1105. The year 1124 was 'very severe. He who had any goods was deprived of them by the great tribute imposed. He who nothing had, died of hunger.'—Ibid. A.D. 1124.—See also Madox, Hist. Exch., pp. 7—9.

[3] 'There was great dread of him, no man durst misdo against another in his time. Peace he made for man and beast.'—Chron. Sax. A.D. 1135.

fortification, when every noble tyrannized over the neighbourhood of his stronghold; 'the twenty years that follow the death of Henry I., and are called the reign of Stephen'[1] (as Professor Stubbs puts it), aptly described by the Peterborough Chronicler as a time when—'All became forsworn and broke their allegiance; for every rich man built his castles and defended them against the king, and they filled the land with castles. They greatly oppressed the wretched people by making them work at these castles; and when the castles were finished they filled them with devils and cruel men. Then they took those whom they suspected to have any goods, by night and by day, seizing both men and women, and they put them in prison for their gold and silver, and tortured them with pains unspeakable. . . . . Many thousands they exhausted with hunger . . . and this state lasted the nineteen years that Stephen was king, and ever grew worse and worse. They were continually levying an exaction from the towns which they called *tenserie*, and when the miserable inhabitants had no more to give, then plundered they and burned all the towns, so that thou mightest well walk a whole day's journey, nor ever shouldest thou find a man seated in a town or its lands tilled.'[2]

---

[1] Select Charters, p. 20.
[2] See Stubbs, Constit. Hist. i. 328; and Professor Stubbs adds:— 'John of Salisbury compares England during this reign to Jerusalem when besieged by Titus.' But read the whole passage, of which the pith only is given in the Constit. Hist. as quoted above, in Chron. Sax. A.D. 1137.

Let us close the Norman period with an observation in reference to Stephen's vow about the Danegeld.[1] The quotation from Hoveden before given is incomplete. There should be added—'Haec principaliter Deo vovit et alia, sed nihil horum tenuit.' These and other things he swore to God to do, but did none of them.

The next inquiry is—How was collected this 'ample revenue wherewith to embellish State'? Collection of revenue.

In the counties, principally by the different sheriffs, many of whom paid for the profits of demesne within the county an annual sum as a composition, termed the 'firma,' or ferm of the shire: in short, farmed them at a rent, as also the Danegeld for the county. In the counties.

In the case of towns, the rent originally was included in and formed part of the ferm of the county, and was collected by the sheriff; who not unfrequently, by extortion from the burghers, made an exceedingly good thing of his bargain with the king. In many cases, however, the burghers early obtained release from the exactions of the sheriff, and a charter granting to them their town at a rent equal to the amount deducted from the ferm of the county. This was termed the 'firma burgi'—the ferm of the town, and this (as well as the auxilium burgi and subsequent tallage)[2] they collected by apportionment amongst themselves, and paid into the Exchequer directly, without intervention of the sheriff. In the case of guilds, the alderman In the towns.

---

[1] See above, p. 37, note 3.
[2] See below, cap. v.

collected the auxilium or tallage of the guild, and accounted for it to the Exchequer.[1]

The Exchequer.

The management and general superintendence of the royal revenue was in the hands of the Court of Exchequer[2] established under the Norman kings, and subsequently reconstructed, or rather re-organized, under Henry II.

Officers of the court.

The officers of the court were the chief officers of the king's household, and such others as the king was pleased to appoint, and were termed Barons of the Exchequer, as appointed from that order. One of the most important of these officers was the treasurer, of whose duties Madox writes:—

The treasurer.

'It seems to have been the duty of the treasurer in ancient time to act with the other barons at the Exchequer in the governance of the king's revenue, to examine and control accountants, to direct the entries made in the Great Roll, to attest the writs issued for levying the king's revenue, to supervise the issuing and receiving of the king's treasure at the Receipt of Exchequer, and, in a word, to provide for and take care of the king's profit.'[3] The treasurer thus appears to have acted in both chambers or divisions of the court,

The Upper and the Lower Exchequer.

for the court was divided into the upper exchequer, the court of account, and the lower exchequer, the court of receipt, which was called the 'Receipt of Ex-

---

[1] Thus, Robertus filius Levestani reddit compotum de 10*l*. de gilda Telariorum Londoniae, the guild of weavers.—5 Steph. Madox, Hist. Exch., p. 323.

[2] From the chequered cloth laid upon the table upon which the accountants told out the king's money, and set forth their account.—Ibid. p. 100.

[3] Ibid. p. 55.

chequer.' In this chamber the money was paid down, weighed, and tested. In that, accounts were passed and legal questions discussed and settled.[1]

Twice a year, at Easter and Michaelmas, full sessions were held in the palace at Westminster, attended by all the barons, with their clerks, writers, and other servants—'In the Exchequer there were, from ancient time, two notable terms or periods of the year, called the Duo Scaccaria; one of them the Scaccarium Paschae, and the other the Scaccarium S. Michaelis. . . . These terms, denoted by the Exchequer of Easter and the Exchequer of Michaelmas, were the times at which the summonses issuing out of the Exchequer for levying the king's debts were wont respectively to be returnable; for which reason, as the *Dialogue*[2] informs us, these two were appointed to be the general or principal terms for making payments into the Exchequer.'[3] At these sessions the sheriffs of counties and other accountable persons appeared and produced their accounts; paying at Easter such instalment as was considered sufficient after allowing for probable future disbursements, and at Michaelmas the balance of receipts for the year. *Easter and Michaelmas sessions.*

A word concerning the Rolls of the Exchequer. Of these Professor Stubbs states—'The record of the business was preserved in three great rolls; one kept *The rolls.*

---

[1] As to the Exchequer, read the Dialogus de Scaccario, written by Richard, Bishop of London, treasurer, son of Bishop Nigel, treasurer and grandson of Robert of Salisbury, justitiar.—Printed in Madox, Hist. Exch., and Stubbs, Select Charters, p. 160.
[2] Dial. de Scacc., ii. 1. 2.
[3] Madox, Hist. Exch., pp. 127, 128.

by the treasurer, another by the chancellor,[1] and a third by an officer nominated by the king, who registered the matters of legal and special importance.[2] The rolls of the treasurer and chancellor were duplicates; that of the former was called from its shape the great roll of the Pipe, and that of the latter the roll of the Chancery. These documents are mostly still in existence. The Pipe Rolls are complete from the second year of Henry II., and the Chancellor's rolls nearly so. Of the preceding period only one roll, that of the thirty-first year of Henry I., is preserved, and this with Doomsday-Book is the most valuable store of information which exists for the administrative history of the age.'[3]

The Angevin kings. The succession to the throne of England of the first of the Angevin kings was signalized by the reorganization of the Court of Exchequer previously mentioned, and the resumption of the royal demesnes, considerable portions of which had been alienated by previous kings. And, before long, an important fiscal alteration was effected in the commutation of knight service for a money payment.

Commencement of Scutage.

Hitherto the attendance on the king in arms

---

[1] The king's Chancellor, who continued up to the end of the reign of Richard I. to perform part of his duty at the Exchequer. After the separation of the Chancery from the Exchequer, it became necessary to appoint a separate high officer to execute the necessary duties at the Exchequer. The earliest record of the appointment of a Chancellor of the Exchequer is in the eighteenth year of Henry III. Return:—Pub. Inc. and Expend. (1869). Part II. p. 335.

[2] Dial. de Scacc., i. 5, 6.

[3] Constit. Hist., i. 379.

according to the array made on every expedition, the most important obligation of tenure by knight service, had been strictly enforced; and failure to attend or render the quota of men required by tenure would have involved seizure into the king's hands of the tenants' lands for non-performance of duty. It is true that not long after the introduction of the feudal system in this island, a practice commenced of allowing essoins or excuses for personal attendance, and attendance by deputy,[1] in the case of spiritual persons[2] unable to attend in the wars, and in cases of sickness, when the tenant of the king was 'ill and languishing.' But with these exceptions (which, indeed, would appear to follow ex necessitate rei), in all the expeditions to the various wars on the continent in which, in consequence of its possessions there, the Crown had so frequently been engaged during the preceding reigns, the military tenants had, as required by tenure, accompanied the king.

Knight service.

An army of this sort was, as may be imagined, not without disadvantages to the king. Delay was occasioned by the late arrival of important barons at the muster of the host. In the field all sorts of difficulties occurred in consequence of the existence of family disputes, jealousies, and wranglings about place and precedence. And the term of forty days which, it will be remembered, was the limit of annual compulsory military service (the usual term during which, under the feudal system, the tenant of a knight's fee

Its disadvantages to the king.

---

[1] Gilbert, Exch., p. 17.

[2] Ecclesiastics as well as laymen held per baroniam. It is on account of the baronies annexed to their bishoprics that bishops are lords of parliament.

was bound to be in the field at his own expense,[1] if we except such peculiar cases as the kingdom of Jerusalem, or castle guard on our northern borders), however sufficient for ordinary purposes of home protection or war on conterminous kingdoms, proved ill-adapted to transpontine expeditions such as those before mentioned. For what could be more inconvenient for the leader of the army than to be under necessity, on expiration of the forty days, either to cut short the campaign, or purchase, by payment or promises, the continued services of his best soldiers?

and to the military tenants. On the other hand, a growing disinclination to foreign service was observable in many of the military tenants. The pleasure of participation in 'the pomp and circumstance of war' was no doubt considerable, and chances opened of additional honours and grants of lands: but such considerations affected principally the great barons, and not directly the major part of the knights, who merely followed to the field some warlike lord whose 'men'[2] they had become, and therefore played but subordinate parts in the military drama. These therefore now began to take seriously into account the more certain results, as abundantly proved by experience, of a prolonged absence from home in those days of iron and blood. By this time the Norman had settled into an English home, and from the circumstances of the times the home tie was a strong one. Who, when he, the strong man armed, was beyond the

---

[1] Hallam, Middle Ages, i. 170.
[2] 'Devenio vester homo,' were the words used in performing homage.

seas, was to take care of goods and castle and fair ladye? And one result of absence was certain; for the warrior, on return, if he found wife and children safe, and castle intact, was sure to see his lands uncultivated and run to waste. It was the old story,

Squalent abductis arva colonis,

and tales are told of crusaders who, after some years of absence, on arrival at home, failed to recognise the place—an overgrown wilderness wholly unlike their cultivated domain.

Under these circumstances, king and subject were alike desirous of a change.

This was particularly the case as regards King Henry II., who might expect more frequent occasions for expeditions to the continent than any previous English king, as lord of wider domains there. For when Eléonore de Guyenne (Eléonore la fière), after the shameful return of Louis VII. from what is termed the second crusade, obtained divorce from a husband she termed a monk,[1] and married Henry Plantagenet, Count of Anjou and Duke of Normandy, she had added to his possessions Western France from Nantes to the Pyrenees; and Henry was, after his accession to the throne of England, in fact, a continental rather than an island king.

Particular reasons for commutation.

The principle of money payment in lieu of personal service, had been in a certain manner recognised in this country as far back as the Laws of Ine,[2] A.D. *cir.* 690, of which cap. 51 was as follows:—

[1] 'Se monacho, non regi nupsisse.'
[2] See Stubbs, Select Charters, p. 61.

'If a gesithcund man (of the rank of gesith or comes—companion of the king) owning land neglect the 'fyrd' (duty of military service), let him pay cxx shillings and forfeit his land; one not owning land, lx shillings; a ceorlish man, xxx shillings, as fyrdwite.' And the doctrine of representation had been admitted in the case of minors and females, as well as ecclesiastics and cases of sickness as before observed. King Henry now determined on further extension of the principle; and the increase of available money favoured his design.

The Scutage of 1156.

The introduction of the thin end of the wedge (so to put it) dates, according to many writers, from the expedition to Wales. Madox quotes from the Red Book of Alexander de Swereford,[1] which contains a collection, from the Rotuli annales or Great Rolls of the Pipe, of memorials concerning scutages, as follows:—

'The first scutage, as far as I can collect out of the annual rolls, was assessed in the second year of Henry Fitz-Empress. It was for the army of Wales; and was assessed only on those prelates who were bound to military services. The quota of it was 20$s.$ for each knight's fee.'[2]—At any rate we find scutage mentioned in the Pipe Roll of the 2nd year of Henry II.; and two years later, A.D. 1159, we arrive at the date fixed by the general consent of all writers on the subject as that of the effective commencement of scutage.

The scutage of Toulouse, 1159.

King Henry was at this time preparing to enforce his title, in right of his wife, to the county of Toulouse.

---

[1] Baron of the Exchequer, temp. Hen. III.
[2] Madox, Hist. Exch., p. 435.

The scene of action was distant; Count Raymond was not the man to submit without a struggle; doubtless he would be backed forcibly by Louis : probably, therefore, the conflict would be long and arduous. It was an occasion on which all the considerations hereinbefore mentioned had peculiar weight. Henry would be in a much better condition for carrying out his plans, aided by a full purse and an army of mercenaries; and as regards the barons and knights, though many of them might willingly embrace this opportunity for display under the banner of the new king—a prince

In the mid might and flourish of his May,

exchanging thus for a time the fog and damps of this island for the delicious sunshine of southern France, the majority of them would probably, if allowed to compound by money payment, prefer to remain at home in supervision of their estates, in lieu of taking a personal part in this foreign expedition for extension of the possessions of the Duke of Acquitaine. Thomas Becket, King Henry's Chancellor, had now become his intimate friend and chief adviser, and was not slow in counselling an arrangement which would, in effect, place in the king's hands the military training of the kingdom. Henceforth Henry should use mercenaries for foreign warfare; for purposes of home defence and order, the old national militia.

'King Henry, therefore, about to go on the expedition aforesaid, and taking into consideration the length and difficulty of the way, being unwilling to disturb either the knights who lived in the country or the burghers and country people generally, taking sixty Angevin shillings[1] in Normandy for each knight's fee, and from all his other possessions, whether in Normandy, England or elsewhere, according to that which seemed to him good, took with him his chief barons,[2] with a few personal followers, but an innumerable host of mercenaries.'[3]

The amount levied in England was two marks for each knight's fee, a knight's fee being of the annual value of 20*l*. The expedition lasted three months.

Thus was introduced the method of taxing the military tenants of the Crown in lieu of military service, termed scutage, from scutum, shield.—' Hoc anno (A.D. 1159) rex Henricus scotagium sive scutagium de Anglia accepit.'[4]

The scutage of Ireland, 1172. The precedent of the scutage of Toulouse was followed in 1172. When Henry collected another scutage from those knights who did not accompany him to Ireland;[5] whither he had hurried with a large force in the previous year, partly for the purpose of

---

[1] The money of the County of Anjou was worth a fourth of the English money of the same name.

[2] Becket is specially mentioned as having accompanied the king. His cortége was magnificent, and strongly impressed the minds of the inhabitants of the country he traversed, who exclaimed, ' What sort of man must the King of England be, since his Chancellor travels in such state ? ' (Michelet, Hist. de France, ii. App. 91.) It may be added that the warlike Chancellor, brave as well as splendid, joined in the fray at Toulouse, and himself—

'bore a knight of old repute to the earth.'

[3] Rob de Monte; Stubbs, Select Charters, p. 122.
[4] Gervas, Hist. Angl. Script., p. 1381.
[5] This scutage was charged under the title, ' De scutagio militum qui nec abierunt, &c.' The scutage of the knights who did not go into Ireland, nor sent thither any knights or money. Madox, Hist. Exch. p. 438, The amount was 20*s*. for each knight's fee.

taking possession of the island, and partly in order to avoid the Papal legation sent in consequence of the murder of Becket.

After this there was the scutage of Galloway;[1] an expedition which fell through in consequence of the submission of Ronald, who met Henry at Carlisle and did homage for the principality. *The scutage of Galloway, 1186.*

Thus it was that Henry practically disarmed the feudal power by accepting money from the knights in lieu of armed service. Michelet describes the process as the provision by the nobles of the bit and bridle for their own restraint.

Taxation of Moveables.

To pass on. Hitherto we have had to deal with the taxation of land; let us change the scene, proceeding to a different class of property, viz., moveables.

The subject that now for the first time claims our attention, viz., the taxation of moveables, in importance and interest is, probably, not excelled by any that has ever occupied the thoughts of financial legislators and others interested in the adjustment of taxation in the various countries of the world. It has presented difficulties varying in character and in degree, in different countries, under different circumstances, and at different times; but in an historical sketch such as the present, dealing professedly only with taxation in this country, we cannot wander far abroad.[2] Keeping at *Importance of the subject.*

---

[1] Madox, Hist. Exch. p. 441.
[2] Should the reader desire a wider investigation of the subject, let

home, where a great variety of knotty points engage the minds of Chancellors of the Exchequer, as suggestion follows on suggestion, proposal on proposal, and occasionally

<small>Quicker than noontide showers comes thought on thought,</small>

in the shape of propositions relating to taxation—it is sufficient to state that, in this country, probably no subject has ever presented itself involving questions more difficult of solution than the taxation of moveables; and that how best to tax personalty is still in the first rank, if not the first, of fiscal questions.

This importance, and the nature of these difficulties, will grow on the reader as he proceeds.

After this special announcement of the arrival of an important character on the stage, we may resume the thread of the narrative. Hitherto, that is, during the Anglo-Saxon and the Norman periods, taxation had reference to land. Moveables, of comparatively insignificant importance, were not directly taxed; though doubtless the baron, whenever moveable property of any amount was observed in possession of any within scope of his power, compelled ample contribution towards payment of the taxes or levies to which he was subject;[1] and, as regards the towns, royal exaction had in later times a certain relation to the value of the moveables possessed by the burghers.

<small>him read De Parieu's chapter on Taxes on moveable property and income from moveable property.—Traité des Impôts, i. 283.

[1] Or, indeed, plundered them at will. 'Ah! Sir,' says (in 'The Rule of the Nuns') the flatterer to the knight who had plundered his villeins, 'truly thou dost well, for men ought always to pluck and pillage the churl, who is like the willow—it sprouteth out the better for being cropped.'</small>

In consequence of the reforms introduced by King Henry, a rapid development was soon observable in the material wealth of the country ; and moveables now began to form a more important item of property. Equally protected by the State, this description of property was clearly in justice equally liable with land to contribute towards maintenance of the State; but the difficult question presented itself—how to discover what moveables an individual possessed ; how to arrive at the true value of moveable property for purposes of taxation ?

Increase of moveables under Henry II.

Under the Roman empire, when moveables as well as land were subject to taxation, 'individuals were compelled to make oath to the accuracy of their returns; and any one detected in making a false return, or in attempting to evade the tax by concealing or underrating property, was punished capitally and his estates were confiscated.'[1]

The tax on moveables levied in several countries of Europe towards the expenses of the first crusade, collected by means of chests erected in the different churches, into which the contributories were compelled to put so much in the pound on the value of their effects and the debts of which they had a certainty of being paid, was enforced in a similar manner by the obligation of an oath that the total was justly summed up ; and the sentence of excommunication was denounced against the fraudulent.

From the military tenants, who, as before stated,

---

[1] McCulloch, Treat. on Taxation, p. 108, 3rd Ed. See, however, as to the method of assessment for the lustralis collatio, Serrigny, Extrait de la *Revue critique de Législation et de Jurisprudence*, Dec. 1861. t. xix., vi^e livraison, p. 513, quoted by de Parieu, Traité des Impôts, i. 288.

were now taxed, not on the hide of 100 acres, but on the knight's fee—which was not a definite area of land, but was fixed by rent or valuation at 20*l.* of annual value, a return or report of the number of fees for which they were liable was accepted as the basis of assessment. But then the king's writ to a tenant-in-chief ran ' per fidem et ligantiam quam nobis debes ; ' true answer, as beseemed his fealty, was required from noble knight ; and to speak the truth—the Spartan rule—was ever a guiding precept of chivalry.[1]

> This is a shameful thing for men to lie.

Moreover, land cannot be concealed from view ; and in those days the approximate annual value of a man's possessions in land was probably no very difficult calculation to those who scrutinized the returns.

The Roman penalty for false return of moveables was probably never present to the mind of Henry. Excommunication (a fearful penalty in those days of Church ascendancy) was available only where the produce of the tax was devoted *in pios usus*—as for a crusade. For the moveables of the baron and the knight, the return of his steward, made under his direction, might probably be accepted. But in the case of the tenant in socage, the mere agriculturist, would his return of his horses, and cows, and sheep, and pigs be trustworthy? Would Cerdric, the Saxon franklin, care accurately to inventory cattle and goods for the purposes of the Norman tax-gatherer? And how could

---

[1] 'The excellent virtue of veracity was held in the same honour (as valour), and an offence against it followed with the like shame.' Mackintosh Hist. En 1   74

his return be checked by sheriff and justice? What answer would Gurth give when it came to the point, and the fiscal question was put. 'Dic mihi, Dameta, cujum pecus?'—Tell me, shepherd, whose herd is this? Again in the towns—as to the Jews, who possessed, be it observed, no inconsiderable portion of the wealth of the kingdom, they were the king's chattels, and the Exchequer of the Jews could deal with them; but would the wealthy burgher, owner of merchandise and other effects, himself by return divulge the existence of property so easy of concealment? Evidently the taxpayer's statement of his own liability in respect of moveables could not be treated as the basis of fair assessment, except in connection with some power of verification. In a word, the neighbours must be consulted.

The method of inquest by jury had been applied in ascertaining the legal and financial consuetudines in the Doomsday survey.[1] This formed a fair precedent; and the jury system was, as we know, a favourite with Henry. In 1181, in accomplishment of his designs for formation of a military force more entirely under his immediate control than were the feudal levies, the king issued the famous Assize of Arms. By this measure he enforced the duty of fyrd (which never had merged in the feudal military service), and re-armed and renovated the force which is our present militia. All freemen were directed to provide themselves with armour according to their means; and the liability of knights was regulated by the number of their knights' *The assize of arms a step towards taxation of moveables.*

---

[1] See Title of the Doomsday Inquest for Ely. Stubbs, Select Charters, p. 83.

fees. But, as regards men not knights, their liability was regulated by reference to their possessions in chattels or rent; and the value of the chattels and rent was to be estimated by chosen knights and freemen in each hundred or borough,[1] the number to be fixed by the king's justices.

By this application to taxation of the principle of assessment by jury the ground had been prepared for introduction of a tax on moveables, when, in 1188, it was decided to impose the celebrated Saladin tithe. It is unnecessary to go into the reasons which may have rendered Henry II. particularly anxious, at this time, to conciliate the court of Rome; the existence of preparations for a crusade was alone quite sufficient cause for a general contribution towards its expense;[2] and however questionable may have been the policy of the foundation of the kingdom of Jerusalem, once founded the kingdom must of course be maintained. The capture of Jerusalem had been a shock to Christendom; a new crusade was to take place for expulsion of Saladin; King Henry himself had taken the cross; and now at the national council held at Geddington it was resolved to levy a tenth of rent and moveables on all except those who took part in the expedition,[3] according to the Ordinance for the

The Saladin Tithe, 1188.

Moveables taxed.

---

[1] Per legales milites vel alios liberos et legales homines de hundredis et de burgis. See Assisa de armis habendis in Anglia, s. 9. Benedictus Abbas, i. 278; Hoveden, ii. 261.

[2] Croisade, c'est un mot sonore; efficace pour lever les décimes et les impôts.—Michelet.

[3] The Saladin tithe was also imposed by Philip Augustus in France, viz., le dixième de leurs revenus et de leurs biens meubles pour les frais de l'armement—c'est ce qu'on appelle la dime Saladine; taxe qui servait

Saladin tithe made by Henry in Council at Le Mans after taking the cross.

The importance of this famous Ordinance, as the first attempt to tax moveables in this country, justifies a detailed statement of its provisions. *The Ordinance of the Saladin Tithe.*

It commences with the charge :—

1. Every one shall give in alms this year the tenth of his rents and moveables. Except, in the case of knights, their arms and horses and clothing ; except also in the case of the clergy, their horses and books and clothing and vestments and church furniture of every sort ; and except the jewels of clergy and laity.

2. The second section has reference to collection. This is to be made in every parish in the presence of the representatives of the Church, the Knights Templars and Hospitalers, the King, the baron, and the clergy ; after excommunication denounced by the ecclesiastical authorities in each parish against the fraudulent. Then follows the jury clause :—' And if any one shall, in the opinion of those presiding at the collection, have given less than he ought, let there be chosen from the parish four or six freemen, who, on oath, shall state the amount which he ought to have stated ; and then he shall add what before was wanting.'

· 3. The third section contains an exemption in favour of the clergy and knights who had taken the cross, that is, would serve personally in the expedition.

4. The fourth section provides for promulgation of the Ordinance in every parish.

de trophée à la gloire du conquérant.—Voltaire, Essai sur les Mœurs, c. 6. Œuvres complètes, xvii. 136. See also Hoveden, ii. 330.

The following is the Latin text of the Ordinance :—

Ordinance of the Saladin Tithe.

1. Unusquisque decimam reddituum et mobilium suorum in eleemosynam dabit hoc anno, exceptis armis et equis et vestibus militum, exceptis similiter equis et libris et vestibus et vestimentis et omnimoda capella clericorum, et lapidibus pretiosis tam clericorum quam laicorum.

2. Colligatur autem pecunia ista in singulis parochiis, praesente presbytero parochiae et archipresbytero, et uno Templario et uno Hospitalario, et serviente domini regis et clerico regis, serviente baronis et clerico ejus, et clerico episcopi; facta prius excommunicatione ab archiepiscopis, episcopis, archipresbyteris singulis in singulis parochiis, super unumquemque qui decimam praetaxatam legitime non dederit, sub praesentia et conscientia illorum qui debent, sicunt dictum est, interesse. Et si aliquis juxta conscientiam illorum minus dederit quam debuerit, eligentur de parochia quatuor vel sex viri legitimi, qui jurati dicant quantitatem illam quam ille debuisset dixisse; et tunc oportebit illum superaddere quod minus dedit.

3. Clerici autem et milites qui crucem acceperunt, nihil de decima ista dabunt, sed de proprio suo et dominico : et quidquid homines illorum debuerint ad opus illorum colligetur per supradictos, et iis totum reddetur.

4. Episcopi autem per litteras suas in singulis parochiis episcopatuum suorum facient nunciari, et in die Natalis, et Sancti Stephani, et Sancti Johannis, ut unusquisque decimam praetaxatam infra purificationem Beatae Virginis penes se colligat, et sequenti die et deinceps, illis praesentibus qui dicti sunt, ad locum quo vocatus fuerit, unusquisque persolvat.[1]

The Saladin tithe as imposed in France. In conclusion of this chapter, it may be interesting to state a few particulars regarding the imposition of the Saladin tithe or tenth in France. According to M. Clamageran, Philip Augustus summoned a meeting

---

[1] Benedictus Abbas, ii. 31; Hoveden, ii. 336.

of all the archbishops, bishops, abbés and barons of the kingdom at Paris, in the month of March, in 1188, when by common consent the following resolutions were passed:—

Every one whether clerk or layman, knight or not, shall pay the tenth of his moveables and of his rents.

The following are excepted: 1. crusaders; 2. the monastic orders; 3. lepers.

Property shall be assessed, without deduction for debts, on the declaration of the tax-payer, who shall make oath thereto under penalty of anathema in case of perjury.

The tenth shall be levied:—on the communes, by their lords;—on church property and goods, by the archbishops, bishops and chapters;—on seigniories or lordships, by the lords having the right of justice.

Part of the produce of the tax is appropriated to the crusaders. The knight crusader, legal heir, son or son-in-law of a knight not crusader, or of a widow, shall have the tenth payable by his father or his mother, as the case may be. The lord crusader shall have the tenth payable by his vassals, his lieges, and those who dwell on his domains, if they are not crusaders.

If any one refuses to pay this tenth he may be arrested by the person to whom it is due, who may dispose of him as he thinks fit.[1]

[1] 'Pour en être par celui-ci disposé selon sa volonté.' Clamageran, Hist. de l'Impôt, i. 279.

CHAPTER V.

FROM THE COMMENCEMENT OF THE TAXATION OF MOVEABLES TO THE TERMINATION OF THE REIGN OF EDWARD THE THIRD, A.D. 1188–1377.

THE period under review in this chapter extends over nearly two hundred years. Three new subjects will be brought under observation, viz., tallage—the arbitrary taxation of towns and royal demesne ; port duties, or 'customs' as we term them ; and, towards the close of the period, the imposition of the first poll tax: and the following is the order of the narrative.

Order of the narrative during this period. It is intended :—To commence with the history of the taxes relating to land, taking scutage first, and afterwards the general land tax. Next, to explain the origin of tallage, and follow that subject down to the time when we find exaction from towns and demesne merged in a more extended system of taxation embracing the whole kingdom. The history of the taxation of moveables will follow next in the order of subjects. After this, will come some observations regarding the origin of port duties or 'customs,' and the history of these duties to the end of the period. And lastly, a few lines regarding the imposition of the first poll tax. In conclusion of all will be added some general remarks relative to events having a bearing on taxation during the different reigns included in the period, inserted more with the view of keeping up a connexion with the general history of the time, than as a mere resumé or summary of preceding details.

The following Table, in which are stated some of the principal taxes of different kinds imposed during the reigns of Kings Richard I., John, Henry III., Edward I., Edward II., and Edward III., may be useful as presenting a bird's eye view, as it were, of the current of taxation during the period in question, and as affording an easy means of reference to dates.

TABLE of the Principal Taxes imposed A.D. 1189—1377.

A.D.	Reign	Land Taxes			Taxes on Moveables, &c.	Tallages	Other Taxes
		Scutage	Carucage, the old Danegeld or hidage				
1189.	RICHARD.	1189. Wales. 10s.	—		—	1189	
		[1]1193. 20s. . . .	1193		1193.4	1193	
		—	1194[2]. 2s.		—	1194. 10[3]	
		1195. Normandy. 20s.	—		—	—	1195–6 tournament tax.
		1196. Normandy. 20s.	—		—	—	
		—	1198. 5s.		—	—	
1199.	JOHN . .	1199. Normandy. 2 m.	—		—	1199[4]	
		—	1200. 3s.		—	—	

NOTE.—Under the head Scutage, m. signifies marks. Under the head Moveables, l. signifies laity; cl. clergy; and d. demesne, including towns; and, later on, c. signifies counties, and t. towns. Under the head Port duties, sub. signifies subsidy in addition to the customs.

[1] A.D. 1193. The taxes of this year were for the King's ransom.
[2] A.D. 1194. In this year Richard seized all the wool of the Cistertians, who compromised by payment of a fine. Hoveden, iii. 242.
[3] This is the first instance of a tallage being called a decima or tenth. See Madox, Hist. Exch. p. 503.
[4] Ibid. p. 487.

HISTORY OF TAXES.

A.D.	Reign	Land Taxes		Taxes on Moveables, &c.	Tallages	Other Taxes	
		Scutage	Carucage, the old Danegeld or hidage				
1201.	JOHN.	1201.[2] 2 m.	—	1201. 40[1]	—		
		—	—	1203. 7[3]	—		
		1204. 2½ m., and on several other occasions the principal being.	—	—	—		
		—	—	1207. 13, 1. & cl.[4]	—		
		1211. Wales. 2 m.	—	—	—		
		1214. Poitou. 3 m.	—	—	—		
1216.	HEN. III.	—	—	—	1218		
		—	1220. 2s.	—	—		
		1221. 2 m.	1224. 2s.	—	—		
		—		1225.[3]15 1.&cl.	—		
		—		1227. 16, cl.	1227		
		—		—	1230[5]		
		1231. Bretagne. 3 m.		—	—		
		—		1232. 40,1.&cl.	1234		
		—		1237. 30,1.&cl.	—		
		1242. Gascony. 20s.		—	—		
		—		—	1243		
		—		—	1246		
		1253. 3 m.		1253. 10, cl.[7]	1255		
				1266. 10, cl.[7]			
		—		1269. 20, 1. & 10, cl.	—	Port Duties	Other Taxes
1272.	EDW. I.	—		—	—	—	
		—		1275. 15, 1. and cl.	—	1275	
		1277. Wales. 40s.		1277. 20, 1. and cl.	—	The old customs	
		—		—	—		
		—		1283. 30, 1. and 20, cl.	—		
		1285. Ditto 40s.		—	—		
		—		—	1288	—	
1290.				1290. 15, 1. & 10 cl.	—	—	

---

[1] Of rent, for the Crusade.
[2] Scutage service for licence to stay at home.
[3] Of the moveables of the Barons.
[4] This 13th had reference also to rent from land.
[5] Granted by Parliament called at Westminster, at Christmas, 1224.
[6] Heavy exactions from London and from the Jews.
[7] Of rent, for 3 years.

A.D. 1188—1377.

A.D.	Reign	Land Taxes	Taxes on Moveables, &c.	Tallages	Port Duties	Other Taxes
1294.	Edw. I.	—	1294. 10, 1. 6, d.	—	—	
		—	1295. 11, 1. 7, d. 10, cl.	—	—	
		—	1296. 12, 1. 8, d.	—	—	
		—	1297. 8, 1. 5, d.	—	—	
		1300—6, Scutages for Scotland	1301. 15, 1.	—	—	
			1302. 15, 1. & cl.	1304	1302. The new customs.	
		—	1306. 30, 1. & cl. 20, d.			

A.D.	Reign	Taxes on Moveables, &c.	Port Duties	Other Taxes
1307.	Edw. II.	1307. 20, 1. 15, d. & cl.	The Old and the New Customs.	
		1309. 25, 1. & d. 10, cl.		
		1313. 20, c. 15, t.	—	
		1315. 15, d.[1]		
		1318. 18, c. 12, t.	—	
		1322. 10, 1. 6, d.	—	
1327. Jan.	Edw. III.	1327. 20, c. & t.	—	
		1332. 15, c. 10, t.		
		1334. 15, c. & 10, t. & cl.	—	
		Tenths and Fifteenths		
		1336. 15, c. & 10, t.	—	
		1337. 15, c. & 10, t.	—	
		3 for 3 years	—	
1339.		—	—	1339. 10th sheaf fleece and lamb [2] for two years
		—	—	30,000 sacks of wool [3]

---

[1] For the war with Scotland. The same year the military tenants were summoned for service. Par. Rolls, i. 351.
[2] By the lords for their demesnes.
[3] By the Commons.

A.D.	Reign	Tenths and Fifteenths.	Port Duties	Other Taxes
1340.	Edw. III.	1340. 15, c.[1] 9, t.	1340. Sub. for little more than a year.	1340. 9th sheaf, fleece, and lamb for two years[2](cancelled 1341) 1340. 20,000 sacks of wool 1341. 30,000 sacks of wool [3]
			1343. Sub.[4] for 3 years	
		1344. 15, c. & 10, t. 2 for 2 years 1346. 15, c. & t. 2 for 2 years 1348. 15, c. & t. 3 for 3 years	1346. Sub. for 2 years	
			1350. Sub. for 2 years.	
		1351. 15 & 10 3 for 3 years		
			1353. Sub. for 3 years 1355. for 6 years 1362. for 3 years 1364. for 3 years [5] 1368. for 2 years [6] 1369. for 3 years [7]	
				1371. 50,000l. levied on parishes
		1372. 15 & 10 for 1 year	1372. for 2 years.[8] Tunnage and poundage 1 year	
		1373. 15 & 10 2 for 2 years	1373. Sub. for 2 years Tunnage and poundage 2 years 1376. Sub. for 3 [9] years	
1377.		—	—	1377. Poll Tax 4d.

[1] Payable by non-agriculturalists.
[2] By the lords and knights of counties.
[3] In lieu of the 9th sheaf, fleece and lamb of second year.
[4] 40s. on wool.
[5] 40s. on wool, 4l. on leather.
[6] 36s. 8d. on wool, 4l. on leather.
[7] At increased rate.
[8] At the same rate.
[9] As granted in 1373.

Taxes Relating to Land.

1. Scutage.

To commence then with the history of scutage, which, as the reader will recollect, was a payment in commutation for military service in the king's expeditions, affecting only the lands of the military tenants in capite of the king, and not the lands of the tenants at fixed rent—the socage tenants. This military tax continued in use for about the next 120 years, and the principal occasions on which it was levied were as follows :—

Three scutages were levied during the reign of Richard I. One in the first year of the reign, under pretence of an expedition to Wales, at the rate of 10s. for every knight's fee;[1] another in 1195, on those tenants in chief who had not accompanied the king to Normandy, at the rate of 20s. for every fee;[2] and the third in 1196, also for Normandy, and also at the rate of 20s.[3] To which it may be added that the ransom of the king (in 1193) was levied partly by a tax of 20s. on the knight's fee. This, however, cannot properly be termed scutage, but ranks under the head of feudal 'aid.' *During the reign of Richard I.*

During the reign of John no less than ten scutages were raised; commencing with that for his expedition to Normandy in the first year of his reign, A.D. 1199, at the increased rate of two marks on the knights' *During the reign of John.*

---

[1] Madox, Hist. Exch. p. 443; Stubbs, Constit. Hist. i. 507.
[2] Madox, Hist. Exch. p. 444.
[3] Ibid.

fee;[1] after which scutage appears to have been levied almost annually.

Constant taxation of the barons. The constant taxation to which the barons were thus subjected formed one of the principal grounds of complaint in their disputes with the king, and had an important bearing on subsequent events in this reign. The king's position as regards demands on the English knights for personal service in foreign expeditions was no doubt in effect somewhat altered after the loss of Normandy through his own fault. This was especially the case as regards the northern barons, who were mostly descendants not of the old feudal families, but of the ministerial nobility of more recent creation, and had little personal interest in Normandy. These now alleged that, as regards defence of the realm, their proper service consisted in the necessary protection of the northern border. At any rate they drew a distinction between hostile excursion preventive to attack—as to defend the possessions of the king when really Duke of Normandy, and expeditions to recover *Refusal of the northern barons to pay scutage.* territory thus lost. Accordingly when called on by the king to follow him in an expedition to the Continent in 1213, they pleaded exhaustion in consequence of previous expeditions in this island, and even went so far as to deny their liability to serve in transpontine expeditions. And when, in the following year, the king, on his return from the Continent, demanded a scutage from them in accordance with precedents of similar payments in the reigns of his father and brother, they flatly refused to pay.

[1] Madox, Hist. Exch. p. 444.

Thus was accelerated the crisis which resulted in the signature by John of the Articles of the Barons, and the issue of the Great Charter. The articles of the Charter relating to scutage are the 12th and the 14th. The 12th follows in its terms the 32nd of the Articles of the Barons, and provides, for the future, that—

The Great Charter, 1215.

The 12th and 14th Articles.

'No scutage or aid shall be imposed in the kingdom, unless by the common counsel of the realm, except for the purpose of ransoming the king's person, making his first-born son a knight, and marrying his eldest daughter once, and the aids for these purposes shall be reasonable in amount.'

And the 14th is to the following effect:—

For taking the common counsel of the realm for imposing an aid in any other case than the three cases before mentioned, or for imposing a scutage, we will cause to be summoned the archbishops, bishops, abbots, earls, and greater barons by our writ directed to each severally; and also all our other tenants in chief by a general writ addressed to our sheriffs and bailiffs; and the summons shall be for a stated day not less than forty days distant, and to a stated place; and in every writ shall be expressed the cause for the summons; and after summons thus made the business shall proceed on the stated day according to the counsel of those who are present, notwithstanding the absence of any who may have been summoned.'

These clauses embody in very clear statement the right of taxation as regards the imposition of scutage; and, as it is not the object of this volume to go deeply into difficult questions regarding the constitutional right of taxation, we need not pause to consider how far they were an innovation, or merely the expression of rights previously existing. Let us continue the list of scutages.

Scutages during the reign of Henry III.

Several scutages were levied in the reign of Henry III.,[1] the principal being: one in 1221, of two marks on the knight's fee;[2] another in 1231, of three marks;[3] another in 1242, of 20s.;[4] and another in 1253, of three marks on the fee[5]:—

During the reign of Edwd. I.

The first scutage of the reign of Edward I., who had succeeded to the throne in 1272, was one levied on his return from Wales, in 1277, at the rate of 40s. for each knight's fee throughout the kingdom; those knights being excepted from payment who went to war with the king personally or by proper substitutes.[6] Again

Conquest of Wales, A.D. 1283.

in 1285 another scutage is imposed throughout England 'pro Wallia,' for the war in Wales.[7] Subsequently to which, as it would appear from the pages of Madox,[8] several scutages were levied for the armies of Scotland

Scotland and Wallace, A.D. 1296-8.

towards the close of the reign. Here, that is with the reign of Edward I., we may consider scutage to have terminated; for though, according to Madox,[9] fines for

---

[1] Madox, Hist. Exch. 445. Stevens states that 15 scutages were granted in this reign (vide p. 47). Probably, however, many of the number were merely voluntary aids from the barons, &c.
[2] Matt. Paris, ii. 247.
[3] Ibid. p. 329.
[4] Ibid. p. 466.
[5] Ibid. iii. 136.
[6] Chron. T. Wykes, Anr. Monast. iv. 274.
[7] Ann. Dunstapl. Ann. Monast. iii. 317.
[8] Hist. Exch. p. 474.
[9] See Writ quoted in Hist. Exch. p. 461.

not serving in the army summoned to march against the Scots were exacted, 16 Edward II., from the archbishops, bishops, clergy, widows and other women, who owed service in that army, and were desirous to make fines for the same, this method of taxation was henceforth superseded by a wider system of taxes on moveables, which included burgher and socage tenant—citizen and agriculturist, as well as baron and knight.

It remains to be explained in what manner scutage, when granted or imposed, was assessed on the taxpayers and collected. The assessment and collection of scutage.

The ancient method of rating land was by the hyde of 100 acres; but when, in lieu of this, it became the practice to rate land by the knight's fee, reports—charters—certificates (they are called sometimes by one name, sometimes by another) were required, if not upon every single occasion of levy of scutage, still as a general rule, from the military tenants, stating the number of fees for which they were liable.[1] These reports were subjected to examination by the Exchequer officers, who tested, as far as in their power, the correctness of the returns. Occasionally disputes arose, in most instances in relation to lands held by ecclesiastics, Certificates of liability.

---

[1] Madox, Hist. Exch. pp. 400, 440. The cartae baronum sent in when the aid for marrying Henry II.'s daughter Maud was levied, were ordered to be laid up and preserved in the Exchequer. A hutch was made to keep them in; but the originals of them were not to be found in the time of Madox, save one, which Madox quotes in full. 'Copies of many certificates of baronies and knights' fees were entered in an orderly manner in the Red Book of the Exchequer.' The hutch for the cartels, it may be observed, cost 22d., a large sum as compared with the price of such hutches subsequently: for a hutch to lay up the memoranda of the great Exchequer costs, temp. 9 Henry III., only 7d.; a hutch to lay the Inquisitions in 2d.; and 'ten dozen of hutches' 20s.

bishops and abbots, claiming probably to hold in frank-almoign [1] and not by baronial and military service : in which cases the entry on the Exchequer Rolls runs :— so and so is charged for so many fees, quos non recognoscit—regarding which he denies his liability.[2] Generally speaking, however, the reports appear to have been accepted at the Exchequer as correct, and they formed the basis of subsequent taxation.[3] The king's writ issued to the barons of the Exchequer to collect his scutage ; and it was paid in directly to the Exchequer by those liable to payment.

In the reign of John when, as before observed, many of the barons were inclined to dispute the legality of his exaction of scutage, difficulties may have arisen in obtaining the usual reports, or it may be that the king only followed his habitual course of extortion ; but from whatever cause, scutages appear to have been sometimes assessed in an arbitrary manner. To remedy this abuse was the principal object of the provision inserted in the Great Charter of Henry III., on the second reissue, in 1217, which, while it asserts the right to take scutage, provides (S. 44) that :—' Scutage shall be taken for the future as it was accustomed to be taken in the time of King Henry, our grandfather '—Henry II.[4] And accordingly the practice of sending in reports would

[1] Scutage was not chargeable upon lands holden in frank-almoign. Madox, Hist. Exch. p. 466.

[2] Ibid. p. 451.

[3] 'The temporal barons and tenants in capite who sent their certificates were generally charged for the number of fees contained in their certificates. But if they sent no certificates, they were charged according to what appeared by the king's records, or the testimony of his officers.' Ibid. p. 403.

[4] Scutagium capiatur de cetero sicut capi consuevit tempore Henrici regis avi nostri.

appear to have been continued under Henry III., and was employed in the 20th year of the reign for the analogous levy for the aid to marry his sister.¹

As far as our investigation of scutage has hitherto proceeded, the tax has the appearance of a charge affecting only the barons and knights who held of the king in capite by tenure of knight service; and such was its immediate incidence. It should be borne in mind, however, that many of the great lords held a considerable number of fees, and had tenants holding of them by knight service the fees for which they paid scutage to the king. These sub-kings (a useful word already previously employed), having themselves paid, or with a view to enable them to pay, to the king *his* scutage for an expedition, had the right of taking what was termed *their* scutage from their tenants according to the quantity of their tenure; indeed, this right extended even to cases where the lord performed personal service in an expedition, and therefore did not pay scutage. The right of taking scutage was unquestionable. Nevertheless sometimes the lord was forced to make fine with the king to have his scutage. Thus, Roger de Verli paid into the Exchequer xxvi*s*. and viii*d*. (21 Henry II.), that he might have the service or scutage of his men (or tenants).² And sometimes the king grants the right without mention of a fine. Thus, Henry III. grants to William de Say his scutages from the fees which he held of the king in chief, because he had done personal service with the king in Gascony³

The incidence of scutage.

---

¹ Madox, Hist. Exch. p. 440.
² Ibid. p. 469. This was for the scutage of Ireland.
³ Ibid. p. 470.

Their scutages the lords collected from their tenants, where they had the power of distraining for the amount, personally ('per manum suam,' as it was termed); in other cases, with the assistance of a writ of aid directed to the sheriff. Thus, Henry de Braybrok (temp. 6 Henry III.) had a writ of aid directed to the sheriff; who is ordered to assist him to distrain his knights who hold of him the fees which he holds of the king in capite, for payment to him of the scutage for those fees, at the rate of two marks a fee, which scutage was charged against him at the Exchequer.[1]

Such was the ancient method of assessment and collection of scutage. In process of time, difficult questions arose regarding the tenure of lands, 'whether they were holden by knight's service or by some other tenure, or (if they were holden by knight's service) whether they were holden immediately of the king or of some other lord,[2] or by how many knights' fees they were holden, and the like; and for these and other causes it became almost necessary that scutage should be collected by the sheriffs of counties, who might make inquisition by the oath of jurors concerning these and such like articles proper to be enquired into."[3] Thus, in the 27th year of Henry III., writs were issued to the sheriffs of counties for collection of the scutage of Gascony, directing them to make enquiry by the oath of twelve knights and lawful men, through whom the truth might best be known, men of substance so as to be responsible to the king in case of default, and

---

[1] Madox, Hist. Exch. p. 469.

[2] For a petition for apportionment of scutage, see Par. Rolls, i. 47, No. 20.

[3] Ibid. p. 472.

find what lands were holden of the king or of others who held of the king in capite, &c., and to distrain the tenants of such fees to pay their scutage for the same.[1] It appears, from the terms of the writ for Middlesex, that the common council of the kingdom had decreed that this scutage should be collected by the sheriffs of counties.[2]

Occasionally, in later times, commissioners were appointed for assessment and collection of scutage. The following is a free translation from a writ (10 Edward II.) appointing William de Hebbeden and Richard de Goldesburgh commissioners to levy and collect the scutages for the armies of Scotland of the 28th, 31st, and 34th years of Edward I., within the county of York, at the rate of 40s. for each fee :—In order thereto, they are to enquire by oath of lawful men of the county what fees were held in capite of the king at the time of those armies. . . . . And the sheriff of the county is commanded to summon lawful men to appear before the commissioners, to make inquisition touching the matters aforesaid. And inasmuch as several persons as well jurors, as bailiffs of the king and of lords of divers liberties, had neglected to attend the commissioners, and to assist or obey them : the king commands the commissioners to amerce severely all such jurors and bailiffs as they should find rebellious or disobedient, and to cause estreats of such amercements to be sent into the Exchequer, that the same may be levied for the king's use.[3]

Form of writ appointing commissioners for assessment and collection.

[1] Writ for Lincolnshire. See Madox, Hist. Exch. p. 472.
[2] Ibid. p. 473.
[3] Writ. Quod rebelles et inobedientes collectoribus scutagii amercientur, &c. Ibid. p. 474.

2. *Carucage.*

Having thus followed to its close the history of the knightly tax scutage, let us pass on to that of the more general tax on all cultivated lands, with this preliminary observation, viz., that little and no very clear information on the subject can be obtained.

Date of cessation of Danegeld.

The Danegeld, already for many years previously a mere composition with the sheriff—a settled revenue and accounted for in like form with the yearly ferm of the county, is not accounted for in the Great Rolls in the same manner after the 2nd year of Henry II.; though some traces of its subsequent existence for one or two years are there to be found.[1] According to Professor Stubbs, 'the ancient Danegeld disappears from the Rolls as a separate item after 1163, and is succeeded by the donum or auxilium (hereinafter mentioned under the head tallage) which 'probably levied on a new computation of hidage, must have been a reproduction of the old usage.'[2]

A similar tax under name of carucage in 1194

A similar tax on agricultural lands, but under the different name of 'carucage,' was levied by Richard I., on his second visit to this country, in 1194, at the rate of 2s. for each carucate or plough land.[3] Again in

and in 1198.

1198, there was levied a 'great' tax, as Tyrrell terms it, at the rate of five shillings for each carucate. For the purposes of this carucage a new survey was made

---

[1] Madox, Hist. Exch. p. 478.
[2] Constit. Hist. i. 582. It would appear, however, that an auxilium comitatus—an aid in the nature of a yearly payment—was rendered by the counties in the reign of Stephen. See Madox, Hist. Exch. p. 418.
[3] At the great Council at Nottingham. Hoveden, iii. 242.

of all lands in the kingdom: and the plan of assessment by jurors, previously adopted, as regards rent and moveables, for the Saladin tithe, was now applied to the assessment of land. A clerk and a knight were sent into every county in England; who, with the assistance of the sheriff of the county and knights chosen for the purpose, after oath taken for faithful performance of duty, summoned before them the stewards of the barons of the county, and, in every township, the lord or bailiff and the reeve and four men free or villein; and two knights for every hundred; who took oath that faithfully and without fraud they would state how many carucates (*i.e.*, what extent of land that could be worked by the plough) were contained in each township (with certain particulars regarding the tenure and liability of lands); and assessed the tax accordingly. The assessments were registered in four rolls, of which the clerk had one, the knight commissioner another, the sheriff of the county the third, and the steward of each baron so much of the fourth as related to his lord's land. The tax was collected by two knights and the bailiff in each hundred; who accounted for the proceeds to the sheriff; who accounted to the Exchequer. The penalties for perjury were severe:— Every villein convicted of perjury was to give to his lord the best ox of his plough team, and render to the king the amount declared to have been lost to the king by his perjury; and every freeman so convicted was to be at the king's mercy, and also was to pay from his own property what had been lost to the king, as in the case of the villein. Each baron was required, with the

Method of assessment

and collection.

Penalties for evasion.

aid of the sheriff, to collect the tax from his tenants : in default the amount was chargeable on his domain. The carucate, or quantity of land that could be ploughed by one plough or team in a season, was fixed at 100 acres.[1]

A similar tax taken by John

King John, in the second year of his reign, A.D. 1200, returns from Normandy to take a carucage of 3s.[2] We have no information how the tax was levied; but it appears to have been considered grievous as coming so soon after scutage of the previous year.[3] The other exactions of this reign have reference principally to the barons and knights, the Jews, the rich burghers, and the clergy.

and by Henry III.

Passing on to the reign of Henry III. In 1220 the king receives a carucage of 2s. for each carucate.[4] The tax is assessed by the sheriff and two knights of the shire, the most intelligent, willing, and able for the business, chosen in full assembly of the county; who collect the tax; and send the proceeds under their seals to London. And in the writ to him the sheriff is enjoined, as he loves himself and his (omnia sua), so to manage the affair that there be no occasion to complain of and inquire into the assessment and collection of the tax, to the great confusion of himself and those connected with him in the said assess-

---

[1] Hoveden, iv. 46; Stubbs, Select Charters, p. 249.

[2] Johannes rex Angliae transfretavit de Normannia in Angliam et cepit de unaquaque carucata totius Angliae tres solidos. Hoveden, iv. 107; Matt. Par. ii. 85.

[3] Rad. Coggeshale, p. 860; quoted, Stubbs, Select Charters, p. 264.

[4] De qualibet caruca sicut juncta fuit in crastino Beati Johannis Baptistae proximo praeterito anno regni nostri quarto duo solidos. Close Rolls, i. 437. See also Ann. Waverl., Ann. Monast. ii. 293.

ment and collection.¹ In 1224 another carucage was levied, at the rate of two shillings for each carucate.² This is the last carucage; henceforth for many years those connected with land were practically taxed by taxes on the produce, mentioned hereafter under the head of Taxes on moveables; and we have to proceed onwards to the 45th year of Edward III., A.D. 1371, for the next succeeding land tax. *The last carucage.*

In that year both Houses of Parliament, 'after that many ways for an aid had been propounded and debated,' consented to grant a subsidy of 50,000*l.*, to be levied of every parish in the land two and twenty shillings and three pence, so as the parishes of greater value should contribute rateably to those of less value.³ The history of the land taxes of this period may be concluded with mention of three circumstances in connection with this tax which make it memorable. *Land tax of 1371.*

These are (1) the occasion for the grant, stated by William of Wickham, Bishop of Winchester, and then Chancellor, to the Parliament assembled, as the cause of summons, viz.:—'That since the last Parliament the *Reasons for the grant.*

---

¹ See Writ for collection of a carucage, A.D. 1220. Close Rolls, i. 437; Stubbs, Select Charters, p. 349. This concluding exhortation to the sheriff to be diligent in the matter is frequent in writs for collection of the king's tallage or taxes. The terms of the exhortation are various; sometimes, as in the case of the Sheriff of Northamptonshire (39 Hen. III.), the sheriff is threatened that the king 'will so chastise him as to make him an example to all the king's other bailiffs.' In the case of the Sheriff of York (52 Hen. III.) the penalty is 'corporal punishment, loss of all his goods, and the king's displeasure—the chastisement to be so severe that others should learn by his example how dangerous it was to disobey the king's precepts.' And the like writs were awarded to the sheriffs of other counties. See Madox, Hist. Exch. p. 244.
² Matt. Paris, Hist. Mag. p. 322. See Tyrrell, ii. 851, 1101.
³ Par. Rolls, ii. 303-4; Tyrrell, iii. p. 779.

king did retake upon him the title of King of France, because his adversary had broke the Peace,[1] and claimed the same ressort or superiority over Acquitaine which had formerly belonged to his father: for which and several other causes he had been at great expences, and sent some great men and others to a mighty number, to recover and conquer his right. And that the king had received news from his friends and allies that his adversary had made himself stronger than he had done before, and ordered so great a number of people to be brought together as in all probability were able this year to put him out of possession of all his lands and countries beyond the sea, as well in Gascoine as at Calais, Guisnes, Ponthieu, and other places. And further that he had such a fleet ready as seemed sufficient to destroy the whole English navy. And also that he was prepared to send over a great army into this land to destroy, conquer, and subject it to his power. Wherefore the king earnestly desired the great men and commons to advise about these points, and counsel him how the kingdom might be safely guarded, the navy preserved from the malice of his enemies, how his lands beyond sea should be kept, the war there maintained, and the reduction carried out.' (2) Secondly, the marvellous miscalculation made by Parliament in the number of parishes in the kingdom. For, a month or two subsequently, on examination of the reports or certificates of the archbishops, bishops and sheriffs, made and returned into Chancery for the purposes of the tax, it appeared necessary, in order to complete the

Marvellous miscalculation of number of parishes.

---

[1] The Peace of Bretigny, May 8, 1360.

sum of 50,000*l.*, to extend the rate for each parish from 22*s*. 3*d*. to 116*s*.[1] (3) Lastly, the manner in which the tax was thus altered. The alteration was made not by Parliament, but by a great council held at Winchester, consisting of four bishops, four abbots, six earls, six barons, and certain of the commons of the last Parliament summoned by the king's writ. 'How such a council could take upon them to alter or add to a tax that had been already given by the whole Parliament I do not well understand,' observes Tyrrell.[2] And, even after due allowance made for the fact that the tax itself had already been granted in full and the principle of charge settled by Parliament, so that the action of the Council was practically limited to rectification of an obvious blunder; and regarding the Council as in sort a representative of the last Parliament, of which all those summoned thereto were members; the proceeding was unusual, and, in a strict sense, unconstitutional. For materially to alter the incidence of a tax amounts in effect to additional taxation of those on to whose shoulders the tax is shifted. In our times, be it observed, so careful is the House of Commons of the right of taxation—'the eternal rock on which they built their power'—that any alteration in the revenue laws can only be made under cover of a resolution of the House. Hence the practice of appending to the resolutions connected with the annual Budget, one to the effect that—'It is expedient to amend the laws relating to the revenue.'

The tax altered by a council.

Vigilance of the House of Commons in modern times.

[1] Par. Rolls, ii. 304.   [2] Vol. iii. p. 719.

Tallage, or the Arbitrary Taxation of Royal Demesne.

<small>The era of tallage, 1163-1304.</small>
What may be termed, for present purposes, the special era of tallage, commences at about the date of the disappearance of the old Danegeld, in the reign of Henry II. A.D. 1163, hereinbefore mentioned under the head Carucage, and extends to nearly the close of the reign of Edward I. A few words of preliminary information regarding demesne may assist the reader correctly to understand what class of persons were liable to the exactions under consideration.

<small>Sub-divisions of royal demesne.</small>
Take a stand-point at, say, the close of the reign of the Conqueror, and turn the eyes to the royal demesne; it is capable of sub-division into forest, field, and town.

<small>1. Forest.</small>
The forest was for the king's sporting and provision of venison for the royal table. Here the king took his pastime, laying aside royal cares, and exchanging for a time court ceremony and city smoke for the natural freedom and fresh air of the forest;[1] and here, as in sanctuary, were guarded the tall deer William loved as if they had been his children.[2] But with this portion of demesne the fiscal historian is little concerned; except perhaps as regards the fines and penalties for offences against forest law, as was termed the savage code of special regulations which secured the king's hunting grounds. The proceeds of these have already previously been mentioned as a

---

[1] See Dial. de Scacc. i. 11.
[2] See Matt. Par. i. 20. 'Amabat enim rex ferus feras ac si esset pater ferarum.'—'Swilce he wære heora fæder.' Chron. Sax. A.D. 1087.

source of revenue (at one time it was considerable) under the kings of the Norman line and their successors; and therefore without further delay we may pass from forest to the open country.

We are now in the royal manors, amidst the tenants of agricultural lands, pasture and arable, meadow and field—the rural tenants. 'The demesne lands,' says the author of the 'Treatise on the Court of Exchequer,' speaking of this sub-division of demesne, 'anciently were to maintain the king's table; and the tenants of them had their living out of the king's land, rendering originally their corn, sheep, oxen, and other produce of the land itself to the king.'[1] This is the ancient feorm-fultum, or rent paid in kind, of the times of the Anglo-Saxon kings; and the system of payment of rent in provisions and accessories for the royal household continued in force after the Conquest,[2] and past our present stand-point, down to the reign of Henry I.; the sheriffs of counties, who were responsible for collection of the king's rents, reckoning, in account with the king's officers, by the value of produce in money—as, for a measure of corn for 100 men, so much; for an ox, 1s.; for a sheep, 4d.; for provender for twenty horses, 4d.; and so on.

2. Demesne in hands of rural tenants.

Rent at first paid in kind,

and collected by the sheriffs.

The exactions of rent in kind appear to have been very severe, and the cultivators flocked to Henry's court with complaints of oppression,[3] or met him in

---
[1] Gilbert, Exch. p. 11.
[2] In primitivo regni statu post conquisitionem, regibus de fundis suis non auri vel argenti pondera sed sola victualia solvebantur; ex quibus in usus quotidianos domus regiae necessaria ministrabantur. Dial. de Scacc. i. 7.
[3] Confluebat interea ad regis curiam querula multitudo colonorum. Ibid.

his progresses, exhibiting their ploughs as useless in consequence of the failure of agriculture. The collection of rent in *specie* was of course exceedingly cumbersome; and Henry was much in want of money for his foreign expeditions. He therefore lent a willing ear to the complaints made to him, and directed prudent and discreet men to go round the kingdom, inspect the farms, and assess the rents to be paid, reducing them to a money value : and for the total amount of all the rents so assessed in each shire the sheriff of the shire was held responsible to the Exchequer.[1]

The ferm of the county.

This was part of the 'ferm of the county,' paid in and accounted for at the receipt of the Exchequer by the sheriff as before mentioned, and recorded in the Rotulus Exactorius.

After this settlement of the rent of the rural tenants, contributions to the royal Exchequer were exacted from them under the name of 'dona' or 'auxilia,' gifts and aids—to what extent the practice prevailed is not clear—and they still paid the danegeld, the tax on agricultural lands, which indeed ere this had as-

The auxilium.

---

[1] Except, indeed, in the case of great nobles who had many farms in their own hands, who themselves collected the amount due for those farms and paid it into the Exchequer.

[2] The revenue was paid principally in gold and silver; but for some time subsequent to this, palfreys, destriers (war horses, led by the right hand), chasseurs, leveriers, hawks, and falcons were taken in payment of rent or fine to the king at so much a-piece. Thus 'Outi of Lincoln fined in one hundred Norway hawks, and one hundred girfals; four of the hawks and six of the girfals to be white ones, and if he could not get four white hawks, he was to give four white girfals instead of them.' Temp. 5 Stephen. Robert de Ellestede gave (temp. 16 John) vi. bald vulperets and six other fox dogs for a writ of pone against Henry St. George. Stephen de Harengot fined in so many shillings and one fox dog (temp. 32 Henry III.) &c. &c. See Madox, Hist. Exch. pp. 186, 187.

sumed the character of ordinary revenue, and was farmed and annually collected by the sheriff. The danegeld disappears from the Rolls as a separate item, as before stated, in 1163. Henceforth the auxilium comes into more continuous use, and may be considered to have assumed a new name, of stronger fiscal import, sometimes applied, in loose phraseology, to all taxes, but which correctly designates only this special form of exaction, viz., Tallage (from the French taillare, tailler, to cut off), the 'carving out by the king of a part or a share of the whole of his tenants' substance, to be paid by way of tribute.'[1]

Tallage.

Let us now turn from demesne in the hands of the rural tenants, tenants in socage, sockmen, men of the plough, to demesne in the hands of urban tenants, tenants in burgage, the artificers, tradesmen, and others of that class dwelling in towns; and it will be well to preface what we have to say regarding the exactions to which they were liable with a few words on the history of towns in this country.

3. Demesne in hands of urban tenants.

Almost all the first towns (to anticipate the use of the word) that ever existed in this country, viz., the cities built by the Romans during their occupation of Britain, all those princely villas of the great Roman families, of which we now and then in these days bring again to light the tessellated pavements, baths, mural paintings, statues, and other remains, and the Christian churches and burial-places,[2] went to ruin in the wreck

History of Towns.

[1] See Tomlin, Law Dict.
[2] 'Here too had been splendid cities, Christian churches, noble public works, and private mansions,' writes Professor Stubbs, from whose admirable work on the Constitutional History of England a considerable

that followed on the departure of the Romans; and, before the time of Bede, relics of Roman roads served only to mark the way from one set of crumbling walls and towers to another, through what is described as a scene of general desolation.

The history of those times is enveloped in obscurity; but, peering through the gloom, we may discover London and some other cities still in existence; and these, and the fortified camps of the German immigrants, retained subsequently as places of habitation, formed, after completion of the English conquest, civil centres *The early township.* for the surrounding districts. The fenced homestead or village, surrounded by the 'tun' or quickset hedge, develops into the 'township.' Whilst the more im- *The burgh.* portant Anglo-Saxon 'burh'—frequently a development of the township, or a large township, or a collection of townships—more strictly organized and more strongly protected than the town, and having a surrounding wall or other solid fence, grows up in positions convenient for trade and commerce, or within the protecting shelter of some powerful man's residence —the house of a mighty eolderman, the monastery where a bishop resides, or a country house of the king.

Little is known regarding the history of the foundation of these earlier towns and boroughs, but it would *Most of the towns situated on royal demesne.* appear that most of them were located (if that be the word) on royal demesne or on the folk-land. Subsequently, after the foundation of the kingdom of Eng-

portion of the next page or two is derived. The reader cannot but recall the lines:—

'Adde tot egregias urbes, operumque laborem,
Tot congesta manu praeruptis oppida saxis.'

land and the establishment of a closer territorial relation between the king and his people, the folk-land, directly subjected to the king as territorial lord, became virtually part of royal demesne. Thus became the king landlord, so to put it, of most of the towns in the kingdom.

The rent of the urban tenants, the owners of tenements in the towns, the rent of the towns we may term it, was collected by the sheriff in each particular shire,[1] being included in and forming part of the ferm of the county for which he paid a round sum annually. In collection of the ferm of the county from the various contributories, the sheriffs appear to have exacted from the towns more than their quota of rent, making considerable profit from them by means of overcharges. Hence arose frequent complaints; and in course of time most of the towns obtained distinct valuations of rent to be made, which precluded the arbitrary exactions of the sheriff, who henceforth, if he still collected the rent, could only collect a certain sum, and this as bailiff of the king. In many cases, however, the town was let to a special custos or committee; in others to the men or burgesses of the town, the guild of the town, or the leet jury; 'which custom so far prevailed' (writes Madox) 'that in process of time most of the towns and boroughs in England came to be let to the respective townsmen or burgesses at fee farm.'[2] This

The rent of the towns.

The towns obtain special compositions.

The firma burgi.

---

[1] Generally speaking, the sheriff exercised, unless excluded by grant, the same superintendence over the town as he did over the country. But in the case of such towns as belonged to great lords or prelates, if any rent was payable, the lord or prelate paid it directly to the king. With these, however, we are not concerned.

[2] Madox, Hist. Exch. p. 230.

is what was termed the 'firma burgi'—the ferm of the town; and the townsmen collected the amount by apportionment amongst themselves, and paid it directly into the Exchequer. In addition to which, when proceeding onwards we arrive at the age of charters, we find most towns of importance in possession of a charter, generally by purchase from the king, granting certain privileges and liberties, and confirming and continuing their local usages and customs.

The towns, however, after that they had thus struggled out of the grasp of the sheriff and obtained many important privileges and concessions from the king, were still liable, as part of royal demesne, to exactions over and above the rent originally fixed, and increment,[1] if any was payable. These exactions at first resembled in kind the occasional dona exacted from the rural tenants; but, increasing in frequency (as the towns increased in wealth), changed from occasional dona into regular contributions corresponding to the danegeld. This was termed the 'auxilium burgi' or 'auxilium civitatis,'[2] and was levied by the towns under assessments made by themselves, and paid by them, in most cases, as they paid their rent, directly into the Exchequer.

The auxilium burgi.

On disappearance of the danegeld,

When, on disappearance of the danegeld, the practice of enforcing the 'auxilium' as a frequent tax was

[1] The crementum firmae was an addition made to the amount of the original rent on a regrant of the charter.

[2] Thus, 'When the county of Lincoln yielded danegeld, the citizens of Lincoln yielded an auxilium and a donum. When the county of York paid danegeld, the city of York paid an auxilium or donum, &c., &c., and other counties and towns paid in the like manner.' Pipe Rolls quoted, Madox, Hist. Exch. p. 480.

extended, as before stated, to the rural tenants, embracing thus all royal demesne, it develops into 'tallage,' as now under consideration—the arbitrary taxation of the tenants of royal demesne, rural and urban, in the mass, or, at any rate, a considerable portion of them.[1]

The principal occasions for exaction of tallage were the expeditions of the king, when the military tenants of the crown either attended the array or paid the composition of scutage. The ground for the exaction appears to have been the obligation of the royal tenants in socage—rent payers—(including urban as well as rural tenants) to contribute, as far as a tenth of their moveables, towards discharge of the king's debt, contracted through necessity of providing for his table and for his host during an expedition, or any other occasion of unusual expense.[2] And the practice was to anticipate the fulfilment of the obligation by existence of a debt, and request an aid or gift from the tenants in order to prevent occasion for incurring it. 'The justices

---

[1] Exactions on a minor scale, as from this or that particular city, or this or that rich citizen, were of frequent occurrence, but require no further notice here.

[2] Gilbert, Exch. p. 19. So inherent in royal demesne was this liability to tallage, that 'if the king granted away a demesne manor or town (that was wont to be tallaged), together with the tallages of the tenants, then such manor or town became tallageable to the grantee. However, when the king demised any such manor, or granted a temporary estate in it, he used to reserve the tallages to himself and his heirs.' Madox, Hist. Exch. p. 502. This right of a grantee to tallage arose whenever the king tallaged his demesne. See, on this subject, Response to a petition of the archbishops, bishops, prelates, earls, barons, and others. Par. Rolls, i. 161, No. 21. Response to petition of Margaret de Clare. Ibid. 171, No. 103. Thus, also, the Bishop of Salisbury is authorized, 'for his necessities and those of his church, to take tallage or reasonable aid from the citizens of Salisbury, whenever the king tallages his demesne.' See Charter, Par. Rolls, i. 174.

The practice in collection.

itinerant'—writes the author of the 'Treatise on the Court of Exchequer'—' before every expedition, went about, to the several tenants in ancient demesne, and the borough holders, in every county within their district; and there they demanded an aid; which was in the nature of a gift or auxilium towards the king's expedition. If they would not give, at the end of the expedition the king might tallage to a tenth, but not to more, towards such expedition.'[1] Application was usually first made to London, demanding of the citizens a certain sum, with the option, in case of refusal, of being decimated towards the discharge of the king's debt, upon which decimation it would be compulsory to swear to the value of the goods. In general the sum so demanded was paid, or a certain sum was settled by arrangement. ' And after such tallaging of the metropolis, the justices in eyre went through their proper circuits, and tallaged all the king's tenants in ancient demesne and burgage tenants,' returning each assessment to the Exchequer. The sum charged was then transferred into the Pipe roll;[2] and the sheriff was made accountable for the collection of the amount.

Review of the principal tallages in the reign of Henry II.

Let us now follow tallage rapidly through the course of its existence; rapidly, for it is not necessary for present purposes to grope into every nook and corner of history for every particular instance of exaction. The principal levies of tallage were as follows :—' In

[1] Gilbert, Exch. p. 20.
[2] The Great Roll of the Exchequer; hence Clerk of the Pipe. See 37 Edw. III. c. 4.

1168, when the whole of England was visited by a small commission of judges and clerks, who rated the sums by which the freeholders and the towns were to supplement the contributions of the knights; and in 1173, when a tallage on royal demesne was assessed by six detachments of Exchequer officers.'[1]

In the first year of Richard I., according to Madox, the King's demesnes were tallaged.[2] The business of the visitation or Iter of the justices in 1194, after the departure of the king for Normandy, includes the exaction of a tallage from all cities, boroughs, and demesne.[3] And this was followed by other tallages in the same reign. *In the reign of Richard I.*

The exactions of King John from individuals, Jews and rich burghers alike, were notoriously severe; but, speaking generally, he was averse to taxation of the lower and middle class in a body, relying in a measure on them for support in his struggles with the barons. *In the reign of John.*

Here let us interrupt for a moment the course of the narrative, in order to answer the inquiry that naturally arises as to what, if any, provision in relation to such arbitrary taxation as before described was made by the great Charter of our liberties. And the answer is, that the Charter does not in its terms refer to tallage at all. In the Articles of the Barons, on which the Charter was grounded, tallage is specially mentioned;[4] *No mention of tallage in Magna Carta.*

[1] Stubbs, Constit. Hist. p. 585. See also Madox, Hist. Exch. p. 485.
[2] Hist. Exch. p. 486.
[3] Cap. Placit. xxii. Praeterea tailleantur omnes civitates et burgi et dominica domini regis.—Hoveden, iii. 264.
[4] Art. xxxii. 'Ne scutagium vel auxilium ponatur in regno, nisi per commune consilium regni, nisi ad corpus regis redimendum, et primogenitum filium suum militem faciendum, et filiam suam primogenitam semel

but all reference to the subject is omitted in the corresponding section of the Charter.¹ Wherefore? it will be asked. To suggest reasons for the omission would be an easy task: historically, it has never been explained.

To resume. The exaction of tallage continued under Henry III.; and, after an interval, was revived by Edward I. In the second year of Henry III. a tallage was set upon the King's manors and the towns.² In 1227 the same king exacted a heavy tallage from the rich, citizens, and burghers.³ In the fourteenth year of the king another tallage was collected.⁴ In 1234 there was a general tallage of all the cities and boroughs and demesne manors throughout England.⁵ In 1243 the citizens of London were 'compelled to that heavy exaction which is termed tallage' in this form: —The tax-gatherer goes to this and that citizen, saying: 'You must accommodate the king, who is carrying on war in foreign parts for the good of the kingdom, and is greatly in want, with such and such monies, until he is restored to his kingdom:' and according to the will and assessment of the extortioners (extortorum) the citizens are mulcted of their money.⁶

Marginal note: Tallages in the reign of Henry III., 1216-1272.

maritandam; et ad hoc fiat rationabile auxilium. Simili modo fiat de tallagiis et auxiliis de civitate Londoniarum, et de aliis civitatibus quae inde habent libertates.'

¹ S. 12, which follows in terms the article above quoted to the word 'auxilium,' and concludes as follows:—

'Simili modo fiat de auxiliis de civitate Londoniarum.'

² Pipe Roll, 2 Hen. III.; Madox, Hist. Exch. p. 488.

³ Ann. Theokesb, Ann Monast. i. 60; Pipe Roll, Madox, Hist. Exch. p. 488.

⁴ Madox, Hist. Exch. p. 489.

⁵ Chron., T. Wykes, Ann. Monast. iv. 77.

⁶ Matt. Paris, Hist. Maj. p. 600; Tyrrell, ii. 924. The King, before leaving England, had, on refusal of the prelates to pay a general tax, ob-

About the thirtieth year of the King, another tallage appears to have been levied; and we may conclude the list of the principal tallages of the reign with what Madox quotes from a writ of the thirty-ninth year of the King, concerning the tallage demanded that year of the citizens of London, which throws considerable light on the subject under consideration :—

'In or about the thirty-ninth year of King Henry III., it was provided by the King's Council at Merton, that the King should tallage his demesnes in England towards the great expenses he had been at in foreign parts. The citizens of London being called before the King and his Council at Merton about tallaging the city, Ralf Hardel the mayor with several others came, and the King demanded of them a tallage of three thousand marks. When they had consulted with their fellow citizens, they came and offered two thousand marks by way of *aid*, saying, they could not nor would give more. Upon this, the King sent his Treasurer Philip Lovell with others to St. Martins, to receive of the city a fine of three thousand marks for tàllage, in case they would enter into such fine, and if they would not, then they were ordered to assess the tallage *per capita*. The city refusing to enter into that fine, the Treasurer and the other commissioners were about to assess the tallage *per capita*, ordering the citizens to swear concerning the value of each other's chattels. The citizens refused to make such oath, or to declare upon the faith they owed to the King the value of each

London acknowledged to be talliable.

tained money by applying to them in the same way, individually. Matt. Par. ii. 401.

other's chattels. So the Treasurer and other commissioners came back *re infecta*. Afterwards the citizens came before the King and his Council at Westminster on the Sunday after Candlemas. It was then disputed whether this should be called a tallage or an aid. The King ordered search to be made, whether the citizens had formerly paid tallage to the King or his ancestors. Upon search, it was found both in the rolls of the Exchequer and of the Chancery, that, in the sixteenth year of King John, the citizens were tallaged at two thousand marks, to have the interdict taken off; that in the seventh year of King Henry III., they were tallaged at one thousand marks; that in the twenty-sixth year of the same King, they paid one thousand marks by way of tallage; and that in the thirty-seventh year they gave one thousand marks and twenty marks of gold by way of tallage. Afterwards, on the morrow, the mayor and citizens came and acknowledged that they were talliable, and gave the king three thousand marks for tallage.'

Tallages in the reign of Edward I.

To pass on to the reign of Edward I. The years 1282 and 1283 form an important epoch in the history of tallage; for at this date negotiation by the Exchequer officers with the burghers and the freeholders in the different towns and counties for grants subsidiary to those of the barons and clergy, which had hitherto been the usual practice, is definitely exchanged for a system of general grants of money made by central representative assemblies. The alteration dates from Edward's expedition to Wales in 1282. He was at Ruddlan, and already had received a grant from the counties and

Ruddlan.

towns after negotiation with his officers; but this proved insufficient, and he was greatly in want of money. A general grant was required; but to summon a parliament at Ruddlan, or to move from Wales in order to hold a Parliament in England, would be equally inconvenient. Under these circumstances the king summoned by writ provincial assemblies at Northampton and York, in which the counties were represented by four knights from each shire, the towns by two men from each city, borough, and market town. The result was a general grant of a thirtieth of moveables (presumably the amount previously granted by the magnates at Ruddlan). This thirtieth was assessed by royal commissioners, and collected by them and the sheriffs of counties.[1]

<small>General grant of a thirtieth.</small>

Practically, tallage may be considered to have terminated at this date; but evil customs die hard; we have yet to record its expiring throes. In 1288, on refusal of the Barons to make a grant for the king's expenses in the war with France, who said 'precisely' that they would give nothing till they had seen again in England the face of the king, the Treasurer appears to have turned an evil eye towards the records of the past, and, in the old form, to have extended a rapacious hand towards the cities, boroughs, and royal demesne throughout the kingdom; beginning to tallage them, and imposing on them intolerable exactions, to be paid at a certain date.[2] And again, in 1294, the year in which

---

[1] See Writ for the collection of a thirtieth, 1283.—Stubbs, Select Charters, p. 458.
[2] Ann, Osney, Ann. Monast. iv. 316.

Edward seized the treasures of the churches and the wool of the merchants, London having granted a sixth of their moveables to the king, there were appointed commissioners to ask, require, and 'effectually induce' in person the men of all the king's demesnes, cities, and towns in all the counties in England, by all ways that they should see expedient, to grant a sixth part, as London had done, that it might show example to others of his demesne towns.[1]

The last of the tallages. Ten years after this, in 1304, the king exacts from his cities and towns the sixth penny, according to the taxation of their goods.[2] This is the last recorded exaction of tallage; for though in strictness the levy was still legal, as not within the terms of the prohibition contained in any enactment on the Statute-book, it was contrary to the spirit of the clause against exaction contained in Confirmatio Cartarum, and moreover by this time had fallen into desuetude, so that the revival amounted in effect to the introduction of a method of taxation wholly new to the existing tenants. The final blow to this species of exaction is usually considered to have been dealt by what is generally known as the 'Statute de Tallagio non concedendo,' and is recited as a statute in the Petition of Right (3 Car. I. c. 1),[3] and which contains provisions to the following effect:—

[1] Int. Record de An. 23. Ed. I. Rot. 73. De sexta parte concessa in London. See Tyrrell, iii. 182.
[2] W. Hemingford, ii. 233.
[3] 34 Edw. I. Stat. 4. Hawkins, Statutes at Large. 'The Articles usually known as the "Statute de Tallagio non concedendo" are not, however, found in any authoritative record, and are now held to be an abstract, imperfect and unauthoritative, of the regent's act of confirmation

CAP. I. 'No tallage or aid shall be taken or levied by us or our heirs in our realm without the goodwill and assent of archbishops, bishops, earls, barons, knights, burgesses, and other freemen of the land.' Statute de Tallagio non concedendo.

CAP. VI. 'And for the more assurance of this thing, we will and grant that all archbishops and bishops for ever shall read this present charter in their cathedral churches twice in the year, and upon the reading thereof in every of their parish churches shall openly denounce accursed all those that willingly do procure to be done anything contrary to the tenor, force, and effect of this present charter in any point and article.'

This branch of our subject may be concluded with the following statement of the effect of the writ for collection of the tallage of 1304.[1]

Three commissioners are appointed, any two of whom are to assess the tallage in 'our cities, boroughs, and demesnes' within the county or counties to which the writ is applicable, separately by heads, or by communities, as they deem most expedient for the advantage of the king. And the commissioners are without delay to proceed to the cities, boroughs, and Writ for collection of tallage in 1304.

and of the pardon of the two earls'—Humfrey de Boun and Roger Bygot. See Stubbs, Select Charters, p. 487. And note the termination of cap. vi. of the Statute, as given in Hawkins, Stat. at Large; W. Hemingford, ii. 153, 154; Select Charters, p. 488. 'In witness of which thing we have set our seal to this present charter, together with the seals of the archbishops, bishops, earls, barons, and others, who voluntarily have sworn that, as much as in them is, they will observe the tenor of this present charter in all clauses and articles, and will extend their faithful counsel and aid to the keeping thereof for ever.'

[1] Par. Rolls, i. 266; Stubbs, Select Charters, p. 491.

demesnes aforesaid, to assess the said tallage according to the ability of the tenants of those cities, boroughs, and demesnes, in the manner before-mentioned; so that the tallage may be assessed as quickly as possible; and so that the rich be not spared, nor the poor too heavily taxed.[1] They are to deliver the tallage rolls, under their seals, to collectors to be chosen by them; who are to collect the tallage without delay, and account for the same to the Exchequer. And they are exhorted to commendable diligence and despatch. For order has been given to the sheriff or sheriffs of the said county or counties, at their request, to compel to appear before them all those of the said cities, boroughs, and demesnes whom they may consider useful for assessing the said tallage, and to aid and assist them in performance of their duty as required by them on behalf of the king.

Ordinary form of writ. This was the ordinary form of writ for collection of tallage; and substantially the same form was used subsequently in the eighth year of Edward II., and the sixth year of Edward III.;[2] when a revival of tallage was threatened but not carried into effect.

The Exchequer of the Jews.

To the foregoing history of the arbitrary taxation of the tenants of royal demesne may be added as a

---

[1] Occasionally, when tallage was collected by poll, (which, however, was rarely the case) cause for complaint had been given to the poorer citizens; who observed that the burden fell upon them, the tax not being fairly assessed according to the value of the property of the citizens. The outbreak in London under William Fitzosbert, in 1196, was caused by such an unjust levy of taxes.

[2] Par. Rolls, i. 449, ii. 446.

pendant a few observations regarding the revenue derived, during a considerable period, by the Crown from the Jews, people whom the king appears to have tolerated, encouraged, and allowed to enrich themselves in this country, as a sponge to be squeezed by him at will. They were the pump, as Michelet puts it,[1] by which kings extracted from below the golden stream.

'Let us now,' writes Madox,[2] 'speak briefly concerning the Exchequer of the Jews.' We cannot do better than take his description. 'The King of England,' he says, 'was wont to draw a considerable revenue from the Jews residing in the realm : namely, by tallages, by fines relating to law proceedings, by amerciaments imposed on them for misdemeanours, and by the fines, ransoms, and compositions which they were forced to pay for having the king's benevolence, for protection, for license to trade and negotiate, for discharges from imprisonment, and the like. He would tallage the whole community or body of them at pleasure; and make them answer the tallages for one another. If they made default at the atterminations or days of payment prefixed to them, they were charged with great fines or compositions for it. In sum, the king seemed to be absolute lord of their estates and effects, and of the persons of them, their wives and children. 'Tis true, he let them enjoy their trade and acquests : but they seemed to trade and acquire for his profit as well as their own : for at one time or other their fortunes or great part of them

The King' treatment of 'the Judaism.'

[1] Pompant l'or d'en bas, et le rendant au roi par en haut.
[2] Hist. Exch. p. 150.

came into his coffers. They were a numerous body (being settled in many, especially the great towns of the realm): and by traffic and taking of usuries and mortgages of the king's subjects, they became very wealthy both in money and land. But as they fleeced the subjects of the realm, so the king fleeced them. These particulars afford a great variety of matter: which I must draw into as narrow a compass as I can.'

<small>Exactions from them.</small>
The more limited space here at disposal admits only of mention of a few of the instances of exactions from Jews and fines imposed on them that Madox quotes from the Rolls of the times of Henry II., Richard, John, and Henry III. Of exactions—how Henry II., about the 33rd year of his reign, 'took of the Jews a fourth part of their chattels by way of tallage;' how John, in 1210, 'imprisoned all the Jews throughout England and despoiled them to the amount of 66,000 marks;'[1] how 'in or about the 28th year of Henry III. the Jews made fine with the crown in 20,000 marks. About which time, there was also imposed upon them a tallage of 60,000 marks; and because some of them had not paid their contingent of this tallage, the king commanded that they their wives and children should be arrested, and their lands rents and chattels seized.'

<small>Fines and amerciaments.</small>
Of fines and amerciaments—in many instances (as in the case of fines for law proceedings) resembling those to which Christians were during these times equally liable; in others, peculiar to the race, as—for trespasses committed by taking in pledge certain vessels appointed for the service of the altar, or certain consecrated

---

[1] Spoliavit eos catallis suis ad valenciam lxvi. mille marcarum.

vestments, for circumcising a Christian boy, &c., &c.[1] The revenue of 'the Judaism,' as it was termed, was managed by a separate branch of the Exchequer, termed the Exchequer of the Jews, with separate curators, who were usually styled 'Custodes and Justiciarii Judaeorum.'[2] But revenue and exchequer both ceased in 1290; when Edward expelled the Jews from this country; reserving, however, to himself their lands and their chattels. Some little money he left them to bear their charges into foreign countries; but of this they were robbed by the inhabitants of the Cinque Ports.

Expulsion of the Jews in 1290.

The Taxation of Moveables, A.D. 1189--1377.

The programme given at the commencement of the chapter has been performed as regards the history of the land taxes of this period, including the special taxation of knights and the more general tax on all agricultural lands, and as regards the special exactions from towns and the tenants of royal demesne. Next in the order of the narrative stands the history of that more extended system of taxation in which scutage,

---

[1] 'Judaei Norwici capti et detenti in prisona regis, pro transgressione quam fecerunt de quodam puero Christiano circumcidendo, debent o. marcas pro habendo respectu.' This case is mentioned by Mathew Paris (ii. 375); and it is stated that the Jews had a mind to crucify the boy at the Passover. Similar practices in conversion were not unknown to the other side. See the Petition of certain Jews, presented to the King in 1290, complaining of the compulsory baptism of a certain Jewish boy, in the church of St. Clements in a suburb of London. Par. Rolls, i. 46.

[2] The following is a form of patent of appointment of such justices, 50 Hen. III.—'Rex omnibus, &c., Salutem. Sciatis quod assignavimus dilectos et fideles nostros Johannem le Moyne et Robertum de Fulleham, justiciarios nostros ad custodiam Judaeorum nostrorum, quamdiu nobis placuerit. In cujus, &c.' Madox, Hist. Exch. p. 159.

carucage, and tallage merged, viz., the taxation of moveables.

Difference between moveables in present and past times.

Before starting to trace through this period the interesting subject now before us, it is well to direct attention to a point of essential importance to a correct understanding of the nature and incidence of taxes on moveables in the days of our ancestors, and that is, the difference between 'moveables' in present and past times.

Moveables in 1875.

The 'moveables' known *in this world of ours* in the year 1875, if we make a rough inventory, sufficient only for present purposes, may be scheduled as follows:—

Money.

A fortunate man may have,—besides cash in the house,[1]

Household and personal moveables.

and a balance at his bankers; valuable furniture in his house, and plate, linen, china, glass, books, pictures, wearing apparel and all the contents of wardrobe and jewel case; a cellar full of various wines, spirits, and other liquors; a stable full of horses, and

Farm moveables.

coach house full of carriages; a farm replete with farming stock live and dead, and on which all the most modern inventions in implements of husbandry are in use. And all this may be maintained by a good round

Investments of various descriptions.

sum in the Funds (Consols, Reduced, and New 3 per cent. Annuities), and income arising from investments in the stocks and shares of various companies—railway, mining, bank, insurance, gas, or dock—or moneys secured by mortgage, bond, debenture, or other marketable security; briefly, from any of those items of investment the rise or fall in which is chronicled in the

---

[1] These particulars follow mainly the Form of Account of Personal Estate for the purposes of the Legacy Duty Acts.

usual Stock and Share Lists of the morning papers, or from moneys secured by private mortgage or bond. He may possess more or less stock-in-trade, safely stowed in shop or warehouse in any of our enormous emporiums of trade; or ships and shares of ships in any of our magnificent harbours of commerce, stored with accumulated wealth— *Stock in trade.* *Shipping.*

> 'the broad arm'd ports
> where sheltered from the storm rich navies glide.'

Of all the great variety of moveables here represented, what descriptions were in existence in *that world of theirs*—England as it was during the period at present under consideration, viz: from 1188 to 1377, or, roughly speaking, during the thirteenth and fourteenth centuries? And as regards such as were then in existence, in what form and to what extent were they possessed by the people of England?

It is easy to perceive at a glance down the foregoing list of moveables that an enormous difference must exist between the moveables of the two periods; nor is it difficult, in some particulars, to draw the necessary distinction between 'Ancients' and 'Moderns.' Let us not, however, rest content with any hazy general idea on the subject, but investigate it with some attempt at method. *Moveables in the 13th and 14th centuries.*

First, as regards money and securities or investments for money. Inasmuch as the commencement of our National Debt dates, in effect, from the time of the Revolution,[1] no difficulty exists as regards the Funds; *No National debt existed.*

---

[1] At the date of the Revolution, the existing Public Debt was 84,888*l*. 6*s*. 9*d*.; an amount which had been borrowed in 1086 on the

representing investments of between seven and eight hundred millions. But to go further, even to the root of all investments whatever. Until the middle of the sixteenth century the taking of interest for money lent was forbidden to Christian men, not only by the canon law, but also by ' divers and sundry acts, statutes and laws ordained had and made within the realm for the avoiding and punishment of usury as a thing unlawful.'[1] Of usurers dead the king and his heirs had cognizance, and might take possession of their wealth; the Holy Church had the cognizance of them in life, to make compulsion, by the censures of the Holy Church for the sin, to make restitution of the usuries taken against the laws of the Holy Church.[2] ' During the dark ages of monkish superstition and civil tyranny,' as Blackstone puts it,[3] ' interest was laid under a total interdict.' Consequently, there was not during this period any means of investing money at interest. The institution of banks was also unknown. The pedigree of the banker in this country is not a long one; the incorporation of the Governor and Company of the Bank of England dating only from July 27, 1694; the introduction of the business of banking into London (where it was at first conducted by the goldsmiths), no further

marginalia: 'Usury' was prohibited.

marginalia: No money was invested,

marginalia: or deposited with others.

security of tallies of anticipation of duties on French linens, under 1 Jac. II. c. 5 (1685). The Bankers' debt, it should be borne in mind, though incurred in the reign of Charles II., was not acknowledged during the reign of James II., nor until 1699. See Return :—Pub. Inc. and Expend. (1869). Part ii. pp. 509–10.

[1] See preamble to 37 Hen. VIII. c. 9. This Act repealed the statutes against usury; but limited legal interest to 10 per cent. It was the first Act that recognised the validity of taking interest on loans.

[2] See Par. Rolls, ii. 133 (1341).

[3] Comm. Lib. II. cap. 30.

back than the commencement of the seventeenth century; before which date the business was in the hands of the Jews and Lombards. Briefly, during this period every man was his own banker; and money, which was comparatively scarce, was usually kept under lock and key in the house, either in the wardrobe or in a hutch in the chamber.[1]

Scarcity of money.

Let us next inquire how the items stock-in-trade and shipping were represented during this period? The answer depends, of course, on the state of manufactures and commerce; and it is obvious that in a country where money cannot be borrowed, except on such terms as may be expected where the bargain involves the infringement of laws human and, as it was imagined, divine, their condition could not be flourishing. But, to proceed to particulars. First, as regards manufactures, it may appear difficult to picture to the mind England, the nation we only know as the greatest manufacturing nation in the world, in the condition of a nation positively without any manufactures at all. Take, however, four of our greatest branches of industry —our cotton trade, our coal trade, our iron trade, our corn trade; and run the eye back over their history.

No manufactures existed.

---

[1] The term 'wardrobe' designated frequently what we should term the safe; but was also applied to the strong room of the house, and even to the 'treasure house of mighty kings.' Thus, when the Treasury of Leagues, one of the four ancient treasuries of the Exchequer, was broken into and robbed in 1303, 'the king's wardrobe, near the Chapter house at Westminster,' is (in an entry in the official records of a payment connected with the robbery), stated to have been broken open. This 'Wardrobe' is now termed the Pyx chamber. It stands on the east side of the cloisters, behind the Chapter house. The door was formerly covered with human skins, nailed to it, said to be skins of Danes, or according to some, of persons executed for sacrilege.

Modern origin of our greatest branches of industry.

About cotton there is of course no difficulty, for the manufacture was in its infancy little more than a century ago; the earliest of the inventions to which are due its growth and present magnitude [1] (the spinning jenny), dating from the year 1767. In 1760, the entire value of the cotton goods manufactured in Great Britain was estimated at about 200,000*l.* a year. Step back half a century, the average annual amount of cotton wool imported into Great Britain, from 1700 to 1705, is not much over a million and a quarter lbs. And the origin of the manufacture dates no further back than about the commencement of the seventeenth century. Before which date, the term cotton, as we find it in several Acts of Parliament [2] applied to goods of English manufacture, denotes a particular description of woollen articles, imitations probably of the cotton fabrics imported from India and Italy.

'But coal and iron and corn' it will be observed— 'were these unknown during the thirteenth and fourteenth centuries? Have we not heard of iron works in the Forest of Dean even in Roman times?' The answer is that, as regards iron, the rise of the manufacture to its present importance is mainly due to the impulse given to it by the great war with revolutionary France and Napoleon, which, increasing the demand for iron, placed obstacles in the way of importation from abroad. Previously, notwithstanding the considerable

---

[1] The spinning jenny of Hargreaves, the spinning frame of Arkwright, the mule jenny of Crompton, and the power loom of Cartwright.
[2] See 5 & 6 Edwd. VI. c. 6. 'An Act for the true making of Woollen cloth,' s. 21; 4 & 5 P. and M. c. 5, s. 13; 23 Eliz. c. 9; 27 Eliz. c. 18; 21 Jac. I. c. 9. 'An Act for the free trade of Welsh Clothes, Cottons, &c.'

impulse to the manufacture resulting from the introduction in 1740 [1] of the use of pit-coal, more than half of the iron made for use was imported. Before the commencement of the use of pit-coal, the manufacture was practically limited to parts of Kent, Surrey and Sussex, where it had been established at an early period in consequence of the existence of abundance of timber near the iron ore; and it had been, as Hume puts it, 'most unprosperous.' This result was mainly due to the action of the Legislature, which, as the only sort of fuel used in the furnaces was of wood, and consequently, as Camden puts it, 'a huge deale of wood was yearly spent,' had condemned the manufacture as tending to the destruction and wasting of timber,[2] so necessary for naval purposes, for building, and for fuel;[3] had restricted the manufacturers in the use of wood; and had even prohibited the establishment of new works in certain places, and the exportation [4] of iron. During the period now under consideration, though the mines in the forest of Dean appear to have

---

[1] At Colebrook Dale and other places. 'A grant or privilege for or concerning the melting of iron ewer and of making the same into cast-works or bars with sea-coals or pit-coals had, by Letters Patent dated as far back as Feb. 1621, been made or granted to Edward, Lord Dudley;' and was included in the reservations in the Statute of Monopolies, 21 Jac. I. c. 3, see s. 14. But the works of the inventor appear to have been destroyed by the populace; and the invention was subsequently neglected.

[2] 1 Eliz. c. 15; 27 Eliz. c. 19.

[3] 'Causing to decay and become scant and raise to great and unreasonable price the necessary provision of wood, as well timber fit for building and other uses as also all other fellable wood serving for fuel. 23 Eliz. c. 5.

[4] See 28 Edw. III. c. 5 (1354); 33 Hen. VIII. c. 7 (1541); 2 & 3 Edw. VI. c. 37 (1548). The prohibition continued in force till 1694. See 5 W. and M. c. 17. 'An Act for the exporting of iron, &c.'

been worked to a certain extent,[1] as well as those in the southern counties before mentioned, the manufacture of iron articles was in a crude state. The agriculturalist usually purchased the iron he required for strakes of wheels (ferramenta), plough shares, &c., in the rough, and sent it to the local blacksmith; fenders, fire-irons, even forks were unknown; and knives, which were usually made by the local smith, were personal possessions, much as watches in the present day.

Some coasting trade in coal, termed sea-coal (carbo marinus), in contradistinction to charcoal (carbones) the coal in ordinary use,[2] existed in this country as early as towards the close of the thirteenth century. Coal was purchased at and used in the castle of Dover in 1279. It was used in Southampton in 1298.[3] There were sea-coal dealers at Colchester in 1295.[4] And about the commencement of the fourteenth century coal was used in London by smiths, brewers, dyers,[5] &c.

---

[1] See writ directing twelve miners of the miners of the forest of Dean to be sent to Gascony (Foedera, Record Edn. iii., pt. ii. 762); and a similar writ directing another dozen miners to be chosen 'from the best and strongest miners of the same forest, to be sent to Edward le Despenser in France.' Ibid. 1021. But see Camden, Britannia, p. 358, where, after mentioning 'the wonderfull thicke forest, shelter of robbers who in the reigne of Henry the Sixt infested all Severn side,' he adds, ' since that rich mines of iron were here found out, those thicke woods began to wax thin by little and little.' See also Atkyns, Hist. Gloucestershire, pp. 199, 200.

[2] Thus the 'cole' mentioned in the Canterbury Tales, as used by the Alchymist, the Chanoune's Yeomannes Tale, is cole of wood; and indeed 'bechen cole' is mentioned.

[3] Rogers, Agriculture and Prices in England, i. 422.

[4] Schedule of Assessment of Colchester. See below, p. 143.

[5] From the Liber Albus we learn that sea-coal was at this date sold in London in sacks and measured by the quarter under the inspection of meters appointed by the Mayor. The coalers discharged their cargo at 'Sea-Coal Lane;' where it was stored.

But coal smoke was considered hurtful to man. Parliament petitioned the King (Edward I.) to prohibit the use of it. Royal proclamations followed, and rigorous measures in the attempt to suppress this novel and 'intolerable nuisance.' Particularly when the Queen resided in London was it considered necessary to prohibit the use of coal, in case it might prove pernicious to her health.[1] Thus discouraged in its commencement, the trade only slowly developed. It was not till the reign of Charles I. that the use of coal became general in London. And even subsequently to that date, according to Macaulay,[2] 'coal was little used in any manufacture.'

Lastly, as regards corn. The cultivation of wheat to any extent was a development of agriculture of a date far subsequent to this period. Bread, indeed, was a usual article of consumption, and ale usually made of a mixture of wheat, barley and oats;[3] but on the other hand, the consumption of mead, made from honey, cider and wine was in the aggregate considerable; and of the

---

[1] Stow, Survey of London, v. 108. According to Lindsay, Merchant Shipping, i. 410, French merchants were the first to export coal from Newcastle, as return cargo for corn. The following is a 'curiosity of legislation' relating to Newcastle.—The king had a custom of 2d. on every caldron of sea-coal sold to people not franchised in the port of the town of Newcastle; and the Act 9 Hen. V. c. 10 makes provision for securing it. The title of this Act, quoted subsequently in 30 Car. II. st. i. c. 8, as referring to keels *at* Newcastle, and obviously so intended, refers in terms (see Hawkins, Stat. at Large, edn. 1735 and Pickering's edn. 1762) to —' Keels that *carry coals to Newcastle,* &c.'

[2] Hist. England, i. 248.

[3] See Assize of Bread and Ale, 51. Hen. III. St. i. (1260), which regulates the price of beer according to the price of the three sorts of grain. N.B.—Hops were introduced only as late as the time of Henry VIII.; and then were at first considered to 'spoile good drynke.'

various sorts of bread mentioned in the Assize of Bread and Ale, the wastel [1] the finest white bread, was a luxury; the cocket,[2] or second sort of bread, was ordinarily used only at the upper table; and the bread of treet (or trite, panis tritici) and bread made of common wheat, our brown or household bread, the ordinary bread of the rest of the household, was largely supplemented by the use of vegetables, such as beans and peas. According to Hume,[3] during the fourteenth century 'the raising of corn was a species of manufactory which few in that age could practise with advantage.' Even at the close of the seventeenth century, according to Macaulay,[4] wheat was cultivated only on the strongest clay, and consumed only by those who were in easy circumstances.

Thus comparatively recent in development are four of the greatest causes of the existence of wealth in moveables in this country. Nor would it be difficult to trace to an origin subsequent in date to this period any other important branch of our national industry, were

---

[1] Wastel. Fine white cakes and bread fit for sopping in the wastel or wassel bowl. The dainty Prioresse of Chaucer's Canterbury Tales feeds her smalle houndes—

'on rosted fleissh, and mylk and wastel bread.'

[2] Made of best corn and bultel or bran, or of corn of lower price than used for wastel. In London a very fine white bread, known as 'demeine' or lord's bread, was sold at double the price of wastel; and a light bread known as Fraunceis (French) and Pouffe, Puff. Horse bread was made from beans and peas without any admixture. The different sorts of bread prescribed by the Assize of Bread and Ale of 1266 were superseded by the (1) white, (2) wheaten, and (3) household bread of the Statute of Anne—8 Anne, c. 18 (1709).

[3] Hist. England, ii. 112.

[4] Hist. England, i. 246.

further prelude necessary to the general statement that:
—with the exception of an inconsiderable manufacture of coarse woollen articles,[1] and the conversion of skins by tanning into leather, there did not exist in England, before the development of the woollen manufacture under the fostering care of Edward III., any general manufacture worthy of mention.

The commerce of a country thus devoid of manufactures and poorly cultivated, foreign or internal, was, as might be expected, inconsiderable. Of the interchange of goods between England and foreign countries before the times of Edward I., the author of the 'Treatise on the Court of Exchequer,' writes:—'The trade of England was originally very small, and carried on merely by those they call Easterlings, which were men of Normandy, Picardy, Flanders, Holland, and so all along the Baltic; they were mere coasters (and indeed all navigation was so before the invention of the needle), and they used in summer time to come over upon our coast and fetch away our wool, woolfells, and leather; and the men of Normandy and Picardy used to bring wines from France.' In short, any foreign trade that existed was in the hands of merchant strangers; who are the 'merchants' alluded to in Magna Carta as permitted 'to have safe entry conduct and return, without payment of any other duties than those accustomed.' And though doubtless the general statement before quoted must be

Commerce of England at this date.

---

[1] Much of the tapestry and cloth of this period, it should be borne in mind, was made at home by the lady and her demoiselles. Weaving was a ladylike accomplishment. Thus, in the Prologue to the Canterbury Tales, it is said of the Wif of Bathe—

'Of cloth makyng she hadde such an hannt
She passed hem of Yprès and Gaunt.'

received with some qualification as regards the commerce of London during and after the reign of Henry III.,[1] it is sufficiently accurate for present purposes. Commerce was inconsiderable. Not till the middle of the fourteenth century had English vessels ventured through the pillars of Hercules into the Mediterranean. Previously to the middle of the thirteenth century, they had not even sailed as far as the Baltic.

The internal trade of the country

The internal trade of the country was extremely slow in development, the principal business taking place at fairs. The difficulty and danger of locomotion was the principal cause, and arose from the condition of the roads, defective police, and the existence in the country of a purely military class. The condition of the highways was so bad as to necessitate, for the sake of the horses, when carts were used, a rest of three days after travelling four. In the cross roads, there was danger of losing the track, and the traveller rarely had the advantage of a bridge.[2] It was usual, therefore, to travel

retarded by bad roads.

---

[1] See the list of articles charged with 'scavage,' or customs for showage of merchandize, and imported by the 'karke,' weighing from three to four hundredweight, given in Liber Albus, Master of the Rolls Series, pp. 223-5. This book contains abundant information on the subject, and is prefaced with a remarkably able Introduction. See also, as to the commerce of England at this date, Anderson, Origin of Commerce; and Lindsay, Hist. Merchant Shipping.

[2] The bad state of even some of the most important bridges is evident from the numerous petitions to the King for pontage, bridge toll, to pay the costs of repairing them. Thus, Wyndesore petitions the King, in 1306, for pontage for eight years, to repair the bridge 'which is very weak, for no cart or any horses can pass it without great danger.' Par. Rolls, i. 193. The nature of pontage appears from the petition of the bridge keeper at Holland, in 1306 (Par. Rolls, i. 199, No. 48), which, stating the dangerous state of the bridge, prays the King to concede 'a certain aid, or toll, to be levied on carts, horses and merchandize crossing the bridge, for repair of the bridge.' The King grants the pontage for seven years.

on horseback, and with only such merchandize as could be carried on pack horses. The trader, as he passed over dreary wold and heath and through marsh and fen and forest, ran the gauntlet through a land where 'robberies, murthers, burnings, and theft were prevalent.' And the offenders, 'being people of the same country,' were concealed by the neighbours, so that 'robberies of strangers frequently passed without pain.'[1] For security, therefore, travellers, where possible, joined company. But combination existed also amongst the robbers; and associated travellers encountered bands of thieves[2]—the 'robberdsmen' whom Coke terms 'a sort of great thieves deriving name from Robin Hood.' But these attacks of the sparrowhawk (so to put it) of the wayside tree and bush[3] were not the greatest dangers of the road. Every castle and fortified house was the eyrie of an equally voracious and more powerful bird of prey; and the merchant stole along past sentinel tower and keep in constant expectation of the swoop of the harpy of exaction; knowing that if passing toll were refused, extortion might be completed in the dungeon of the castle. 'Havoc and spoil and ruin were the gain' of men having no occupation but that of arms. To them, indeed, a raid upon the merchants afforded pastime[4] as

Defective police

and the men in armour.

---

[1] i.e. penalty. See 13 Edw. I. st. 2. (The Statute of Winchester) c. 1.

[2] Hence the commissions of trail-baston—the appointment of justices by Edward I., during his absence in the Scotch and French wars, specially to make inquisition throughout the country regarding offenders of this class. See Mat. West, pp. 450, 451.

[3] The Statute of Winchester required all trees and bushes to be cleared within a distance of 200 feet on each side of every highway from one market town to another. See c. 5.

[4] Passages confirmatory of this view might be adduced, to any number, from the mediæval romances and stories. See, on this subject, Wright, Domestic Manners during the Middle Ages, p. 327.

well as more solid advantage; and occasionally the quarry was pursued into cover and struck even in town. Thus, in the histories which treat of this period, Mr. Thomas Chamberlain is regarded only as a specimen of an existing class. He was 'a gentleman of some note,' who, assembling his friends at Boston in Lincolnshire under pretence of a tournament, set fire privately to the town, and while the inhabitants were employed in endeavouring to put out the flames, broke into the booths and carried off the goods from the fair held there.'[1]

The dread of tallage prevents accumulation of wealth in towns.

Such were the impediments which prevented the development of any trade throughout the country. Within towns, the obstacles were of a different character. The town wall—for during this period every town was more or less a camp or fortress secured by

'High raised battlement and labour'd mound,
Thick wall and moated gate,—'.

the town gates, closed by command of the King from sunset to sunrise; the prohibition of entertaining strangers in the suburbs at night; the night watches kept at the gates, who were to arrest strangers; these precautions,[2] defied the smaller and, generally speaking, the greater thief.[3] They afforded, however, to the burgher no protection from the rapacious hands of the

---

[1] As to this act of incendiarism, A.D. 1288, see Rishanger, p. 117. According to him all the money in England would scarcely restore the damage done.

[2] 13 Edw. I. st. 2, c. 4.

[3] Nevertheless 'robberdsmen wastors and drawlatches' so increased in numbers, 'committing manslaughter, felonies and robberies,' as to necessitate an enactment giving power to the constables of towns to arrest suspected strangers by day as well as by night. See 5 Edw. III. c. 14 (1331).

king or the sub-king to whom the town belonged. And the dread of tallage—arbitrary exaction not satisfied by the payment of lump sums from the community, but requiring also special payments from individuals who appeared richer than their neighbours [1]—this dread of extortion, was for ages the principal check to the accumulation of wealth and stock in trade in the towns, and supplies the reason for the non-existence of any considerable amount of moveables during this period, except in the hands of the Jew usurer and some few of the principal merchants.

If, in prosecution of our search for moveables, we enter the castle of the period, in wardrobe and hutch there may be, under lock and key, some silver in money, some plate, a few handsome drinking vessels for lords and ladies and guests, a silver saltseller or two, and some silver spoons. The arms, armour and trappings of the knights, and the principal dresses of lord and lady are in many cases splendid and costly; [2]

Moveables in the castle.

---

[1] Thus, when the citizens of London (19 Hen. II.) paid 666*l*. 13*s*. 4*d*. de Novo Dono, for their *donum* (see above, p. 86), Reiner son of Berenger, Ralph Bucel, and William son of Isabel each paid 100 marks *de promissione sua*, according to promise. These men had frequently been sheriffs of London, and probably were '*sub nexibus curiae regis.*' Madox, Hist. Exch. p. 405.

[2] For a good description of a mediæval lady in full costume, see Philippe de Reimes' Romance, 'Blonde of Oxford and Jehan of Dammertin,' where the cote de drap d'or bien taillie—gown of cloth of gold well cut, mantle with tassels worth 14 marks, chaplet of fine gold—capeles de fin or, with its fremail—clasp, 'as rich as any of the kings,' aumosniere —purse, and girdle are all described. These last are worked with precious stones and pearls as big as peas—

'd'or et de pieres est ouvrée
et de pelles gros comme pois.'

The lady is being arrayed for her wedding.

though only the more ostentatious of the nobility possess the embroidered girdles and flowered shirts and silk waistcoats mentioned occasionally in the old chronicles, and those velvet beds and silken robes which were put into settlement in the same manner as manors and estates.[1] The general furniture and household appliances are surprisingly rude. But castles are exceptional cases; let us enter the ordinary manor[2] house of the period, taking stand in the hall, principal living room for all the household, sleeping room for most. There is no carpet on the floor, boarded only on the raised part whereon stands the dais,[3] rush strewn as to the rest, which is but puddled earth and clay. There are no curtains to the windows, 'wind-doors' indeed, covered with a rude sort of canvas in lieu of glass,

<small>In manor and other houses.</small>

---

[1] An interesting list of bequests of gorgeous beds, &c., is given in Sir S. Meyricks Introduction to Shaw, Ancient Furniture, p. 15.

[2] The country house was now termed a Manoir (Fr. from manere, to reside); the larger manor houses, Courts. Thus in the Sompnoures tale, Canterbury Tales,—

'Down to the Court he goth
Where as there wonyd (dwelt) a man of gret honour.'

As regards furniture and domestic moveables there was but slight difference between the Court and the ordinary manor house; and what is above stated applies to both, as also, with a difference of course as regards the hall, to the better class of houses in towns.

[3] Dais, deis, sometimes denoted the cloth with which the high table was covered, and hence the table itself; sometimes, the cloth of state or canopy over the raised part of the hall. The dais table was at this time the only fixed table in the hall, and hence was termed the table dormant. Thus, in the Prologue to the Canterbury Tales, in mention of the hospitality of the Frankeleyn, it is said—

'His table dormant in his halle alway
Stood ready covered al the longe day.'

The other table or tables of the hall, formed of benches or trestles removeable at will, were usually removed after a meal. 'Dais' is also used to denote the raised or upper part of the hall.

then a luxury limited almost to royal palaces. We find no pictures, no books, hardly anything that in our days we should term a chair;[1] for the benches at meals as well as the table are formed of planks and trestles easily removeable. A perch or two for hawks, or for hanging up articles of clothing, a rude cupboard, and a hanging of cloth behind the chief seat at the dais, complete the rude furniture of the place. Enter the ladies' chamber, for it is open to visitors, the moveables it contains are the bed, a chest, coffer or hutch for money and special valuables—as the silver or mazer cups of the master and mistress, a silver broach and buckle or two—perhaps a cupboard, and another perch for wearing apparel. Complete the domiciliary visit by inspection of the solarium, or upper chamber and the kitchen, and the list of moveables is lengthened only by addition of a brass caldron for boiling, the usual existing method of cooking meat, and the other vasa and utensilia of the period—leathern cups, horns and wooden mugs for drinking, a variety of bowls, platters and spoons, some of brass, but most of wood, and pitchers jugs pots and pans of earthenware.[2] If we include articles of consumption, we may find, in the cellar, a cask or two of Gascoine wine, from which is made the "clairet" drunk at the high table; in the

In camera.

In coquina.

In cellario.

---

[1] 'It took centuries of blockheads'—writes De Quincey, when mentioning Cowper's playful history of the slow development of the sofa through successive generations of immortal dullness—' it took centuries of blockheads to raise a joint stool into a chair.'

[2] See, as regards the furniture of houses in the 13th and 14th centuries, Wright, 'Domestic Manners'; and Turner, 'Domestic Architecture in England.' An interesting picture of the state of England in the 13th century, condensed principally from the book last mentioned, is given in Mr. Longman's Lectures on Hist. Eng. i. 251.

In larderio.	wood-cellar, store of wood for fuel; and, if it be winter time, in the larder, abundance of salted beef and mutton, cheese and honey.
In grangia.	For the principal moveables of the period we must look, not into the habitable part of the house, but into granary and store-room, and a-field. Here it is that are to be found the "mobilia" which the taxors were sworn faithfully to assess "dehors meson"—outside the house; and they consisted principally of cattle, horses, oxen, kine, bullocks, sheep, lambs and pigs; beasts of the plough, and carts, ploughs and other implements of husbandry; and the contents of barn and granary—wheat, barley, oats, &c., when the crops had been ingathered. The wool, skins, and leather usually formed special subjects for taxation.
Taxes on moveables fell on the landowners.	When, therefore, we bear in mind that, during this period, it was not the usual custom, as at present, to parcel out estates in farms, but to keep them in hand under superintendence of bailiffs,[1] we see clearly that these taxes on moveables fell mainly on the great landowners.
History of taxes on moveables.	To proceed with our history. The method of taxation by grant of fractional parts of moveables, introduced, as before noticed, for the Saladin tithe, continued in force in this country for about a century and a half; and rent, which did not come under the general head 'moveables,' was occasionally included specifically in the grant.
The earlier grants.	The earlier grants are various in amount; a fortieth,

[1] This statement applies to spiritual as well as to temporal lands. And we see the reason for the greater objection, on the part of the clergy, to taxation of their moveables than to taxation of their rents.

a thirtieth, a twentieth, an eighteenth, a sixteenth, a fifteenth, a thirteenth, a twelfth, an eleventh, a tenth, a ninth, an eighth, a seventh, a sixth, or a fifth is granted. Subsequently, the practice settles down to the uniform grant of tenths and fifteenths.

For sake of clearness, let us first follow the progress of the use of this method of taxation; reserving for future consideration the inquiry into the incidence of these taxes and the manner of collection, when it will also be explained why different fractional parts, as for instance, tenths *and* fifteenths, were granted simultaneously.

The heavy ransom of King Richard is levied, in 1193, partly by exaction of a fourth of revenue and goods from every person in the kingdom. In the reigns of Richard I. and John.

In the reign of John, in 1201, a fortieth of rents is granted for the crusade;[1] in 1203, the king exacts a seventh of the moveables of his barons, on the ground that by their defection he had lost castles in Normandy;[2] and, in 1207, a thirteenth of moveables from the whole kingdom.[3]

In the reign of Henry III., in 1225, the king, now of age, receives on reissue of the charters, for defence of the kingdom then threatened by Louis VIII., a general fifteenth of moveables;[4] in 1227, a year of tallage, a Henry III.

---

[1] Hoveden, iv. 187-9. This is of course exceptional.
[2] Matt. Paris, ii. 08.
[3] Decimam-tertiam partem catellorum suorum de immobili et mobili. Ann. Waverl. Ann. Monast., ii. 258. Ex omnibus mobilibus et rebus aliis. Matt. Paris, ii. 108. For particulars of writ for collection, see below, p. 125.
[4] Matt. Paris, ii. 268; Ann. Dunstapl. Ann. Monast., iii. 93. Matt. Westm. p. 284. For particulars of writ for collection, see below, p. 126.

fifteenth from the religious orders, and a sixteenth from the clergy ;[1] in 1232, a fortieth from clergy and laity ;[2] in 1237, a thirtieth of all moveables ;[3] in 1253, a year of scutage, from the clergy a tenth of rents, for three years, for the king's expedition to Gascony ;[4] in 1266, from the clergy another tenth, for three years ; and in 1269, another tenth, from the clergy, and a twentieth of all moveables from the laity.[5]

Edward I. In the reign of Edward I., the system of taxation by reference to moveables continues in use, in preference to any taxation having direct reference to the value of lands ; the reason being, according to Carte, the state of confusion into which the accounts of the Exchequer had fallen in the previous reign. 'So ill had these been kept, that to attempt to discover the true value of lands was an endless task, and could not but create numberless disputes and a deal of ill blood among the nobility, which Edward was desirous to avoid ; for which reason he was tacitly content to take taxes which he could collect without collision with the barons.' In 1275, a year not to be passed over without mention of the first appearance of the sheep disease termed 'the scab,' so serious to landowners during this period, a fifteenth is granted by the prelates, earls, barons and others in the kingdom ;[6] in exaction of which both

[1] Ann. Theokesb. Ann. Monast., i. 69.
[2] Matt. Paris, Hist. Maj. Edn. 1684, p. 320. For particulars of writ for collection, see below, p. 128.
[3] Tricessima regni pars, omnium scilicet mobilium. Matt. Paris, ii. 395. For particulars of writ for collection, see below, p. 129.
[4] Matt. Paris, iii. 136.
[5] T. Wykes, Chron. Ann. Monast., iv. 225, 227.
[6] W. Rishanger, Chron. p. 86. For writ, see Par. Rolls, i. 224.

clergy and laity are taxed to the utmost, 'in a manner before unaccustomed;'[1] and, in 1277, a twentieth, as a subsidy towards the expenses of the war with Llewelyn.[2] In 1283, the important date when the system of negotiation with the towns and the freeholders in counties is exchanged for general parliamentary grants, a thirtieth is granted by the laity, and a twentieth, by the clergy.[3] In 1290, on expulsion of the Jews, 'very pleasing,' we are told, 'to English church and people,' the king not only acquires their lands and goods, but also receives from the clergy a tenth of spiritualities, and from barons and clergy a fifteenth of all temporal goods, to be taxed according to their real value.[4] In 1294, a year of great scarcity, and the year in which the treasures of churches and the wool of the merchants are seized, and a moiety of the goods of the clergy is demanded—'in order,' as the king puts it, 'that out of the goods of the land the land itself might be preserved unhurt'—a tenth is granted by the earls, barons, knights, and all others in the kingdom in aid of the war,[5] and a sixth is collected from London and the other towns.[6] Then follows, in 1295, from earls, barons, knights and others in the kingdom, an eleventh; from towns and

Severe taxation, 1290-97.

---

[1] Quintam-decimam omnium bonorum inaudito more ad unguem taxatam rex jusserat levari et confiscari. Ann. Waverl. Ann. Monast., ii. 386.
[2] W. Rishanger, Chron. p. 92.
[3] W. Rishanger, Chron. p. 105; Ann. Dunstapl. Ann. Monast., iii. 294. As to assessment of this thirtieth, see below, p. 131.
[4] Ibid. p. 362. As to assessment of this fifteenth, see below, p. 131.
[5] Par. Rolls, i. 226.
[6] Matt. Westm. p. 422. See also W. Rishanger, Chron. p. 143.

demesne, a seventh; and a tenth from the clergy;[1] in 1296, from earls, barons, knights and laity outside towns and demesne, a twelfth, and from towns, of whatever tenure, and demesne, an eighth.[2] In this year the clergy make no grant, in consequence of the Bull of Pope Boniface (*Clericis laicos*);[3] but in the following year find themselves practically compelled to pay a fifth.[4] In this year, 1297, the king again levies considerable sums by seizure of the wool of the merchants, receiving 40s. for every sack, and compels the counties to send provisions to the seaports for use in the expedition to Flanders;[5] and 'earls, barons, knights, and other laity of the kingdom, outside cities boroughs and demesne,' grant an eighth, and cities towns and demesne, a fifth.[6]

Complaints caused thereby.

If we pause for a moment to listen to the protestations and complaints caused by exactions so frequent and so severe as those of the last few years, we find the people representing that hardly enough is left them for food, and that they are unable to till their lands. More particularly do they complain of the exactions from wool. 'The wool of England,' they say, 'is equal to half the value of the whole land, and the tribute exacted from it amounts to the fifth of the value of the land.'[7] Nevertheless, in

---

[1] Matt. Westm. p. 425; Patent Rolls, Dec. 4; Par. Rolls, i. 227.
[2] Patent Rolls, Dec. 16; W. Rishanger, Chron. p. 165.
[3] Which prohibited, under penalty of excommunication, the payment of taxes to secular princes out of the goods of the Church. Ibid.
[4] W. Rishanger, Chron. p. 168; W. Hemingford (Hearne), i. 108, 109.
[5] W. Hemingford, i. 110, 111.
[6] Patent Rolls, July 30; Par. Rolls, i. 239.
[7] W. Rishanger, Chron. p. 176; W. Hemingford, i. 116.

the same year, on confirmation of the Charters (the Great Charter and the Charter of the Forest), the laity (magnates and commons) grant a ninth, as an aid for the king's war in the kingdom of Scotland, the clergy of the province of Canterbury, a tenth, and the clergy of the province of York, as 'nearer the danger,' a fifth.[1] In 1300, the earls and barons grant a fifteenth, in consideration of the confirmation of the perambulations of the Forest.[2] In 1301, a general fifteenth is granted by the commonalty of the counties.[3] In 1302, a year of scutage, the king not only attempts to exact the aid pur fille marier granted in 1290,[4] and to increase the duty on exported wool woolfells and leather,[5] but also exacts a fifteenth from the clergy and the people.[6] The last grant from moveables in this reign, following two years after the tallage of 1304, is the thirtieth granted, in 1306, by the archbishops, abbots, priors, earls, barons, knights, freemen and commonalty of the counties of the kingdom, and twentieth from towns and demesne,[7] in the nature of an aid towards the expenses of knighting the king's eldest son.

In the reign of Edward II., grants in relation to moveables are made on several occasions. The principal grants are stated in the Table of Taxes prefixed to this

Reign of Edward II.

[1] W. Rishanger, Chron. p. 182. Patent Rolls, Oct. 14. See also Par. Rolls, i. 241.
[2] Matt. Westm. p. 433.
[3] Patent Rolls, Oct. 24; Par. Rolls, i. 242.
[4] See Par. Rolls, i. 25.
[5] See Writ of Summons to a 'Colloquium' of Merchants. Parliamentary Writs, i. 134, 135; Stubbs, Select Charters, p. 490.
[6] W. Hemingford, i. 198; Par. Rolls, i. 266.
[7] Patent Rolls, Nov. 10; Par. Rolls, i. 269, 270.

chapter, and it is unnecessary here to recapitulate them.[1] This method of taxation is now well established; and on two occasions the amount of grant is a twentieth, and from towns and demesne, a fifteenth. In 1322, the grant is of a tenth and a sixth.

Cessation of this system of taxation in the reign of Edward III.

On our arrival at the eighth year of the reign of Edward III., we have to note, in relation to the present subject, one of the most important alterations ever made in the taxation of this kingdom. In 1327, the first year of the reign, a general twentieth of moveables had been granted by earls, barons, and commonalty of counties, and towns and demesne, and had been assessed and collected in the usual manner.[2] In 1332, the king had attempted to revive tallage, and writs had issued for the collection of a fifteenth of moveables and a ninth of rents from royal towns and demesne,[3] in form similar to those issued for the tallage of 1304; but no levy had ensued, for the king withdrew the writs on the grant by Parliament, in the usual manner, of a fifteenth and tenth. For assessment of this fifteenth and tenth, writs in the usual form had issued; but the assessments had been more strictly made than theretofore. Moreover, the taxors and collectors, and their clerks and assistants, had 'levied divers sums of money from many in the kingdom, that they might spare them in the assessment and collection, and had extorted certain other sums from others under colour of office, applying the proceeds to their own use, and in-

Severe assessment in 1332.

[1] The Table may be verified by reference to Par. Rolls, i. 442, 445, 448, 351 and 450, 454 and 455, and 457.
[2] Par. Rolls, ii. 425.
[3] See Par. Rolls, ii. 446.

flicting other hardships on the people.' Thus assessed and collected, the tax seemed to be four times heavier than the last fifteenth and tenth. Serious complaints had arisen; of which we now have to note the result; which is that, on the grant, in the following year (the eighth of the reign) of another fifteenth and tenth, an alteration is made in the writs for assessment and collection; and 'in order as far as possible to avoid the oppression, extortion, and hardships that occasioned the complaints, and to promote the advantage and quiet of the people,' a power is inserted in the writs, amounting to a direction to the royal commissioners to treat with the communities of cities and boroughs, the men of townships and ancient demesne, and all others bound to pay the fifteenth and tenth, and settle with them a fine or sum to be paid as a composition for the fifteenth and tenth. The sum thus fixed is entered in the Rolls as the assessment of the particular township; and the taxpayers assess and collect the amount from the various contributors. Only in case of refusal to compound is the usual machinery of assessment and collection to be enforced; and even then the amount to be levied is not to exceed the amount assessed for the last fifteenth and tenth.[1] *Composition for the fifteenth and tenth, 1334.*

Henceforth the sum thus fixed by composition for the 'fifteenth and tenth' of 1334, is accepted as the basis of taxation; and on grant of a fifteenth and tenth it is usual to declare that they shall be levied in the ancient manner according to the ancient valuation,[2] that is, without any *Henceforth established sums are levied on counties and towns.*

[1] Par. Rolls, ii. 447.
[2] A lever meisme la somme en la manere come la darreine quinzisme a lui grantez feust levee, et ne mye en autre manere. Par. Rolls, ii. 148. (1344.)

fresh assessment, each particular county or town paying the usual sum. In the aggregate, these sums amounted to about 39,000*l.* ;[1] and from this point in the narrative it should be borne in mind that, as regards the revenue, 'fifteenth and tenth' are merely an Exchequer expression for 39,000*l.* or thereabouts.

Total of the sums charged for a fifteenth and tenth, in 1373.

Thus is relinquished the old system of taxation by grants of fractional parts of moveables;[2] and the ad valorem principle vanishes for a while from taxation in this country. A fifteenth and a tenth, or more correctly, the established sums of money charged on the different counties and towns as for a 'fifteenth and tenth,' are granted to the king in 1336; in 1337, for three years; in 1344, for two years; in 1346, for two years; in 1348, for three years; in 1351, for three years; in 1372, for a year; and in 1373, for two years:[2] and the same method of raising revenue, for it cannot properly be termed taxation, is continued in the following reign and subsequently. Counting from the date of its commencement in 1334, it endured for very nearly three hundred years.

The incidence, assessment

Having thus run the eye down the list of grants, let us proceed to a more close examination of this

---

[1] See Return of the XVe & X^e of 1373, printed in Archæologia vii. 337. This return specifies the sum raised in each respective county and town therein mentioned, but does not include the counties Palatine of Chester and Durham. The total is 38,170*l.* 9*s.* 2½*d.* Penalties recovered under the Statutes of Labourers went 'in aid of the fifteenth and tenth,' that is, the amount was deducted from the contributions required of the poorer class of taxpayers. See Par. Rolls, ii. 238.

[2] Par. Rolls, ii. 148, 159, 201, 238, 310, 317. On the Rolls 'quinszime en ancienne manere' means 'quinszime et disme;' compare the record of the grant of 1373 with the Return above quoted.

system of taxation, and endeavour to ascertain from the writs for assessment and collection, and any other available sources of information, what was the incidence of these taxes on moveables, and what the method of assessment and collection usually employed. A reference back to a previous page will enable us to start with the Ordinance for the Saladin tithe. Passing on to the thirteenth exacted by John at the Council of Oxford in 1207, for 'recovery of his dominions in Normandy and elsewhere,' we find on inspection of one of the writs for collection[1] that:— *and collection of the earlier grants. Writ for the thirteenth, 1207.*

The charge includes rent as well as moveables; for 'every layman of the whole of England who has in England rent and chattels' is taxed; and the rate is one shilling for each mercate (13s. 4d.) of his annual rent, and one shilling for each mercate (13s. 4d. worth) of any sort of moveable chattels which he had on the (octave) eighth day after Candlemas[2] (February 2nd), that is to say, at the termination of the council, and so for more or less.—Sworn statements, to be made before the king's justices, are required from the stewards and bailiffs of earls and barons, stating the value of the rents and moveable chattels of their lords; and every man, not earl or baron, is to swear personally to the value of his own rents and chattels in such manner as the king's justices think fit.[3]—A conviction for fraudulent removal or concealment of chattels, or transfer of chattels to the *The charge. Sworn statements required. Penalties.*

[1] Patent Rolls, i. 72; Stubbs, Select Charters, p. 275.
[2] In Octavis Purificationis Beatae Mariae. Any day between a feast and the octave was said to be within the utas, octava.
[3] It will be observed that the method of assessment by jury adopted for the Saladin tithe is not applied in assessment of this thirteenth. It is, however, again employed in the next reign.

custody of another, or for undervaluation of chattels, involves total forfeiture of all the chattels of the offender, and imprisonment during the king's pleasure.—Separate registration of every hundred in each county, and of every parish in each hundred is required, to the intent that the king's justices may be able to answer for each vill separately.—When the justices have assessed the tax in any hundred, city, or vill, they are forthwith to cause the particulars of the assessment to be transcribed from their rolls, and deliver the same to the sheriff, for collection of the tax in fifteen days; retaining the rolls safely in their own custody till they bring them to the Exchequer.—An oath is to be taken by all clerks of the king, king's justices and their clerks, and all who in any way take part in the business in hand, that they will faithfully, to the best of their ability, perform the business as ordered, and without any reserve.—Then follows the appointment of commissioners for assessment of the tax in the particular county to which the writ is applicable; and the writ concludes with an injunction to the sheriff to assist them in performance of their duty.

Let us next take a writ for assessment and collection of the fifteenth of 1225, granted to Henry at the general council at Westminster, on his coming of age, and in consideration of the reissue of the charters.[1]

The writ commences with the appointment of commissioners or justices (to whom it is directed) for the purpose of assessment and collection of the fifteenth of all moveables in the manner following:—The sheriff of the county is to cause to come before them all the knights

---

[1] Foedera, Record Edn. 1. 177; Stubbs, Select Charters, p. 346.

of the county, on a stated day, at a stated place; on which day the justices are to cause to be elected four knights in each hundred or wapentake, or more or less according to the size of the hundred or wapentake; who are to go through the several hundreds and wapentakes and assess and collect the fifteenth of the said moveables. The charge is general in its terms, including all moveables, but the following are specifically exempted :— (1) As regards archbishops, bishops, abbots, priors and the rest of the clergy, earls, barons, knights, and freemen not merchants — their books of all sorts, ornaments of churches and chapels, riding horses, cart and sumpter horses, and arms of all sorts; their jewels, vasa, utensilia,[1] larders, cellars, and hay; and except corn bought for the garnishing of castles. (2) As regards merchants, who will give a fifteenth of all their merchandise and moveables—the arms to which they are sworn,[2] their riding horses, their household utensils, and the food contents of cellar and larder. (3) And as regards villeins—the arms to which they are sworn, their utensils, their flesh, fish, and drink not for sale, and their hay and provender not for sale.

each hundred assessors.

The charge and the exemptions.

The elected knights are not to act in the hundred or wapentake in which they are resident, but in the others adjoining.

Every person not earl baron or knight, is to swear to the number, quantity, and value of his own moveables, and of those of his two nearest neighbours. And

Sworn statements required.

---

[1] Vasis, utensilibus. Vasa may mean pots and pans; utensilia, anythings necessary for use and occupation in a house, as household stuff, &c.

[2] Jurati ad arma, the local force armed under the Assize of Arms.

in case of dispute between the person to whom the moveables belong and his neighbours jurors as aforesaid, concerning the said moveables, the knights are to inquire into the truth by means of a jury of twelve of his neighbours or as many as they consider sufficient for the inquiry, and assess the tax accordingly. In the case of earls barons and knights, the stewards and bailiffs of their manors, or, in the absence of stewards, the bailiffs only, are to swear to the value of the moveables of their lords in each township.—The fifteenth is to be paid in moieties; and is to be collected by the reeve and four freemen of each township, and by them paid to the elected knights; who are to bring the money to the justices to whom the writ is addressed; who are to place it in a safe place, either in a cathedral church or in an abbey or a priory in the same county, until further orders for remitting it. An oath for faithful performance of duty is to be taken by the elected knights, in the presence of the justices, and by the justices, before the sheriff and knights assembled on the day before mentioned.

In the writ for the collection of the fortieth in 1232[1] the grant, though expressed to have relation to all moveables, is limited by subsequent definition to:— Corn, ploughs, sheep, cows, pigs, horses, cart horses, and horses used for agricultural purposes.[2] The method of

Marginalia: Disputed cases to be settled by jury. Collection by reeve and four freemen in each township. Oath. Writ for the fortieth, 1232. The charge.

---

[1] M. Paris, Hist. Maj. Edn. 1084, pp. 320, 321; Stubbs, Select Charters, p. 351. The grant is stated to have been made by the archbishops, bishops, abbots, priors and clergy having land not belonging to their churches, earls, barons, knights, freemen, and villeins; but the manner in which the freeholders and villeins may have been consulted, or how their consent was given, is not known.

[2] De bladis, carucis, ovibus, vaccis, porcis, haraciis (haras Fr. stud), equis carettariis (Fr. charette), et deputatis ad waingium in maneriis.

TAXATION OF MOVEABLES.

assessment and collection is as follows:—In each township four of the most substantial freemen are to be elected; who, with the reeve of the township, are on oath, to assess the fortieth of the moveables aforesaid on each individual, in the presence of knights assessors assigned for the purpose. After which, the fortieth is to be assessed on the aforesaid four freemen and reeve, on oath, by two freemen of the township. A schedule of particulars is then to be made, and delivered to the stewards of the barons, or their attorneys, or to the bailiffs of liberties, in order that the barons or lords of liberties may, if able and willing so to do, collect the fortieth. In cases where they are unwilling or unable, it is to be collected by the sheriff of the county; who is not to make profit in the collection, but deliver the whole over to the said knights assessors at the safest township in the county, to be placed by them in a safe place in the said township. Nothing is to be taken for the fortieth from any man who has not moveables of the kind specified to the value of forty pennies at the least.

Assessment by four elected freemen and the reeve in each township.

Collection.

The minimum taxable.

In the writ for the collection of the thirtieth in 1237 [1] the grant is expressed to be of 'a thirtieth of all moveables, in the autumn on completion of the harvest,[2] that is to say, of—corn, ploughs, sheep, cows, pigs, horses, cart and agricultural horses, *and other cattle and goods*,[3]

Writ for the thirtieth, 1237.

The charge.

---

[1] Foedera, Record Edn. i. 232; Stubbs, Select Charters, p. 357. This grant is stated to have been made by the archbishops, bishops, abbots, priors, and clergy having lands not belonging to their churches, earls, barons, knights and freemen, for themselves and their villeins.

[2] Sicut ea habebunt in crastino Exaltationis Sanctae Crucis, anno regni nostri vicesimo primo, quando blada sua fuerint coadunata.

[3] Note the extension of the charge as compared with that of 1232.

K

130   HISTORY OF TAXES.

Four knights and a clerk appointed commissioners.

except silver and gold, palfreys, sumpter horses, war horses, cart horses,[1] arms, utensilia, and vasa.'—Four knights and a clerk, appointed by the writ, are to cause to be elected, in every township, four freemen as assessors; who are to be sworn, in presence of the knights and clerk, faithfully to assess the tax and reasonably to value all things to be valued, according to an ordinary and fair estimate and valuation. And afterwards they are to state the particulars of all chattels and their value to the four knights and clerk,

Collection by the elected freemen assisted by the sheriff.

collect the tax according to their orders, and pay the proceeds to them; and if necessary the sheriff is to assist them in distraining for the tax. The four elected freemen are to be assessed by four other men of the township chosen for the purpose by the knights aforesaid. An exemption is allowed in respect of poverty,

The minimum taxable.

similar to that for the fortieth in 1232, as follows:— 'No poor man or woman shall contribute anything to this tax unless he or she has in goods more than the value of 3s. 4d.'

The probable practice in assessment.

If, after this investigation of the area of the charges and the method of assessment and collection provided by writ in the case of several of the earlier grants of a fractional part of moveables, we enquire what was the usual practice in assessment of these taxes, we find that, probably, it tended rather to undervaluation than

---

[1] Dextrariis, runcinis.. The dextrarius was the war horse, led by the squire with his right hand; the runcinus, the horse of servants and attendants, which Chaucer, in his description of the seaman in the Prologue to the Canterbury Tales, terms a rouncy:—

'He rood upon a rouncy, as he couthe.'

The palfrey was more particularly the ladies' horse.

to rigid assessment; for when the people are taxed for the fifteenth of 1275, '*ad unguem*,' that is, up to the full value of property, such a proceeding is characterised as most unusual and unheard of.[1]   And, in the following year, the king, willing to spare the poor, ordains that those who had not the value of 15*s*. in goods shall not be compelled to contribute.[2] *The fifteenth, 1275.*

Again, for the thirtieth of 1283, which is charged on all who have over half a mark in chattels, and is assessed by twelve jurors in each neighbourhood, all moveables outside towns being taxed there locally, moveables within towns, by the burghers—the assessments appear to have been moderate.[3] *The thirtieth, 1283.*

But when the fifteenth of 1290 is assessed (by twelve jurors in each hundred) according to the true value of goods, that proceeding is followed by grievous complaints regarding the valuations. *The fifteenth, 1290.*

In 1297, when we may consider the practice as regards assessment and collection of this description of tax as definitely settled, the eighth and fifth are assessed and collected as follows:— *The fifth and eighth, 1297.*

A writ is issued for each county, appointing taxors for the county, and to the following effect:—The King to the knights freemen and whole community of the county, greeting. Whereas the earls, barons, knights and other laity of our kingdom living outside the cities boroughs and royal demesne, have *Writs appointing taxors in each county.*

---

[1] Inaudito more ad unguem taxatam. Ann. Waverl. Ann. Monast. ii. 386. For form of writ for assessment and collection of the fifteenth, see Par. Rolls, Appendix, i. 224.
[2] Ann. Winton. Ann. Monast. ii. 120.
[3] Ann. Dunstapl. Ann. Monast. iii. 294.

granted to us an eighth part of all their moveable goods; and the citizens burgesses and others (probi homines) of all and every the cities and boroughs of the kingdom, of whatever tenure and liberty, and of all our demesne, a fifth part of all their moveable goods—those things excepted which in the ordinance for assessment of the said eighth and fifth are excepted—in consideration of the confirmation by us of the Great Charter of King Henry, our father, of the Liberties of England, and also of the confirmation of the Charter of the Forest of our said Father. We, wishing to provide that the said eighth and fifth may be levied and collected as fairly and easily as may be for the people of our kingdom, have appointed two knights, (naming them) or either of them, in any case where both, through the absence of one of them from necessary cause, cannot be present, to assess, tax, levy, collect, and pay over to us, the said eighth and fifth for the said county, according to the form contained in a certain Roll which we have caused to be delivered to the said knights. And therefore we order you to attend to, answer, advise and assist in this matter the said knights or one of them as aforesaid, when thereunto required by them on our behalf.[1]

The Roll or ordinance for assessment.

The Roll or ordinance for assessment referred to in the writs is in the form of an ordinance of the king and his council that the gift granted to the king by the laity of the kingdom shall be levied in the manner following, that is to say:—

[1] Taxatores assignati in singulis comitatibus Angliae. Par. Rolls, i. 239.

TAXATION OF MOVEABLES.   133

First, In each county two knights are to be taxors and collectors, or one knight and one serjeant, the most responsible that man can find, not belonging to the county for which they are appointed, or having land in the county; and these taxors and collectors are in each county faithfully and by careful examination to cause to be selected from each township in the county four or two lawful [1] men, or less or more, according to the size of the township, the most trustworthy responsible and capable for the business.

These men of the township, as soon as chosen, are to take oath faithfully to assess all the goods of every township in which they make the assessment, as existing in field or house or elsewhere, on the day of the nativity of the Virgin next ensuing, and fairly and faithfully to value them, and faithfully to enroll all the parcels and totals of the said goods so valued and assessed, without any omission or fraud by reason of relationship, favor, or friendship. Assessment by selected men of the township.

The two chief assessors and taxors, after receiving the oath of the said men of the township, are to go from hundred to hundred and from township to township, as soon as they can, to see and enquire if the goods of every one are assessed taxed and valued well and faithfully, as according to right and reason they should be, by the said men of the townships. And they are to enquire if any township has concealed any goods so as to escape taxation with the other goods on the aforesaid day. And if such be the case, such Chief taxors to be surveyors,

---

[1] Loiaux hommes—legalis homo was one possessed of all the rights of a freeman.

goods are to be assessed in the same manner as the others. And if they discover that the men of the townships or any of them have concealed, or by gift or favor undervalued anything, they are to make the requisite additions to and complete the assessments according to their discretion in the most lawful manner they can, for the service of the king. And they are to report to the Treasurer and Barons of the Exchequer the names of those who have thus trespassed against their oath.

<small>and make surcharges.</small>

The assessment of the goods of the selected men of the township is to be made by other lawful men of their neighbourhood, not related to them, assigned on oath for that purpose by the knights' chief taxors. The assessment of the goods of the chief taxors and collectors is reserved to the Treasurer and Barons of the Exchequer.

As soon as the assessments are completed, the chief taxors and collectors are to cause the tax to be levied and collected according to the form delivered to them from the king.

The assessment is to include the goods of the clergy as well as the laity, if not annexed to their churches; and the goods of villeins of archbishops, bishops, religious orders, and all the rest of the clergy whoever they be.

<small>Exemptions (1) as regards knights and gentlemen.</small>

The following articles are exempted from assessment:—The armour, riding horses, jewels and clothing of knights and gentlemen, and of their wives, and their vessels of gold, silver and brass.

All cities and boroughs of the kingdom, small and great, of whatever tenure or franchise, and all the king's demesnes are to be taxed to the fifth. And in cities boroughs and mercate towns, the following articles are exempted from assessment:—A robe [1] for the man and another for the woman, and a bed for both of them, and a ring and a buckle of gold or silver, and a girdle of silk in ordinary use by them, and a cup of silver or mazer from which they drink.

(2) as regards citizens and burgesses.

The goods of artizans governed by a head master are not to be taxed; but the goods of artizans governed by their own master are to be taxed as in the case of other men.

The goods of any person not amounting in value in the whole to 5 shillings are not to be taxed.

The minimum taxable, 5s.

A Schedule or Roll of assessment is to be made in duplicate by the taxors, containing the name of every one taxed, and the amount with which he is charged for the eighth or fifth as the case may be; of which when completed, one part is to be retained by the taxors, the other, to be forthwith sent, under their seals, to the Treasurer and Barons of the Exchequer.

Schedule of Assessment.

The taxors and their clerks are not to take any recompense for anything appertaining to the business. If necessary, a good and lawful person is to be sent into each county, sworn to the king to survey, see, enquire and examine if the assessment has been made and levied well and faithfully in the form prescribed, and that the people have not been wrongfully grieved, or in other manner damaged by the sheriff or other officers of the king, except only in payment of the gift aforesaid.

The Rolls of the fifteenth [2] as far as they apply to

[1] Robe, suit of clothes.   [2] The fifteenth of 1290.

the particular county; a transcript of the form of this ordinance; and a transcript of the form of the oath they are to make, are to be delivered to the chief taxors and collectors.[1]

<small>Oath.</small>

A form of oath is prescribed to be made by the chief taxors and by the sub-taxors.[2] And the clerks who transcribe the Rolls or Schedules are to be sworn faithfully to enroll all names and sums, and to commit no fraud whereby the king may incur loss, or any other be damaged, and to take nothing from any one under colour of office, as fee or otherwise, except only meat and drink.

<small>Writs of assistance sent to the sheriffs.</small>

A Writ is also issued to the Sheriff, directing him to assist, and cause his bailiffs and officers to assist, the knights taxors and collectors and their clerks in the levy of the said eighth and fifth in the county.[3]

We are now rapidly approaching the termination of taxation by grants of fractional parts of moveables. Henceforth there is little material alteration in the method of assessment and collection employed; but before concluding this portion of the subject, it may be interesting to give a specimen of one of the later Tax Acts or ordinances in the language of the Parliamentary Rolls. The following is the form of ordinance for assessment of the 10th and 6th of 1322; it is, in effect, similar to that for the 8th and 5th of 1297 above mentioned; and is almost verbatim the same as the ordinance for the last tax of this description, viz.: the

---

[1] Forma taxationis octave et quinte regi concessarum. Par. Rolls i. 230.

[2] Forma sacramenti taxatorum. Par. Rolls, i. 240.   [3] Ibid.

15th and 10th of 1334. It is selected for insertion in the text in preference to the form for the tax of 1334, as less obscured by contractions difficult to understand. But, first, it may be observed that the usual writs appointing taxors in the different counties of the realm are issued; to the following effect:—The king to his well beloved and faithful earls, barons, knights, freemen, and the whole commonalty of the county of . . . . as well within liberties as without, and also to the bailiffs of communes,[1] cities, boroughs, and our ancient demesne in the same county, greeting. Whereas the earls, barons, knights, freemen and commonalty of the counties of our realm have granted to us a tenth of all moveables which they had at the feast of St. Andrew the Apostle last past, and, in our ancient demesne, a sixth, and the citizens and burgesses of the cities and boroughs of the said counties of the realm, in like manner, a sixth of all the goods which they had on the said feast, lately in a certain treaty had between ourselves and the prelates magnates and counties of our kingdom at York;[2] to be collected, levied, and paid into our Exchequer.— Then follows the appointment of two knights (named in the writ); who, with the assistance of a clerk to be chosen

[1] A chartered town was sometimes termed a commune, communitas.

[2] Regarding the grant of this tenth and sixth to the King, at York, towards his expedition against the Scots, Tyrrell says:—'The reader may here observe the great violence of these times; for as the King by his late success against the earl of Lancaster and the barons of his party was now able to procure a Parliament that would do whatever he and the Despensers would have them: so when the tide turned, and the Queen and her adherents (who were the greater part of the barons) got the better over the King, and these his favourites were executed, all the proceedings in this Parliament at York were looked upon as null and void, as being procured by force and fear, as you will find hereafter, towards the latter end of the reign.' Tyrrell, iii. 299.

by them for the purpose, and for whom they are responsible, are to assess and collect the said tenth in the said county, and the said sixth in the cities boroughs and ancient demesne in the said county, as well within liberties as without, according to the form delivered to them under the royal seal, &c., &c. The usual writs for assistance are also issued to the sheriffs of counties; and the following is the form of—

The Ordinance for Assessment.

<small>Ordinance for assessment, original text, 1322.</small>
Ceo est la fourme quele les Asseours et Taxours du disme graunte a nostre Seigneur le Roi a Everwyk, au Tretiz eu illoques, le demeyn proscheyn devant la Feste de Seint Martyn, l'an de son regne seszime, par countes, barouns, francs hommes, et les communaltez de tous les countes du roialme, Et ensement du sisme graunte au Roi illoques en totes les cities, burghs, et les auncienes demeignes le Roi du mesme le Roialme, de touz lour biens qe eux averoint le jour de Seint Andreu prochein a venir, deivent garder en meismes les disme et sisme affeer, taxer, cuiller, et lever. C'est a saver qe—

<small>Assessment by selected men of the towns, &c.</small>
Les chiefs Taxours sanz delai facent venir devant eux de chescune cite, burgh, et autre vile du counte, deinz fraunchise et dehors, les plus loials hommes et mielz vanez de meismes les lux, a tiele noumbre dount les chiefs Taxours puissent suffiseament eslire qatre ou sis de chescune ville, ou plus si mester feit, a lour discrecion, par lesqueux la dite taxacion et ce qe a ce appent a faire mielz purra estre faite et acomplie.

Et quant il averont tieux eslutz, adonques les

facent jurer sur Seintes Evangeles, seit a saver ceux de chescune ville par eux, qe ceux issi juretz loialment et pleinement enquerront queux biens chescun de meismes les villes avoit le jour de Seint Andreu avant dit, en meson et dehors, ou q'il fuissent, saunz nul desporter, sur greve forfeture. Et touz ceux biens, ou q'il seient devenuz depuys en cea par vente ou en autre manere, loialment taxerount solom lour vereie value; sauve les choses desoutz forprises en ceste forme. Et les frount enbrever et mettre en roule endente tut pleinement, le plus en haste q'il purrent, et liverer as chiefs taxours l'une partie desoutz leur seals, et reprendre devers eux l'autre partie desouz les seals des chiefs taxours.

Et quant les chiefs taxours averont rescu en tiel manere les endentures de ceux qe serront juretz a taxer en citez, burghs, et autres villes, mesmes les chiefs taxours loialment et peniblement examinent celes endentures; et si eux entendent q'il eit aucune defaute, ceux tantost l'adressent, issi qe rein seit concelee, ne pur doun ne pur reguard de persone meyns taxe qe reson demande.

Et voet le Roi, qe les chiefs taxours ailent de hundred en hundred, et de vile en ville, la ou mester serra, a surveer et enquere qe les souztaxours en les meismes viles eient pleynement taxe, et a eux presente les biens de chescun, et s'il troessent rien concele, meintenaunt l'adressent et facent asavoir au Tresorer et as Barons de l'Escheker les nouns de ceux qe issint auront trespassez, et la manere de lour mesprise. *Chief taxors to be surveyors.*

Et la taxacion des biens des souztaxours des viles

soit faite par les chiefs taxours, et par autres prodes hommes qe eux eslirront a ce faire, issi qe les biens de ceux seient taxez bien et loialment, en mesme manere qe les autres.

La taxacion des biens as chiefs taxours, et de lour clers, soit reserve au Tresorer et Barons de l'Escheqir.

<small>Collection.</small>

Et les chiefs taxours, si tost com il averont receu presentement des souztaxours, facent lever les disme et sisme a l'oeps le Roi, sans delai, et sans desport faire a nuli, en la fourme qe enjoint lour est par com-

<small>Schedule of assessment.</small>

mission. Et facent faire deux roules de la dite taxacion, acordanz en touz pointz; et retiegnent l'un devers eux, pur lever la taxacion, et l'autre cient a l'Escheqier a lendemein de la cluse Pasqe proschein a venir, a quel jour il frount lour primer paie.

Et fait a savoir, qe des propres biens les Prelatz, et des Religious, et des autres clercs, lesqueux biens sount issauntz des temporautez qe sount annex a lour eglises, rien ne seit fet, tan que le Roi eit autrement ordene. Nequedent, si Prelat, homme de Religion, ou autre clerk, eit terre ou tenement de heritage, ou de purchaz, ou a ferme, ou en noun de garde, ou par eschete ou eu autre manere, seit taxacion faite de touz les biens qe lour furent en meismes les lutz, le jour de Seint Andreu avantdit, en la fourme qe ceste taxacion se fra des biens des lays.

<small>Exemptions (1) as regards knights and gentlemen.</small>

Et set assavoir qe en ceste taxacion des biens de la communalte de touz les countes, serrount forpris armure, monture, joeux, et robes as chivalers, et as gentyshommes, et a lour femes, et lour vessele d'or, d'argent et d'arrein. Et en citez, et en burgs, soient forpris une robe pur le homme, et un autre pur la femme, et un lyt pur ambdeux, un anel, et un fermail d'or ou d'argent, et un cent de seye q'il usent touz les jours, et ausi un hanap d'argent ou de mazre, dount il beyvent. *(2) As regards citizens and burgesses.*

Et les biens de meseaux, la ou il sount governez par soveregn messeal, ne seient taxez, ne prises. Et s'il scient meseaux governez par meistre seyn, soeint lour biens taxez come des autres.

Et fait a remembrer qe les biens des gentz des countez hors des cites, burghs et demeyns le Roi, q'en tut ne passent la value de dis souldz, ne seit rien demande ne leve; ne des biens des gentz des citez, burghs, ne demeignes le Roi, qe ne passent la value de sys souldz en tut, rein de seit demande, ne leve'.[1]— *Minimum taxable (1) to the 15th (2) to the 10th.*

As before stated, the form of ordinance for the assessment of the 15th and 10th of 1334 is practically the same as that above given [2]—and after 1334 the method of taxation by grants of fractional parts of moveables is changed for grants of established sums of money charged on the different counties and towns, and levied by self assessment.

Of the Schedules of assessment made for the different taxes on moveables the only specimens [3] that exist are two of assessments for the borough of Colchester, one for the seventh of 1295, the other for the fifteenth of 1301. The length of these schedules prevents their insertion in full in the text, but the following are some of the most interesting particulars they contain:— *Specimens of assessment schedules.*

[1] Par. Rolls, i. 457.
[2] Ibid. ii. 447.
[3] *Optima* istiusmodi Taxationum *Specimina.* Par. Rolls, i. 228, 243.

Assessment for the 7th of 1295. *Burgus Colchestr.*

<small>Schedule of assessment for Colchester, 1295.</small>
In the 24th year of the reign of King Edward, son of king Henry, an Assessment was made within the precinct and liberty of the Borough of Colchester of the goods and chattels of every one as possessed on Michaelmas day last past .... for the grant to the said king Edward made for the defence of the kingdom and as an aid for his war lately commenced against his enemies and the rebellious in France, by twelve burgesses of Colchester, that is to say (*here follow their names*) who say on their oath that:—

<small>The Prior.</small>
Richard, prior of the Church of St. Botolph at Colchester, had on Michaelmas day last past:—10 quarters of wheat (siliginis, gros blé), at 5*s.* a quarter; 12 quarters of barley, at 4*s.* a quarter; 8 quarters of oats, at 2*s.* a quarter; 4 beasts of the plough, at 3*s.* a beast; 4 oxen, at half a mark (6*s.* 8*d.*) an ox; 1 bull, value 5*s.*; 6 cows, at 5*s.* a cow; 32 sheep, at 8*d.* a sheep; and 7 lambs, at 6*d.* a lamb.—Total, 10*l.* 12*s.* 6*d.* The 7th of which = 30*s.* 4¼*d.*[1]

<small>A vicar.</small>
Master William Waryn, (who, we learn from the subsequent assessment for 1301, was a vicar) had on the same day chattels and goods to the amount of 16*l.* 9*s.* 8*d.* In most particulars the assessment of the vicar resembles that of the prior, including a bull;[2] but it also includes two poor horses and a cart, valued at 10*s.*; 3 calves, at 12*d.* a calf; 12 pigs, at 12*d.* a pig; and hay, valued at 3*s.*

---

[1] The farthing (quadrans) was first made in 1278, the year in which the half-penny (obolus) previously semicular, as a penny cut in two in the middle, was made round. Walsingham, i. 19.

[2] This is usual, in provision for tithe of cattle.

Following the items of assessment, two items from the last mentioned, we come to a sea-coal dealer, Edward de Berneholte, who has :—30 quarters of sea-coal, at 6*d*. a quarter; 12½ quarters of salt, at 5*s*. a quarter; iron valued at 25*s*.; 2 cups of silver, valued at 12*s*.; a cup of mazer,[1] value 3*s*.; a brass caldron, value 2*s*. 6*d*.; and 4 silver spoons, at 10*d*. a spoon. The total of his assessment is 6*l*. 3*s*. 4*d*.

<small>Sea-coal dealer.</small>

A little further on we find, from the assessment of Edward Talbe, that the value of a cart and horses, (not stated to be poor), is one mark, that is, 13*s*. 4*d*.

The next item (the assessment of Henry Godyer) is the first that includes a bed; which is valued at 4*s*.

The next, is the assessment of a tanner; who has besides wheat, barley, oats, pigs, &c., leather bark and utensils for his tannery, valued at 5 marks (3*l*. 6*s*. 8*d*.); garments (robam) valued at half a mark; three pounds of wool, at 2*s*. per lb.; a piece of woollen cloth, valued at 10*s*.; and a stack of wood (talewoda[2] fagat) valued at 5*s*. Altogether, he appears to be a man of substance, for he is assessed to a total value of 7*l*. 8*s*. 10*d*. The same may be said of the person

<small>Tanner.</small>

---

[1] To the enquiry what was a *mazer* cup? (as to the enquiry what was the Murrhine Vase of the Romans) no clear answer has yet been given. See, on this head, Du Cange. But whether it was made, as some have conjectured, of beech wood (See Turner, Domest. Architecture) or, as others have surmised, of metal, or of agate, or of onyx, or, as appears most probable, of coloured glass or porcelain, the mazer cup was precious. 'My Lord' Bishop Swinfield, (see his Household Roll, Mar. 6, 1290,) uses a mazer cup. When the cell at Hatfield is burnt, in March 1231, several ciphi argentei et maserini with other valuables are destroyed. Matt. Paris, ii. 330. The value of the mazer cup varies in these two assessments for Colchester from 3*s*. to 1*s*.

[2] Firewood cleft and cut into billets of a certain length. See 34 & 35 Hen. VIII. c. 3.

next named in the Schedule, also a tanner, who is assessed at 8*l*. 1*s*. 4*d*.

Small assessments. The total value in many of the succeeding items is insignificant:—8*s*. 8*d*.; 11*s*. 4*d*.; a peperer, 14*s*. 4*d*.; a miller (who appears to have a good pig, for its value is 2*s*.) 7*s*. 4*d*.; two dyers, one of whom has woollen cloth to the value of 15*s*. : his total is 28*s*. 4*d*.; the other, a piece of woollen cloth, value half a mark, and 4 lbs. of wool : his total is 3*l*. 15*s*. 3*d*. Then comes a glovemaker, who has white leather and gloves valued at 18*s*., and a total value of 30*s*. Roger Lomb, a butcher, has (besides other moveables) 6 carcasses of beef, at 5*s*. a carcass; 16 carcasses of sheep, at 6*d*. a carcass; and tallow and fat, &c. In two cases of shoemakers, the assessment gives the value of their leather and shoes at 7*s*., and they have no other goods. A little further on we come to another sea-coal dealer, John Bonlefe, who has, besides other chattels, 18 quarters of sea-coal, at 6*d*. a quarter; iron, valued at 2*s*. 6*d*.; and a quarter of salt, 5*s*.

Number of tanners. As might be expected, the schedule includes a number of tanners, Colchester being one of the chief export towns for leather; only, however, in a few cases, according to the assessment, does the tanner possess much besides his leather, bark, and tanning utensils. There are also linendrapers, assessed for their merchandise; more butchers:—'Randolph the butcher had on the said day, flesh, value 7*s*.: the 7th=12*d*.;' fishmongers:—Henry Pungston had on the said day herrings, value 10*s*., a cow, value 5*s*.: total 15*s*., and William son of Henry Pungston had two quarters of wheat, frumentum, at 6s. 8d. a quarter; and 9s. in fish and herrings: total 22s. 4d.; and several other descriptions of small dealers and tradesmen.

The Schedule concludes with the assessments for the townships of Miland, Grinsted, Westdonilaunde and Lexedene which are included in assessment as forming part of the borough. In these assessments rarely is more than a cow and a small quantity of corn returned; and the corn is principally oats and barley. To pass from particulars to a consideration of the most striking features of the Schedule taken in the whole—1. The inconsiderable amount of stock in trade and goods of that class assessed in a place of such importance as Colchester may be noticed as remarkable. 2. The scarcity of valuables and household furniture: for the cases are few in which we find even a silver or mazer cup or one or two silver spoons included in assessment; and as far as is to be gathered from the assessments, a bed would appear to have been, at this date, an exceptional luxury in the borough; and the same may be said as regards the brass caldron, and as regards any dress of assessable value. 3. Another remarkable feature of the Schedule is the insignificant total of the vast majority of the assessments. And the last noteworthy point has relation to the nature of moveables assessed, which, taken in the aggregate, consist chiefly of animals, beasts of the plough, horses, cows in abundance, sheep and pigs, and of corn, principally barley and oats.

The most striking features of the Schedule.

The other Schedule of assessment is that for the 15th in 1301. On reference to this a considerable

<small>Schedule of assessment for Colchester, 1301.</small>

development in the art of assessment since 1296 is at once apparent. The sweep of the net is wider; as shown by the increased number of taxpayers inscribed in the Schedule. There is more definite system in the operations of the assessor. And in particular detail of existing moveables the schedule is more strict and complete. We gather that the assessor, on his visit of valuation, inspects first the money bag or pouch and the treasure chest of the taxpayer; then,

<small>Improvement in the art of assessment.</small>

the chamber; then, the rest of the house; taking seriatim—where the house is so subdivided—kitchen, brewery, larder, and granary. His attention is next directed to any existing stock in trade or implements of handicraft. And, lastly, he values animals— horses, cows, sheep, pigs; and hay and fuel. (In the smaller cases, the assessment is of course not so

<small>Particulars of assessment.</small>

detailed.) This done, he enrols the particulars in detail, specifying the value placed upon each heading of property; and thus supplies us with an interesting list of the moveables possessed by the inhabitants of a considerable borough at this date, and their values for purposes of taxation. The following are some of the

<small>In pecunia nummata.</small>

principal moveables assessed:—Money, but this only in a number of cases easily counted on the fingers, and, in those few cases, the amount is generally insignificant—two shillings it may be, or four shillings, six shillings and eightpence, ten shillings, or one mark, but,

<small>In thesauro.</small>

in one instance, two marks (1*l.* 6*s.* 8*d.*) Valuables, such as silver buckles, a frequent item—valued at 4*d.*, 6*d.*, 8*d.*, 9*d.*, 12*d.*, and even as high as 1*s.* 6*d.*; silver rings, valued at from 6*d.* to 1*s.*; silver spoons, scarce articles, valued at about 8*d*. or 9*d*.; silver cups and cups of mazer, the value of the mazer cup being 1*s*., 1*s*. 4*d*., 1*s*. 6*d*., in many cases 2*s*., and in one case 3*s*.

In the chamber (to follow the assessor in his visit), *In camera.* the principal moveables assessed are:—Articles of clothing, such as mantles and robes, valued at from five to ten shillings; supertunics or cloaks; tunics and linen (lintheamina,[1] which may include shirts as well as sheets); beds, valued at from two to five shillings: in a few cases there appear to have been two beds in the same house; household linen—the table cloth (mappa) valued at ninepence to two shillings, and napkins or towels (manutergia), valued at five or six pence each; kitchen utensils—the almost universal olla enea, patella enea, and pocinetum eneum, brass caldron or pot, valued from one shilling and sixpence to three shillings, brass platter or dish, valued at from eight to eighteen pence, and brass bowl, probably for soup, valued at from 6*d*. to 1*s*.[2]; the tripod, valued at from three to eight pence, and the craticulum. Other articles, sometimes

---

[1] Griffin, eldest son of the Prince of North Wales, endeavours to escape from prison in the Tower (A.D. 1244) by means of a rope made of his sheets—facta longa reste de lintheaminibus. Matt. Paris, ii. 482. In these assessments the word may be considered to apply also to shirts. Night-shirts were, according to most authorities, unknown—people slept naked; see, however, on this point, Mr. Riley's observations in Liber Albus, Introduction, p. 92.

[2] Brass was used chiefly for the domestic utensils of this period. 'Every farmhouse of any importance had one or two brass or copper pots, a jug and basin of the same material, used apparently for washing hands, and a few dishes, the last being generally of more slender construction. These articles are universally named in the inventories of effects and in the registers and indentures of farm stock.' Rogers, Agriculture nd Prices, i. 602.

described as in the kitchen, sometimes as in the house are :—the basin and ewer (lotor cum pelvi), and andirons or firedogs. The contents of brewhouse, larder, and granary need not be specified; for, in these particulars, the assessment resembles that for 1295; as also in regard to the animals, corn, and fuel assessed.

<small>Comparison of the two Schedules.</small>

It is interesting, however, to compare values; and we find that, as regards animals, beasts of the plough remain as before at 3s., cows at 5s., and lambs at 6d. each; but sheep have risen from 8d. to 12d. each.[1] Grain of all sorts has decreased in value; wheat, frumentum, from 6s. 8d. to 4s., siligo, from 5s. to 3s. a quarter; barley, from 4s. to 3s.; and oats, from 2s. to 1s. 8d.[2] Passing on to stock in trade and

---

[1] These values may be compared with the Table of averages of prices of live stock in Rogers, Agriculture and Prices. In London, *temp.* Edw. I., the carcase of the best ox sold for 13s. 4d.; of the best cow for 10s.; of the best pig for 4s.; of the best sheep for 2s. See Liber Albus, Introduction, p. 81. The following are the prices fixed by ordinance in 1315, a year of famine, it must be remembered, after several years of bad harvests :—For the best fat ox, not fed on grain, 16s., and no more; if fed on grain, and fat, 24s.; for the best cow, fat, 12s; for a pig of twelve—duodecim—years old (a mistake for duorum, two; see ordinance, 'porc gras de deus aunz'), 40d.; a fat sheep, unshorn, 20d.; a fat sheep, shorn, 14d.; a fat goose, 2½d.; a good fat capon, 2d.; a fat hen, 1d.; two chickens, 1d.; four pigeons, 1d.; and for 24 eggs, 1d. See Writs to the Sheriffs of Counties, and to the Mayor and Sheriffs of London, Par. Rolls, i. 295. The ordinance was repealed in the following year. Walsingham, i. 145.

[2] According to the Table of Averages of Grain, in Rogers, Agriculture and Prices, the price in 1295 is for wheat, 6s. 9d., for barley, 4s. 4⅜d., and for oats, 2s. 4¾d.; in 1301, for wheat, 5s. 0½d.; for barley, 3s. 7⅞d.; and for oats, 2s. 0⅜d. In regard to the price of corn at this date, it should be borne in mind that a series of bad years had commenced with the great storm of St. Margaret's Even (9th July), 1290, when 'there fell a wonderful tempest of haile, that the like had never been seene nor hearde of by any man living. And after these issued such continuall raine, so distempering the ground, that corne waxed very deare, so that whereas wheat was sold before at three pence a bushel, the market so

implements of handicraft, we are struck with the insignificance in amount of the assessments, and even more so with the variety of trades and occupations. Let us take position for a moment, and pass under review these tax-payers assessed within the precinct and liberty of the Borough of Colchester. First pass the Rector Ecclesiae and several other clergymen; then comes the barber, largo al factotum, surgeon,[1] at any rate as far as blood-letting, as well as barber; then follow miller, baker, cook, mustarder, spicer, butcher, fisherman, brewer, and wine seller; then, tanner, skinner, shoemaker, weaver, fuller, dyer, tailor, linendraper, girdlere, glovere, and taselere; then, tiler, glazier (verrer), carpenter (W. Dumberel, with ' an ax termed " brodex," valued at 5*d*., another ax, valued at 2*d*., and the instrument which is termed " squire," valued at 1*d*.'), cooper, ironmonger, smith, and potter; then, the sailor; then, the bowyer; the wood seller, and the sea coal dealer; and lastly the local representative of the Fripperers (Pheliparii) the

Personal review of the Taxpayers.

> Jews from St. Mary's Axe, for jobs so wary
> That for 'old clothes' they'd even ax St. Mary.

Wool, in small quantities, appears in one or two

rose by little and little that it was sold for two shillings a bushel. And so the dearth increased almost by the space of 40 years till the death of Edward the Second, insomuch that sometime a bushel of wheat, London measure, was sold for 10*s*.' Holinshed, Chron. i. 284. As to the fluctuation of the price of grain at different seasons, and the difference in the metropolitan and provincial markets, &c. see Household Roll of Bishop Swinfield, 1289–90.

[1] Thus, in Edw. I.'s reign, barbers in London are forbidden to expose blood in the window, ne mettent sanc en lour fenestres: they are to carry it privily to the Thames. Liber Albus, Introduction, p. 53, and see p. 714.

assessments, the value is 3*d.* per lb. ; an advance of 1*d.* on the value in 1295.

<small>Small assessments.</small>

The insignificant amount of many of the totals is as remarkable a feature in this Schedule as in that for 1295. The following are specimens of small totals :—Saman the carpenter has a tunic, value 2*s.* 6*d.*, an ax, value 2*s.* 6*d.* : total, 5*s.* ; William of Tendring the tailor has an old cloak, value 3*s.*, a bed, 2*s.* 6*d.*, a brass pot, 1*s.* 6*d.*, and a pair of scissors, 3*d.* : total, 7*s.* 3*d.* ; Alexander at the bridge has a boat, value 10*s.* ; Cecilia the widow of Le Vaus, 3 sheep, at 12*d.* a sheep : total 3*s.* ; Gilbert the taselere, an old supertunic, value 1*s.* 3*d.*, a sheep, value 12*d.*, and a lamb, 6*d.* : total 2*s.* 9*d.* ; and Walter the Weaver, a surtout valued at 2*s.* 8*d.*—nothing more.

The following are some of the principal assessments :—

<small>Principal assessments.</small>

Henry Pakeman the tanner has (with other goods) a mazer cup ; a silver buckle ; four silver spoons ; two table cloths and two towels ; and altogether, including moveables in house granary and larder, bark skins and utensils for tanning, and barrels and vats for brewhouse, a total of 9*l.* 17*s.* 10*d.* : the 15th being 13*s.* 2¼*d.* William Proucale, a butcher, has a total of 7*l.* 15*s.* 2*d.* Henry Persun, another butcher, has a silver buckle ; a gold ring, value 12*d.* ; two silver spoons ; a mazer cup ; and altogether, including carcasses of beef, muttons, pork, fat, cloth of russett, 4 pounds of wool, two horses, a cart, &c., a total value of 5*l.* 3*s.* 1½*d.* Richard of Wyseton has (with other goods) a gold ring, value 12*d.* ; in money, 3*s.* ; a hackney, valued at

6s. 8d.; and wax, silk purses, gloves, girdles, leather purses, and needlecases,[1] flannel, silk, and lining material, giving a total value of 4l. 1s. 11d.

Wine is mentioned in two assessments only. John Colyn has a cask, valued at 40s.; and Henry of Leycester (whose assessment is the last item in the Schedule) has one pipe[2] of wine of the value of two marks (1l. 6s. 8d.), 'which he has received from Ralph Stacey of Herewyc for sale.' Henry affirms that for this Ralph has been taxed, and therefore that it should not be taxed in his hands. 'It remains to be seen by inspection of the Roll for Herewyc whether the said pipe is assessed among the goods of the said Ralph or not; for it is right that our Lord the King should have his tax either from Henry or from the said Ralph.' {Wine.}

The total assessment for the borough is stated to be 518l. 1s. 4¾d.: the total of the fifteenths, 34l. 12s. 7d. The number of assessments is about 390; which would give an average value of 1l. 6s. 6d. for property, and about 1s. 9d. for tax, per head.

Customs and Port Duties.

The student of our fiscal system finds, amongst

---

[1] Acularia. The use of these needlecases is not at once apparent; but according to Chaucer's 'Romaunt of the Rose,' they were necessaries for a young gentleman's morning toilet:—

—'Up I roos and gan me clothe. . . .
a sylvre nedle forth Y droughe
out of an aguler queynt ynoughe
and gan this nedle threde anon. . . .
with a threde bastyng my slevis
alone I went in my plaiyng.'

[2] The pipe contained 126 gallons.

the preliminary difficulties he encounters, not the least, in the necessity of acquiring a knowledge of the meaning of our fiscal terms; many of which are obscure and some misleading. It is well, therefore, before proceeding to investigate the origin of our revenue from customs, to explain that 'customs' is the term applied in the fiscal language of this country to frontier or port duties—toll levied at the ports for goods *in transitu*.

Explanation of the term 'Customs.'

Origin of taxation by toll.

In western Europe, to go no farther, taxation by toll from merchandize *in transitu*, according to the common observation of all historical writers who have devoted attention to the origin of taxes, appears to have originated in arbitrary exactions from the merchants. Any other conclusion would be surprising: for in the olden time every highway, every pass, every river at every turn seems to have been commanded by castle, tower and keep. Their picturesque ruins yet remain, objects of admiration to the continental tourist. He thrusts neck out of railway carriage window, snatching, under difficulties, transitory glimpses of them, when rushing along beside the Rhine. They give a sentimental charm and interest to his musings on the banks of the Main. They stand, grim grey sentinels, in the gorge of every valley of the Alpine passes. But exceptionally good specimens for present purposes overhang the Danube between Lintz and Vienna. We have now arrived, in the narrative, at about the middle of the fourteenth century. Take, for purposes of illustration, this date. The principal merchandize of the world passes from Alexandria to Venice and the other

Italian ports;[1] and thence, if intended for a northern mart, to Cologne down the Rhine, or through the Tyrol and along the Danube towards Augsbourg or Vienna. Take ship with the merchant, and proceed down the river till you see the dash of waves against the Strudel, the Scylla of the Danube. Henceforward you must advance in daylight and hug the shore, or perish; that you will also have to do further on in avoidance of the Wirbel or whirlpool, the Charybdis of the Danube. Nature has rendered the passage perilous, but man more; for 'twixt rock and whirlpool the river banks are lined with castles.[2] Every cruel loophole scans the passer-by. The other toll-houses higher up the river you may perchance have avoided. Here it is doomed:—'Stop, merchant, and pay.' Briefly, in days of yore the merchant, wholly in the power of the sovereign of any country into or through which he passed, was compelled to submit to the terms imposed for permission to pass, and for safe conduct, which was equally necessary; and accordingly was by king and sub-king so fleeced and pillaged that 'pillé comme un marchand' became a proverbial expression.

On changing time and place, withdrawing the eye from foreign parts, and fixing it on a sea port of England at an early date—any time antecedent to Magna Carta—we see the merchant stranger, on arrival here with his casks of Gascoine wine or other merchandize, between plundering people and stormy sea, in no better position than the merchant of the Danube scene, filing along among rocks and whirlpools

Its origin in England.

---

[1] Having already paid a toll of over 30 per cent. to the Sultan.
[2] The distance is about three-quarters of a mile, the number of castles, five.

under observation from the various castles on the banks. Here, as on the continent, the king may condition further progress as he wills, and no doubt did so; therefore, in the absence of historical enactment, it is not unreasonable to conjecture that port duties in this country, as tolls abroad, originated in arbitrary exactions levied by toll at the sea ports. To descend, however, from conjecture to ground of historical fact. We know that certain tolls levied at the sea ports had, before the date of Magna Carta, obtained by continuance the force of 'customs,' and were therefore so termed. These, as probably not in their nature unreasonable, were by Magna Carta established and legalized in the following terms :—' Let all merchants have safety and security to depart from England and to come into England, and to remain in and go throughout England both by land and by water, for the purpose of buying and selling, without any evil or unjust tolls, paying the ancient and rightful customs.'[1]

Customary tolls legalized by Magna Carta in 1215.

The nature of these customs it is not possible now to state with certainty. Reference may have been made to a disme or quinzime, tenth or fifteenth, payable on the value of merchandize, or to certain rights of pre-emption and prelibation (for the jus prelibationis pervaded the whole feudal system), or it may be that the reservation in the charter was in the nature of a salvo of general import, and the draftsman of the charter or any of the signatories would have been

---

[1] Omnes mercatores habeant salvum et securum exire de Anglia, et venire in Angliam, et morari et ire per Angliam, tam per terram quam per aquam ad emendum et vendendum sine omnibus malis toltis, per antiquas ut rectas consuetudines.

puzzled to state precisely the nature of the customs in question. After all, as Chief Baron Gilbert puts it — 'though knowledge is no burden, the question is not much material to us.'[1]

To return to facts. Before the date of Magna Carta, there existed the following custom regarding wine, the principal import of this country:—From every wine-laden ship the king took two tuns, one before, the other behind the mast, at the price considered reasonable by his officer. This customary right of pre-emption was termed the King's Prisage of Wine.

Prisage of wine.

Before the year 1266, there existed also a custom regarding wool, the principal export of the country, in the nature of a money payment or duty collected at the ports, and certain other customary payments of the nature of which we have no precise information. The Statutum de Scaccario of that year provides that:—'the principal collectors of the custom of wools at the two terms before mentioned (Michaelmas and Easter) shall pay all such money as they have received of the said custom, and shall make account from year to year clearly of all parcels received in any of the ports or other places of the realm, so that they shall answer for every ship (issint gil respoigne de chescun neef) where it was charged, and how much it carried, and whose the wools were, and for every other charge of the ship whereof custom is due, and for the whole receipt.' Starting then with the king's prisage on wines, a custom (amount unknown) on wool exported, and some minor customary tolls or port duties, let us assume a revenue

Custom of wool.

[1] Gilbert, Exch. App. p. 271.

of 6,000*l.* per annum from 'customs' in the reign of Henry III.[1]

<small>Legislative commencement of port duties.</small>

In the first Parliament of the succeeding reign, the revenue from port duties had its legislative commencement in a grant made, in what Professor Stubbs terms 'a semi-constitutional manner,' at the request of the merchants,[2] of duties on wool, woolfells and leather exported from England and Wales, the amount being:—For every sack of wool (26 stone), half a mark (6*s.* 8*d.*); for every 300 woolfells, half a mark; and for every last of leather, a mark (13*s.* 4*d.*), under the name of 'customs.'[3]

The produce of these duties or customs and the various taxes on moveables granted to the king proved insufficient for his necessities; and, in 1297, he attempted to levy a further tax on wool by seizure of the wool in the hands of the merchants. This occasioned the insertion, in the famous statute termed 'Confirmatio Cartarum,'[4] of an article stigmatizing the new exaction on wool as mala tolta,[5] an evil toll or tax, and its con-

<small>The malotoute.</small>

---

[1] Hume, Hist. Engl. i. p. 170, note C.

[2] Ad instantiam et rogatum mercatorum.

[3] Dimidiam marcam de quolibet sacco lanae, et dimidiam marcam pro singulis trescentis pellibus lanutis quae faciunt unum saccum, et unam marcam de qualibet lesta coriorum exeuntibus regnum Angliae et terram Walliae. According to the author of the Treatise on the Court of Exchequer, this demi mark for each sack of wool is termed, in a Record in the Tower of the date of 3 Edward I., nova custuma, 'which plainly intimates that there were others before that time.' See Gilbert, Exch. App. 208. Similar duties were granted to the king in Ireland, to be collected at the ports.

[4] 25 Edw. Stat. 1.

[5] Mala-tolta—sometimes mala-tollia, from tollo, to take or toll—the unjust custom on wool, the evil tolta or tax. See Glossary to Stubbs, Select Charters. According to Sinclair, some writers have supposed

sequent release by the king. But, at the same time, the export duties on wool, woolfells and leather granted to the king and his heirs as aforesaid, under the name of 'customs,' were recognised and established. Henceforth these duties were termed 'Antiqua Custuma,' the ancient customs.[1]

Antiqua Custuma.

A few years after this establishment of 'the ancient customs,' the heavy expenses of the wars in France and Scotland compelled the king to have recourse to further means of recruiting his revenue; and he commenced the practical application of those eastern experiences which the author of the Treatise on the Court of Exchequer describes in the following terms:—'Edward had travelled into the Levant,[2] and from thence had fetched many new institutions: for there he found that upon all commodities, both exported and imported, a vectigal or tribute was paid to the state or prince where such importation or exportation was made; and that this acknowledgment was founded upon the protection that such princes or states gave to their foreign traders, and therefore by them cheerfully submitted to. It was paid upon goods imported, because the merchant had liberty to sell them in that prince's dominions, and was protected by him in the recovery of the price from any of his subjects: it was likewise laid upon the goods exported, and that was by way of ascertaining the

that maltoltes were duties upon malt! The same word was used in reference to illegal taxes in France. See Clamageran. L'impôt en France, i. 311.

[1] For the text of this Article, see below, p. 178.

[2] It will be remembered that Edward had been abroad three years when his father died, having, in 1269, joined what proved to be the last Crusade.

158   HISTORY OF TAXES.

quantities and values of what was to be sold to the merchant.'[1] The king's prisage of wine was particularly objectionable to the merchant, because, from his inability to take the measure of the conscience of the king's officer, he never could calculate beforehand the terms on which he could import his wine; and, on the other hand, vessels were enlarged, and other practices occurred in fraud of the rights of the king. It was, therefore, a change as acceptable to the foreign merchant as beneficial to the revenue, when, in 1302, Edward, by agreement with the foreign merchants for themselves and all others from their countries,[2] commuted prisage for certain duties to be paid in money, *i.e.* for every hogshead of wine imported, 2*s.* to be paid within 40 days after the wine was landed; for every sack of wool and every 300 woolfells exported, 3*s.* 4*d.*; and for every last of hides exported, 6*s.* 8*d.*; for every scarlet cloth dyed in grain, 2*s.* 0*d.*; for every other cloth, 1*s.* 0*d.*; for every quintal of wax, 1*s.* 0*d.*; and for all other goods and merchandize exported and imported, 3*d.* in the pound: in collection of which, credence was given to the merchants upon the value of the merchandize imported 'by letters which they might show of the same goods of their lords or companions (principals or partners); and if they had no letters, they were to be believed by their oath of the value.'[3] The duties thus granted were additional to the ancient customs (antiqua custuma), and as such were termed nova custuma, the

Commutation of prisage in 1302.

Nova custuma.

---

[1] Gilbert, Exch. p. 205.
[2] 'Pro se et omnibus aliis de partibus suis.'
[3] See recital in the Statute of the Staple, 27 Edw. III. st. 2, c. 26.

new customs. Henceforth, therefore, the merchant stranger paid as export duty:—On every sack of wool and every 300 woolfells, 6s. 8d. + 3s. 4d.=10s.; and on every last of hides, 13s. 4d. + 6s. 8d.=1l. The fixed duty on wine paid by the merchant stranger was termed 'Butlerage,' as in commutation of the rights of the king's butler. Butlerage.

In May in the following year, the king endeavoured to extend to the native merchants the fiscal arrangement thus made with the merchant strangers; and issued writs to London and the other towns principally concerned, to the following effect:—
'I am given to understand (says the king in the writs) that certain merchants of our kingdom, with a view to being quit of our prisage and the enjoyment of certain privileges granted by us to merchant strangers, desire to pay to us from their goods and merchandize certain new duties and customs which the said merchant strangers pay to us from their goods and merchandize within our kingdom;' and accordingly the mayor and sheriffs are directed to send to a Colloquium at York two or three citizens armed with full powers to treat on behalf of the community of the town. To this Colloquium forty-two towns sent representatives; and the king's proposal was carefully considered, but meeting with strong opposition, ultimately was rejected. The king, therefore, still continued to take prisage from wine imported by a subject. The King attempts to extend it to native merchants.

Such was the origin of port duties or customs in this country, and the duties previously mentioned, antiqua and nova custuma, continued payable during the reigns of Edward II. and Edward III.; increasing in yield. Indeed, to the improved yield of the port duties in the last-mentioned reign is mainly due the popular belief that the king had been at work with the alchymists in the transmutation of metals, and had taken counsel with the celebrated Raymond Lulli; who for him, so said report, passed over to England, and there, in the Tower of London, manufactured six millions of gold, the material for the rose nobles, which bear to this day the name of the nobles of Raymond.[1] It was not, however, by the use of the crucible in the attempt to find that short cut to riches which was the 'quest' of the age, but by taking at the turn that tide which, in the affairs of nations as of men, so taken, leads on to fortune, by availing himself of the opportunities of the times, and increasing the commerce of the nation that Edward discovered the art of making gold. The survivors of the crusades had returned from the East with new tastes, as well as new ideas; they loved to wear the fine fabrics of the East, to drink out of the jewelled cup, to sleep beneath the purple coverlet, to deck their wives and ladies with 'all that's bright and rare, the zone, the wreath, the gem,' jewelled girdles of curious device, circlets for the hair, and ausmonieres studded with orient pearls. Sugar, which the crusader had first tasted on the plains of Tripoli, now a necessary of life, had almost displaced honey in rich households, at any rate as regards the high table. Cinnamon and other spices of the East were in common use for flavouring dishes and drinks,

Improved yield of the Customs in the reign of Edward III.

[1] See Michelet, Hist. de France, iii. 71.

especially the ale of the period, which, no better than sweet-wort, was consumed as soon as made, and 'probably was so thin that it might be drunk in "potations pottle deep" without disturbing the equilibrium of the drinker';[1] but for his stomach's sake must have required the addition of a stimulant. Ginger, rhubarb, aloes and canella, commodities which, according to Joinville, the crusaders imagined to be found in the morning in nets set overnight by cunning hands in the waters of the Nile before it entered Egypt, the débris of trees shaken by the breeze in that terrestrial Paradise from whence the river flowed,[2] were now commonly sold by the pound, and, with pepper and other articles of that description, formed part of the ordinary stock of grocers in towns.[3] Briefly, the experience acquired by the crusaders had added considerably to the list of available conveniences and luxuries of life. The crusades had given the first impulse to commerce.

In this increasing business of interchange what had England to give? Of tin some small amount, it is true;[4] but she continued to be, as in the time of Cæsar, the great

[1] See Liber Albus, Introduction, p. 60.
[2] Hist. de St. Louis, c. 40. The water of the river was of a mysterious nature; for when suspended from the ropes of the pavillions, in the pots of porous earthenware used in the East, it became, even at midday, as cold as spring water!
[3] 'In the store (of Bishop Swinfield) at Sugwas, and amongst his purchases in London in 1290, we find aniseed, cinnamon, carraways, coriander, cubebs, cummin, draget (buck-wheat), galingal, ginger, gromil, liquorice, pepper and saffron; some of them in large quantities.' See Household Roll of Bishop Swinfield, ii. 51.
[4] Tin, of which, till its discovery in Germany by an exiled Cornish miner about 1241, Cornwall had the monopoly (Matt. Paris, ii. 453), was subject to a customary duty on exportation; but the contribution to the Exchequer from this source was insignificant.

M

producer of animals, flocks, and herds. She had to give her wool, and it was the best in the world. Accordingly, to the safety of the sack of wool in its passage across the sea; to keeping open the communication with our greatest customers, the Flemish towns; to the interchange of wool and skins for all these necessaries and luxuries from the East, as well as French and Spanish wines and other European commodities, Edward's attention was constantly directed. The 'father of English commerce'[1] had no need of occult operations such as those attributed to Nicolas Flamel or Raymond Lulli.

This increase in the revenue from port duties was not the produce of the antiqua and nova custuma alone. To pass over any irregular exactions of maletoute, and the grant of a subsidy for about a year in 1340,[2] after that the great semi-naval victory of Sluys and the capture of Calais had secured the sack of wool in its passage across the Channel, subsidies—extraordinary grants—of additional port duties were frequently granted to the king.

Subsidies of port duties granted to him.

In 1343, on augmentation of the fixed price for wool in the different countries of the kingdom, the Lords and Commons, with consent of the merchants, grant, for three years, a subsidy of 40s. on every sack of wool exported.[3] This duty is renewed, for two years, in 1346, in aid of the war and for defence of the kingdom.[4] And there are added, in the following year, duties on cloth and worsted exported, at the rate of 14d. for each cloth, from merchants denizens, and

---

[1] Hallam, Middle Ages, ii. 384.   [2] 14 Edw. iii. c. 21.
[3] De chesun sak de leyne que passera. Par. R°lls, ii. 138.
[4] Ibid. 161.

21*d.* from merchant strangers; and for cloth of worsted: for each cloth, from denizens, 1*d.*, and from strangers, 1½*d.*; and for every lit, from denizens, 10*d.*, and from aliens 15*d.*—duties which caused considerable complaints, but were confirmed to the king on the ground that it was 'reasonable that the king should have the same profit from cloth made in the kingdom and exported, as from wool exported, according to the total amount of cloth made from a sack of wool.'[1]

In 1348, in reply to a request for a subsidy, 'his poor Commons' present to the king a lengthy list of their previous contributions to the exchequer:—' by reason of which your said Commons can hardly bear or support any charges.' One item in the list has relation to the subsidy of wool, stated to amount to 60,000*l.* per annum, 'by reason of which each sack of wool, which is the treasure of your land, is sold at less its value by 40*s.*'[2] And the Commons are careful to state that the fifteenths, which they grant for three years, are granted on condition that the subsidy of 40*s.* on each sack of wool shall cease at the expiration of the time for which it has been granted, viz., at Michaelmas next, and that in future no such grant be made by the merchants, 'because such a subsidy is, in effect, a charge on the Commons and not on the merchants, who simply give so much the less for the wool they purchase.' Therefore, at last, wise Commons! *Important discovery by the Commons.*

In 1350 the Commons again petition the king regarding the subsidy of 40*s.* per sack of wool (which would appear again to have been granted to the king

---
[1] Par. Rolls, ii. 168. [2] Meins de la value de xls. Ibid. ii. 200.

by the merchants) repeating their observations made in 1348 regarding the incidence of the tax—that it was in effect a charge on the people and not on the merchants. They pray, however, that should the king in his great necessity require such a subsidy for half a year or a year, he will 'inform them of his will, to their comfort.' And on representation by the king that the subsidy was granted to him ' for his great necessity which still continues, and indeed increases day by day,' the Lords and Commons, by common assent, grant the said subsidy from Michaelmas next for two years.[1]

In collection of the export duties 300 woolfells were at this date charged with the same amount as a sack of wool.[2]

In 1353, the staple of wools, skins, and leather is fixed at certain towns in England, for that the king understands that in consequence of the staple of the wool of England, ' which is the sovereign merchandize and jewel of his kingdom of England,' having been held, before now, out of the kingdom, people of foreign lands are enriched, and the profit which thence should have accrued in his kingdom to the people in general from sale of their wool, had been appropriated by a few individuals of his kingdom, to the great damage and impoverishment of the said kingdom ;[3] and the king takes the opportunity of asking the prelates, lords, and commons to

[1] Par. Rolls, ii. 229.
[2] See Petition, Par. Rolls, ii. 230.
[3] Par. Rolls, ii. 246. The staple towns are :—for England, Newcastle, York (Everwyk), Lincoln (Nicole), Norwicz, Westminster, Canterbirs, Cicester, Wyncester, Excester, and Bristol (Brustuyt); for Wales, Cermerdyn; and for Ireland, Dyvelyn, Waterford, Cork and

grant him the subsidy on wool, woolfells, and leather for a term, the last grant having expired at Michaelmas past; which accordingly they do, for three years.[1] In the Parliament held at Westminster after Martinmas in 1355, the Commons, after a brief conference with the Lords in the White Chamber, grant unanimously the subsidy of wool, skins and leather to the king, for six years, to be levied in the same manner as at present, on condition that, during that time, the king shall not impose other taxes or charges on the said Commons.[2]

In 1362, the Lords and Commons with one assent grant to the king a subsidy of wool, skins and leather exported, at the rate of 20s. for every sack of wool and every 300 woolfells, and 40s. for every last of leather, for three years from Michaelmas.[3]

In 1364, the Chancellor informs the Lords that:—certain lords had been with the king, and that, in his presence, his estate had been fully explained to him, and how he stood, and in what a plight he was (comment et en quele plit il estoit), and he was openly informed of what he had; the amount of the revenues of his kingdom; the fees and annuities with which he was charged; the great amount of the payments he had made for the establishment of Gascony, Calais, and certain castles and towns towards the north; and for the wars in Ireland and elsewhere; and the costs and gifts incurred and

Droghda. The staple of lead was held at the same towns—the custom paid for lead exported was 3d. for every 20 pounds—vint soldѳe.

[1] Par. Rolls, ii. 252.
[2] Ibid. 265.
[3] Ibid. 273.

made in respect of several strangers who visited him for divers causes. And it was clearly proved that all the revenues of his kingdom were not sufficient to meet the moiety of his expenditure; and that therefore the king prayed an aid. And after deliberation as to the best manner of aiding the king, and saving his honor and estate, the Lords and Commons grant the king a subsidy on wool, woolfells, and leather exported, at the rate of 40s. for every sack of wool and 300 woolfells, and 4l. for every last of leather, for three years.[1]

In 1368, a time of peace, except indeed on the Scottish border, where 'war's the borderers' game,' and therefore the state of things appeared more like war than peace ('semble plus la guere qe pees'), another subsidy is granted, but at a different rate, viz., for every sack of wool and every 240 woolfells 36s. 8d., and for every last of hides 4l., for two years.[2] This grant is expressly stated to be additional to the ancient custom of half a mark for every sack of wool and twelve score woolfells and a mark for every last of leather.

In 1369, affairs had assumed a warlike aspect on the continent; and another subsidy is granted at the following rates:—1. From denizens, for every sack of wool and every 240 woolfells, 43s. 4d.; and for every last of leather 4l., 'in addition to the old customs.' 2. From aliens, for every sack of wool and every 240 woolfells, four marks (2l. 13s. 4d.); and for every last of leather, eight marks (5l. 6s. 8d.)[3]

[1] Par. Rolls, ii. 285.   [2] Ibid. ii. 295.
[3] Ibid. ii. 300. The charge on aliens would appear to include the old and the new customs as they are not specially mentioned.

In 1372, the war, 'which for a space did fail,' has recommenced, and accordingly Parliament renews the subsidy, for two years, at the rate fixed in 1369.[1] But this is not all, for after the 'chivaliers' of counties have received their 'congé' and have departed, the citizens and burghers members of Parliament are ordered to remain, 'for certain reasons.' To whom, assembled before the Prince and other prelates and lords in a chamber near the White Chamber, it is shown that:—in the year last past there was granted, for a certain term, for the safe and sure conduct of the ships and merchandize coming inwards to this country by sea, and passing outwards, a subsidy, that is to say, for each tun (tonelle) of wine imported, 2s.; and for each pound (£) of every sort of merchandize imported or exported, 6d.; which term is just expired. And it is suggested that they, having regard to the perils and mischiefs that might happen to their ships and merchandize by the enemy at sea, should grant a similar subsidy, for a year, for the said causes. Which subsidy they grant to the king. And then depart.[2] The subsidy and tunnage and poundage are renewed, in 1373, by Lords and Commons, for two years.[3]

[1] Par. Rolls, ii. 310.
[2] Ibid. ii. 310. In collection of this poundage, questions appear to have arisen similar to those which always, in modern practice, arise in working a new tax act, in relation to the area of charge. The fishermen of the Eastern coast were required to pay 6d. in the £ value on their fish caught and brought home, as for so much 'merchandize or goods imported.' And it became necessary to issue Writs to the collectors of the poundage, stating that it was not the intention to tax fish caught in the sea and not exported, and accordingly that they were not to charge the said fishermen. Writs to the collectors of the subsidy in the ports of Holkam, Welles, Blakeneye, Wyveton, Claye, Salthous, Skiryngham and Croumere. Foedera, Record Edn. iii. part ii. 1004.
[3] Par. Rolls, ii. 317.

In 1377, the subsidy, as granted in 1373, is renewed for three years; the Commons excusing themselves from further grant because of late they have so severely suffered from the ravages of the pestilence among the people and servants, murrain of cattle, and failure of corn crops and other fruits of the earth, that they can do no more at present.[1]

This concludes the grants of subsidies of port duties in the reign of Edward III. We leave the collection of the duties in London in the hands of Geoffrey Chaucer; to whom had been granted, in 1374, the office of Comptroller of the custom and subsidy of wools, skins and woolfells in the port of London; he 'taking in that office such fees as previous comptrollers of the custom and subsidy in the said port have hitherto been accustomed to receive. He is to write with his own hand official accounts; continue in residence; and perform his duties personally and not by deputy. And one of the two parts of the seal termed "cocket" is to remain in his custody, as long as he is in office.'[2]

Chaucer a Comptroller of Customs.

The Poll Tax.

The first Poll Tax.

The first Poll Tax on native inhabitants ever imposed in this country was granted in 1376. The king was ill at Shene, and Parliament was opened under commission by Richard of Bordeaux, Prince of Wales; the Chancellor stating the principal cause of summons to be:—
'Information that the king had received of preparations

---

[1] Par. Rolls, ii. 322.
[2] 'Officium contrarotulatoris in portu London' Galfrido Chaucer conceditur. Rymer, Foedera vii. 38; Record Edn. iii. part ii. 1004.

made by his adversary of France, during and under cover of the truce, for war by land and sea, and of overtures and alliances made by him to and with those of Spain, Scotland, and others our enemies, who almost surround us, for the purpose of destroying our lord the king, his kingdom of England, and abolishing the English language, which God forbid; and that the king was desirous of their advice, counsel, and assistance in his necessity; bearing in mind how, by the Grace of God and their good aid and counsel, the kingdom had been in his time maintained and guarded in great honor and prosperity. In answer to this request, Parliament granted for maintenance of the war and defence of the kingdom, a tax of Fourpence to be taken from the goods of each person of the kingdom, men and women, over the age of fourteen years, except only real beggars (verrois mendicenbs sans fraude).[1] Praying the king to hold them excused for not being able to grant a greater subsidy, because of their recent losses on the sea, and bad years which had happened of late.[2] From a Return of the monies levied by the collectors of the tax in the different counties, cities, and principal towns in England[3] it appears that the sum received amounted to 22,607*l*. 2*s*. 8*d*., and that 1,376,442 lay persons paid the tax. This novel tax—'tax hitherto unheard of,' as Walsingham has it, provoked considerable complaints.

The amount of yield.

[1] The clergy also granted 12*d*. from every beneficed person, and 4*d*. from every other religious person, except mendicant friars. Par. Rolls, ii. 364.   [2] Ibid.

[3] Chester and Durham, having their own receivers, are not included. And observe:—the sum raised does not correspoond with the stated number of taxpayers. See Subsidy Roll, printed in Archaeologia, vii. 337.

General Remarks.

We have now passed under review the principal taxes imposed in England from 1188 to 1377; which with the profits of royal demesne and the other sources of ordinary revenue hereinbefore mentioned, supplied the king's exchequer during ——.

The Reign of Richard I.

1. The ten years' reign of Richard I., or rather government of the kingdom by his justiciars—William Longchamp, Walter de Coutances, Hubert Walter, and Geoffry Fitz-Peter successively, for the king was a continual absentee. Educated in Southern France, land of sunshine, land of love and song, accomplished in those arts, and prone, as was the troubadour, to wandering adventure; large and powerful in frame, and in the highest degree ambitious of renown for personal valour, King Richard was connected by the fact of possession, as the only tie, with what seemed a damp and dismal island, where the guitar was rarely heard, and rarely 'morn brought forth a noble chance;' and he regarded its inhabitants chiefly with an eye to fiscal advantage, as subjects—for exaction. His valiant deeds in the unfortunate crusade gained for him, indeed, such renown in the East that, according to Joinville, the Saracen mother stilled her squalling brat with, 'Stop, here comes King Richard,' and when the horse of Saracen or Bedouin shied at a bush, the rider would say; 'What, think you 'tis King Richard.'[1] But crusades were expensive proceedings, and the

---

[1] 'Cuides-tu que ce soit li roys Richard.' Joinville, Hist. de St. Louis, c. xvii.

expenditure on that account, as well as for the king's ransom from the Austrian dungeon, and for the continual pottering and uneventful war with Philippe Augustus in which he spent the concluding years of his reign, to say nothing of the two coronations and royal progresses in which were consumed the four months of his two visits to England, concurred to render Richard a costly king to his subjects. Large portions of the demesne lands, and dignities, and offices of trust were sold; the vassalage of Scotland, together with the fortresses of Roxburgh and Berwick went for 10,000 marks; but for London no purchaser could be found;[1] and the free application of all the usual methods of taxation was supplemented by extortions from individuals as by way of loan, various compulsory resealings of royal charters attended with payments of fines as for renewal, and the seizure, on the occasion of the king's second visit, of the wool of the Cistertians, who as sworn to poverty possessed at that time no other chattels.[2]

The means by which the ransom of the king was raised, before mentioned piecemeal under different headings, were (1) a tax on the lands of barons and knights, of 20s. for each fee, the hybrid scutage before mentioned; (2) a hidage or carucage—a general tax on lands holden by some other service than that of the shield, assessed on the hide lands of the different counties by the king's justiciars, and collected by the

The ransom of the King, how raised.

---

[1] The king is stated to have expressed a willingness to sell London if he could find a purchaser. W. Hemmingford, p. 519.

[2] The Cistertians compounded by payment of a fine.

sheriffs; (3) a tallage on cities and boroughs; (4) seizure of the wool of the Gilbertines and Cistertians, and the plate and jewels of the churches; and (5) a fourth of revenue or goods from every person in the kingdom.

The tournament tax.

Lastly, before passing to the next reign, a word concerning a tax more consonant in nature with popular tradition of the doings of Cœur de Lion; who if a bad king, at any rate equalled in fame King Arthur, when he—'with spear in rest, from spur to plume a star in tournament, shot through the lists.' 'A tournament of doves'—says Corisande in 'Lothair' to the hero of the pigeon shooting match—'a tournament of doves. I would sooner have seen you in the lists at Ashby.' Lothair's precise rank is not stated, but as noble, or as knight, before entering the lists for 'the joyous passage of arms at Ashby,' he would have paid a tax, then recently imposed[1] on jousts, as follows: —For an earl, 20 marks of silver; for a baron, 10 marks; for a knight having lands, 4 marks; and such as had no lands, 2 marks.

The Reign of John.

2. During the reign of John, extortioner, unjust &c., whose exactions, frequently conducted with great cruelty, licentiousness, and cowardice, left him at last no friend—a reign which presents little difficulty in fiscal summary, we may follow Tyrrell:—

[1] The king had encouraged tilting with the lance in order to practice his knights for the crusades; but subsequently may have found that the martial appetite for such exercises required restraint rather than encouragement. The celebrated description of the tournament at Ashby in 'Ivanhoe' and the authorities there quoted, prove that encounters in the lists had, at that date, an earnestness about them very different from the hastiludia of a subsequent date, when what Byron terms the 'monstrous mummeries of the middle ages' were in full swing.

'As for his taxations and ways of raising money, they were so many, so various, and so arbitrary, that it may almost be said his whole reign was but one continued taxation and oppression of his subjects.'

3. During the long inglorious reign of Henry III., a period of fifty-six years, capable of division into three epochs—the first, from 1216 to 1232; the second, from 1232 to 1252; and the third from 1252 to 1272. Of these the second was, as stated by Professor Stubbs:—'A period of great exactions and unfeeling tyranny on the king's part .... the political history being little more than a detail of heavy demands for money, ineffectual protests, and ever-increasing irritation.' To this epoch, therefore, let our attention be for a few moments directed. It commences in 1232, with a refusal by the barons to grant an aid towards the expenses incurred in the king's late expedition to foreign parts. 'The earls, barons, and knights tenants in capite had accompanied the king in person; had spent their money in a useless attempt; and had returned poor. Under these circumstances an aid could not rightly be required of them.'[1] Then in the same year, we find the king excusing his remissness in repelling the incursions of Leolinus (Llewellyn) Prince of Wales and his Welsh marauders, on the ground of want of money. 'I have heard from my treasurer,' he answers Peter des Roches and others with a sigh, 'that the whole revenue from the Exchequer hardly suffices me for simple food, and accustomed alms; wherefore poverty does not permit me to undertake

[1] Matt. Paris, ii. 339.

hostile expeditions.' Then answered his councillors:
—'If thou art poor, impute it to thyself, who dost
transfer to others honors and wardships and vacant
dignities in such a manner, alienating them from the
treasury, that neither in riches of gold or silver, but
only in shadowy name canst thou be called king. For
thy predecessors, magnificent kings, most rich in all
glory of riches, not from elsewhere, but from the
profits and emoluments of the kingdom collected price-
less treasure.' After this, a strict inquiry into the conduct of the sheriffs, king's bailiffs and other officers,
followed by demands for, payment of arrears in all
cases of fraud and default, a thousand marks of silver
taken from Ralph Brito on his removal from the office
of treasurer, and other proceedings of that sort, filled,
according to Matthew Paris, the king's empty coffers in
a very short time.'[1] Nevertheless, ere many years are
past, the king is in the same position of pecuniary difficulty, and we find him, on refusal of a general aid
towards prosecuting with a strong hand his claims on
foreign lands, making application to the prelates first
in a body, but with no success, afterwards to them
individually ' with sweet words exacting money from
them in this form :—You know how destitute I am of
all money and treasure, and how I am called on to
recover land belonging to me by a clear and incontestable title, were I not hindered by poverty. Now
you ought to assist me in my necessity.'[2] And in
November in the same year, ' Because he was bound by

His fiscal difficulties.

---

[1] Matt. Paris, ii. 342.
[2] Ibid. ii. 401; and see note as to the original text.

no small debts to the merchants in wine, wax, and foreign cloth, the king extorted much money from citizens of London and Jews; nor even thence did the merchants receive full payment.'[1] But the straits to which the king was reduced are notorious.

The reign was a period of misrule, leading up to the Barons' war; of lavish generosity to foreign relatives and friends; of excessive tallage of the towns, principal cause of that dislike to the king which induced them to side with the Barons.[2] But the prominent feature in the history of the reign, from any point of view, is the king's desire to regain lost territory on the continent—his foreign proclivities, principal cause of all the difficulties of the reign. The current of national feeling, including the nobles, had, since the loss of Normandy, set inwards. Henry's thoughts and wishes were ever fixed on continental position; his eyes, ever strained across the strait. He stood, as it were, on the shore of England waiting for 'a sail'— *His foreign proclivities.*

> Orans primus transmittere cursum,
> Tendebatque manus ripae ulterioris amore.

4. During the reign of another crusader, as valiant as King Richard, and ever ' foremost in the fight and victor at the tilt and tournament ; ' whether we regard him in single combat, as with Adam de Gurdon, strongest of ' the disinherited ; ' in tournament, as at Chalons, where he plucks their Count out of saddle ; or in battle, as at Lewes, in the utter rout of the Londoners opposed to him in the Barons' line ; and at Evesham, against a *The Reign of Edward I.*

---

[1] Matt. Paris, ii. 406.
[2] An event impressed on the memory from the summons of their representatives in conjunction with those of the counties to Simon de Montfort's famous Parliament of 1265.

former friend and teacher in war, now his foe, whose eye had previously marked his orderly advance. 'By the arm of St. James!' exclaims the great earl, 'these advance wisely. They have not this of their own knowledge, but have learned it from me. Let us commend our souls to God, for our bodies are theirs.' But, in addition to this, Edward had other and more lasting titles to renown: Wise administrator, to whose ability is due the consolidation and arrangement, the practical formation of our constitution in its modern outline; our English Justinian: from his useful legislation; and, last and greatest, that of first truly English king.

When, however, we regard the reign from a fiscal point of view, undoubtedly it was, from the expenses of the wars in Wales and in Scotland and the hostilities with France which intervened, a period of considerable fiscal difficulties. To meet these, as stated by Professor Stubbs:—'Edward's expedients for the raising of money are most diversified: the petition for thirtieths, twentieths, fifteenths, twelfths, elevenths, tenths, ninths, eighths, sevenths, sixths, fifths, thirds, runs up the whole scale of fractions, reaching the climax in the demand of a half of clerical revenue, or rather, perhaps, in the seizure of all the wool. When direct request for a subsidy is hopeless, he falls back upon the old feudal aids: his daughter is to be married, or his son to be knighted; or the scutage; or respite of distraint of knighthood, itself an expansion of the scutage system; or an increase in the customs; or, last and meanest, a revival of the almost forgotten tallage on demesne.'[1] Only, however, from 1290 to 1297 was

Edward's expedients for raising money.

[1] Select Charters, p. 410.

the taxation of the kingdom very serious. It reached the culminating point in the year last mentioned; when in a general petition archbishops, bishops, abbots, priors, earls, barons, and the whole commonalty (who deny their obligation to accompany the king in his expedition to Flanders because their ancestors never did military service in that land) add that:—'Even were they bound to go, they have not the means so to do; because they are prostrated by divers tallages, aids, and prises, that is to say, of wheat, oats, malt, wool, skins, oxen, cows, and salt flesh, without the payment of a penny, and these are their only means of sustenance.[1] And they state that they are not able to grant an aid, on account of their poverty occasioned by the said tallages and prises; having, indeed, hardly the means of sustenance; and complain that the whole community is oppressed by the tax on wool, which is too heavy— 'for the wool of England amounts almost to the value of half the whole land, and the tax paid thereon amounts to the fifth part of the value of the whole land.'

The following are the terms of the new Articles inserted in that famous statute which Hallam, in allusion to the immunity from arbitrary taxation it secured to us, says 'is inadequately denominated "The Confirmation of the Charters," for it added another pillar to our constitution not less important than the Great Charter itself':— {The new articles in 'Confirmatio Cartarum,' 1297.}

---

[1] 'Quia nimis afflicti sunt per diversa tallagia, auxilia, prisas, videlicet, de frumento, avenis, braseo, lanis, coriis, bobus, vaccis, carnibus salsis, sine solutione alicujus denarii de quibus se debuerant sustenasse.' Rishanger, Chron. p. 175.

First, in the original text:

Original text.

V. E pur ceo qe aucunes gentz de notre roiaume se doutent qe les aides e les mises, les queles il nous ount fait avant ces oures pur nos guerres e autre bosoignes, de leur grant e leur bone volunte, en quele manere qe faitz seient, pussent turner en servage a eus, e a leur heirs, par ce qil serroient autrefoitz trovez en roule, e ausi prises qe ont este faites par my le roiaume par nous ministres en notre noun, avoms grante pur nous et pur nous heirs, qe mes iceles aides, mises, ne prises, ne treroms a custume, pur nule chose qe soit fait ou qe par roule ou en autre maniere peust estre trove.

VI. E ausi avoms grante pur nous e pur nos heirs as ercevesques, evesques, abbes, e priurs, e as autres gentz de seinte eglise, e as contes e barons e a tote la communaute de la terre, qe mes per nule busoigne tieu manere des aides, mises, ne prises, de notre roiaume ne prendroms, fors qe par commun assent de tut le roiaume, e a commun profit de meisme le roiaume, sauve les auncienes aides e prises dues e custumees.

VII. E pur ceo qe tut le plus de la communaute del roiaume se sentent durement grevez de la male toute des leines, cest asavoir de chescun sak de leine quarante soudz, e nous ont prie que nous les vousissoms relesser, nous a leur priere les avoms pleinement relesse; e avoms grante qe cele ne autre mes ne prendroms sanz lour commun assent e leur bone volunte; sauve a nous e a nos heirs la custume des leines, peaus e quirs avant grantez par la communaute du roiaume avantdit.[1]

[1] Hawkins, Statutes at Large.

Of which the following is a translation:

V. And for so much as divers people of our realm are in fear that the aids and tasks which they have given to us beforetime towards our wars and other business, of their own grant and goodwill (howsoever they were made), might turn to a bondage to them and their heirs, because they might be at another time found in the rolls, and likewise for the prises taken throughout the realm by our ministers; we have granted for us and our heirs, that we shall not draw such aids, tasks nor prises into a custom, for any thing that hath been done heretofore be it by roll or any other precedent that may be found.

VI. Moreover we have granted for us and our heirs, as well to archbishops, bishops, abbots, priors, and other folk of holy Church, as also to earls, barons, and to all the commonalty of the land, that for no business from henceforth we shall take such manner of aids, tasks, nor prises, but by the common assent of the realm, and for the common profit thereof, saving the ancient aids and prises due and accustomed.

VII. And for so much as the more part of the commonalty of the realm find themselves sore grieved with the maletote of wools, that is to wit, a toll of forty shillings for every sack of wool, and have made petition to us to release the same; we, at their requests, have clearly released it, and have granted for us and our heirs, that we shall not take such things without their common assent and goodwill; saving to us and our heirs the custom of wools, skins, and leather granted before by the commonalty aforesaid.

The Reign of Edward II.

5. During the reign of Edward II., memorable for unworthy favourites, defeat in battle, famine, pestilence, discord between the king and the barons—sad times; but, on the other hand, a reign of comparatively light taxation.

Suppression of the Knights Templars.

On suppression of the Order of the Temple, in 1312, (as useless since the capture of Acre, the last stronghold of the Christians in Palestine; dangerous, certainly to the Pope, if not indeed to society generally; and for many excellent reasons which he who wills may read), their lands, it might be imagined, would have reverted in fact, as they did in law, to the king. But that was not the case. The Pope interfered, insisting on the appropriation of these lands to purposes similar to those for which they had been granted. And, in the result, the lands of the Order of the Temple in England, as well as in France and Italy (portion of those nine thousand manors the Order possessed in Europe) were conferred on the Hospitallers, who had taken the Island of Rhodes from the Turks, and had kept it with a courage which, as Voltaire remarks, 'deserved at least the spoils of the knights of the Temple for their recompense.'[1]

The following extract from a ballad of the reign of this king[2] is interesting as referring to inequalities, or rather injustice, in the practical assessment of taxes in towns at this date. The evils against which the complaint is directed had relation, probably, to the action

---

[1] Essai sur les Mœurs, cap. 66. Œuvres complètes, xxvii. 242.
[2] Percy Society, vol. xxviii.

of the town guilds, between whom and the craft guilds the struggle still continued, rather than to valuation by assessors appointed by the king. After allusion to the conscription of 1315–16,¹ the poem proceeds :—

>Whan the kyng into his werre
>wol have a taxacion
>to help him at his need
>of each town a portion,
>Hit schal be to-tolled ²
>Hit schal be to-twyzt ³
>Hit schal half-del ⁴ be go
>into the develes fist
>   of helle,
>ther beth so many parteners
>ne dar no pore mon telle.⁵
>A man that hath an hundred pound
>schal pay xii pens round :
>and so mych schal a pore mon pay
>that poverte hath brout to ground,
>that hath a housful of chyldre
>sitting about the flete.⁶
>Christis cors hab thei !
>but⁷ that be well sette
>   and sworn,
>the pore schal be i-pylt⁸
>and the rych schal be forborn.

6. And during 'the most active and prosperous reign of Edward III.,' as Rymer terms it;⁹ date of the effective commencement of our national greatness—

<small>The Reign of Edward III.</small>

---

¹ In 1315, the citizens, burgesses, and knights of counties granted a 15th of moveables from cities, towns, and royal demesne; but the Lords and Commons, one strong well armed (potentem et defensibilem) foot soldier, from each vill (cities, boroughs, and royal demesne excepted), his expenses to be paid until he arrived at the host, and for 60 days afterwards, at 4*d.* a day; and market towns that could bear the expense of more than one foot soldier were to be further charged. Par. Rolls, i. 351. This was afterwards commuted for a 16th of moveables. Par. Rolls, i. 451. ² Levied in full, or divided out. ³ Snatched away. ⁴ One half. ⁵ Give information. ⁶ Floor. ⁷ Unless. ⁸ Robbed. ⁹ Dedication of the Foedera to Queen Anne.

date of Crécy and of Poitiers, where, on the hill slope where Edward stood at bay in retreat from the raid on Normandy, and in the narrow way between the vineyards where the Black Prince had intrenched the little mixed army of freebooters with which he had penetrated into the heart of France, our bowmen and bill-men first established the renown of the English foot soldier for unrivalled stability in the battle-field, since retained down to Waterloo and Inkermann. Date of our first effective command of the English Channel, gained by the semi-naval victory of Sluys and the capture of Calais, and of the victory in the Channel over the Spanish fleet[1] whence Edward acquired the title of 'King of the Seas;' first item in a brilliant list that concludes with The Nile and Trafalgar. Date of the introduction into this country of the Flemish weavers, and the improvement of our woollen manufacture, forming the foundation of that industry in manufacture, by which, even more than by warlike qualities, we have attained our present high position amongst the nations of the world. Date of the commencement of our commerce, hitherto almost entirely in the hands of merchant strangers, the tenants of the Steel Yard, i.e. the German merchants, and others. For when a fair sea-way was opened for our shipmen, they soon acquired practical acquaintance with all the sea-board of western Europe. And therefore Chaucer, who ever represents the class rather than an individual, in portraiture of a typical 'schipman' from the West

---

[1] Known as 'Les Espagniols sur mer.'

GENERAL REMARKS. 183

of England, from Dartmouth or thereabouts, 'for ought I wot he was of Dertmouthe,' says :—

> 'He knew wel alle the havenes, as thei were,
> 'From Scotlond to the cape of Fynestere,
> 'And every cryk in Bretagne and in Spayne.'

Nor was this for long the extreme of their experience; they followed the returning vessels of the Genoese, and themselves sailing round between the Pillars of Hercules, extended their ventures into the Mediterranean Sea. Date also of the commencement of English literature and of the use of the English language, of which Chaucer may be considered the father in verse, Wycliffe in prose, particularly of its use among the higher classes, whose children henceforth were taught to speak English, and to translate Latin into English, instead of French; and of its legislative recognition, viz. by the statute of 1362, which enacts that pleas in the Law Courts shall be in the English tongue.[1]

Take for a moment a wider view of things. It is an age when commercial tendencies originating with the Crusades curiously intermingle with that ultimate phase of the feudal system termed 'chivalry.' 'The strange characteristic of the time is that it is warlike and mercantile. The history of the period is epopée and story, romance of Arthur, farce of Patelin. The whole epoch is double-faced and squinting. Contrasts prevail; everywhere prose and poetry contradict each other, make game of each other. The two centuries of interval

The intermixture of feudalism and commerce.

[1] 36 Edw. III. c. 15.

between the dreams of Dante[1] and the dreams of Shakespeare create themselves the effect of a dream. It is "A Midsummer Night's Dream," where the poet mingles at will artizan and hero; noble Theseus figures there by side of weaver Bottom, whose beautiful ass's ears turn Titania's head.'[2] During this critical time, also a period of peculiar difficulty to our nation from the antagonism which sprung up between this country and France, we possessed, to our inestimable advantage, a ruler equal to the occasion, in all, from the prosaic as well as from the poetic point of view, Father of our Commerce, as well as Founder of the Order of the Garter and the Round Table at Windsor. 'No manlier prince, and none more prudent or successful, ever occupied the English throne.'[3] In a word, we had *the man.*

Edward as 'greatest knight.'

Assume a few moments' conversation with a gallant knight of the period; one, shall we say, who, on accompanying Edward to Amiens to do homage to Philippe de Valois for Guyenne, heard of the brilliant French Court, tournaments, joustings, one eternal fête, making Paris '*the most chivalresque residence in the world,*' and of the splendours of Vincennes, where of a morning four kings would enter the lists to joust before his Most Christian Majesty. Ask him a few questions regarding Halidon Hill, regarding Sluys, regarding that morning when, as the fog cleared off, the heralds recognized by their insignia eleven princes, forty barons, and twelve hundred knights among the thirty thousand dead on the

[1] The Divina Commedia seems to have been commenced before Dante's exile from Florence in 1304.
[2] Michelet, Hist. de France.
[3] Foster, Debates on the Grand Remonstrance, 1641, i. 42.

hill side at Crécy. Did Edward really, at the banquet after his single combat with Eustace de Ribeaumont, greatest of French knights, present to him a circlet of pearls, to be shown to his lady love as a gift from his hand? And what Knights of the Garter, after return of the Black Prince from Bordeaux with the valiant and valuable captive he so scrupulously treated as the King of France, sat at the Table Round at Windsor with Edward, and the Black Prince, and De Maunay, and Chandos? briefly—regarding the military and chivalresque glories of the reign. With justice he might dilate on the subject, and compare with the French Court. at its best the court of that prince who, at the beginning of his reign, was 'a petty prince indeed in comparison with the most puissant Philippe de Valois;'[1] the difference being that kings were captives, not visitors.

Next, regard the reign from the commercial point of view. The king is equally prudent, equally energetic, equally successful; renewing the Carta Mercatoria; encouraging the foreign merchants, in lieu of repelling them, as did Philippe; affording facilities to commerce, in lieu of fettering it with regulations and oppressing it with taxes; introducing Flemish weavers, and cherishing the manufacture of the great staple article of his country; clearing the seas of wool pirates, and securing the passage of wool and cloth across the strait. Never, in war or in peace, is the king's eye off the sack of wool. Hence all his attempts to prevent the severance by the French king of our commercial con-

Edward as 'the father of English commerce.'

---

[1] 'Edouard était un bien petit prince pour s'opposer à cette grande puissance de Philippe de Valois.' Michelet, Hist. de France, iii. 187.

nexion with Flanders. Hence his alliance with Artevelde, the all-powerful Flemish brewer. Hence his assumption of the formal title of King of France when he could not otherwise secure the effective co-operation of his allies. Hence the obstinacy with which he prosecuted the siege of Calais; building a town [1] round the place, for residence, till capture of that stronghold of the wool pirates. The statute-book of the reign is thick strewn with enactments relating to wool, to cloth, to the staple, to subsidies from wool, &c. &c. down to the last, which have reference to:—'Woollen cloths not to be transported before they are fulled,' and 'Certain cloths whereof no subsidy or aulnage shall be paid.' [2] 'Thus endeth the statutes made in the time of the noble King Edward the Third.' And, if a commercial counterpart is desired to the picture of Edward and his Table Round, it may be found in the description, by Stow, of the banquet given by Henry Picard, ex-Mayor of London, who, in 1363, at his house in the Vintry, entertained the King, the Black Prince, the King of France, the King of Scotland, and the King of Cyprus, 'besides many others, noblemen.' [3]

Popularity of Edward's policy.

In this policy and line of action the barons and knights followed Edward with a will, mindful of the source that supplied the means for their magnificence—their hosts of retainers, damaskened blades, splendid armour, gorgeous apparel—and of the necessity of keeping open the market for that wool which was the

---

[1] He named this new town Villeneuve la Hardie. Guizot, Hist. France, ii. 101.
[2] 50 Edw. III., cc. 7 and 8.
[3] 'And, after that, kept his Hall for all comers, that were willing to play at dice or hazard.' Survey of London, i. 260.

principal product of their estates. To anyone familiar with the history of the times, the story of the Vows on the Heron is well known. Robert of Artois, exiled from France, and residing at the English Court, brings to the banquet of Edward a heron he has killed, and, after the manner of the times, persuades king and knights to make a vow thereon. A lady closes with her hand an eye of her admirer; and he vows, and others after him, to wear a patch over one eye till released by valiant deed performed in the enemy's country of France. Now these knights, patch on eye and sworn as aforesaid, were, it has been shrewdly observed, very wide awake; and in the gallant blow that enabled the removal of the patch, struck, as knights for lady, but as landowners, for sheep. In lieu of repelling, it is well to accept with grateful acknowledgment of the fact, the imputation that we were at this date a nation of herdsmen. 'What else but animals does England rear?'[1] says a satirical poem of the period. The knight who bargained for ransom with any of that crowd of captives, 'the gentlemen who had proved themselves so useless to France,' and whose extortions for levy of ransom maddened the French peasantry to 'the Jacquerie,' might well smile at such a sneer; as in after times, his descendants, again victorious, but then—'a nation of shopkeepers.' The rose noble, if stamped with a shep instead of a ship,[2] might have been also

---

[1] 'Quos praeter pecudes alit Anglia.' See the first of two sets of verses in which Englishman and Frenchman engage in a regular slanging match, in true Billingsgate fashion; and which are interesting as evidencing the hatred that existed at this date between the two nations. Political Poems and Songs (Master of the Rolls Series), i. 91, 92.

[2] 'Our enemies bid for the shippe sette a shepe.'

inscribed with 'Honi soit qui mal y pense'—Shame to him that thinks ill of it. And had Edward anticipated Philip of Burgundy, he would have used, in establishment of his Order of knighthood, a more appropriate symbol, in the Golden Fleece, than the thing which may have fallen from the pretty Countess of Salisbury. 'One thing I advise you,' said, in after years, the Emperor Sigismund on visiting King Henry V., 'keep Dover and Calais as your two eyes.' (The modern version is :—'Keep up your Channel fleet.') By that means Edward not only secured the commerce of England, but commanded the highway along which passed the trader between Spain and the Flemish cities, and, as still more important, the trader between those cities and the East and Mediterranean, when the Venetians and Genoese, obstructed in their continental route by fiscal exactions and mercantile regulations, took ship, and by the sea route round the western coast of Europe, communicated with Bruges and the other cities that rendered Flanders at that date the emporium of trade.[1]

Edward as 'King of the Seas.'

The Black Death.

In conclusion may be added a few words regarding an event which, in its consequences, meets the student of the history of this reign at every turn; which created an economical revolution, changing the price of labour and commodities; and which is not without a certain importance from our present point of view. During

---

[1] Ffor if this see be kept in tyme of werre,
Who can here passe withought daungere and woo?
Who may eschape, who may myschef differre?
What marchandye may for by be agoo?
Ffor nedes hem muste take truse every ffoo:
Fflaundres, and Spayne, and othere, trust to me,
Or ellis hyndered alle for thys narrowe see.

The Libel of English Policy, Political Poems and Songs, ii. 158.

the middle ages Western Europe was frequently devastated by pestilence. Wars were frequent, producing, as a necessary consequence of devastation, famine; then came pestilence—war, famine, pestilence, that was the ordinary cycle of events; and the most serious pestilence happened in the middle of the fourteenth century. Arriving by the old route of the East, in 1347 it struck Florence, prepared as victim by the famine of the previous year, with that fatality which Boccaccio describes in the prologue to the Decamerone. In 1348, it ravaged France in the manner described by Michelet and other historians; and, in sombre Germany, originated that frenzy in mortification of the flesh which produced the order of the Flagellants. And in England, which it reached in 1348-9, in interruption of the revelry of the victor of Crécy and his new Knights of the Garter, it destroyed about one-half of the population.[1] After the angel of destruction had stayed his hand, there resulted, from the depopulation caused in this country by 'the Black Death,' the scarcity of labour that occasioned the famous Statutes of Labourers and other provisions to obviate the rise of wages, and compel workmen, servants, labourers and others[2] to work for certain fixed wages; and, as another consequence, the introduction

[1] According to Sismondi, it is calculated that in the whole of Europe, which was subjected, from one extremity to the other, to this dreadful scourge, three-fifths of the population were destroyed. Repub. Ital. iv. 96. According to Froissart, if he is any authority on such a point, a third perished. According to Walsingham (i. 273), 'AEstimabatur a pluribus quod vix decima pars hominum fuisset relicta ad vitam.'

[2] Extending even to parish priests: for when the Commons petition that 'chaplains have become too dear since the pestilence, to the great grievance and oppression of the people,' their wages are fixed at six marks the year.

of a more extended system of tenant farming. Hitherto, the great landowners, including the religious orders, who indeed, and particularly the Cistertians, were the chief agriculturists of that day, had, speaking generally, farmed their estates by means of bailiffs or reeves. Chaucer gives us a picture of such a reeve :—

> 'his lordes scheep, his neet, and his dayerie,
> 'his swyn, his hors, his stoor, and his pultrie
> 'were holly in this reeves governynge.'

The few hundred acres that the largest modern landowner may keep in hand for purposes of 'shorthorns,' for preservation of the rabbit, or that he may, unrestrictedly, shoot partridges in standing barley, are but a garden patch when compared with the home farms of the middle ages. Of these an idea may be formed from the Petition of the elder Spencer, in which he complains that from his manor of Fastern in Wiltshire and other manors in that and other counties (naming 63 manors) his enemies had driven away— 28,000 sheep, 22,000 oxen, heifers and cows, 600 horses and mares, besides taking away a vast quantity of provisions of all sorts;[1] or from the quantity of live stock possessed by the Bishop of Winchester in 1331, viz. : 1,683 oxen of all ages, and 11,548 sheep. The tenant farmer was not, indeed, unknown, paying rent in money or in kind, or partly in money and partly in kind. And, indeed, the class had lately increased in numbers, as the nobility required more and more money to meet a growing expenditure in luxuries, in

[1] Rot. Claus. 15 Edw. II. See Tyrrell, iii. 206.

jewels, in splendid armour and costly horses. But, as a rule, estates were kept in hand. Subsequently, however, to the visitation of the Black Death, such were the difficulties in working large estates occasioned by the scarcity of labour, that the landowners found it convenient, if not necessary, to adopt a new system; and now began to parcel out their estates in farms, letting these farms to tenants either with the stock thereon (which was at first the usual practice, in consequence of lack of capital) or without. Thus, therefore, the Black Death of 1349 connects itself easily with our present subject. By some persons it may be remembered more particularly as 'the pestilence of Florence,' occasion of the retreat to the Gardens of Pampinea, and the composition of the amusing stories of the Decamerone, models for Chaucer, Ariosto, and many other writers; by others, as cause of the death, at Avignon, of that lady who yet lives in song, the celebrated object of Petrarch's sonnets, Laura de Noves, wife of Hugues de Sade; or in connection with the peculiarities of the Flagellants; or as affording, in Boccaccio's description, a subject for curious comparison with similar horrors as described by Thucydides as regards the plague at Athens, and by De Foe as regards the Great Plague of London. From our present point of view it is memorable, not only from the frequent references to its ravages in the various Rolls of grants of taxes during this period, but also as main cause of the existence of the tenant farmer—that is, speaking in fiscal language and in reference to the income tax, the taxpayer under Schedule (B).

Rise of the tenant farmer.

CHAPTER VI.

FROM THE COMMENCEMENT OF THE REIGN OF RICHARD THE SECOND TO THE COMMENCEMENT OF THE CIVIL WAR, A.D. 1377–1642.

Chart of the period. THE period under review in this chapter extends over two hundred and sixty-five years, including the last quarter of the fourteenth century, the whole of the fifteenth and sixteenth centuries, and the first half of the seventeenth century. It comprises, to take first, running in a well-worn groove, the reigns of our kings *1. Reigns of kings.* and queens :—The reigns of Richard II. ; Henry IV., Henry V. and Henry VI. ; Edward IV., Edward V. and Richard III. ; Henry VII., Henry VIII., Edward VI., Mary and Elizabeth ; and James I. and Charles I., that is, the last of the Plantagenet line, 1377–1399 ; the lines of Lancaster and York, 1399–1485 ; the House of Tudor, 1485—1602 ; and the first and *2. Wars.* second kings of the House of Stuart. It comprises, to take the principal fighting events, as having a direct and special bearing on taxation :—The latter part of the protracted contest between this country and France *The hundred years' war.* termed by French historians 'The Hundred Years' War,' the principal events in the first scene being the battle of Azincourt, and the capture of Rouen, leading to the treaty of Troyes, by which, on the death of Charles VI., Henry was to succeed to the crown of France, and, in the final scene, the awakening of France under that stout amazon, 'the Maid of Orleans,' Jeanne d'Arc or Darc,[1] whichever the correct name, the death of Talbot at Castillon, and the subsequent loss of Bordeaux, Bayonne, and indeed all our continental possessions except Calais. The long period of contest and confusion known as the 'Wars of the Roses,' including the battles of St. Albans (1455), Northampton, Towton, Hexham, Barnet and Tewkesbury (1471), and Bosworth (1485), with, intervening in date between the two last-mentioned battles, Edward the Fourth's costly expedition to France. Henry the Seventh's war with France in 1492. Henry the Eighth's war with France and the Battle of the Spurs in 1513, and in the same year the repulse of northern invasion at Flodden. Another Scoto-French war in 1544, costing about 1,340,000*l*., and including the capture of Boulogne. Queen Mary's war with France, memorable for that loss of Calais which on her death, said the Queen, would be found to have graven the name on her heart. And, as the principal event of this description subsequent to the foregoing, our long struggle with Spain in the reign of Elizabeth, including the defeat of the Armada in 1588.

The wars of the Roses.

Flodden.

Armada times.

The period commences in times of castle and

[1] Darc would appear to be the correct writing. See Nouvelles Recherches sur la famille et le nom de Jeanne Darc. Paris, Dumoulin 1854; Michelet, Hist. de France, v. 33. Employment in farm work connected with the use of horses is sufficient to account for the Maid's ability in management of them.

During this period. chivalry; with Lollardry in its infancy; and Chaucer's Canterbury's Tales copied in manuscript; in a narrow world, beyond whose confines are obscure vallies and undiscovered countries, therefore supposed to be 'landes full of deviles;'[1] and the innumerable stars above us shine fixed in the floor of heaven. It concludes after 'the great bravery of building that set in in the times of Elizabeth'[2] had 'beautified the land' and the loopholed castle had been superseded by the 'Hall' so be-windowed that Bacon cannot escape sun or draught; in times of buff jerkin, arquebuss, and *Gunpowder,* rapier, when the 'bombards' had accomplished their destiny in the destruction of chivalry and feudalism, and the old nobility had perished almost to a man in the 'Wars of the Roses.' The Reformation is past, England is no longer under the religious domination of the Pope of Rome, and indeed has become 'Puritan England.' And the 'Faerie Queen,' 'Hamlet,' the 'Novum Organum,' and that History of the World the *the printing press,* long labour of years of imprisonment uncompleted in consequence of the axe of the executioner, are in our hands in print,[3] with 'the one English book which was *the mariner's compass,* then familiar to every Englishman.'[4] The discoveries of Columbus, Sebastian Cabot, and Amerigo Vespucci, the exploring expeditions we have for years been furnishing out, the adventurers we have equipped, and the colonists who have left our shores, have enlarged the world. We are on tolerably intimate terms with the

---

[1] See Mandeville. [2] Camden.
[3] Caxton's first printing press was set up at Westminster about 1474.
[4] 'England became the people of a book, and that book was the Bible.' Green, Hist. of the English People, p. 447.

Great Mogul.[1] And the East India Company has existed for nearly half a century. Those hazy dark dreams of foreign lands have long since faded away, replaced by dazzling visions of El Dorado, and lands and cities full of silver, gold, and diamonds. What the mariner's compass has effected for the world,[2] the telescope has effected for the skies;[3] we are now engaged in investigating boundless space, and *and the telescope*

> 'Some had lately in the moon
> Found a new world to th' old unknown;
> Discovered sea and land Columbus
> And Magellan could never compass.'

Briefly, the period includes a total change in the names and families, the dwellings, the arms, dress, manners, thought, habits, religion, and in many respects the food of Englishmen. Awake old John of Gaunt to look at Buckingham, he would with difficulty recognise that he was in England—till reminded by a requisition to pay his contribution to the last 'fifteenth and tenth;' for during the whole of this long period of changes there was little practical alteration in our system of taxation. The fiscal history of the times is therefore easily accomplished. After a few minutes' delay at starting, to consider the memorable Poll Tax *changed the world.*

But there was little change in taxation in England.

---

[1] See commission to H. Heydon and C. Glemham. 'Whereas wee (Jac. I.) have been moved by sundrie letters, messages, and requests from the Great Mougull to gratifie him with some choice arts and rareties which our dominions are famed to afford no lesse usefull than unknown in those parts, &c.' 14 Sept. 1622. Foedera, xvii. 407.

[2] La boussole ouvrit le monde. Voltaire.

[3] The revival of astronomy may be referred to the time of Copernicus, which for present purposes may be stated roughly as the first half of the sixteenth century. In the same manner the date of Galileo and the telescope may be stated as the first quarter of the seventeenth century.

of 1380, it is a straight run all down the road. The principal points for attention are the rise in the produce of the port duties, and the manner in which the area of direct taxation was extended so as to include rent and land. The order of the narrative is as follows: First, it is intended to treat of poll taxes; secondly, of the other direct taxes of the period, i.e., those imposed on property and persons in relation to property; and thirdly, of the customs and port duties. Subsequently, after some words concerning forced loans and benevolences, a few general remarks will be added in conclusion of the chapter and this Part of the subject.

Order of the narrative.

1. *Poll Taxes.*

To commence with the Poll Taxes. The advantages in rapidity of assessment and collection which this form of taxation was at this date considered to possess, led to the imposition of another capitation tax in 1379, when an immediate sum of money was required. But in order to avoid the unpopularity caused by the obvious unfairness of a mere poll tax such as 'the tallage of groats,' as it was termed, of 1377, a more equitable system was introduced. The taxpayers were classified by reference to rank (which it should be borne in mind had in those days a more direct relation to property than it has at present), condition in life, and property, and were charged accordingly.[1] The object evidently was to cast the burden on the rich to the relief of the poor; but this equitable and beneficial policy

Their advantages in rapidity of collection.

---

[1] As thus imposed, the tax was in effect a mongrel kind of property tax. It therefore falls, for mention in detail, under the subsequent head of Taxes imposed in relation to property. See below, p. 200.

THE POLL TAX OF 1380. 197

was reversed in 1380, when another poll tax, resembling in the form of charge the poll tax of 1377, was imposed, under the following circumstances:—

The expenses of the expedition to France under the Earl of Buckingham had absorbed the proceeds of the last Parliamentary grants. There was an arrear of a year and a quarter's pay to the garrisons of Calais, Brest and Cherburg. An expedition was in course of preparation against Scotland. The crown jewels were in pawn; and the king was deeply in debt—outrageousement endettez. The subsidy of wools had produced little in consequence of the disturbances in Flanders. And a demand was made to Parliament for the large sum of £160,000. A long consideration of the state of affairs by the prelates and lords resulted in their suggesting to the Commons three methods of taxation as the best under existing circumstances:—(1.) A grant of a certain number of groats from each person (male and female) throughout the kingdom, the strong aiding the weak.[1] (2.) A tax, for a certain term, on all manner of merchandizes bought and sold in the kingdom, payable, on sale, by the vendor; and (3.) The grant of a certain sum by the old method of 'fifteenths and tenths.' To these suggestions, however, they added the observation that 'fifteenths and tenths' were very grievous in many ways to the commonalty; before assessment no one could tell in advance what sum he would have to pay; and a long time must elapse before any considerable sum could be levied from any such grant; whereas such a tax as they suggested of four or five groats

In 1380 a large sum is required immediately.

The lords suggest three kinds of taxes,

[1] Le fort aident al feable. Par. Rolls, iii. 80.

on each person would produce a considerable sum for an immediate aid to the king; and every one in the kingdom could well bear the tax, because the strong would be compelled to aid the weak. And therefore, it appeared to the Lords that this method of levy by a groat tax would be the best, and the least grievous as aforesaid.' The Commons assented to the views thus expressed, and in the result a tax was granted of three groats, 12*d.*, from each lay person in the kingdom, within franchise as without, male and female, of whatever estate or condition of life, over the age of fifteen years, except real beggars.[1]

<small>but incline to advise a poll tax.</small>

<small>Imposition of the poll tax.</small>

The provisions regarding the manner in which the tax was to be levied explain the meaning of the suggestion that 'the strong should help the weak.' Which words, as well as the whole plan of the tax, it may be not uninteresting to add, are obviously borrowed from the French 'fouage' as imposed in 1369, and assessed in the Langue d'oïl provinces, 'le fort portant le faible.'[2] These provisions were to the following effect:—In payment of the sum total assessed in every township, persons of substance were, according to their property, to assist the poorer persons; provided that the most substantial should not pay more than 60 groats, 20*s.*, for himself and his wife (pour lui et pur sa femme), and no person less than one groat for himself and his wife. Every one was to be charged at the place of residence of himself his wife and children, or at the place where

<small>Provisions for mitigating the incidence of the tax.</small>

---

[1] Forpris les verrois mendinantz qi ne serront riens chargez. Par. Rolls, iii. 90.
[2] See Clamageran, L'Impôt en France, i. 391.

he resided in service. Every artificer, labourer, servant, and other lay person, whether a servant residing with any prelate, lord temporal of any rank, abbot, prior, clerk of the chancery common bench king's bench exchequer or receipt, or with any other officer, knight, esquire, merchant, citizen, or burgess, or with any other person, was to be included in assessment and to be charged according to the amount of his estate.[1] And commissioners were to be appointed in counties and in cities and towns, to be collectors and controllers of the tax; and were to be sworn to faithful performance of their duty.

The taxgatherer, in seeking a direct money payment, however small, from the poor, has never at any time, in any country of which we have fiscal record, had an easy task to perform. Hence the origin of that minimum taxable introduced in the direct taxes of many countries, in infringement of the rule that a tax to be fair should be general, which applies no less to direct than to indirect taxation—a concession of principle to stubborn fact admitted, as previously noticed in the narative, in several of the Ordinances for taxes on moveables in this country. But, mitigated in its incidence as the poll tax of 1380 was by the provisions before mentioned—amounting in effect to a demand of fourpence only from the poorer classes, it appears insufficient to account for events that followed. It was not the real cause of those events. The minds of the peasantry had been prepared for, had been impelled

Difficulties in collection of direct taxes from the poor.

This tax of 4d. not sufficient to account for the peasant revolt.

The real cause.

---

[1] Que chescun de eux sois assis et taillez selonc l'afferant de son estat. Par. Rolls, iii. 90.

towards revolt against feudal oppression by other circumstances. Step back a few years in history, to times when the expenses incurred by the nobles in the first expeditions to the continent in the reign of Edward the Third, and the life of splendour and feasting in which they indulged caused them to have recourse to all means in their power to procure money. Their wool was the principal, but an insufficient, source of profit. Next in importance was their manorial revenue; and a reference to any of the old manor accounts will prove the vigilance with which the mediæval baron, abbot, or other lord exacted his fines, quit rents, compositions, heriots, tolls from various sources, &c., &c. Every little peddling item is booked; every driblet and drop is sucked in. Another source of revenue was opened in the sale of freedom to the serf and exemption from personal service to the villein. Edward himself joined in the generous course of liberation—on payment of the proper fines prescribed;[1] and the Church was not tardy in furthering the pious work of manumission—

[1] The following is the text of a charter of manumission:—Rex omnibus ad quos, &c. Salutem. Sciatis quod per Finem quem Johannes Simondson nativus noster manerii nostri de Brustwyk fecit coram delectis et fidelibus nostris Johanne de Molyns Nicholao de Bokelond et Hugoue de Berewyk, quos assignavimus ad hujusmodi Fines, ad opus nostrum, de nativis nostris partium illarum, pro manumissione eorundem, recipiendum, Manumissimus praefatum Johannem Simondson et totam sequelam suam, et ipsos ab omni opere servili exuimus, et erga nos exoneravimus. Volentes et concedentes pro nobis et haeredibus nostris quod idem Johannes Simondson et tota sequela sua praedicta imperpetuum Liberi sint et Liberae conditionis; ita quod nec nos nec haeredes nostri praedicti a praefato Johanne Simondson seu sequela sua praedicta ratione villenagii sui quicquam exigere seu vendicare poterimus in futurum. Teste Rege apud Turrim London. decimo sexto die Maii. (A.D. 1338.)

Consimiles literas regis de manumissione habent subscripti; videlicet (Here follow the names of two other nativi.). Foedera, v. 44.

for slaves belonging to lands not her own. Thus it was that free labour was increasing in the land, when came 'the Black Death;' depopulation; great scarcity of labourers; demands for increase of wages; the landowner in difficulties, unable to pay for free labour, or to find tenants for his farms—to cultivate, or to let his demesne.

Of knighthood in the 14th century it has been observed that the mission was, not the mission of the romances, but—to crush the feeble. Correct as regards France, where the peasant was feeble, and was, for maintenance of magnificence and for payment of ransoms, crushed—even *into* the ground,[1] the observation applies to this country only in a limited degree. The race that provided archers and bill-men for Crécy was not wholly weak, nor had there existed hitherto the same reasons for extortion. At any rate, the Sire d'Aubrécicourt, who 'plundered and killed *at random*, to merit well of his lady Isabelle de Juliers,'[2] had no counterpart in this country; any more than subsequently the pastime existed of shooting peasants when thatching, because they looked so funny when rolling off the roof; or ever any 'custom' which a Deputy Lapoule could adduce as a right that had existed for the seigneur to kill, on returning from hunting, a limited number of serfs for refreshment of his feet in their warm entrails and blood.[3] Nevertheless, the English noble of this period was not slow,

---

[1] As to the souterrains, see Michelet, Hist. de France, iii. 259.
[2] Froissart.
[3] Hist. de la Révolution Française, par Deux Amis de la Liberté, i. 217. Quoted Carlyle, Fr. Rev. B. i. c. ii.

under pressure of circumstances as aforesaid, in recourse to deeds for which excuse can be asked only on the ground of 'necessity, the tyrant's plea.' Hence the Statutes of Labourers limiting wages, and when the labourer refuses to work, compulsion under penalty. He runs away—brand him on the forehead with a red hot iron. Then follow un-English attempts to meet the difficulty:—cancellation of instruments of manumission and exemption; the lawyer at work picking holes in charters of freedom; the steward of the manor giving, in the manor court, decisions in favour of the lord. Such was the process of oppression. Is it surprising if there was a counter process of resistance?

The statutes of labourers.

Cancellation of charters of freedom.

A broad gap had been made in that divinity which hedged the knight, when the knife of the artizan found its way through the armour of the noble in the ditch at Courtrai. Knights did not win at Bannockburn. Knights did not win at Crécy. Knights did not win at Poitiers. And there was in England many a peasant hand familiar with the process of taking or if need be of finding a way into the moving fortresses of iron. Lions rampant, green dragons, unicorns, wiverns, bulls, griffins, and other emblems previously terrible, acquired a new significance, and aroused the feeling which in later times found expression in Blucher's: 'Mein Got, what a city for to take!' To terrify the horses by bombards which shot out round balls with fire and noise, or madden them with arrows shot from the long bow, no longer aimed at the impenetrable things above, this became the object of the foot-soldier; whose awe

Diminished respect for men in armour.

for the man in armour on horseback altered during the wars in France to a desire to take him captive. I have secured him—Knight of the Star.[1] 'Je l'ai pris! je l'ai pris!'[2] The Black Prince dies. The victor of Crécy also dies, in a dishonoured old age. No more victories abroad. The importation of captive kings, princes, dukes, counts, barons, and chevaliers ceases. The golden stream of ransom is dried up at the fountain head. Disasters to our arms follow at sea and on land. 'Is it to supply the means of magnificence to gentlemen who prove themselves so useless to England that we, who have purchased our own blood, should return to renewed serfdom?'[3] says the nativus. '*They* have fine houses, velvets and furs, spices, wines, and white bread and ease; and *we* the rain, the wind and rags, and pain, and labour, and hunger,' joins in, in general chorus, the peasant class. Agitators are abroad, and thousands are repeating John Ball's lines :—

> 'When Adam delved and Eve span
> Who was then the gentleman?'

It needed but some general cause of complaint to combine in revolt all those who were desolate and oppressed. And for the purpose nothing more effective could well have been imagined than a poll tax, touching all, imposed to meet the expenses of a disastrous

[1] The Order of Notre-Dame de la noble maison ou de l'Étoile was founded by K. Jean in 1351, in imitation of Edward's Order of the Garter. Guizot, Hist. de France, ii. 117.

[2] See description of the scramble for the captive King Jean, at Poitiers. Ibid., 121.

[3] As to the right of a villein to purchase his own blood (sanguinem suum emere), see Blunt's Tenures, sub tit. Bosbury, Hereford, p. 486.

campaign, and significant of the intention of the landowner to lay the burden of failure on the poor.[1]

Rapacity and insolence of the farmers of the tax.
Under the best and most careful method of collection it would have been difficult, in the existing spirit of the times, to collect the new poll tax; and when, subsequently, it was found necessary to get in the arrears by farming the tax, the rapacity and insolence of the farmers in collection hastened the crisis of the peasant revolt. Endless contentions occurred in adjustment of the supreme difficulty with reference to age; and the immediate cause of the outbreak is stated to have been an act very similar to that which caused Sicilian Vespers, viz., the attempt of one of the collectors to ascertain in a rude manner the age of a girl for whom exemption was claimed on the ground of youth.

Brief history of the revolt.
The proximate cause of the revolt, its real object, and, indeed, its history as far as necessary for present purposes, are thus given in a political poem of the period:—

> Tax has tenet us alle,
> *probat hoc mors tot validorum,*
> The Kyng thereof had smalle,
> *fuit in manibus cupidorum;*
> Hit hade harde honsalle,
> *dans causam fine dolorum;*
> Revrawnce nede most falle,
> *propter peccata malorum.*

---

[1] Compare with this imposition of the poll tax Michelet's description of the imposition by the Black Prince of the fouage in Acquitaine, which in effect cost him the principality:—' Le prince de Galles choisit, avec le tact Anglais, ce moment de mauvaise humeur pour mettre sur leurs terres un fouage de dix sols par feu. . . . un fouage aux maigres populations des landes, aux pauvres chevriers des montagnes,' &c., &c. Hist. de France, iii. 298.

> Bondus they blwun bost,
>   *nolentes lege domari;*
> Nede they fre be most,
>   *vel nollent pacificari;*
> Charters were endost,
>   *hos libertate morari;*
> Ther hor fredam thay lost,
>   *digni pro caede negari.*[1]

'They refused to listen to any terms until they were freed from their servile bondage, and obtained, in effect, charters of their freedom; but the advantage they supposed they had thus gained only led them into still greater bondage, which they had merited by the outrages they perpetrated.'[2]

Who that has read, in the pages of Macaulay,[3] the description of what proved to be a death-blow to Omichund, will not easily recollect the passage:— 'Omichund, the red treaty is a trick. You are to have nothing,'—and has not felt pity even for him notwithstanding his rascality and crimes? But a more melancholy picture is presented by the page of history which describes the result of the peasant revolt of 1380 to the poor *nativus*, if criminal, criminal through desire for freedom (and who loves not his own flesh and blood?): 'Villein, the king had no power to grant your charter of freedom. You are still a slave.'

The King's charters declared invalid.

The peasant revolt of 1380, which may be compared in some respects to the Jacquerie in France, was, however, more happy in the consequences that

---

[1] Political Poems and Songs, i. 224.
[2] Ibid., Introduction, p. 56.
[3] Essay on Lord Clive.

resulted. In France, before the Jacquerie, 'Bonhomme crie, mais bonhomme payera,' had been the tax-gatherer's text;[1] and, after the suppression of the Jacquerie, it continued to be the same. Jacques paid as before. 'Il paya la taille, les aides, la gabelle, les droits de marché, de péage, de douanes, de capitation, les vingtièmes, etc., etc.'[2] Every sort of tax and toll continued to be exacted from him. It was not so in England. 'During the century and a half after the peasant revolt villeinage died out so rapidly that it became a rare and antiquated thing;'[3] and the condition of the people steadily improved; so that, writing of England in 1477, Commynes expresses an opinion that the people of England are, in their relations with the higher classes, the happiest of any nation with which he is acquainted.[4] And as regards taxation, in 1382, the year after the revolt, the landowners undertook the entire payment of a 'fifteenth and tenth;' and henceforth the gradual introduction of the subsidy, a form of tax which had a more direct incidence on rent and land, evidences that they were not reluctant to bear the weight of taxation. The hated form of poll tax appears no more during the whole of the period, except as a method of obtaining from aliens, who could not be reached by the ordinary fifteenths, tenths, and

---

[1] Ils supportaient et supporteraient tout, disait-on; on les appelait Jacques l'onhomme. Guizot, Hist. de France, ii. 148.
[2] Thierry, Lettres sur l'histoire de France. Dixième Édn. p. 471.
[3] Green, Hist. of English People, p. 250.
[4] Or, selon mon advis, entre toutes les seigneuries du monde dont j'ay congnoissance, où la chose publicque est mieulx traictee, ou regne moins de violence sur le peuple. . . . . c'est Angleterre. Commynes, Mémoires, Mlle. Dupont, Edn. 1840, ii. 142.

subsidies, some contribution towards the exigencies of the State in which they maintained a thriving trade. Thus, a poll tax on aliens was granted to Henry VI. in 1439, and again in 1442;[1] and in 1453 (aliens were not then in high favour in the kingdom) a similar tax, to be paid yearly during the life of the king, the amount of charge being :—For every person not born within the realm, Ireland or Wales, or in the duchies of Gascony, Guyenne or Normandy and subject of the king (under his obeisaunce), if a householder, 16$d.$, and if not a householder, 6$d.$ For every stranger merchant broker or factor or their attornies, not denizens, if householders, 40$s.$; and if not householders, but resident six weeks within the realm, 20$s.$, to be charged, in case of their departure without payment, on the persons with whom when here they resided. And for every stranger merchant broker or factor made denizen by letters patent or otherwise, 10 marks yearly.[2] *except on aliens.*

The stranger merchants are thus enumerated:— Every Venetian, Esterling, Italian, Januay (Genoese), Florentine, Milaner, Lucan, Catelonian, Albertyn, Lombard, Hansard, and Prucier. *List of merchant strangers in 1453.*

On one or, at the most, two occasions during the period, a graduated poll tax was imposed, in clumsy attempt by this means to tax persons in relation to property; but such taxes fall for mention under the next subsequent heading in the narrative.

---

[1] Par. Rolls, v. 6, 38. A similar tax on secular, stipendiary, and chaunting priests, was granted in the year 1449. Ibid, 144.
[2] Concessio subsidii de alienigenis infra regnum commorantibus. Par. Rolls, v. 230.

2. *Taxes Imposed in Relation to Property.*

<small>Fifteenths and tenths continue in use.</small>

To deal, next, with taxes imposed on property and persons in relation to property. During the whole of the period, or, more precisely, down to the end of the reign of James the First, the previously established practice of raising extraordinary revenue by grants of nominal 'fifteenths and tenths' continues in force. On the grant of a fifteenth and tenth, every county and town knows the sum of money to be raised, and probably has its own favourite established method of assessing the amount on the various taxpayers. To enumerate all the grants of this description made during the period is unnecessary for present purposes; it will be sufficient when, in the course of the narrative, anything occurs of special importance in relation to fifteenths and tenths—such as, for instance, the grants of total exemption made to particular towns greatly decayed, and the general provision for the other decayed towns by allowance of a certain stated sum out of the total of the grant, to be apportioned between such towns —to note the fact. And, briefly stated, the narrative, except as far as it relates to fifteenths and tenths, re-

<small>Subsequent introduction of subsidies.</small>

solves itself into a record of the gradual introduction of another form of taxation, as supplementary to fifteenths and tenths, generally known as and termed, *par excellence*, 'the Subsidy,' in the attempt to tax the increase of wealth in towns that had prospered, and to reach land and rent as well as moveables.

<small>Two fifteenths and tenths granted in 1377.</small>

To start with fifteenths and tenths. In October 1377, the first year of Richard's reign, a grant is made of two fifteenths for outside cities and boroughs, and two tenths within cities and boroughs; that is to say, 'the old established sums accustomed to be levied when such fifteenths and tenths had been granted,' for two years, for the purposes of the war.[1] And as it would appear that certain great seigneurs, especially of the religious order, had hitherto escaped contributing to this kind of tax in respect of certain of their possessions, the king, in response to a petition of the Commons on the subject, ordains that all religious persons (gentz de seinte Eglise) are to pay their proportion with the laity in respect of all their possessions which have come into their hands or which they have purchased since the 20th year of King Edward, son of King Henry.[2]

The supposed advantages of capitation taxes in rapidity of collection have previously been noticed under the head of Poll Taxes. Accordingly, in April 1379, when 'a present sum of money is required for instant operations on the continent,' certain port duties granted in the previous year, which of course only brought in money by degrees, are repealed; and Parliament, in lieu of adopting the old form of fifteenth and tenth, grants, in addition to new port duties, a tax in form a capitation tax, but so charged as in effect to fall 'on the goods of certain persons throughout the kingdom.'[3] Briefly, it is an attempt to tax persons

Tax by reference to rank, condition of life and substance. 1379.

---

[1] Par autielles sommes de deniers et nemye greignours ne meindres come ont este acustumez estre levez des villes parmy le Roialme quant tielles dismes et quinszismes ont este grantez. Par. Rolls, iii. 7.

[2] Ibid., 24.

[3] Un autre subside a prendre des biens de certaines persones parm le Roinulme, &c. Ibid., 57.

in classes, by reference to their rank, condition of life, and substance.

Schedule of charge.

In the schedule of charge, approved by Parliament, the grant is stated to be of 'a sum of money to be levied of the different persons of the kingdom in manner following, as well within franchises as without; that is to say :—[1]

Earls, barons, knights, and esquires.

	£	s.	d.
The Duke of Lancaster and the Duke of Bretagne, each	6	13	4
Item, every earl of England, and every countess widow in England, the same as the earls, viz.	4	0	0
Item, every baron and baneret, or knight who can spend as much, and every baroness widow shall pay as the baron, and banresse as the baneret, viz.	2	0	0
Item, every bachelor, and every esquire who by statute should be knight, and every widow dame, wife of bachelor or esquire as aforesaid	1	0	0
Item, every esquire of less estate, and every woman, widow of such esquire, or substantial merchant (marchant suffisant)	0	6	8
Item, every esquire having no possessions in land, rent, or chattels, who is in service or follows the profession of arms	0	3	4

The Knights' Hospitallers.

Then follow special heads of charge for the Order of the Hospitallers :—The chief Prior of the Hospital of St. John is to pay, as a baron, 40s.; every commander of the order in England, as a bachelor, 20s.; every other brother, knight of the said order, 13s. 4d.; and every other brother of the said order, as an esquire without property, 3s. 4d.

Lawyers.

The judges and legal profession are charged as follows:—Every justice, of whatever Bench, and ex-justices, and the chief baron of the exchequer, each 5l.;

---

[1] This interesting classification of taxpayers may be compared with Camden's chapter on 'The States and Degrees of England.' See Britannia, p. 163.

every serjeant and grand apprentice of law, 2*l.*; every other apprentice to the profession of law, 1*l.*; all other apprentices of less estate, and attornies, each, 6*s.* 8*d.*

The commercial and trading classes are charged as follows:—'The mayor of London pays, as an earl, 4*l.*; the aldermen of London, each, as a baron, 2*l.*; the mayors of the great towns of England, each, as a baron, 2*l.*; the other mayors of the other small towns, according to the amount of their estate, 1*l.*, 10*s.*, or 6*s.* 8*d.*; all the jurates[1] of considerable towns (des bones villes), and great merchants of the kingdom, pay, as bachelors, 1*l.*; all other substantial merchants, 13*s.* 4*d.*; all smaller merchants, and artificers 'who have gaine of the land,' according to the amount of their estate, 6*s.* 8*d.*, 3*s.* 4*d.*, 2*s.*, 1*s.*, or 6*d.* Trade and commerce.

In the rural population, every serjeant, and franklin of the country is charged, according to his estate, 6*s.* 8*d.* or 3*s.* 4*d.*; and the farmers of manors parsonages and granges, cattle dealers, and dealers in all other mean merchandise, according to their estate, 6*s.* 8*d.*, 3*s.* 4*d.*, 2*s.*, or 1*s.* The franklin and farmer.

Item. All advocates, notaries and proctors married,[2] pay, as serjeants of the law, apprentices of the law, and attornies, each according to his estate, 40*s.*, 20*s.*, or 6*s.* 8*d.*; pardoners and summoners married, each according to his estate, 3*s.* 4*d.*, 2*s.*, or 1*s.* Advocates proctors, &c.

Item, all hostelers, who are not merchants, each according to his estate, 3*s.* 4*d.*, 2*s.*, or 1*s.* Hostelers.

Lastly, are charged the capite censi, the proletariat; The general.

---

[1] Jurati. Officers sworn for the government of corporations.
[2] The unmarried are taxed with the clergy, see below, p. 212, note.

and the amount is, for every married man, for himself and his wife, who are not of the estates aforesaid, over the age of sixteen years, except real beggars (forspris verroies mendinantz), and every man and woman sole, of such estate, and over the age aforesaid, 4*d*.

Merchant strangers. Every merchant stranger, of whatever condition he be, pays tax according to his estate, as others denizens.

No person is to pay tax except in the place where he resides. And in all cases where the charge is not fixed for certain in the schedule, the amount is to be assessed in the discretion of assessors and controllers appointed for that purpose.[1]

Small yield of the tax. The tax, calculated to produce over 50,000*l.*, yields not half that amount. More money is required, for 'our lord the king and his kingdom are, as it were, surrounded and besieged on every side by their enemies, who in great multitude endeavour with all their might, as well by land as by sea, to destroy the same our lord the king and his said kingdom (which God forbid), and what is more, to eradicate entirely the English language (d'ouster oultreement la Langue Engleise).' And for defence and salvation of the kingdom, and for an expedition ordered to Brittany,

---

[1] Par. Rolls, iii. 57, 58. The clergy adopt the following scale :— For the Archbishop of Canterbury, 6*l.* 13*s.* 4*d.* For bishops, mitred abbots, and other spiritual persons, peers, 4*l.*; others having benefice or office of the value of 100 (sic. qy. 400) marks a year, 3*l.*; of the value of 200*l.* and under 100 (qy. 400) marks, 2*l.*; 100*l.* and under 200*l.*, 1*l.* 10*s.*; 100 marks to 100*l.*, 1*l.*; 40*l.* to 100 marks, 13*s.* 4*d.*; 20*l.* to 40*l.*, 10*s.*; 10*l.* to 20*l.*, 5*s.* All other beneficed clergy, 2*s.* Monks and nuns, and other men and women of any religious order, according to the value of the house to which they belong, 3*s.* 4*d.*, 1*s.* 8*d.*, 1*s.*, or 4*d.*; and for all unbeneficed clerks, 4*d.* Persons under sixteen years of age and mendicants excepted. And for all advocates, proctors, and notaries, unmarried, 3*s.* 4*d.* Wilkins, Concilia, iii. 141, 142.

which if God pleases shall prove a good remedy under existing circumstances, and a great succour and salvation to the said kingdom, and destruction to the enemies aforesaid, the Lords and Commons, although it is a grievous charge for them to bear—reverting to the old form of imposition—grant one fifteenth and a half for outside cities and boroughs, and one tenth and a half for inside cities and boroughs, to be levied and collected in the same form and manner as the last two fifteenths and tenths.[1]

<small>Grant of a fifteenth and tenth in the usual manner.</small>

Then comes the poll tax of 1380, and the Peasant Revolt. After which, in 1382 the landowners take upon themselves the whole burden of a fifteenth and tenth, in the following manner. The same sums that were levied in towns and other places on the grant of the last fifteenth and tenth are to be levied on this occasion; but they are to be assessed on—dukes, earls, barons, banerets, knights and esquires, and all other secular lords of manors, townships, and other places in the kingdom, in respect of the amount and total of all their crops and cattle, or the total and amount of the profits of all their demesne lands in each township or other place throughout the kingdom, and in the same manner of the profits of all lands and tenements appropriated to mortmain since the 20th year of King Edward, son of King Henry, between Michaelmas and the feast of the Purification. Great care, however, is taken to provide that only for this occasion, 'for reverence of God (al reverence del Dieux), and for support, aid, and relief of the poor commonalty, who appear to be weaker and poorer

<small>The landowners defray the tax of 1382.</small>

[1] Par. Rolls, iii. 75.

than heretofore,' is so unusual a tax granted. It is not to be considered as a precedent for charging, hereafter, the landed interest otherwise than they formerly have been, and ought, reasonably, to be charged.[1]

This tax not to be considered a precedent.

The produce of this fifteenth and tenth is taken by the warlike Bishop of Norwich 'for the service of God and the holy Church in the crusade granted to him by Pope Urban,' otherwise, for his year's campaign in France against the anti-pope and for relief of the city of Ghent.[2]

Fifteenths and tenths continued.

In the following year the Lords and Commons revert to the old system, granting a fifteenth 'to be levied in the ancient manner.'[3] In 1384 there is a grant of a half of a fifteenth. And a reference to the Parliamentary Rolls will show the subsequent grants of fifteenths and tenths in this reign.[4]

Assessment of fifteenths and tenths.

It has been previously stated that there is ground for believing that the method of assessment in relation to fifteenths and tenths was by no means uniform throughout the kingdom, but varied in different districts and towns, each of which had probably certain convenient rules and a settled practice for getting in the sum established. In some cases, however, it would appear that the proper method of assessment formed a subject of dispute between the taxpayers. Such, for instance, was the case as regards Oxford. The University had, it would appear, purchased a great part of the city since the 20th year of Edward I.; and the question was whether they should or should not be charged to

Instance of dispute as to proper assessment.

---

[1] Par. Rolls, iii. 134.　　[2] Ibid., iii. 145, 146.　　[3] Ibid., 151.
[4] See Par. Rolls, iii. 167, 185, 204, 221, 244, 285, 301, 330, 368.

the tenth in respect of the rents derived from their tenants. The collectors distrained the masters and scholars; and, in 1389, 'the devout orators, chancellor, guardians, provosts, and masters, and scholars of the University,' present a petition praying that, as their tenants are charged to the tenth and pay according to the amount of their moveables, they may not be charged in respect of the rents derived from the tenements occupied by such tenants.[1] A counter-petition is presented by the commons, praying that the University may not be discharged from payment of such manner of taxes, 'to the great destruction of the poor burghers of the said city.' No order appears to have been made in response to the said petitions.

The Parliamentary Rolls of the same year supply an instance of a special grant of exemption on the ground of poverty. The poor lieges of the counties of Northumberland, Cumberland, and Westmoreland have been ravaged by the French and Scots and are greatly impoverished, and some of them are utterly destroyed. They now pray for remission of fines, issues, amerciaments, arrears of the ferm and the last fifteenth. The king grants the petition. And subsequently the Council grant and allow that the tenth payable by the clergy, and in cities and boroughs 'shall be included in the exemption, according to the intent of the petition, though they be not specified therein.'[2]

Exemption granted in certain cases.

Hitherto the almost invariable method of taxation had been the old 'fifteenth and tenth'—grants of the old-established sums set on counties and towns; and

[1] Par. Rolls, iii. 276.   [2] Ibid., 270.

these sums, it will be in the recollection of the reader, were levied on the possessors of 'moveables.' At the commencement of the fifteenth century, in 1404. (6 Henry IV.), we have to note the first symptom of a tendency to change; and the bias is in the direction of the more immediate taxation of land according to value, and inclusive of rent. The Welsh rebellion (under Owen Glendower) is in full blaze, and the trumpet is sounding for a renewal of hostilities abroad.

Grant of 5 per cent on land and rent in 1404. The Lords and Commons grant 'two fifteenths and tenths, to be levied in manner accustomed,' and certain port duties; and, in addition to these, the lords temporal (les seigneurs temporelx pur eux et les Dames temporelx et toutz autres persones temporelx) grant, for defence of the kingdom : 'of every 20*l*. of land or rent in their hands, being of the value of 500 marks a year and upwards, 20*s*., to be levied at the feasts of Christmas and St. John the Baptist next ensuing'— in short, a tax at the rate of 5 per cent. on land and rent.[1]

Another tax on land and rent in 1411. Again, towards the close of the reign, in 1411 (13 Henry IV.), another tax of the same description is granted by Lords and Commons (in addition to certain port duties); but wider in its incidence, as commencing at a lower figure of charge—viz. of every man and woman, of whatever estate or condition, having lands or rent to the value of 20*l*. a year, net (outre les charges et reprises duement trovez), 6*s*. 8*d*.; and so upwards, for every full 20*l*. of land or rent, clear of all charges, 6*s*. 8*d*. But care is taken to provide that

---

[1] Par. Rolls, iii. 546.

this grant shall not be treated as a precedent for the future.[1]

To pursue the subject of direct taxation into the reign of Henry V. The connexion that existed between the House of Lancaster and the clergy, the liberal offers of Archbishop Chichele to the king for promotion of foreign conquest in diversion of public thought from religious inquiry, and the fact that the clergy bore a considerable portion of the burden of the war, are notorious. Moreover, the war was in a great measure self-supporting, that is, was conducted on the principle of pillage. Sufficient consideration is not given to these circumstances by those writers who total up Henry's available revenue, and add—'with these revenues Henry V. set out to conquer France.'

It must be owned, however, that the king seems to have started on his expedition of conquest without any very careful deliberation regarding payment of expenses; as appears from what may be termed the parliamentary record of the recommencement of the war, and the first taxes granted to the king for the purposes of the war. At the meeting of Parliament the Bishop of Winchester, Chancellor of England, declares, by command of John Duke of Bedford, Guardian of England, the reasons for summons of the Parliament, in a short sermon of which the text is: 'As he has done to us so let us do to him.'[2] And subsequently the Commons— 'considering that the king their sovereign lord, to the

Recommencement of the war with France.

---

[1] Par. Rolls, iii. 648. There was not any grant of fifteenth and tenth that year.
[2] Prist pur son Theame: 'Sicut et ipse fecit nobis, ita et nos' faciamus.' Par. Rolls, iv. 62.

honour of God, and for avoiding effusion of Christian blood, had made to his adversary of France divers requests for restitution of his heritage, according to right and justice; and how thereupon there had followed divers conferences, on this side of the sea and on the other, to the great cost of their said sovereign lord the king; nevertheless, the king had not been able by the said requests and conferences to obtain his said heritages or any notable part of them. And because the king, although he had not sufficient from the ordinary revenues of the kingdom or from any grant of subsidy theretofore made to him, effectively to prosecute his claim, yet trusting in God that in his just quarrel he would see himself sustained and supported, had courageously undertaken an expedition to foreign parts, pawning his jewels for provision of money, and in his own person had crossed the sea, and arrived before the town of Harfleur, and had besieged and taken it, and then held it. . . . . and with a small force (ovesq. poy de gentz) in comparison with the power of France, had marched towards the marches of Calais, where, on the way, many dukes, earls, and other lords, with the power of the realm of France to an excessive number, encountered him in battle, when God gave the victory to the king, to the honour and exaltation of his crown, his own renown, and the especial comfort of his loyal subjects, and to the fear of all his enemies, and apparently the eternal profit of all the kingdom'—for these reasons, grant, with the assent of the lords spiritual and temporal (in ad-

The victory of Azincourt, in 1415,

dition to the port duties, granted to the king for life but not as a precedent for future kings), a fifteenth and tenth, 'to be levied in the accustomed manner.'[1]   *and consequent grant of taxes.*

After the death of Henry V. we still continued, at first, victorious on the continent; and, 'my lorde of Bedford chevid many great and faire things, and in especial, ye Batayle of Vernule, ye which was ye grettest dede doon by English men in our dayes, save the Battaille of Agyncourte, in the which Bataille of Vernule was slayne and taken ye flour of knyghthede, as well of ye kyngs partie adverse of ye same cuntre, as of Scotland, and of oyer strange nations, yat were yere in assistence and helpe of ye kyngs partie adverse.'[2] *Verneuil, 1424.* To meet the expenses of the war, a new kind of tax, charged on all inhabitant householders in certain parishes, rural and in towns, by reference to the rating of the parish church, supplemented by a tax on owners of knights' fees, was imposed in 1427. And as it is interesting to follow the alteration in the language used on the Rolls, the following is given in the original text:—

'And also ye saide commens, graunten to oure saide soverain lord, for ye said defense, yat all inhabitantz, housholders, withynne every parische of this saide royaume, so yat yer be inhabited in ye saide parische X persones there holdynge housholde, alway citees and burghes excepte, of wiche parisches the chirches be not extented, or singulerly beth afore yis tyme extented withynne ye annuell value of X marc; paie to oure saide soveraine lord, al onely VIs. VIIId. of her godes   *Tax on inhabitant householders, in 1427, in rural parishes,*

[1] Par. Rolls, iv. 64 (3 Hen. v. 1415).   [2] Ibid., 423.

moebles.' Where the church is valued at X marks, all inhabitant householders are to pay 13*s.* 4*d*; 'and so in to ye hiest extente afore yis tyme made, aftre ye rate.' 'And yat ye inhabitantz, housholders, of every parische, withynne citees and bourghes of this saide royaume, in like wise and forme inhabite, beynge ye chirche ther of annuell value of XX*s.*, pay to oure saide soverain lord, ii*s*. And so above, aftre ye rate, to ye hiest value of parische chirches, be due inquerrez yerof to be hade. Salvyng alwaies in suche inquerrez to ye saide citees and burghes, her fraunchises and libertees.

and in urban parishes.

'And also ye saide Commens graunten to oure saide soverain lord, for ye defense aforsaide, that every persone withynne ye saide royaume, beynge seysed of londes and tenementz withynne ye same royaume, in his demesne as of freehold; which londes and tenementz ye said persone possessour, or persones possessours, holdeth immediatly be a hool knyghtes fee; paie to our saide soverain lord, VI*s*. VIII*d*.; and so aftre ye rate, to ye fourthe part of a knyghtes fee, al temporell possessions dymeable and ye possessioners of ham for the same possessions except.' . . . . 'Trustynge alway, that for ye omission and exception of ye saide temporel possession, yat ye lordes spirituel wolle graunte to our saide soverain lord, a hool dyme, for ye defense aforsaide.'[1]

and on knight's fees.

The hool dyme is granted; and the proceeds of tax and dyme go towards the expenses of the war with France, soon about to take a disastrous turn, com-

[1] Par. Rolls, iv. 318.

mencing from 'the tyme of the siege of Orleans, taken in hand God knoweth by what advis.'¹

The first grant of a fifteenth and tenth in this reign was made in 1429, on 'ye morne next after the Fest of Seint Mathewe the appostell, the yeer of the regne the VIII., viz. of an hole quinszisme and an hole disme of the lay people, to be arered in manere accustumed, paiable the morne after Seint Hillarie day next comyng.'² This was the year of the raising of the siege of Orleans and of the coronation of the young king at Paris; and the before-mentioned grant was almost immediately followed by another similar grant. <small>The siege of Orleans raised.</small>

In 1430 another 'hole quinzisme and hole disme, and the thridde part of an hole quinzisme and of an hole disme,' are granted, 'to be paied and arezed of the moeble godes of the laie poeple of the roialme in manere accustumed;'³ and, in addition to these, a tax on all freeholders of lands held by knights' service, or otherwise, viz. :—(1) · 'Of every lay man and woman seized in their demesne as of freehold of any manors, lands or tenements in the kingdom, held by knight service, according to the amount of their holding'—*i.e.*, 'for every whole knight's fee, 20*s*.' And the same, from all spiritual persons seized in their demesne as of freehold, and any other person seized to the use of any spiritual person, of any manors, lands or tenements purchased since the 20th year of the reign of King Edward 'the First since the Conquest,' held by knight service. And according to that rate, for 'all manors, lands and <small>A tax on knights' fees, in 1430,</small>

---

[1] Petitio ducis Bedford, Par. Rolls, v. 435.
[2] Par. Rolls, iv. 336.   [3] Ibid., 368.

tenements, of similar tenure, but held by less service than the service of a whole knight's fee (par meyndre service que par service de entier fee de Chivaler),' down to and including the tenth part of a knight's fee. But spiritual persons were not to be charged in respect of manors, lands and tenements amortized before the aforesaid 20th year. And (2) 'Of every lay man and woman seized in their demesne as of freehold, of any manors, lands or tenements held by other service than knight service, or seized of any rent-seck,[1] or rent-charge, of the annual value of 20*l*. after deducting reasonable and necessary charges, 20*s*. ;' and the same, from all spiritual persons, as in the case of the foregoing tax, and according to that rate for any less annual value down to and including 5*l*.

and on other lands not held by knight service, and rents seck and rent-charges.

The Chancellor of England for the time being is to send commissions into every county in England to certain substantial persons named by the Council of the king, to make inquiry as well within franchises as without, by the oath of the 'prodes hommes' of the said counties cities and boroughs, of all the manors, lands and tenements held by other service than knight service, and of rents seck and rent-charges of the annual value of 20*l*. after deducting expenses, and from 20*l*. down to and including a value of 5*l*. as aforesaid, and of the persons seized thereof in the manner aforesaid; and of

Commissioners to make inquisitions.

---

[1] Rent, redditus, rendered or lands for tenements may, for present explanatory purposes, be stated to be of three kinds:—1. The ordinary rent of a tenant. For this, power of distress exists as of common right. 2. Rent-charge, issuing out of land specially *charged* by deed with power of distress for payment; and 3. Rent-seck, *siccus*, reserved by deed without any clause of distress.

TAXES IN RELATION TO PROPERTY. 223

the persons seized of the said manors, lands and tenements held by the said (knights') fees, and parts of fees as aforesaid, and of their names and surnames, and the towns, hamlets, places and counties where they dwell, and of what estate, degree, art, occupation, or condition they are. The inquisitions are to be certified to the Exchequer. And the tax is to be collected by the sheriffs of counties.[1]

The tax on knights' fees is kept distinct from the tax on other lands of freehold, by insertion of a proviso that:—'No man or woman, spiritual or lay, who pays tax for any manors lands or tenements held by tenure of knight service, is to pay anything for manors lands or tenements held by other service than knight service, nor for any rent-seck or rent-charge;' and *vice versâ*. No one is to pay, in respect of lands held by any other tenure than knight service, or for rent-seck or rent-charge, more than 20*s*. And if anyone feels himself aggrieved by any of the said inquisitions taken as aforesaid, he may question their correctness.[2]

It is also provided that no one shall be put to loss or prejudice by force of the inquisitions, after payment of the tax; but this provision does not suffice to allay the fears of the taxpayers. As might be expected, difficulties soon arise in regard to the inquisitions. It is discovered that 'divers ambiguities, doubts and grievances, may arise to the king and to his liege subjects by the levy and execution of the aforesaid taxes.' And in the result, the king, in response to a petition of the Commons on the subject,

Difficulties in the levy of these taxes.

The inquisitions &c. are 'entirely cancelled.'

[1] Par. Rolls, iv. 370 (1430, 9 Hen. VI.).   [2] Ibid., 370.

releases the grants, and ordains that 'all the commissions, inquisitions, briefs, and returns relating to them shall, one and all, be entirely cancelled, taken out of his courts, and held not to be of record; so that none of them shall remain, in any manner, of record, or be taken for a precedent in future times.'[1]

Reverting to the subject of fifteenths and tenths, we may take, from the Parliamentary Rolls of 1432, another instance of exemption of a town from tax on the ground of poverty:—The poor tenants and landowners of the town of Malberthorp, in Lincolnshire, which had been, and still is, utterly destroyed and wasted by the overflowing of the water of the sea, 'which town is, and of olde tyme has bee, charged at every graunt of ony hole taxe to oure soverayn lord, to the some of $6l.$ $14s.$ $5\frac{1}{3}\frac{1}{4}d.$,' pray respite of taxation for ten years. It is granted for two years.[2]

<small>Another instance of total exemption from tenth.</small>

<small>General provision for relief of decayed towns.</small>

In this manner total exemption from payment of the established sum as for their 'tenth' was granted to particular towns, under special circumstances. For relief of decayed towns in the aggregate, provision was made as follows:—A stated sum, at first 4,000*l.*, subsequently raised to 6,000*l.*, was expressly deducted from the sum that 'the fifteenth and tenth attained unto, in part relief and discharge of the poor towns, cities and boroughs, desolate, wasted or destroyed, or over greatly impoverished, or else to the said tax over greatly charged.' This sum in relief was divided between the various shires rateably, according to the proportion they paid of the whole fifteenth and tenth. And the sum al-

[1] Par. Rolls, iv. 409.   [2] Ibid., 385.

lowed for the particular shire was repartitioned between the decayed towns cities and boroughs by Parliamentary Commissioners, being a lord and the two knights of the shire. In cities and boroughs being shires incorporate, a commission consisting of a lord and the two citizens or burgesses representing the city or borough in Parliament, apportioned the sum in relief between the decayed parishes or wards in the shire so incorporate. The various Commissioners, under their letters, sealed with their seals, certified to the collectors of the fifteenth and tenth the towns, cities, boroughs, parishes and wards, and the sums of them so to be discharged; and the collectors acted on such certificates.[1] This system of allowing relief for decayed towns was continued in 1433,[2] and subsequently, and became the settled practice.[3]

The usual practice.

The next tax on landowners, granted subsequently to that of 1430, viz., in December 1435, includes in one charge all freeholds, and extends not only to rent, but also to annuities, and offices[4] of freehold. It is charged on:—'Every person seised of manors, lands, tenements, rents, annuities, offices, or of any other possessions temporal, as of freehold in England, to his own

Tax on land, rent, annuities, and offices of freehold, in 1435.

---

[1] Par. Rolls, iv. 425.   [2] Ibid., 487.
[3] See Par. Rolls, v. 142, 144, 228, 407, 623; vi. 438, 442, 514, &c.
[4] ANNUITY.—A yearly payment of a certain sum of money, granted to another for life, for years, or in fee, to be received of the grantor or his heirs, so that no freehold be charged therewith; whereof a man shall never have assise or other action, but a writ of annuity.—Terms de Ley, 44; Reg. Orig., 158; Co. Lit. 144 *b*; Tomlins, Law Dict. AN OFFICE is the *right* to exercise a public or private employment and to take the fees and emoluments thereunto belonging, whether public, as those of magistrates, or private, as of bailiffs, receivers, or the like. Blackstone, Comm., ii. c. 3.

proper use, or of any other person or persons to his use, of the yearly value of 5*l.*, over the reprises and charges' at the following rates :—For a yearly value of 5*l.*, 2*s.*6*d.*; and so for every entire 20*s.*, 6*d.*, ascending from the said 5*l.* unto the yearly value of 100*l.* And for every person seised of possessions as aforesaid of the yearly value of 20*s.* over the said 100*l.*, for the said 20*s.*, 8*d.* ; and so for every entire 20*s.* ascending from 100*l.* unto the yearly value of 400*l.* And for every person seised of possessions as aforesaid of the yearly value of 400*l.* or more, for every 20*s.* of the said 400*l.*, 2*s.*; and so for every entire 20*s.* unto the highest value of his said possessions.

Commissioners to make inquisitions.
The Chancellor of England is to send commissions into every shire to certain substantial persons to be named by the Council, empowering them to make inquiry regarding the freehold possessions as aforesaid, with power to summon all freeholders liable, under the estate of baron, and examine them, and cause them to be sworn of their freehold in the shire. All persons of the estate of baron, and every estate above, are to be examined of their freehold before the Chancellor and Treasurer, or other persons specially appointed by the king, and are to be charged according to their examination.[1]

The collectors of fifteenths and tenths, how appointed.
The practice in nomination and appointment of collectors of the fifteenths and tenths when granted, appears from a petition of the commons to the king presented to Parliament in 1439. The Parliamentary representatives of cities and boroughs, on coming up to Parliament, used to deliver into the king's Chancery the names of certain persons, to be collectors of the tenth

---

[1] Par. Rolls, iv. 486.

in the particular city or borough. Whereupon the king sent his letters patent to the persons named, appointing them to be collectors. And these collectors were accountable for their receipt directly to the Exchequer. The complaint now made was that, in several cases, persons whose names had been so returned by city or borough members had been appointed collectors of the fifteenth in the county in which the town was situated, as well as of the tenth in the particular town, 'to the great loss and damage of the county.' The king answers that henceforth 'no man dwelling within any city or borough' in which the practice of sending up names for collectors as aforesaid has prevailed, shall be appointed collector of the fifteenth for the shire, ' olesse he mowe spende in the shire, oute of the saide citee or burgh, in londes or tenementz to the value of 5*l*. by yere, over the charges and reprises.'[1] Qualification for collectors for shires.

The sweep of the fiscal net is again enlarged in 1450; when a tax or subsidy is granted to Henry VI. wider in the area of charge than previous taxes. The charge extends to—(1) Every person having full estate of freehold in any lands, tenements, rents, services, annuities, offices, fees, profits, or commodities[2] temporal, within the kingdom, to the yearly value of 20*s*., clear of charge. (2) Every person having estate term of life, in any annuity not to be taken at any place certain, to the yearly value of 20*s*. And joint tenants and tenants in A tax, in 1450, on (1) land, rent, annuities, offices, fees, and profits of freehold; (2) other life annuities;

---

[1] Par. Rolls, v. 25.
[2] COMMODITY, commoditas, interest, advantage, profit. 'They knew, that howsoever men may seek their own commodity; yet if this were done with injury unto others, it was not to be suffered.' Hooker. Johnson's Dictionary.

common in any of the premises are to be charged as one person. And (3) Every copyholder and customary tenant of any manor for life, or 'to hym, or to eny of his heirs, after the custom of maner.'[1] The amount to be paid is, for the first 20s., 6d.; and so for every whole 20s., from the yearly value of 20s. to and including 20l., 6d. For every person having over 20l. up to and including the sum of 200l., for every 20s. of such value, 12d. And for every person having over 200l., for every 20s. of such value, 2s.

(3) copyholds;

Possessions in the hands of persons corporate are expressly declared subject to the subsidy; and lords and other persons holding lordships or seignories of the king immediately in Wales. Guardians are chargeable where lands are in wardship; and spiritual persons as well as temporal, for possessions purchased or amortized since the 20th year of Edward I.

Then follows a charge on: Every person having any office, wages, fee or fees, term of years or otherwise than of the estate of freehold, to the yearly value of 2l.; at the same rates of charge as in the case of freeholders and copyholders.

(4) certain offices, wages, and fees, less than freehold.

---

[1] COPYHOLD, tenura per copiam rotuli curiae, is a tenure of lands in England, for which the tenant hath nothing to show but the *copy* of the *rolls* made by the steward of the lords court; on such tenant's being admitted to any parcel of land or tenement belonging to the manor. A copyhold tenant had originally, in judgment of law, but an estate at the will of the lord; yet custom so established his estate, that by the custom of the manor it was descendible, and his heirs inherited it; and therefore the estate of the copyholder is not merely at the will of the lord, but *at the will of the lord according to the custom of the manor:* so that the custom of the manor is the life of copyhold estates. Customary freeholds are estates held by copy of court roll, but not at the will of the lord.—See Tomlins, Law Dict.

Three knights and a squire are appointed Treasurers and Receivers; and they are to take 4s. a day each for their wages.

Commissions under the great seal are to be directed to 'divers notable persons' into every shire of the kingdom, to take examination of all persons residing or being in the shire regarding the value of their chargeable property—of the value of their havoyre of the premises. And any person appearing and before the commissioners examined 'by his othe uppon a boke' regarding the value of his chargeable property, is not to be charged to the subsidy except according to the value of his chargeable property as appearing by such examination. *Commissioners to be appointed*

This grant is, however, to be considered exceptional; and care is taken to provide against any precedent:— 'And we, your said Commons, in all humble wise as we can or may, pray and beseech your highness of your most abundant grace tenderly to consider the universal poverty and penury of your liege people of this your realm, so that we can, may, nor dare not, in any wise charge your said people with such usual charges as before this time to you have been granted in your Parliaments; and thereupon of your most especial grace to admit and accept this our grant of the said subsidy, and that it be not taken in any example hereafter, but as a thing granted for the defence of this your realm in this your most grettest necessite.'[1] *The tax not to be a precedent.*

Through lack of diligence in the commissioners appointed and the sheriffs of counties, and lack of attendance of persons chargeable, this subsidy continues *Additional provisions required for enforcing the tax.*

[1] Par. Rolls, v. 172–174.

unlevied and unpaid. Therefore, in the Parliament of November in the same year, it is enacted:—that writs shall be directed to the various sheriffs, commanding them to make open proclamation, in places convenient, that the several commissioners be ready at certain stated days and places, to examine all persons chargeable to the said subsidy; and that every person chargeable be then there ready to be examined. The attendance of the commissioners is enforced by a penalty of 20*l.*, and by 'a reasonable daily reward to every commissioner for his labour and costs,' the amount to be fixed by the advice of the king's Council. The attendance of persons chargeable is secured by penalty of treble duty,—'the forfeiture of the treble of that that the same person shall be found chargeable by virtue of the said grant, be it by inquiry or otherwise, at the discretion of the said commissioners.' Provision is made that every person examined before any commissioners, in any shire, is to be examined of 'all the livelihood that he hath in all the shires of the realm; and then by that examination is to be quit and discharged of examination for the premises in all other places.' The attendance of the sheriff or his deputy at days and places assigned by the proclamation, to assist the commissioners, and execute their precepts and warrants, is enforced under penalty of imprisonment, and of making fine and ransom with the king. And the minimum taxable is extended, in the case of freeholders and copy-holders, to 2*l.*, and in the case of persons having office, wages, fee or fees, term of years or otherwise, to 3*l.*[1]

[1] Par. Rolls, v. 211.

During the Wars of the Roses, confiscation of the lands of the other side by the party in power is the rule. The expenses of the contest thus fall mainly on the landowners: the people generally are not severely taxed. The old 'fifteenth and tenth' form of levy continues in use. Any other form of tax attempted proves, in a greater or less degree, unsuccessful. In 1463, Parliament grants to Edward the Fourth 'for the hasty defence of the realm,' an aid of the sum of 37,000*l*. Of this, 31,000*l*. is to be levied and charged on the shires, cities, boroughs, towns, hamlets, and other places of the realm, in the like sums and in the manner and form of payment of the fifteenth and tenth last granted, when the sum of 6,000*l*. was deducted in respect of decayed towns; and the assessments are to be made by such and the like persons as have afore this time assessed the fifteenths and tenths when granted. But certain new provisions as to the minimum taxable are added, viz., that no person not having lands rents or hereditaments to the yearly value of 10*s*., nor goods and chattels to the value of 5 marks, is to be chargeable.[1] And the residue, 6,000*l*., is to be levied by a rate on the inhabitants of the said shires having lands, tenements, rents, possessions, or hereditaments to the yearly value of 20*s*., or goods or chattels to the value of 10 marks; every shire or town, being a shire incorporate, to be charged after the rate of the deduction allowed, in respect of decayed cities, from the last fifteenth and tenth. The assessments are to be made by particular assessors, royal commissioners, who are

[1] Par. Rolls, v. 497.

Failure of an attempted alteration in 1463.

to send their certificates to collectors, also to be appointed by the Crown, stating the names of the persons assessed and the sums charged upon them. The innovation is not great; but the plan has to be abandoned almost immediately. The king remits the 6,000*l.*; and it is 'ordained and established' that—the 31,000*l.* shall be paid, had, and levied 'only by the name of a fifteenth, and under the general form and order of a fifteenth heretofore used and accustomed, over the deduction of 6,000*l.*, and not by or under any other name, order, or form, the said Act notwithstanding.'[1]

A similar result follows on the imposition, in 1472, of a new kind of tax for the maintenance of 13,000 archers for an expedition against 'oure auncien and mortall ennemyes.'

The king, in league with Charles of Burgundy, has stipulated to pass the seas with an army of over 10,000 men. Parliament, for the hasty and necessary defence of the realm, and—'to assiste your roiall astate, ye verraily entendyng in youre princely and knyghtly corage, with all diligence to youre highnes possible, all youre bodely ease leyde apart, to resiste the seid confedered malice of youre and oure seid ennemyes, in settyng outeward a myghty armee, able by the helpe of God to resiste the seid ennemyes, so that youre highnes myght of us youre true subgettes have lovyng assistence,'—grants to the king 13,000 men, archers, to serve one year; 'every of the said men to have and perceyve 6*d.* by the day only.' And for payment of the wages of the archers, (1) the Commons grant to the king,

[1] Par. Rolls. v. 498.

from all except lords of Parliament, 'the tenth part of the value of a year, of the issues and profits of all manner of lands and tenements, rents, fees, annuities, offices, corrodies,¹ and pensions, held in fee simple, fee tail, or for term of life, and of similar copyhold and customary possessions; and (2) the lords of Parliament, temporal and spiritual, 'of their fre wille, toward, herty and lovyng dispositions, over and beside all other promyses made by any of the seid lords temporell to attende in their persones apon the king in his seid armee,' grant the tenth part of value for one year, of the issues and profits of all honours,² castles, lordships, manors, lands, tenements, rents, fees, annuities, offices, corodies, pensions, and fee-farms³ held by them for term of life or any greater estate, and of similar copyhold and customary possessions.⁴

Tax of the tenth part, for payment of 13,000 archers, in 1472.

¹ CORODY, corodium, a sum of money, or allowance of meat, drink, and clothing, due to the king from an abbey, or other house of religion, whereof he was founder, towards the sustentation of such a one of his servants as he thought fit to bestow it upon. The difference between a corody and a pension seems to be—that a corody was allowed towards the maintenance of any of the king's servants in an abbey; a PENSION is given to one of the kiug's chaplains, for his better maintenance, till he may be provided of a benefice. Corodies also belonged sometimes to bishops, and noblemen, from monasteries.—Tomlins, Law. Dict.

² HONOUR is used especially for the more noble sort of seigniories, on which other inferior lordships or manors depend, by performance of some customs or services to those who are lords of them. In such cases the superior lord is called the lord paramount over all the manors included in the Honour.—Ibid.

³ FEE-FARM, feodi firma, or fee-farm rent, is when the lord, upon the creation of the tenancy, reserves to himself and his heirs, either the rent for which it was before let to farm, or was reasonably worth, or at least a fourth part of the value; without homage, fealty, or other services, beyond what are especially comprised in the feoffment.—2 Inst., 44; Tomlins, Law Dict.

⁴ Par. Rolls, vi. 4-6.

These taxes are to be assessed and levied in the different shires and places of the kingdom by royal commissioners; but, as late as the eighth of January 1473, to which day Parliament was prorogued, divers commisioners for assessment of the tax in divers shires and other places have not sent in certificates as required by the Act, so that the proportion of the tax for those shires cannot be ascertained. Other provision is, therefore, necessary for payment of the archers. And, again, Parliament reverting to the customary mode of taxation, grants a fifteenth and tenth in the old form, with the old deduction of 6,000*l*., &c., &c.[1]

Inadequate yield of the tax.

This fifteenth and tenth yields 30,683*l*. 6*s*. 2¾*d*., making with the produce of 'the tenth part' of 1472 from those shires which sent in certificates — viz., 31,410*l*. 14*s*. 1½*d*., a total of 62,094*l*. 0*s*. 4¼*d*. A sum of 51,147*l*. 4*s*. 7¾*d*. remains to be raised for payment of the wages of the archers;[2] and this sum the Commons grant to the king, to be paid as follows:—Certain sums are fixed for and charged on the shires and towns specified in the Act. Royal commissioners are to be appointed for every specified shire and town; who are to subdivide the sum thus locally fixed, and appoint a sum certain upon every city, town, burgh, hamlet, and other place within the limits of their commissions. This sum is to be calculated with reference to the amount of goods

The residue charged in a novel manner.

---

[1] Par. Rolls, vi. 39, 40.

[2] The counties from which certificates had not been sent in were saddled with the payment of 500 archers, leaving 12,410 to be provided for.

and chattels of every person inhabitant and residing in the particular locality; which are to be taxed 'afore any land or other possessions. The goods and chattels of such persons not having any or but little land or other freehold, nor to fifteenth and tenth aforetime but little or not charged, in ease and relief of other persons to the said tenth part and other charges aforetime greatly charged, specially at this time to be chargeable.' And if the said taxation of goods fails to accomplish the whole sum specified in the commission, the commissioners are to charge the deficiency on all lands, tenements, annuities, corodies, rents, pensions, and other possessions, in which any person has any manner of freehold.[1]

The foregoing is but a brief abstract of some of the lengthy and perplexing provisions of the Act which imposed this novel form of tax; and it is not surprising to find that the form of levy proves 'so diffuse and laborious' as to render impracticable the collection of the tax at the times specified in the Act. In a word, this new kind of tax 'for the hasty expedition of the king's viage roiall' has broken down— *(Collapse of the new tax.)*

Saepe viatorem nova non vetus orbita fallit.

The Commons, informed of the circumstances by the Chancellor, 'lovyngly' ponder and weigh them; fix a near day for payment; and—'forasmuch as they do remember that the most easy, ready and prone payment, of any charge to be borne within the realm by the commons of the same, is by the grant of

[1] Par. Rolls, vi. 115-117.

The Commons revert to the fifteenths and tenths.

fifteenths and tenths, the levy whereof amongst your people is so usual, although it be to them full chargeable, that none other form of levy resembleth thereunto,'—pray the king to remit the said sum of 51,147*l*. 4*s*. 7¾*d*., and in lieu thereof to take 'a hoole fifteenth and tenth, and three parts of a hoole fifteenth and tenth; the soomes whereof exceden the foreseid soome: to be taken and levied of the goodes and catels and other thynges usuelly to fifteenth and tenth contributorie and chargeable, within shires, cities, burghs, tounes and other places in this your reame in maner and fourme aforetyme used.'[1]

The foregoing are instances of the difficulty experienced in introduction of new forms of tax in this country at the date in question, and sufficiently prove the correctness of the observation made by Coke in the fourth volume of the Institutes, who says:—'It is worthy of observation how quietly subsidies (i.e. taxes) granted in forms usual and accustomable (though heavy) are borne; such power hath use and custom: on the other side what discontents and disturbances subsidies framed in new models do raise (such inbred hatred novelty doth hatch).' And to these may be added an instance adduced by the same author, of a tax—the particulars of which it is of no importance here to mention[2]—imposed in the fourth year of Henry VII.,

Coke's observations on old and new taxes.

---

[1] Par. Rolls, vi. 151.

[2] The grant was of—the tenth part of a year only of the issues and profits of all possessions temporal; and of the goods and chattels of every person being of the value of ten marks, 20*d*., and so upwards after the rate. The whole produce was only 27,000*l*., or thereabouts. And it was, subsequently, necessary to supplement the grant (which was for the maintenance of 10,000 archers) by a grant of a fifteenth and tenth.—Par. Rolls, vi. 421, 438.

and collected in an irregular manner, which Coke stigmatises as 'a new found subsidy, which raised a rebellion in the north, in which the noble Earl of Northumberland, a commissioner in that subsidy, was by rebels cruelly and causelessly slain.'[1]

On the other hand it is worthy of remark that when, in the fourth year of Henry VIII., a tax similar to that of 1379[2] is imposed as follows:—For every duke, 10 marks; earl, 4*l.*; baron, 2*l.*; knight or man worth 800*l.* in goods, 30*s.*; for every man who has 40*s.* in wages, 12*d.*; and for every man of fifteen years of age and upwards, 4*d.*;[3] the tax, though novel in form, is paid without much opposition. It yields, however, not one-third of the amount expected.

The history of direct taxation during the remainder of the period is easily told.

Fifteenths and tenths, sometimes now shortly termed 'fifteenths,'—for tenth, it will be in the recollection of the reader, merely expressed the tax as paid in towns—grants of the old-established sums for the various counties and towns specified, continue in use down to the year 1624. In which year three fifteenths and tenths are granted to James I.[4] This is the last grant of the kind: for, subsequently, when, in the first Parliament of Charles I., a motion is made for adding two fifteenths to the subsidies granted to the king, it is rejected; and the next Parliament is dissolved before the vote they make of three fifteenths passes into law.

Direct taxes during the remainder of the period.

The last fifteenth and tenth.

---

[1] Institutes, iv. (Edn. 1797) 33, 34; and see Holinshed, Chron. iii. 493.
[2] See above, p. 209.   [3] Lords' Journal, i. 25.   [4] 21 Jac. I., c. 34.

As regards other direct taxes. To quote the words of the author of the Treatise on the Court of Exchequer :—' In the times of Henry VIII., Queen Elizabeth, and King James I., we find that they raised both subsidies and fifteenths ; this was because the value of things increased, and therefore fifteenths were not according to the true value of the townships. And therefore they contrived that the subsidy should be raised by a pound rate upon lands, and likewise a pound rate upon goods.'[1] We are now, therefore, face to face with the memorable Subsidies. Let us inquire more particularly into the nature and history of the Subsidy.

The capitation tax of 1512 (4 Hen. VIII.), previously mentioned, was calculated to produce 160,000*l*. The actual yield was only 50,000*l*. The deficiency, 110,000*l*., Parliament grants to the king, in 1514, to be charged and paid, in the manner of the subsequent Subsidies, *i.e.*, by a pound rate on the value of moveables, and a pound rate on the annual value of land. This is effected by the Act 6 Hen. VIII. c. 26, which may fairly be considered the first of the Subsidy Acts. The amount of charge, under the Act, is 6*d.* in the pound and, if required, a second subsidy of the same amount. The first subsidy produces only 45,637*l.* 13*s.* 8*d.* And in order to complete the 110,000*l.*, it is found necessary, not only to raise the second subsidy, but also to grant in addition a whole fifteenth and tenth. Henceforth it becomes the usual practice to grant, as supplementary to the old-esta-

[1] Gilbert, Exch. 194.

blished fifteenths and tenths, in the same Act, a subsidy or subsidies of the nature before described. Thus, Henry VIII. has, in 1534, one fifteenth and tenth, and a subsidy of 12*d*. ;[1] in 1540, four fifteenths and tenths, and 1*s*. in the pound from lands, and 6*d*. in the pound on moveables ;[2] and, in 1545, two fifteenths and tenths and a subsidy.[3] Queen Mary has, during her reign, according to Stevens,[4] grants of three subsidies and five fifteenths. Queen Elizabeth has twenty subsidies and forty fifteenths ;[5] and King James, nine subsidies and ten fifteenths.[6] King Charles has seven subsidies,[7] but, as before stated, no fifteenths.

<small>and subsidies at the same time.</small>

To go into the particulars of all the various Subsidy Acts, and the lengthy and elaborate provisions they contain, would be an endless task. It may be remarked, however, that the Acts are ably and carefully drawn, and that for any one familiar with the provisions of the existing Income Tax Act, it may not be altogether uninteresting to trace the connexion that exists between the present and the old legislation on the subject. The existing Act of 1842 is a reprint (with certain alterations of minor importance) of the Act 46 Geo. III. c. 65, passed in the year 1806, when the income tax was raised to two shillings in the pound (i.e. 10 per cent.) in order to meet our enormous expenditure during the final years of the war with

<small>The Subsidy Acts.</small>

<small>Connexion between them and the Income Tax Act.</small>

---

[1] 26 Hen. VIII. c. 19.   [2] 32 Hen. VIII. c. 50.
[3] 37 Hen. VIII. c. 25.   [4] Hist. of Taxes, p. 234.
[5] 1 Eliz. c. 21; 5 Eliz. c. 30; 8 Eliz. c. 19; 13 Eliz. c. 27; 18 Eliz. c. 33; 23 Eliz. c. 15; 27 Eliz. c. 29; 29 Eliz. c. 8; 31 Eliz. c. 15; 35 Eliz. c. 13; 39 Eliz. c. 27; and 43 Eliz. c. 18.
[6] 3 Jac. I. c. 26; 7 Jac. I. c. 23; 18 Jac. I. c. 2; 21 Jac. I. c. 34.
[7] 1 Car. I. c. 6; 3 Car. I. c. 8.

France. The last-mentioned Act is grounded, in the main, on the provisions of the Act 43 Geo. III. c. 122, passed in the year 1803, when the income tax was reimposed, in consequence of the recommencement of war, after the short interval of quiet which followed the peace of Amiens. And the pedigree of the Act may be followed backwards through the old annual 'Land Tax' Acts, as they are termed (but which, in their provisions, relate also to the taxation of moveables), past the times of the Revolution, and those of the Civil War, to the Subsidy Acts which form the subject of our present consideration. In this place it will be sufficient to treat the subject broadly, stating:—

Avi numerantur avorum.

Review of the Subsidy Acts.

(1) The nature of the tax thus distinguished by the name of the Subsidy. (2) The usual amount of charge. (3) The incidence of the tax. And (4) The provisions for management, assessment, and collection.

1. Nature of the Subsidy.

1. The subsidy is a parliamentary subvention to the king levied by—a pound rate on the value of moveables, and a pound rate on the annual value of and yearly profits from land, or, more accurately—a tax on persons in respect of their reputed estate in moveables including the products of land, or in annual value of and profits from land. Generally speaking, aliens pay double tax. Occasionally the Subsidy Act includes a poll tax on aliens not liable to the subsidy.

2. The usual amount of charge.

2. The amount of charge for a full or entire subsidy is 2*s.* 8*d.* for moveables, and 4*s.* for land; but occasionally the subsidy is collected in parts, as 1*s.* 8*d.* for a first payment, followed by a second of 1*s.*, for moveables; and 2*s.* 8*d.* and 1*s.* 4*d.* in the case of land.

TAXES IN RELATION TO PROPERTY. 241

3. As regards the incidence of the tax. The charge includes— *3. Incidence of the tax.*

(a) Every person and every fraternity, guild, corporation, mystery, brotherhood or commonalty, in respect of every pound, as well in coin, as the value of every pound that they have of their own, as also plate, stock of merchandise, all manner of corn and grain, household stuff, and all other goods moveable, and of all sums of money owing to them: a deduction being allowed of such sums of money as they really owe; and an exemption, in respect of the apparel of the person charged, his wife and children, but not including jewels, gold, silver, stone and pearl. *(a) As regards moveables.*

Exception of apparel.

And (b) Every person for every pound yearly that he hath in fee simple, tail, or for life, in any honors, castles, manors, lands, tenements, rents, services, hereditaments, annuities, fees, corodies, or other yearly profit from land, according to the clear yearly value thereof. *(b) As regards land.*

The tax on moveables is kept apart from the tax on profit from land, by a provision that persons charged in respect of their moveables are not to be charged in respect of profit from land, and vice versâ— 'None are to be doubly charged.' *None are to be doubly charged, i.e., in respect of moveables and of land.*

The charge on aliens resident here is, usually, double the amount charged for persons born under the king's obeysaunce. *Higher charge on aliens.*

A minimum taxable is always allowed, that is, taxation commences at a certain stated value of moveables and in profit from land. And, occasionally, a lower charge is imposed between the minimum *The minimum taxable.*

R

taxable and another stated sum at which the full charge comes into play.

Exemption of inhabitants of the northern counties.
The inhabitants of the northern counties—Northumberland, Cumberland, Westmoreland, the towns of Berwick-upon-Tweed and Newcastle-upon-Tyne, and the bishoprick of Durham—are exempted,[1] and the Universities of Oxford and Cambridge.

4. Provisions for management, assessment, and collection.
4. As regards the provisions for management, assessment, and collection. The Act is put into execution by commisioners appointed by the Lord Chancellor, the Lord Treasurer and other great officers of the crown, or any two of them, the Lord Chancellor being one. And it is evidently the intention that they shall be persons of the highest respectability and integrity (a certain number of 'the most sadd and discrete

Commissioners.
persons,'[2] &c., &c.) The commissioners are to divide themselves for distinct hundreds, wards, &c., within the limits of their commission; and issue precepts to the constables and other inhabitants to attend and be examined.

Assessors appointed by commissioners.
The assessors are appointed by the commissioners, and return their assessments to them; and persons dissatisfied with the assessments are allowed an appeal to the commissioners.

The high-collectors and sub-collectors.
The collectors are also appointed by the commissioners; and their names are to be returned to the High Collector, an officer to be appointed in each

---

[1] As liable to be ravaged by the incursions of the Scotch.

[2] 6 Hen. VIII. c. 26, s. 4.—'Sad men' was an expression not unusual. For instance, in 3 Hen. VII., c. 14: 'Against conspiring to destroy the king, or any lord, counsellor or other great officer,' power is given to enquire into confederacies, &c., by twelve 'sad men and discrete persones, &c.'

shire and division by the commissioners; to whom the sub-collectors are accountable; and who himself is accountable to the Exchequer. One duplicate of the schedule of assessment is to be given to the High Collector, and the other is to be returned into the Exchequer, to be a charge upon the High Collector's receipt. Schedules of assessment.

The High Collector gives security to the commissioners to answer for the money by him received.

To the sub-collectors precepts and assessments are to be delivered; and, under such precepts, they have authority to distrain the lands and goods of persons assessed by virtue of the Act. Precepts to collectors.

Such is, briefly stated, the general plan of the Subsidy Acts; and the subsidy is, it will be observed, in effect, an attempt to return to *ad valorem* taxation of property. Two fifteenths (2*s.* 8*d.* in the £) of moveables, and three fifteenths (4*s.* in the £) of annual profit from land throughout the kingdom— in the sixteenth century what may such a tax be calculated to produce?[1] And what an index is here afforded, in this proportionate tax, continued through the century and so on down to the Civil War, of the progress in wealth of the kingdom. You have hand on the pulse of the kingdom; and need not in history any Annalis Conclusio, 'Transit annus frugifer,' &c.; the yield of the revenue proving the abundance of the harvest and the prosperity of the

---

[1] In the reign of Henry VIII. a general survey was made of the whole kingdom, by which the income of the kingdom was estimated at four millions.—Parl. Hist. iii. 26; Sinclair, Hist. Rev. i. 186.

nation, or the reverse, as the case may be. Vain expectation! The original produce of a subsidy is comparatively insignificant; and the yield, instead of increasing with the wealth of the country, falls off, till a subsidy produces little more than 70,000*l.*

Reasons for the small yield of a Subsidy, If we inquire into the reasons for this, they are not difficult to discover. The tax, it will be observed, is personal. A, B, or C, assessed at the place where he lives, ranges in the assessment schedule as a man of so much estate, his possessions in other counties included. The assessment is based, mainly, on the declaration of the taxpayer regarding his property, and subsequent assessments will probably be based on those preceding, and A, B, and C be rated as before, or their successors, at about the same fortune or estate. The old valuation will not only regulate the payment on one occasion, but will stand as a precedent in future years. There is, therefore, every inducement for as low an estimate in the declaration of property as

and its decrease. the conscience of the taxpayer permits. Hence the originally low valuation of property. And, subsequently, the number of cases in which assessments are raised, is as nothing compared with those in which they are lowered: for any increase of fortune by rise of rent or by new purchases is, naturally, seldom divulged to the assessor; whilst, on the other hand, any loss or diminution of property is sure to be pressed on his notice.

The average yield. The highest recorded produce of a subsidy is 120,000*l.*; but so carelessly and inefficiently do the assessors perform their office, that it dwindles subsequently down to between 70,000*l.* and 80,000*l.*; which for present purposes may be considered as the average yield. 'So loose indeed was the whole method of rating subsidies,' writes Hume, 'that the wonder is not how the tax should continually diminish, but how it yielded any revenue at all.'[1]

It is the rule, down to 1589, not to grant more than one subsidy and two fifteenths at the same time. In that year, however, when a considerable supply is required to meet the expenses of defence against the Spanish Armada, two subsidies and four fifteenths are granted at the same time.[2] This course is afterwards followed in 1593, when three subsidies and six fifteenths and tenths are granted at once.[3] In 1597 a similar grant is made.[4] And in 1601 the grant is of no less than four entire subsidies and eight fifteenths and tenths.[5]

A practice commences of granting several subsidies at once.

Thus also James I. receives, in 1605, three entire subsidies and six fifteenths;[6] and in 1623, when it is expected 'that the King may be engaged in a present war by breaking of the two treaties with Spain, viz., the one of the Marriage, and the other of the Restitution of the Palatine, three entire subsidies and three fifteenths and tenths, whereof 18,000 is to be employed towards the repair of certain decayed cities and towns, and the residue is to be expended in the managing of the expected war.'[7] And thus Charles I.

---

[1] The five subsidies granted to Charles I. in the third year of the reign were computed at 100,000*l.* each subsidy, the five amounting to 500,000*l.*—Stevens, Hist. of Taxes, p. 275.
[2] 31 Eliz. c. 15.   [3] 35 Eliz. c. 13.   [4] 39 Eliz. c. 27.
[5] 43 Eliz. c. 18.   [6] 3 Jac. I. c. 26.   [7] 21 Jac. I. c. 34.

has from his first Parliament, in 1625, a grant of two entire subsidies[1]; and, in 1627, a grant of five subsidies,[2] at one and the same time.

The history of direct taxation during this period may be completed by mention of the capitation tax of 1641, and the famous ship writs.

The capitation tax of 1641.

The capitation tax is imposed by Parliament for payment of the army and other debts of the kingdom. It may be compared with the tax of 1487 (4 Hen. VIII.) and the tax of 1379;[3] and the charge is as follows:— For every duke, 100*l.*; marquess, 80*l.*; earl, 60*l.*; viscount and baron, 40*l.*; knight of the Bath, 30*l.*; knight bachelor, 20*l.*; esquire, 10*l.*; every gentleman spending 100*l.* per annum, 5*l.*; and for all others of ability a competent proportion—'the meanest throughout the kingdom was not excused under 6*d.*'[4]

The Ship Writs,

The famous Ship Writs are issued, not on Parliamentary authority, but by order of the king. In 1634, questions regarding mare liberum and mare clausum[5] —the dominion of the sea, involving a probable contest with the Dutch, fishing in 'British waters;' and the damage done to our merchant shipping by the Barbary

---

[1] 1 Car. I. c. 6.
[2] 3 Car. I. c. 8.
[3] See above, pp. 209, 237.
[4] Stevens, Hist. of Taxes, p. 287. And see proclamation for the speedy payment of the monies assessed by Parliament for disbanding the armies. Foedera, xx. 403.
[5] For a brief statement of the purport of Hugo Grotius' treatise, 'Mare Liberum, sive de jure quod Batavis competit ad Indicana commercia Dissertatio,' 1612; and W. Welwood's treatise, 'De Dominio Maris,' 1615, in answer, see Anderson, Commerce, ii. 255-57. As to Selden's Mare Clausum, 1635, see ibid. 361; and for Sir P. Medow's Summary thereof, ibid. iii. 345, Appendix.

pirates have rendered advisable an increase in the navy. Money is required for that purpose. The king desires to obtain it without recourse to a Parliament. Can this be done?—that is the question; and if so, how?

The highest legal authority is consulted; and Noy, the attorney-general, having searched for any previous cases that might stand for precedents, 'with his own hand'—according to Clarendon—'draws and prepares the ship writs' for the maritime towns and counties; which are issued on October 20, 1634.[1] 'Noy,' writes Selden, in his Table Talk, 'brought in the ship money for maritime towns, which was like putting in a little finger that afterwards you may put in a greater. He that pulls down the first brick does the main work; afterwards, it is easy to pull down the wall.' {drawn by Noy, attorney-general. First issue, in 1634.}

The grounds for the issue of the writs are stated in the writs; 'His Majesty having vouchsafed, even by his writ, to declare enough to satisfy all well minded men, and to express the clearness of his princely heart in arming at the general good of the kingdom.'[2] And the reason for limiting the writs to the maritime towns and counties is expressed to be:—that 'although that charge of defence, which concerneth all men, ought to be supported by all, as by the laws and customs of the kingdom of England hath been accustomed to be done: notwithstanding this, we consider that you constituted in the sea coasts, to whom by sea as well great dangers are imminent, and who by the same do get more plentiful {Reasons for changing only maritime places.}

[1] For the form of writ, see Rushworth, ii. 257. Noy died before the issue of the writs.
[2] Speech of Lord Keeper Coventry, June 17, 1635, Rushworth, ii. 297.

248   HISTORY OF TAXES.

gains, for the defence of the sea and the conservation of our princely honour in that behalf according to the duty of your allegiance against such attempts are chiefly bound to set your helping hand.'[1]

<small>A second issue intended, to extend to inland places.</small>

On June 17, 1635, Thomas Lord Coventry, Lord Keeper of England, by command of His Majesty, in his address to all the judges of assize in England in the Star Chamber previous to their circuits,[2] informs them that the king, by advice of his council, has determined on a second issue of writs, to extend, not only to the maritime towns and counties as heretofore, but also to the inland counties, in short to all the kingdom: 'For, since all the kingdom is interested, both in the honour, safety and profit, it is just and reasonable that they should all put to their helping hands.' Accordingly, on

<small>Second issue, in 1635.</small>

August 18, 1635, a second issue of ship writs is ordered, to extend to inland as well as maritime counties and towns, the requisite alteration having been made in the recital to the writs; in the following manner:— The king, by special warrant, directed to the Keeper of the Great Seal of England, Lord Coventry, requires him to issue out of the Court of Chancery 'the ensuing writs, in the form following, unto the counties, cities, towns, and places' mentioned in the warrant.

The following, to select one as a specimen, is, in substance, the form of writ for the county of Dorset:—

<small>Form of writ for Dorsetshire</small>

'DORSET.—The king, &c., to the sheriff of our county of Dorset: to the mayor, baliffs, burghers, and community of the town of Poole, and to the sheriff of that town; to the mayor, baliffs, aldermen and burgesses of the borough of

---

[1] See recital in the form of writ.   [2] Rushworth, ii. 294–8.

Dorchester; to the mayor and burgesses of the town and borough of Wareham;—(and so on, for Weymouth and Melcombe, Lyme Regis, Bridport, Corfe, Shaftesbury, and Blandford Forum), and to the loyal men of those towns and boroughs, and their members, in the town of Poole, and the Isle of Purbeck, and the towns of Portland, Burton, Sherborne, Cranborne, and Sto-borough, and all other towns. boroughs, townships, hamlets and other places in the said county of Dorset, greeting.

' Whereas we are informed that certain pirates, enemies of the Christian name, Mahometans, and others in bands have nefariously taken and despoiled ships and goods and merchandise, not only of our own subjects, but also of the subjects of our allies, in the sea which has used of old times to be defended by the English nation, and have taken them off at will, and have reduced the men in them to a miserable captivity. And whereas we see them daily preparing a navy further to molest our merchants and harass the kingdom, unless a more speedy remedy be applied, and their endeavours be met with stronger opposition. Considering also that the peril which threatens from all sides in these warlike times, renders it necessary for us and our subjects to hasten as speedily as possible the defence of the sea and the kingdom,—

' We wishing, with the help of God, to provide for the defence of the kingdom, the safeguard of the seas, the security of our subjects, the safe conduct of ships and merchandise coming to our kingdom of England, and from the same kingdom passing to foreign parts, especially since we and our ancestors, kings of England, have hitherto been lords of the said sea, and we should much regret if this royal honor should in our time perish, or in anything be diminished. And inasmuch as this burden of defence which relates to all should be borne by all, as by the law and custom of the kingdom of England has hitherto been the case.'

After this recital of the reasons for the levy, there follows a direction—to equip one ship of war of 500 tons (portagii quingenti doliorum) with men, skilled masters, and strong expert sailors, 200 at the least, and cannon and small arms and gunpowder, (tormentis tam majoribus quam minoribus, pulvere tormentario) and spears darts and other necessary ammunition sufficient for war, with double equipage, and also with provision and necessaries for twenty-six weeks at least—to be at Portsmouth on such a day, &c., &c.

Provisions are added—for assessing the burden to be borne by the different towns in the county; for sub-assessment of the contributions to the sum assessed on each town, upon the men of the town according to their condition and ability; and for appointment of collectors. And the writ concludes with an injunction not to collect more than is absolutely necessary for the purpose in hand.

<small>Similar writs for the other counties, &c.</small>

The like writs are to be directed (mutatis mutandis) unto the counties, cities, towns and places hereafter ensuing—videlicet *(naming them)*. And each county and town to which a writ is directed is charged with a ship of a certain tonnage, and a certain number of men.[1]

<small>Commission for ships in aid, Nov. 16.</small>

Subsequently, a special commission is issued for the loan of ships and pinnaces of the king's own to those counties and places which cannot of themselves find such ships and pinnaces for the service as required by the ship writs, and the arming and furnishing them in warlike manner with ordinance and munition of all sorts; and giving authority to the Treasurer of the navy to receive of and from the several officers of the

---

[1] De warranto speciali Thome Domino Coventry Custodi Magni Sigilli Angli c.—Foedera, xix. 658 et seq.

counties and towns aforesaid all such monies as shall be paid in for the said ships and service.[1]

This introduction of a larger finger meets with some opposition, not only in inland, but also in maritime places where the previous levy had not encountered resistance. And therefore, Feb. 2, 1636, the king submits a case to the judges for their opinion; which they express, in terms following the wording of the questions put to them, as follows:— *Opposition to the tax.* *A case is submitted to the judges.*

The opinion of the Judges:—
May it please your most excellent Majesty,—
We have, according to your Majesty's command, every man by himself, and all of us together, taken into serious consideration the case and questions signed by your Majesty, and inclosed in your royal letter; and we are of opinion, that when the good and safety of the kingdom in general is concerned, and the whole kingdom in danger, your Majesty may, by writ under your Great Seal of England, command all the subjects of this your kingdom, at their charge to provide and furnish such a number of ships, with men, victuals, and munition, and for such time as your Majesty shall think fit, for the defence and safeguard of the kingdom from such danger and peril; and that by law your Majesty may compel the doing thereof in case of refusal or refractoriness. And we are also of opinion that in such case your Majesty is the sole judge, both of the danger, and when, and how the same is to be prevented and avoided.[2] *Their opinion.*

   John Bramston,   George Crooke,
   John Finch,   Thomas Trevor,
   Humphrey Devenport, George Vernon,
   John Denham,   Francis Crawly,
   Richard Hutton,   Robert Berkley,
   William Jones,   Richard Weston.

[1] Foedera, xix. 697-9. And for the instructions and directions from the Lords of the Council for assessing and levying the ship-money against the next spring, see Rushworth, ii. 259-64.

[2] Rushworth, ii. p. 355.

This opinion, it will be observed, has reference only to cases in which *the whole kingdom is in danger*. It must be assumed that the king is advised that the whole kingdom is in danger. At any rate, a third issue of ship writs similar to those issued on the last occasion is ordered on August 12, 1636;[1] a fourth, on September 19, 1637;[2] a fifth, in 1638;[3] and a sixth in November 1639.[4]

Third and subsequent issues.

The produce is, for the year 1636, i. e., from the writs issued that year, 202,240*l*. 2*s*. 3*d*.;[5] and the average produce may be stated as about 200,000*l*.

Produce of the tax.

The following is a list of the 'distribution of ships to the several counties of England and Wales, with their tonnage and men, as the same was ordered to stand' in the year 1639, taken from Stevens, Hist. of Taxes.[6] A similar list for the year 1636, that is for the writs of 1635, is given in Anderson, Hist. of Commerce,[7] and may be compared with the writs in Rymer's Foedera, or in Rushworth,[8] where the sum set on the corporate towns in each county is given. The charge for that year is calculated at 10*l*. per ton, viz., for a ship of 500 tons, 5,000*l*. The proportion of men to tonnage is always two men to every five tons.

Distribution of ships to the several counties.

---

[1] Foedera, xx. 56; Commission for ships in aid, Jan. 31, 1637, ibid.
[2] Foedera, xx. 169; Commission for ships in aid, Dec. 28, 1637, ibid. 184.
[3] See Commission for ships in aid, Feb. 3. Foedera, xx. 286.
[4] See Proclamation for levying arrears. Foedera, xx. 432.
[5] Rushworth, ii. 344.
[6] P. 285.
[7] Anderson, Commerce, ii. 362.
[8] Rushworth, ii. 335 et seq.

	Ships.	Men.	Tuns.
Berks.	1	128	320
Buckingham	1	144	360
Bedford	1	96	240
Bristol	1	26	64
Cornwall	1	176	440
Cambridge.	1	112	280
Cumberland and Westmoreland	1	45	112
Chester	1	96	240
Devon	1	288	720
Darby	1	112	280
Dorset	1	160	400
Duresm	1	64	160
Essex.	1	256	640
Gloucester.	1	176	440
Hampshire.	1	192	480
Hereford	1	112	280
Huntington	1	64	160
Hertford	1	128	320
Kent and Ports	1	256	640
Lancaster.	1	128	320
Leicester	1	144	360
Lincoln	1	256	640
London	2	448	1220
Middlesex.	1	160	400
Monmouth.	1	48	120
Northampton	1	192	480
Nottingham	1	112	280
Northumberland.	1	64	168
North Wales	1	128	320
Norfolk	1	253	624
Oxon.	1	112	280
Rutland	1	26	64
Somerset	1	256	640
Surrey	1	112	280
Sussex	1	160	400
Suffolk	1	256	640
Stafford	1	96	240
South Wales	1	160	400
Salop.	1	144	360
Warwick	1	128	320
Worcester.	1	112	280
Wilts.	1	224	560
York.	1	384	960

Such are the reasons for the levy of ship money by the king; the mode of issuing the ship writs; the form of writ; the opinion of the judges in categorical answer to the questions put to them by the king; and the distribution of the charge between the several counties.

<small>Attempts to test the legality of ship writs.</small>

An attempt, in 1636, to test the legality of the ship writs, by Mr. R. Chambers, of London, fails: Sir Richard Berkeley, one of the justices of the Court of King's Bench who signed the opinion aforesaid, stating openly in Court:—'There is a rule of law, and a rule of government, and many things which may not be done by the rule of law may be done by the rule of government;' and 'refusing,[1] on that ground, to suffer the point of legality of ship money to be argued by counsel for Chambers.'[2] Then comes Hampden's case.[3]

<small>Hampden's case, May 22, 1637.
The Act against ship-money, 1640.</small>

Then, the Parliament of 1640. And then the Act of 1640, 16 Car. I., c. 14: 'An Act for declaring illegal and void the late proceedings touching ship money, and for vacating of all records and process concerning the same,' which is in the terms following, and tells its own story:—

<small>Issue of ship writs.</small>

Whereas divers writs of late time issued under the Great Seal of England, commonly called *Ship Writs*, for the charging of the ports, towns, cities, boroughs and counties of this realm respectively, to provide and furnish certain ships for his Majesty's service: And whereas upon the

---

[1] This refusal formed one of the grounds of his impeachment by the House of Commons. See Rushworth, ii. 609.

[2] Rushworth, ii. 323.

[3] For Report of the Proceedings in the case of Ship-money between the King and John Hampden, Esq., in the Exchequer, 13 Car. I., A.D. 1637, see Howell, State Trials, iii. 826–1315; Rushworth, ii. 480–600.

execution of the same writs, and returns of certioraries thereupon made, and the sending the same by mittimus, into the Court of Exchequer, process hath been thence made against sundry persons pretended to be charged by way of contribution, for the making up of certain sums assessed for the providing of the said ships, and in especial in Easter term, in the 13th year of the reign of our Sovereign Lord the King that now is, a writ of scire facias was awarded out of the Court of Exchequer, to the then sheriff of Buckinghamshire, against John Hampden, Esquire, to appear and shew cause, why he should not be charged with a certain sum so assessed upon him; Upon whose appearance and demurrer to the proceedings therein, the Barons of the Exchequer adjourned the same case into the Exchequer Chamber, where it was solemnly argued divers days, and at length it was there agreed by the greater part of all the Justices of the Courts of King's Bench, and Common Pleas, and of the Barons of Exchequer there assembled, that the said John Hampden should be charged with the said sum so as aforesaid assessed on him; The main grounds and reasons of the said Justices and Barons which so agreed, being, that when the good and safety of the kingdom in general is concerned, and the whole kingdom in danger, the king might by writ under the Great Seal of England, command all the subjects of this his kingdom, at their charge, to provide and furnish such number of ships with men, victuals and munition, and for such time as the king should think fit, for the defence and safeguard of the kingdom from such danger and peril, and that by law the king might compel the doing thereof, in case of refusal or refractoriness; And that the king is the sole judge, both of the danger, and when, and how the same is to be prevented and avoided; According to which grounds and reasons, all the Justices of the said Courts of King's Bench and Common Pleas, and the said Barons of the Exchequer, having been formerly consulted with by his Majesty's command, had set their hands to an extrajudicial opinion, expressed to the same purpose; which opinion, with their names thereunto, was also by his Majesty's command inrolled in the Courts of Chancery, King's Bench,

Necessity of enforcing payment by process of law.

Proceedings against John Hampden.

Case solemnly argued in the Court of Exchequer Chamber.

Judgment against Hampden.

Grounds for that decision.

Extrajudicial opinion given by the judges previously to the same effect.

Common Pleas and Exchequer, and likewise entered among the remembrances of the Court of Star-Chamber, and according to the said agreement of the said Justices and Barons, judgment was given by the Barons of the Exchequer:—That the said John Hampden should be charged with the said sum so assessed on him. And whereas some other actions and process depend, and have depended in the said Court of Exchequer, and in some other Courts against other persons, for the like kind of charge, grounded upon the said writs, commonly called *Ship Writs*, all which writs and proceedings, as aforesaid, were utterly against the law of the land;

The House of Commons declare their view of the law as antagonistic to the decision of the judges,

II. Be it therefore declared and enacted by the King's most excellent Majesty, and the lords and commons in this present Parliament assembled, and by the authority of the same:—That the said charge imposed upon the subject, for the providing and furnishing of ships, commonly called ship money, and the said extrajudicial opinion of the said Justices and Barons, and the said writs, and every of them, and the said agreement or opinion of the greater part of the said Justices and Barons, and the said judgment given against the said John Hampden, were, and are contrary to and against the laws and statutes of this realm, the right of property, the liberty of the subjects, former resolutions in Parliament, and the Petition of Right made in the third year of the reign of his Majesty that now is.

and proceed to enforce it.

III. And it is further declared and enacted by the authority aforesaid, that all and every the particulars prayed or desired in the said Petition of Right, shall from henceforth be put in execution accordingly, and shall be firmly and strictly holden and observed, as in the same petition they are prayed and expressed; And that all and every the records and remembrances of all and every the judgment, inrolments, entry and proceedings, as aforesaid, and all and every the proceedings whatsoever, upon, or by pretext or colour of any of the said writs, commonly called *Ship Writs*, and all and every the dependants on any of them, shall be deemed and adjudged to all intents, constructions and purposes, to be utterly void and disannulled; and that all and every the said judgment, inrolments,

All proceedings connected with the ship writs declared to be void.

entries, proceedings, and dependants of what kind soever, shall be vacated and cancelled in such manner and form as Records use to be that are vacated.¹

The judgment of the judges cancelled.

The Royal Standard was raised at Nottingham on the evening of the 23rd of August, 1642.

Civil war.

Without departure from the course of the narrative, as confined to the history of taxation in this country, we may, in progress, put forth a hand and cull by the way a flower, if the reader will allow the expression, from under Italian skies.

Specimen of an Italian tax on moveables in the sixteenth century.

'In Florence,' according to Sismondi, 'the method of assessing the taxes had been always almost absolutely arbitrary; and it was perhaps impossible to avoid entirely this inconvenience in a mercantile republic, where the burden must necessarily fall most heavily on the profits of commerce, and where every declaration of fortune would, from its liability to shake the credit of the merchants, be extremely odious. The land tax was based on a valuation made with great care. Indirect taxes seem, in their nature, to be voluntary and do not detract from liberty; but the direct tax on moveable property, or on the unknown profits of commerce, was that which it was especially difficult to regulate; it was reserved for occasions of pressing necessity and extraordinary subsidy.' The celebrated

---

¹ Statutes at Large. The marginal notes in the text are not those printed in the Statute book, but may prove of more assistance to the reader's eye. Marginal notes to Acts of Parliament, it may be observed by the way, are not of any authority. They do not afford a scintilla of argument regarding the proper construction of enactments or the intention of the Legislature, though they may prove perplexing and misleading to those ignorant of the fact. They are useful as finger posts, in indication of the locality of enactments.

Nicolas Capponi introduced, about 1528, with other reforms, the following regulations regarding the assessment of the tax on moveable property :—' The great Council, after having decreed the sum to be levied in this manner, named twenty citizens, and imposed on them the duty of dividing the sum fixed amongst the taxpayers. It required, under heavy penalties, their work to be completed in a certain stated number of days; and it established a minimum and a maximum for each item of contribution. The commissioners performed their work each one separately, and forthwith delivered to the monks of some convent, specified by a public decree, each one a schedule of taxpayers, stating the sums he had adjudged them to pay. The monks, in order to determine the contribution of a citizen, brought together the twenty propositions of the commissioners regarding him. They first put aside the six highest and the six lowest as possibly suggested by hatred or by favour; then they added together the eight moderate assessments, and divided the sum by eight. They were sworn to secrecy for all their work; and after finishing it, they burnt all the materials.'[1]

Customs and Port Duties.

The third sub-division of our subject comprises the customs and the port duties, but attention need only be fixed on the port duties; and the reader will not fail to have observed that the port duties hitherto granted admit of classification under the following heads :—

[1] Sismondi, Répub. Ital. x. 64, and the authorities there quoted.

THE PORT DUTIES. 259

(1) The subsidy (as distinguished from the custom) of wool, woolfells, and leather exported; (2) Tunnage—the duty on wine imported, at so much the tun; and (3) poundage—the duty on merchandise, other than that specially charged, exported or imported, at so much per £ value; and they may be termed shortly, for present purposes, the duties on wool and leather, tunnage and poundage.

Comprising (1) duties on wool and leather, (2) tunnage, and (3) poundage.

The duties on wool and leather granted to Edward III. in the 50th year of his reign, for three years, on the expiration of the grant, are regranted to his successor, for a short term; and also certain new duties of the same description; and poundage, at the rate of 6d., for a short term.[1] But the new duties and the poundage are repealed in 1379,[2] on the grant, as before mentioned, of the capitation tax.

In 1381, the duties on wool and leather, from which 'the greatest revenue the king has from his kingdom towards payment of the expenses of the war is derived'—de quoi le greindre profit que le Roi prent en son roiaulme sourde, are renewed to the king, for less than a year, and with an intermission of one week, 'lest the king by continual possession of the said subsidy might claim it as of right and custom.'[3] Subsequently in the same year, these duties are granted to the king, for four years.[4] And in 1397, the king has a grant of them for life—care being taken to provide that the grant shall not be made a precedent in the time of his successors, Kings of England.[5]

Duties on wool and leather granted to Richard II. for life,

[1] Par. Rolls, iii. 37, 38.   [2] Ibid. 58.
[3] Ibid. 104.   [4] Ibid. 114.   [5] Ibid. 368.

s 2

To particularise the various grants of the duties on wool and leather, and tunnage and poundage, made subsequently during this period, would answer no good purpose, but only confuse the reader. Henceforth, although there are occasional intermissions, and sometimes, on renewal, the rate is altered, briefly, though precautions are taken to prevent the uninterrupted continuance of the duties, in the endeavour to prevent any claim by the king to take the duties as 'customs,' port duties on wool and leather, and tunnage and poundage, may be considered practically established as a branch of revenue.

<small>and to Hen. V., after Azincourt, with tunnage and poundage.</small>
Henry IV. has not any life grant of port duties, either on wool and leather, or tunnage and poundage; but both are granted to Henry V. for life, after the victory of Azincourt, in 1415.[1] In the earlier grants of tunnage and poundage the rates had varied as follows:—Tunnage 2s., and poundage 6d.; tunnage 3s., and poundage 6d.; tunnage 3s., and poundage 1s.; tunnage 1s. 6d., and poundage 6d.; tunnage 2s., and poundage 8d. The life-grant to Henry V. is at the rate of 3s. for tunnage, and 1s. for poundage: the charge of tunnage extending to exported as well as to imported wine; the poundage being general—'on all manner of merchandize coming into the kingdom, and passing out of the same—inwards and outwards—except wool, woolfells, and leather, and wine (as contributories to the revenue under the special charges relating to them) and except 'chescun manere de blee floure, et pesson rees et bestaill entrant en le dit roialme.'

[1] Par. Rolls, iv. 64.

Henceforth we may tie the three—the duties on wool and leather, tunnage, and poundage—in one bundle under the more convenient term for present purposes and the correct designation for this branch of the revenue, viz., the port duties.

After several grants for years, Henry VI. has, in 1452, a grant for life.[1] Edward IV. has a grant for life.[2] So also has Henry VII., the rate being—for tunnage 3s., and for poundage 12d.[3]; and in 1490, a new duty on malmsey, at the rate of 18s., besides the old custom, for every butt imported by any merchant stranger; the butt to contain 126 gallons, and no butt to be sold for above 4l.; this additional duty to continue 'until the Venetians abate their new impositions of four ducats at Candy.'[4] Henry VIII. has a life grant of the duties,[5] and so have Edward VI., Queen Mary, and Queen Elizabeth.[6] *Grants of the duties for life to Henry VI., Edw. IV., Hen. VII., Hen.VIII., Edw. VI., Mary, and Elizabeth.*

After the foregoing rapid run down the history of the port duties during Lancaster and York and Tudor times, we may, on entering the Stuart period, direct a more close attention to the terms of the usual port duties Act, as declaratory of the legal position of this branch of the revenue. The duties are granted to James I. for life, in the first year of his reign; and the Act by which they are imposed[7] commences:—'In *'The Act of a subsidy of tunnage and poundage,' 1603.*

[1] See recital to 31 Henry VI. c. 8.
[2] See 12 Edw. IV. c. 3. Several ordinances made for the true payment of a subsidy of tunnage and poundage granted to the king during his life, by a statute not printed made ann. 4 Ed. IV.
[3] Par. Rolls, vi. 268.   [4] 7 Hen. VII. c. 8.
[5] Gilbert, Exch. p. 286; and see 6 Hen. VIII., c. 14.
[6] See 1 Edw. VI. c. 13; 1 Mar. Sess. 2, c. 18; 1 Eliz. c. 20.
[7] 1 Jac. I. c. 33, 'An Act of a subsidy of tunnage and poundage.'

A subsidy granted to the king of tunnage, poundage, wools, &c.

their most humble wise show unto your most excellent Majesty, your loyal and obedient subjects and commons in this present Parliament assembled, That whereas well your noble great grandfather of worthy memory, King Henry the VII., the noble king of famous memory, King Henry the VIII., the late king of worthy memory, King Edward the VI., the late Queen Mary, and the late renowned Sovereign Lady, Queen Elizabeth, as other your right noble and famous progenitors, kings of this your realm of England, time out of mind, have had and enjoyed unto

What subsidies the kings of this realm have had, and for what causes.

them, by authority of Parliament, for the defence of this your realm, and the keeping and safeguard of the seas for the intercourse of merchandise safely to come into and pass out of the same, certain sums of money, named subsidies, of all manner of goods and merchandise coming in or going out of the same your realm. And forasmuch as we your said poor commons, undoubtedly and most assuredly do trust, and have sure confidence in your Majesty's good favour and will towards us your said commons, in, and for the keeping and sure defending of the seas against all persons, intending, or that shall intend the disturbance of us your said commons, in the intercourse, and the invading of this your realm, to our molestation, unquieting and loss, which at any time cannot be borne without the great excess and intolerable costs, charges and expenses of your Majesty, which is not when need shall require in such cases to be lacked at any time, but rather we your said commons wishing that such furniture of all things may be had in readiness from

THE PORT DUTIES. 263

time to time, when necessity shall require; For the speedy indelayed provision and help, for the suppressing of such inconveniences, disturbances and invasions . . . by the advice and consent of the Lords spiritual and temporal in this present Parliament assembled, and by the authority of the same,' give and grant to the king:—

One subsidy called tunnage, that is to say, Of every tun of wine that is or shall come into this realm, or any your Majesty's dominions, by way of merchandise, the sum of three shillings, and so after that rate; And of every tun of sweet wines, as well malmsey as other, that is or shall come into this realm by any merchant alien, three shillings, and so after the rate, over and above the three shillings above mentioned; And of every awm[1] of Rhenish wine that is or shall so come in, twelve pence. Grant of tunnage of wine,

And also one other subsidy called poundage, that is to say, of all manner of goods and merchandise of every merchant, denizen and alien, carried or to be carried out of this realm, or any your Majesty's dominions, or to be brought into the same by way of merchandise, of the value of every twenty shillings of the same goods and merchandise, twelve pence, and so after the rate. and poundage on value of goods.

And of every twenty shillings value of tin and pewter vessel carried out of this realm by every or any merchant-alien, twelve pence, over and above the twelve pence aforesaid.

Except and foreprised out of this grant of subsidy of poundage, all manner of woollen cloth made or

---

[1] An awm or aume (Teut. ohm., i.e. cadus vel mensura) contained forty gallons.

Exceptions out of the subsidy of poundage.

wrought, or which shall be made or wrought within this realm of England, and by every or any merchant denizen, and not born alien, carried or to be carried out of this your said realm; and all manner of wools, woolfells, hides and backs of leather, that is or shall be carried out of this your said realm; and all wines not before limited to pay subsidy or tunnage; and all manner of fresh fish and bestial coming, or that shall come into the same your realm.

Duties on wool and leather.

And further, one other subsidy, that is to say, of every merchant born denizen, of and for every sack of wool, 1l. 13s. 4d.; and of and for every 240 woolfells, 1l. 13s. 4d.; and of and for every last of hides and backs, 3l. 6s. 8d., and so after the same rate, for every less or greater quantity for any the same merchandise more or less; And of every merchant-stranger not born denizen, of and for every sack of wool, 3l. 6s. 8d.; and of and for every 240 woolfells, 3l. 6s. 8d.; and for every last of hides and backs, 3l. 13s. 4d; and so of all the said wools, woolfells, hides and backs, and of every of them after the rate.

Penalty and other clauses.

The duties, as before stated, are granted to the king for life. And the Act contains:—A forfeiture clause in the case of shipment or landing of goods without payment of duty; A provision, that on proof of capture of goods by enemies or pirates, or their loss at sea, other goods to the same value may be shipped at the same port as the lost goods, without payment of duty; A proviso that for goods shipped in any carrick or galley by a merchant denizen he shall pay duty as an alien; and, An exemption in favour of herrings or other sea fish taken by a subject upon the seas and exported by a subject.

At the date of the accession of Charles I., in 1625, in consequence of the repeated grants of the port duties to a succession of sovereigns for life, they have come to be regarded as forming, in effect, a recognised part of the ordinary revenue of the Crown. The annual produce is considerable; and it is difficult to see how the Crown can possibly carry on government if deprived of this branch of revenue. Moreover, there exists a pressing demand for money, to meet the expenses of the intended war with Spain. But the question of the right to impose port duties has assumed a different aspect since the commencement of the preceding reign. The imposition of duties on merchandise by the King appears to be sanctioned by the judicial decision in the celebrated currant Case (Bates' Case),[1] grounded on the principle that such duties are 'the effects of foreign commerce; but all affairs of commerce and treaties with foreign nations belong to the king's absolute power. He, therefore, who has power over the cause, must have power over the effect.' It is necessary, therefore, to take a firm stand, and maintain the constitutional right of Parliament to grant such duties. Hence the grant by the Commons in the first Parliament of Charles I. of the port duties for a year only. The Lords, however, refuse to pass the Bill. The plague rages in London; Parliament is transferred to Oxford, and shortly afterwards is dissolved. And the port duties are for

Reasons for the grant of the duties to Charles I. for only a year.

[1] See below, General Remarks, reign of James I.

many years levied under royal warrant by order of the Privy Council without any Parliamentary authority.[1]

Yield of the port duties.

A few words now regarding the yield of this branch of the revenue.

According to a statement made in certain Articles presented to Parliament in 1409, the produce of the duties on wool and leather, which had been very considerable[2] in the 14th year of Richard II., had diminished in the reign of his successor, in consequence, partly, of corrupt collectors, who committed and connived at fraud.

In 1421.

In the ninth year of reign of Henry V. the annual produce is as follows:—

	£	s.	d.
Parva custuma on wools	3,976	1	2
Magna custuma	26,035	18	8½
Parva custuma on goods	2,438	9	1¼
Subsidy of tunnage and poundage	8,237	10	9½
	40,687	19	9¼ [3]

In 1431, 2 and 3.

In the years 1431, 1432 and 1433, it is (not to take account of anything under pounds) as follows:—

	1431 £	1432 £	1433 £
The custom of wool and small customs	7,780	6,996	6,048[4]
The subsidy of wools	20,151	16,808	14,259
Tunnage and poundage	6,920	6,998	6,203
	34,851	30,802	26,510

[1] Feodera, xviii. 737; xx. 118.
[2] £160,000. This seems a large sum, but 'Be it trowe, or be it fals, it is as the copie was'—'Il fuist respondu a son Escheqer de CLXM li et pluis par an del subside et custumes des layns et pealx lanutz.' Par. Rolls, iii. 625.
[3] Declaratio proficuorum regni et onerum supportandorum. 9 Hen. V. 1421. Foedera, x. 113.
[4] Except from Newcastle.

or for present purposes, say, on an average, about 30,700*l.* a year.[1]

Our commerce makes rapid progress during the fifteenth century; and Canynges of Bristol (temp. Henry VI. and Edward IV.), who had ships of 900 tons burden, may be ranked as a proxime accessit to the celebrated Jacques Cœur, to whom—'a vaillant *cœur*—rien d'impossible.' During the reign of Henry VIII. the yield of the port duties at first improves, but falls off towards the close of the reign.

At the commencement of the reign of Elizabeth, it is found necessary to make additional provisions for securing payment of the duties. The Act by which this is effected[2] recites that:—'the sums of money paid in the name of customs and subsidies of wares and merchandises transported out and brought into the realm of England by any merchant stranger or denizen, is an ancient revenue annexed and united to the imperial crown; and hath in the time of King Edward III., and other the Queen's most noble progenitors, amounted to great and notable sums of money, till of late years many greedy and covetous persons, respecting more their private gain and commodity, than their duty and allegiance, or the common profit of the realm, have and do daily, as well by conveying the same their wares or merchandises out of creeks and places where no customer is resident, as also by and through the negligence or corruption of the customer, searcher or other officer, where they be resident, as by divers other fraudulent,

---

[1] Status Revent. Annal. Regni. 12 Hen. VI. Par. Rolls, iv. 435.
[2] 1 Eliz. 1558. c. 11

undue and subtle practices and devices, convey their goods and merchandises as well brought from parts beyond the sea as transported out of this realm of England, without payment or agreeing for the payment of the customs and subsidies therefore due; whereby the yearly revenue aforesaid is very much impaired and diminished, to the great loss and damage of the Queen's Highness, and to the great burden and charge of her loving subjects, who by occasion thereof have of late years been more charged with subsidies and payment for the supplement of the said loss and damage, than else they should have been.' And, accordingly, the Act contains stringent enactments regarding the lading and discharge of goods, and for preventing frauds by custom house officers. In consequence of these protective enactments and the increase of commerce, the revenue, previously about 24,000*l.*,

In 1590. increases, in 1590, to 50,000*l.* a year; and as we are told, Sir Thomas Smith, by whom the duties had been farmed, is compelled to refund some part of the profits he has received.[1]

In 1604. In 1604 the duties yield about 127,000*l.* a year.[2] In 1613, according to *The Circle of Commerce*, published in the year 1623 by Edward Misselden, an eminent merchant, they yield:—

	£	*s.*	*d.*
At the port of London:— outwards,	61,322	16	7
inwards,	48,250	1	9
Total custom of the port of London	109,572	18	4

[1] See Sinclair, Hist. Rev., i. 207, and the authorities there quoted. See, however, Camden, p. 440, there referred to.
[2] Journal, 21 May, 1604; Hume, Hist. Eng., iv. 357.

At all the out-ports:—

	£	s.	d.		£	s.	d.
outwards,	25,471	19	7	}	38,502	9	4
inwards,	13,030	9	9				

Total amount of customs of England in 1613, 148,075 7 8[1] In 1613.

'In King James' reign, when I was Commissioner of the Treasury (writes Coke), these subsidies, granted for life, amounted to 160,000*l.* per annum, and so letten to farm.'

In 1617 the annual revenue has increased to about 190,000*l.*[2] In 1617.

In 1622, according to *The Circle of Commerce,* above mentioned, the yield of the customs, outwards and inwards, is 168,222*l.* 15*s.* 11*d.*[3] And, according to a publication of the year 1641, the yield is then put at about 500,000*l.*; though, as a fact, the amount is probably overstated.[4] In 1622. In 1641.

It remains to explain the manner of arriving at the rate to be paid for poundage on goods. The tunnage on wine, a duty regulated by the contents of the vessels, is easily ascertained; but poundage has reference to value, and the question is, how was that value determined? Method of valuation for 'poundage.'

The author of the Treatise on the Court of Exchequer writes :—'The book of rates seems to be as ancient as the 31st of Edward I.; for thereby the merchants agreed to be charged with the pound rate

---

[1] Anderson, Commerce, ii. 260.
[2] Abstract of His Majesty's Revenue, Hume, Hist. Engl., iv. 356.
[3] Anderson, Commerce, ii. 297.
[4] Mr. Lewis Roberts, Treasure of Traffic, published in 1641. See Anderson, Commerce, ii. 391. See also Sinclair, Hist. Rev., i. 260, who quotes Hume, vii. 340.

according to value, and such a pound rate could hardly be well and equally assessed without a book of rates; since, without such a book, the customs would be liable either to the oath of the merchant, or the oppression of the officer.'[1] This, however, is mere conjecture; there is no historical record of the existence of a book of rates in the earlier history of the port duties; and the original plan of taking the oath of the merchant appears to have continued as late as the reign of Edward IV. In collection of the poundage on merchandises granted to that king for life in 1472, the merchandises are to be valued—'After that they cost at the first biyng or achate, by their othes, or of their servauntes, biers of the said merchandises in their absence, or by their letters, the which the same merchantes have of such biyng from their factours, and in noon otherwise.'[2]

Queen Mary's orders in Council.

Queen Mary, by order in Council, increases the customs in some of its branches; and probably a book of rates is put out in her reign, after the loss of Calais, when it is necessary to increase the rates because the Calais duties are at an end.[3] Queen Elizabeth follows the precedent;[4] and a new book of rates, in which the various commodities are stated in alphabetical order and valued according to the real price, and which refers to the Act by which the duties were granted to Queen Mary for life, and mentions a former book of rates, is printed 14th October, 1586.

Queen Elizabeth's book of rates.

This book of rates continues in force during the reign of Elizabeth, and till the 6th year of James I.,

[1] Gilbert, Exch., 223. [2] Par. Rolls, vi. 154.
[3] Gilbert, Exch., p. 225.
[4] See Bacon, iv. 362, quoted Hume, iv. 192.

1609; when, 'the value of commodities having considerably increased,' the king 'rectifies that' by his Letters Patent; and in a new book of rates the goods that have not altered in value are charged according to the old subsidy, and where the value of goods have increased, a corresponding additional charge is stated by way of impost.[1]

<small>The rates are 'rectified' by James I.</small>

This is probably the book of rates mentioned by Coke, where, speaking of this branch of the revenue, he says:—'The values of the merchandise for which the subsidy of poundage is paid do appear in a book of rates in print, whereby the merchant knows what he has to pay.' And he adds the excellent observation that, 'seeing that nothing is more uncertain than the values of merchandises wherefor the subsidy of poundage is paid, it were good at every grant of them, to set down rates in a schedule annexed to the Bill.'[2]

In 1604 King James charges a special duty on tobacco; an important future contributory to our revenue introduced in this country by Raleigh, as will be remembered from the story of the waiting-woman's attempt to put out her 'smoking' master with a pot of beer. The amount is six-and-eightpence per lb. over and above the custom of twopence upon the lb. weight usually paid before.[3] But the tax is not successful from any point of view. It does not diminish the importation of the unnecessary weed, and the duty is not punctually paid.[4] The king's aversion to

<small>Duty on tobacco.</small>

[1] Gilbert, Exch., pp. 224, 225.　　[2] Institutes, iv. 38.
[3] Commissio pro Tabacco. Foedera, xvi. 601.
[4] See 'Commissio specialis concernens le garbling herbae Nicotianae.' Apl. 7, 1620. Foedera, xvii. 190.

tobacco is well known. And in a subsequent proclamation the plant is stigmatised as :—'A weed of no necessary use, but of late years brought into the kingdom, amongst other vanities and superfluities which come from beyond the seas;' the planting of tobacco in England and Wales is prohibited; a special licence is required for importation of tobacco; and it is required to be sold, in future, in roll marked with a mark or seal appointed for the purpose.[1]

Charles I., book of rates. Lastly, a new book of rates was made and enforced by Charles I. in 1635; and was subsequently altered by him as to various items of charge.[2]

The ancient port officers of the customs. A few words may be added regarding the ancient port officers of the customs. They are (1) customer, (2) comptroller, and (3) searcher. The customer receives the customs. The comptroller enrolls the payments at the custom house, and raises a charge against the customer. The searcher receives from the customer and comptroller the document authorising the unlading or shipment, as the case might be, of the goods for which customs have been paid.

Documents in use. The document authorising the landing of goods is termed the warrant: the license to export them, the

The Warrant and the Cocket. cocket. Regarding this document the author of the Treatise on the Court of Exchequer says :—'This word Cocket, Skinner derives from the Cockboat, because the taking in this schedule was an emblem that the ship was going to sail.' An amusing derivation;

---

[1] A proclamation for restraint of the disordered trading of tobacco, June 29, 1620. Foedera, xvii. 233-5.
[2] Foedera, xx. 118.

but cocket or corket is simply an abbreviation of the terms of acquittance expressed in the receipt given to the merchant on payment of the duty—' quo quietus est,' qo qetus est; as will be seen from the following form of a cocket:—

'Edwardus, omnibus ad quos, salutem. Sciatis, quod A. B. nobis solvit in portu nostro London. custumas nobis debitas pro tribus saccis lanae, *quo quietus est,* testibus collectore et contrarotulatore custumarum nostrarum in portu praedicto, die, anno, &c.'[1]—A. B. has paid the customs due for three sacks of wool, whereof he is quit. 'Quietus est' is the usual form of acquittance in entries in the old Exchequer Rolls; in which, after reciting a payment, the entry usually concludes with 'Et quietus est.'—Et. Q. e., as it is to be found abbreviated in Madox's History of the Exchequer.

Form of a cocket.

Particular seals are used for the cockets, and are delivered to the customers on appointment. Thus, the seals appointed for the cocket which the customers are to use in the customing of wools and skins in the port of Lenn are to be delivered to them in a purse sealed with the Exchequer Seal.[2]

Seals for the cockets.

A statute of Hen. VI. imposes a penalty for sealing or using cockets in blank—blankes escrowes en parchemyn appellcz blankes cokkettetz—to deceive the king of his customs; and the penalty is forfeiture of goods and chattels, as in case of felony, and imprisonment for three years.[3]

[1] Hale, De Portibus Maris, cap. xi. Hargrave's Tracts.
[2] Illa sigilla quae deputantur pro cokotto quo dicti custodes uti debent custumando lanas et coria in praedicto portu de Lenn. See Madox, Exch., p. 536. [3] 11 Hen. VI., 1433, c. 16,

The Surveyor.

Practices such as those at which the enactment last mentioned was aimed induce the appointment of the Surveyor as a check upon the searcher, in order to prevent fraud in allowing more goods to be exported or imported than were mentioned in the cocket or the warrant. Hence the surveyor is termed, in the Act of the 20 Hen. VI. c. 5, the surveyor of the searcher.

Legal disabilities of officers.

'All customers, controllers of the custom, clerks, deputies, ministers, and their servants, factors, and searchers, controllers or surveyors of searchers, and their clerks, deputies, ministers, and factors are forbidden to have any ships of their own; to buy or sell by way or by colour of merchandise; to meddle with freighting of ships, or have or occupy any wharfs or quays; or hold any hostries or taverns; or be any factors or attornies for any merchant, denizen or alien; or be hosts to any merchant-alien, upon the pain of 40l., to be forfeit as often as they do the contrary.'[1]

The tide waiters.

The tide waiters and land waiters are, originally, only servants to the searcher and surveyor.[2]

Before concluding the history of port duties during this period, the following Petition of the House of Commons (temp. Henry V.) may be inserted, as one of those curiosities which occasionally enliven the process of search through the Parliamentary Rolls. It embodies a remarkable proposition for deriving fiscal profit from our command of the Channel. The date is 1420, the year following that of the assassination of Jean Sans

---

[1] 20 Hen. VI., 1442, c. 5; see also 11 Hen. IV., 1409, c. 2.
[2] Gilbert, Exch., p. 230.

Peur, Duke of Burgundy. His successor, Philippe, has formed a league with Henry; and the result has been the treaty of Troyes, by which, on the death of Charles, Henry is to succeed to the crown of France.

> The king had granted every article,
> His daughter, first; and in sequel, all
> According to their firm proposed natures.

The fortune of England has reached the zenith: 'most greatly lived this star of England.' It descends almost to the nadir in the following reign, when our historical records are dark with licenses to convey pilgrims to St. James of Galicia, licenses to export tin for payment of ransom, licenses for the transmutation of metals, or for discovery of the philosopher's stone, under 'a king over-subjected and over-wived,' as Fuller puts it, and 'fitter for a cowl than a crown.'

To the most gracious and puissant prince the Duke of Gloucester, Guardian of England, the poor Commons of the kingdom of England, &c., &c.

Proposal, in 1420, to tax all strangers passing along the Channel.

Item, the said Commons pray, that whereas our most Sovereign Lord the king and his noble progenitors time out of mind (de tout temps), have been lords of the sea, and also by the grace of God it happens that our said lord the king is lord of the sea coast on both sides of the sea (des costes d'ambeparties del Meer), it be ordained, that from all strangers passing along the said sea, such tax for the assistance of our said lord the king shall be taken as to him may seem fit, for the safeguard of the said sea.[1]

Loans and Benevolences.

Our kings, for many generations, exercised the right of begging and borrowing; and sometimes, as Macaulay

[1] Par. Rolls, iv. 126.

puts it, 'begged in a tone not easily distinguished from that of command, and sometimes borrowed with small thought of repaying.' It is not intended in this volume to enter into the details of every exaction of this sort. It matters little in what particular form this or that king borrows, whether by means of 'rag-man' or 'privy seal.' Under any form of loan the lender to the king loses for a time the use of his money. He is fortunate if the capital is eventually repaid; an uncertain result even in the case of compulsory loans; as may be seen by reference to the Act of 1543 (35 Hen. VIII., c. 12)—an abstract of which is given in Hawkins' Statutes at Large, as follows:—

Nature of loans to the king.

The Lords and Commons do remit unto the king all such sums of money as he hath borrowed of them or any other, by way of prest or loan, by his privy seal sithence the first day of January, anno 33 of his reign. And if the king have paid to any person any sum of money which he borrowed, by sale of land or otherwise, the same person, his heirs, executors, or administrators, shall repay the same to the king. And if any person hath sold his privy seal to another, the seller shall repay the money to the buyer thereof.

It is worthy of note that in collection of these loans in the reign of Henry VIII. the people are compelled to reveal the extent of their fortune on oath, a circumstance which renders the loans extremely unpopular.

Benevolences.

To pass from borrowing to begging. It would not be difficult to form an amusing catalogue of the various demands of this sort of which record has been preserved—for aid on different occasions, new year's gifts, &c.; the wealthy citizens of London and the principal merchants being the chief sufferers. But such proceedings have little connection with taxation; and it is intended to limit the remarks here made to what is known more especially as the period of benevolences, which, commencing during the turbulent times of the Wars of the Roses, terminates with the Petition of Right.

During the struggle between the two parties, it is obviously an object to both not to risk by unjust taxes any diminution of popularity; and hardly an instance occurs of any attempt to impose a tax without Parliamentary sanction. But considerable sums are extorted from the richer classes as for gifts; and this method of recruiting the Exchequer assumes in Edward the IV.'s time such unusual proportions as to be regarded as an innovation.

Edward IV., when he ascended the throne—'estoit fort jeune, et beau prince entre les beaux du monde.'[1] By Bacon he is bracketed with 'Augustus Cæsar, Titus Vespasianus, Philippe le Bel, Alcibiades of Athens, and Ismael the Sophy of Persia, all high and great spirits, and the most beautiful men of their times.'[2] According to Rapin, he was 'one of the handsomest men in England, and perhaps in Europe. His noble mien, his free and easy way, his affable carriage, won the hearts of all at first sight.' And the historian adds, that these qualities 'gained him esteem and affection, which stood him in great stead in several circum-

Benevolences during the reign of Edw. IV.

---

[1] Commynes, Mémoires, Mlle. Dupont, ii. 281.
[2] Viri prorsus magni, et nihilominus perpulchri. Sermones Fideles sive Interiora Rerum, De Pulchritudine.

stances of his life.' From the pictures we have of him we know that—

> He, like Sir Topas, dressed with art,
> And if a shape could win a heart,
> He had a shape to win.

And Philippe de Commynes goes so far as to say that 'his restoration to the throne was due in no small degree to the inclination the principal London ladies felt for him.' However that may have been, these good looks and this free and easy way are of material assistance to him in personal collection of a benevolence about the thirteenth year of his reign.

<small>Edw. IV, and the widow.</small>

A rich widow, asked for a contribution by the handsome king, assents, saying 'by my trothe for thy lovely countenance thou shalt have even twentie pounds.' 'Looking scarce for half that sum,' the king 'thanks her, and lovinglie kisses her.' The free and easy way completes the charm: for, in the words of the chronicler, 'whether the flavor of his breath did so comfort her stomach, or she esteemed the kiss of a king so precious a jewele, she swore incontinentlie that he should have twentie pounds more, which she with the same will paied that she offered it.'[1]

The attractions that collection of benevolences in this manner may have for ladies fail to recommend the practice to the commons in general; who, in lieu of regarding this method of increasing the Royal revenue with favour, stigmatize benevolences as 'new and unlawful inventions.' Accordingly, one of the first acts of Richard III., 'obliged to support

---

[1] Hall, Chron. p. 308.

by popular measures a somewhat shaky title to the throne,' is an endeavour to ingratiate himself with the people by abolition of the new method of exaction. This is effected, by the Act of 1483 (1 Rich. III., c. 2), in the stringent terms following:—

The king remembering how the commons of this his realm, by new and unlawful inventions, and inordinate covetise, against the law of his realm, have been put to great thraldom and importable charges and exactions, and in especial by a new imposition called a Benevolence, whereby divers years the subjects and commons of this land, against their wills and freedoms, have paid great sums of money to their almost utter destruction: (2) For divers and many worshipful men of this realm, by occasion thereof, were compelled by necessity to break up their households, and to live in great penury and wretchedness, their debts unpaid, and their children unpreferred, and such memorials as were ordained to be done for the wealth of their souls anentized and annulled, to the great displeasure of God, and the destruction of his realm: (3) Therefore the king will it be ordained, by the advice and assent of the Lords Spiritual and Temporal and the Commons of this present Parliament assembled, and by the authority of the same:— That his subjects and the commonalty of this his realm, from henceforth in no wise be charged by any such charge, exaction, or imposition, called a Benevolence, nor by such like charge; (4) And that such exactions, called Benevolences, before this time taken, be taken for no example to make such or any like charge of any of his said subjects of this realm hereafter, but it shall be damned and annulled for ever. [Statutes of the Realm.]

The Statute against Benevolences.

This compendious anathema does not prevent a revival of benevolences by Henry VII., more especially memorable from the benevolence levied (but with

Revival of Benevolences by Henry VII.

quasi-Parliamentary consent of a great council)[1] in 1491, in collection of which the Commissioners are ordered to act on the principle that 'such as are sparing in their manner of living must have saved money, whilst those that live in a splendid and hospitable manner give ample evidence of wealth and ability to pay '—instructions which emanate from Archbishop Morton; the dilemma is therefore termed 'Morton's fork.'

Morton's fork.

In the person of Henry VIII. again appears a king little if at all inferior to Edward IV. in fulfilment of the requirements for personal collection of benevolences; but there is no record of any such use of his advantages. Moreover this king, though otherwise absolute, is not always fortunate in the levy of benevolences. Although over one irregularity of this sort he is careful to throw the cloak of respectability, an 'amiable graunte' he terms it—hoc praetexit nomine culpam, the *invitation* to *benevolence* is met by 'the cry of hundreds of thousands that they are English and not French, freemen and not slaves.' In Kent the royal Commissioners flee for their lives; and in the result, the king finds it necessary to cancel his commissions.

The 'amiable graunte' to Hen. VIII.

'The Petition exhibited to His Majesty by the Lords spiritual and temporal and Commons in the Parliament of 1627 assembled, concerning divers rights and liberties of the subjects'—the famous Petition

---

[1] See writ de pecunia mutuanda pro expeditione Franciae. Foedera, xii. 404; and the 'shoaring or underpropping Act,' 11 Hen. VII., 1494, c. 10. 'A remedy or means to levy a subsidy or benevolence before granted to the king.' See also Bacon, Hist. Hen. VII., Works, Spedding, vi. 121, 161.

of Right,[1] death warrant of benevolences and forced loans, tells its own story. After referring to the Statute against Tallage of 1306,[2] the Statute against Benevolences of 1483,[3] and other enactments to the same effect, it proceeds as follows :— *End of benevolences.*

By the statutes before mentioned, and other the good laws and statutes of this realm, your subjects have inherited this freedom, that they should not be compelled to contribute to any tax, tallage, aid, or other like charge not set by common consent in Parliament. *The Petition of Right.*

II. Yet nevertheless, of late divers commissions directed to sundry commissioners in several counties, with instructions, have issued; by means whereof your people have been in divers places assembled, and required to lend certain sums of money unto your Majesty, and many of them, upon their refusal so to do, have had an oath administered unto them not warrantable by the laws or statutes of this realm, and have been constrained to become bound to make appearance and give attendance before your Privy Council, and in other places, and others of them have been therefore imprisoned, confined, and sundry other ways molested and disquieted; (2) and divers other charges have been laid and levied upon your people in several counties by lord lieutenants, deputy lieutenants, commissioners for musters, justices of peace and others, by command or direction from your Majesty, or your Privy Council, against the laws and free customs of the realm.

. . . .

X. They do therefore humbly pray your most excellent Majesty :—That no man hereafter be compelled to make or yield any gift, loan, benevolence, tax, or such like charge,

---

[1] Entered in the Statute Book for 1627, 3 Car. I., as c. 1. Only so much of the 'Petition' as relates to the subject of impositions is given above.

[2] See above, p. 95.   [3] See above, p. 279.

without common consent by Act of Parliament; (2) And that none be called to make answer, or take such oath, or to give attendance, or be confined, or otherwise molested or disquieted concerning the same, or for refusal thereof.

. . . .

XI. All which they most humbly pray of your most excellent Majesty, as their rights and liberties, according to the laws and statutes of this realm; and that your Majesty would also vouchsafe to declare:—That the awards, doings and proceedings to the prejudice of your people in any of the premises shall not be drawn hereafter into consequence or example; (2) And that your Majesty would be also graciously pleased, for the further comfort and safety of your people, to declare your royal will and pleasure, That in the things aforesaid, all your officers and ministers shall serve you according to the laws and statutes of this realm, as they tender the honour of your Majesty, and the prosperity of this kingdom. [Statutes at Large.]

General Remarks.

Reign of Richard II. His enormous household. Such are the methods of taxation that assist in maintenance of the army of ten thousand persons that constitutes the 'household' of Richard II. In Edward's reign, France had become, as a French historian puts it, 'the farm of England: they worked only to pay the ransoms of king and nobles.' And receipts, to any number, for such ransoms may be found in the pages of Rymer's Foedera, our principal historical record. In Richard's reign, as may be remembered from the last words of Shakspeare's 'John of Gaunt, time-honoured Lancaster,' the com-
England let to farm. plaint is, that England 'is now leased out . . . like to a tenement or pelting farm,' for benefit, prac-

tically, of the king's favourites. And Fabyan remarks of this king that—'as for taxyng and exactyng of the commons, it was the usuall thynge with hym.'[1]

From these resources, partly, the bowmen for Azincourt are equipped, and the herrings paid for, so valiantly defended by Sir John Falstaff on the road to Orleans.

The Hundred Years War. Azincourt Battle of the Herrings.

Then comes the struggle for land. Now the Red Rose is in the ascendant, now the White, as Fortune turns her wheel. But at every revolution, battle; confusion; noise, and garments rolled in blood; prodigious slaughter of landowners; statutes, gleaning the refuse of the sword; and lastly, confiscation of the lands of the 'party adverse.' Nearly one fifth of the land in the kingdom, according to Sir John Fortescue, comes at one time or another into the hands of Edward IV.

The Wars of the Roses.

To state that during this contest the old nobility are absolutely swept away, is to use a high-coloured expression, admissible, perhaps, if for the purpose only of directing attention to a circumstance which, in its general bearings, it is absolutely essential to keep in mind in study of subsequent English history. The old nobility do not, however, perish to a man; as did the Fabii in the ambuscade, who *all* went, *all* perished. But they do perish as a powerful class. Many perish by the sword, for this now is not ordinary fumbling of tournament, or pastime of warfare with French chivalry; many, by the executioner's axe; and many wander in exile on the Continent, melancholy pictures for

[1] Chron. Sept. Pars Rich. II.

Commynes—relations of kings, in want and rags; and Plantagenets, begging their bread in the train of the Duke of Burgundy.[1] What remain never henceforth fill the same position of importance in the State. The old feudal nobility are no more, and Warwick is indeed, and not only in picturesque nomenclature, the 'last of the Barons.' What Hall terms 'the Politike Gouvernance of Kyng Henry the VII.,' in summary of his reign, is principally directed towards prevention of any re-establishment of the old feudal nobility. Hence his revival of the Star Chamber.[2] Hence his rigid enforcement of Statutes of Liveries:—' My Lord ' (this to De Vere, Earl of Oxford), 'I thank you for your good cheer, but in respect of your retainers, my attorney-general will speak with you.' Wise precaution against new king-makers. Gentle prelude to the 'Heads off' of his violent son,[3] and the collared 'dogs' of his imperious granddaughter. By these means Henry firmly establishes what has been termed, with a view to mark the constitutional change introduced first under Edward IV., 'the New Monarchy,' between which and the usual term for its later development, 'the despotism of the Tudors,' there is little practical difference.

According to Sinclair, Henry VII. 'probably re-

[1] Mémoires, Dupont, i. 231.   [2] See 3 Hen. VII., 1487, c. 1.
[3] Henry VIII. appears to have been so confident in the success of his policy as to recommend it to the French king, for application in that kingdom. At the 'Field of the Cloth of Gold,' in allusion to the haughty bearing of the Constable de Bourbon:—'If I had a similar subject in my kingdom,' said Henry to Francis, 'I would not long leave his head on his shoulders.' Guizot, Hist. de France; Michelet; &c.—This was indeed New Monarchy.

ceived more money, and spent less than any of his predecessors on the throne of England.' But his demands for grants are not frequent, the object of the king's parsimony being, indeed, to avoid any necessity for appeal to Parliament. Nor, with the exception of the tendency towards benevolences hereinbefore noticed, is there any attempt to levy taxes without authority of Parliament. To the rapacity in collection of revenue shown by the king's creatures, Richard Empson and Edmund Dudley, and to his strict enforcement of the feudal rights of the Crown, is due the fiscal disrepute of the reign. Empson and Dudley.

The first outcome of the 'all excellent things that might be hoped,' on the accession of Henry VIII. is the rapid dissipation by the handsome and lusty young king, in tournament, masquerade, feasting, and that expedition to France memorable for the 'Battle of the Spurs,'[1] of the two millions accumulated by his predecessor. The reign of Henry VIII.
1513.

Then follows the Wolsey period. More feasting and revelry, but a policy of peace and alliance with France, and the meeting of the two monarchs on 'The Field of the Cloth of Gold.' At home, concentration of authority; a cardinal, legate of the Pope, but himself in revenues, in palaces, in number of household, in magnificence, in authority, practically Pope; but withal ever submissive to the royal will. All verges towards absolute despotism, except in this, that the king has not the power of the purse. For, when desire The Wolsey period.
1520.

---

[1] For spurs were used more than swords. Amongst the prisoners were La Palise, De Longueville, and Bayard. Guizot, Hist. de France, ii. 559.

Despotism in all but the power of the purse.

1523.

for military glory and the re-conquest of his 'hereditary dominions in France,' urges him to war, and money is required to meet a war expenditure, and a forced loan is tried, and produces little, and Parliament is summoned, and a grant of a fifth from the laity is requested, and hardly half the required grant is conceded, and subsequently an attempt is made to levy tax by royal commission and by a benevolence, and resistance is encountered in London, Kent, and Suffolk—that is, when it comes to the point, the king yields, and releases the royal demand.

The fall of Wolsey.

The fascination of the royal lover by Anne Boleyn, and the fall of the great minister who opposes, as involving an irremediable rupture with Catherine's imperial nephew, the will of the amorous and headstrong king, form the next scene.

The Cromwell period

The decade that follows is the Cromwell period, with an ecclesiastical policy, and the suppression of all that opposes it. The nation, accustomed to the existence of practically supreme ecclesiastical authority at home, easily acquiesces in the rejection by the king of asserted domination abroad. The Statute of Appeals is passed.[1] The firstfruits of archbishoprics and bishoprics in England are not henceforth to be paid to the Bishop of Rome, otherwise called the Pope.[2] 'The intolerable exactions of great sums of money claimed to be taken out of this realm by the Bishop of Rome, called the Pope,

TheStatute of Appeals.

---

[1] 24 Hen. VIII., 1532, c. 12. 'For the restraint of appeals;' 25 Hen. VIII., 1533, c. 19. 'The submission of the clergy and restraint of appeals.'

[2] 25 Hen. VIII., 1533, c. 20. 'An act for nonpayment of firstfruits to the Bishop of Rome.'

and the see of Rome, as well in pensions, censes, peter-pence, procurations, fruits, suits for provisions, and expeditions of Bulls for archbishoprics, and bishoprics, and for delegacies, and rescripts in causes of contentions and appeals, jurisdictions legatine, and also for dispensations, licenses, faculties, grants, relaxations, writs called *perinde valere*, rehabilitations, abolitions, and other infinite sorts of bulls, breeves, and instruments of sundry natures, names, and kinds, in great numbers heretofore practised and obtained, otherwise than by the laws, laudable uses, and customs of this realm should be permitted, the specialities whereof being over long, large in number, and tedious here particularly to be inserted'—'whereby,' says the Act, 'the subjects of this realm, by many years past have been, and yet be greatly decayed and impoverished'—these—a long roll of the loaves and fishes—are all abolished.[1] Briefly, 'the extort exactions of innumerable sums of money craftily exhausted out of this realm by colour of the said usurped authority of the Pope, are removed.'[2] And, finally, the king is declared to be 'the only Supreme Head in earth of the Church of England, called Anglicana Ecclesia.[3]

The first blow of 'the Hammer of the Monks'[4]

Prohibition of the intolerable exactions of the Pope.

The king head of the Church.

Dissolution of the

[1] 25 Hen. VIII., 1533, c. 21. 'An act concerning peter-pence and dispensations.'
[2] See Preamble to 32 Hen. VIII., c. 24.
[3] 26 Hen. VIII., 1534, c. 1. 'The King's Grace to be authorised Supreme Head.'
[4] Cromwell was termed 'The Hammer of the Monks.' Thus Sprenger's famous Manual of the Inquisition was termed 'a Hammer for the Sorceress,' Marteau pour les sorcières, Malleus maleficarum. Michelet, Hist. de France, vii. 86, 126. Thus, also, subsequently Prynne's enormous quarto was termed 'Histrio-mastyx,' a Whip for the Stage Player.

<small>monasteries.</small> destroys only the lesser monasteries (1536). The greater abbeys fall subsequently in 1539. The other strokes of the king's minister are with a sharper instrument, and fall on whatever of learning or feudal power opposes or seems to oppose the establishment <small>'The Terror.'</small> of royal supremacy in the Church.[1] Bishop Fisher, Sir Thomas More, the leaders of the 'Pilgrimage of Grace' in the north, and, in the west, Henry Courtenay, Marquess of Exeter, and Lord Montague, elder brother of Cardinal Reginald Pole, share the same fate; and there is a sad scene by the block-side between the executioner and old Lady Salisbury, her gray hairs dabbled with blood.

<small>Fall of Cromwell.</small> Cromwell himself follows next, for, though considerations of policy render it advisable to endeavour to conciliate the North German powers, with a view to a combination against Charles V. as the principal opponent to be feared to the progress of the Reformation, and Cromwell may rightly have advised the marriage with the Protestant princess, still he who forges the link to bind Henry to too plain a wife works in peril—the peril of his head. Between the Queen as she is and Holbein's portrait of Anne of Cleves the difference is too great. Accordingly, on Cromwell quick work is done, as <small>1540.</small> indeed he requests it may be, the quick work of those times.

It has been observed by an illustrious writer[2] that 'the variations of policy in this reign have generally

---

[1] Henri dressa d'une main des échafauds pour des catholiques, de l'autre des bûchers pour les protestants qui refusaient de souscrire le symbole et d'approuver le gouvernement que la nouvelle église recevait de lui. Guizot, Charles I. i. 132.
[2] Mackintosh, Hist. Engl. ii. 114.

some connection with revolutions in Henry's palace and bed.' Never was history of reign of monarch more personal. Throughout it is, as later on in France with Louis XIV.—'L'état c'est Moi.' The rupture of those bonds that enthralled us—our emancipation from foreign hierarchic domination, is a personal act of the king; to whom we owe it that our Church is the Church of England, and not part of the Church of Rome. The rest is also personal and, in the main, a fearful chronicle. The page of history is bespattered with blood spots that will not 'out.' Not only those ladies whom, as it has been put, he 'first caressed and then mangled'—the 'little neck' of Anne Boleyn and other necks, and the gray hairs of Lady Salisbury, his relative, and seventy years old—but all the others, a long roll of names, many noble, others more illustrious than by ordinary nobility, in which are included Fisher, Surrey and More,[1] glue with their blood the label of 'tyrant' to this king. There is no mystery, no fog, no dimness about the acts of Henry VIII. and all that he did. All are written in clear page of history. And concerning them it is as easy to form an opinion, as concerning the king's person from the portrait of Henry, the beautiful young man, or the more familiar portrait of Henry, the royal Falstaff of later years, a mountain of flesh.[2]

Personal character of the reign of Hen. VIII.
Rupture of the Roman bonds.
'The river of blood.'
Queens.
Nobles.
Illustrious men.

---

[1] 'Quique sacerdotes casti dum vita manebat.'
'Quique pii vates et Phaebo digna locuti.'
'Quique sui memores alios fecere merendo.'

[2] The following is an interesting specimen of severe legislation extracted from the statute book of this reign:—'It shall be lawful for any of the king's subjects, if themselves do perfectly know, or by vehement presumption do

Distribution of the lands of the monasteries and abbeys,

The dissolution of the monasteries (completed by suppression of the greater monasteries, 1539), a source of wealth ever within reach of the king on an emergency, has been termed 'the killing of the goose that laid the golden eggs.' Their lands enriched the courtiers, to whom they were lavishly granted—the new aristocracy, Russells, Cavendishes, Fitzwilliams, rather than the royal exchequer. And the same may be said of the lands of 'the Knights of Rhodes, otherwise called Knights, or Friers of the religion, of St. John of Jerusalem in England, and of a like House in Ireland,' which, after a life provision for the two Priors and certain of the confreres, were granted by Parliament to the king in 1540. The principal reasons being: that

and Knights of St. John.

'the knights abiding in the parts of beyond the sea had unnaturally and contrary to their allegiances maintained the usurped power and authority of the Bishop of Rome, lately used and practised within this realm'; that it was 'dangerous to permit within the realm any religion being sparks, leaves and imps[1] of the said root of iniquity (*i.e.* usurped authority); that the isle of

---

perceive, any will, act, or condition of lightness of body in her which shall be the Queen of this realm, to disclose the same to the king, or some of his Council. . . . If the king, or any of his successors, shall marry a woman which was before incontinent, if she conceal the same, it shall be high treason; and so shall it be in any other knowing it, and not revealing it to the king, or one of his council, before the said marriage, or within twenty days after. . . . If the Queen, or wife of the Prince, shall by writing, message, words, tokens, or otherwise, move any other to have carnal knowledge with them, or any others shall move either of them to that end, then in the offender it shall be adjudged High Treason.' See 33 Hen. VIII. 1541. c. 21. ss. 7–10.

[1] Imp—a shoot, a sprout, a sprig (Johnson). It is thus used by

Rhodes, from which the said Religion took their old name, is surprised by the Turk; and that it were better that their possessions in this realm should rather be employed and spent within this realm, for the defence and surety of the same, than converted to and among such unnatural subjects.'[1]

'Tall in stature; beautiful in figure; with a countenance expressive of the highest dignity and sweetness; and with splendid health'[2]—such is the picture drawn by Bacon of the Queen who ruled England during the latter half of the sixteenth century, the chronicle of whose reign fills so brilliant a page in our national history. The two Cecils are there— Lord Burghley and his son, Robert; Walsingham, sage in council; Sir Thomas Gresham, prince of merchants; Howard of Effingham; rougher figures—the 'Sea-Dogs'—Drake, Hawkins, and Frobisher; more courtly countenances — Sir Walter Raleigh and Sir Philip Sidney; and Hooker; and Spenser; and Bacon, 'the wisest, greatest of mankind;' and 'the protagonist on the arena of modern poetry, and the glory of the human intellect,' William Shakspeare.[3]

The reign of Elizabeth.

But the prominent features in the history of the

Shakspeare, Henry V.:—'A lad of life, an imp of fame;' meaning, not 'diable d'importance' (see Le Sage, Diable boiteux), but in the sense of our 'sprig of nobility.'

[1] 32 Hen. VIII., 1540, c. 24. 'An Act concerning the possessions of St. John of Jerusalem in England and Ireland.'

[2] 'Aderant ei et externa; statura procera; corporis decora compages; summa dignitas oris cum suavitate; valetudo maxime prospera.' Bacon, In Felicem Memoriam Elizabeth. Works, v. 504.

[3] De Quincey. And, as to the orthography of the name Shakspeare,

292   HISTORY OF TAXES.

<small>Establishment of Protestantism.</small> reign are—the completion of the work commenced in the reign of Henry VIII., in firm establishment of Protestantism; and the loyalty amounting to enthu-
<small>Unbounded popularity of the Queen.</small> siastic devotion in the nation towards the Queen, its champion.

The loyalty and liberality of the Commons commence with the reign. The terms of the recital to the first subsidy Act of the reign[1] are not merely rigmarole of parliamentary draftsman.

<small>Animated recital to the first Subsidy Act.</small> 'The care which we do perceive your Majesty hath, most noble and redoubted sovereign, to reduce this realm and the imperial crown thereof now lately so sore shaken, so impoverished, so enfeebled and weakened, into the former estate, strength and glory, doth make us not only to rejoice much in the bounteousness of Almighty God, who hath so marvellously, and beyond all worldly expectation preserved your Majesty in these late difficult and dangerous times, but also to study and bend all our wits and force of understanding, how we may like loving and obedient subjects, follow our head, in this so noble and so necessary an enterprise.

'And considering with ourselves, that the decay hath been, besides many other things, especially in these three : First, wasting of treasure, abandoning of strength, and in diminishing of the ancient authority of your imperial crown; We do most earnestly and faith-

---

see de Q., Works, xv. 312. The letter of Sir F. Madden to which he there refers is printed in Archaeologia, xxvii. 113.

[1] Eliz., 1558, c. 21. 'An Act of a subsidie and two fifteenes and tenth, by the temporaltie.'

fully promise to your Highness, that there shall lack no good will, travel, nor force on your behalf, to the redress of all this: but we shall be ready, with heart, will, strength, body, lives and goods, not only to recover again that which is thus diminished, but if need be, to recover further (as far as right, and the will and pleasure of God shall suffer) the old dignity and renown of this realm.

'The time and place whereof doth not rest in us, but, as most reason is, in your most noble Majesty, with the advice of your honourable counsell; Nevertheless, since it doth so manifestly appear to us all what inestimable wasting and consumption of the treasure and ancient revenues of this realm hath been of late days, and what great new charges, and intolerable expenses your Highness is forced now to sustain, by reason of the decay and loss of parcel of your ancient crown: so, being not ignorant that no worthy enterprise, no noble attempt, no not so much as the preservation of a strong and puissant estate, may be without some mass of treasure presently to be had, and ready against all occurrents; Therefore we your most obedient and loving subjects, the lords spiritual and temporal, and the commons in this present Parliament assembled, to show our willing hearts and good minds, upon mature consultation had, have condescended and agreed with one voice and most entire affections, to make your Highness at this time a present, not such indeed as in our affections we do wish it, and as we know most certainly ought to be: but yet of your accustomed clemency which you do show to all men, we humbly on our knees pray your Highness not to reject it, but to accept our good wills and hearty desires herein, and that this our small gift may be by your Highness, the lords spiritual and temporal, and the commons in this present Parliament assembled, and by the authority of the same enacted.'

<small>Elizabeth's rule of conduct towards her people.</small>

Such feelings influenced the Commons towards their Queen. On the other hand, the precept of conduct observed by Elizabeth towards her people was—to rule by love rather than by fear. 'Gain their heart,' was Burghley's advice; and she did gain their heart. 'I have few such gifts,' says she kindly to the Mayor of Coventry, who presents a handsome and well-filled purse, 'it is a hundred pounds in gold!' 'Please your Grace,' replies the Mayor, 'it is a great deal more we give you. It is the hearts of your loving subjects.' And the Queen answers—'We thank you, Mr. Mayor, it is, indeed, a great deal more.'[1]

<small>She 'is of all men enchantingly beloved.'</small>

By acts of kindness such as this even more than by that eminently practical turn of mind, truly English in dislike of speculation and 'ideas;' that economy in fiscal management which avoided too frequent appeals to her people for grants of taxes; that sagacity in discernment of merit which surrounded her throne with great men for counsellors; the splendour in the dress, appearance and surroundings of their Queen; and that success in internal administration which established

---

[1] See Mackintosh, Hist. Eng. ii. 433. Appendix.

tranquillity and order at home, so conducive to the prosperity of the nation, did the Queen gain their heart. So that when, following after the attempted interference of the foreigner by the Bull of Deposition; the fearful accounts of the bloody system adopted by the Catholics, as announced by the fugitives from Alva's shambles in the Low Countries, and by La Motte Fénelon when he confirmed the news from France of the work of Charles IX. and Catherine de Medicis, advancing to the Queen through ranks of courtiers, silent, clothed in mourning—'stately forms, black-stoled, black-hooded, like a dream'; when, after this, last of all invasion is sanctioned by the antagonistic religion, and the Armada is blessed by the Pope, every feeling that can animate a nation as one man and combine all in resistance to foreign invasion is aroused; and the world holds record of no more enthusiastic exhibition of loyalty than that when the Queen, then queen for thirty years, no brother, no uncle, no relation near, alone, in disregard of all personal peril,[1] rides amongst her soldiers at the muster at Tilbury: Scene at the muster at Tilbury.

[1] Elizabeth's courage braved the precedents of numerous previous conspiracies. Many of these are notorious facts of history; but from a minute of Secretary Cecil, in 1560, it appears that every development of the arts of assassination (and a moment's consideration of Italian history at this date will show how various they were) was feared by the Queen's advisers. The minute is headed 'Certayne cautions for the Queen's apparell and dyett,' and states that: 'We think it very convenient that your Majestie's apparrell and specially all maner of thyngs that shall touche any part of your Majestie's body bare be circumspectly looked into,' and so on—concerning perfume in gloves, forrayn meate and dishes, &c., and the precaution of 'receiving wekely twice some preservatiff contra pestem et venena; keeping the back doores to the chamberors chambers safe,' &c. &c. Burghley, State Papers, Haynes, p. 368.

Elizabeth's words to her soldiers.

'Let tyrants fear: I have always so behaved myself, that, under God, I have placed my chiefest strength and safeguard in the loyal hearts and goodwill of my subjects. And therefore I am come amongst you at this time, not as for my recreation or disport, but being resolved, in the midst and heat of the battle, to live or die amongst you all; to lay down, for my God, and for my kingdom, and for my people, my honour and my blood even in the dust. I know I have but the body of a weak and feeble woman, but I have the heart of a king, and of a King of England too; and think foul scorn that Parma or Spain or any prince of Europe should dare to invade the borders of my realms.'

The struggle with Spain.

To meet the expenses of this contest with the most powerful monarch in Europe, Philip of Spain, master also of Naples, of Milan, of the Low Countries, and of the New World in the West, the nation granted the necessary supplies so willingly, that some persons, failing to regard the question from all points of view, have objected to Elizabeth's policy that her demands for subsidies were not frequent enough, that she ought to have asked for more, and to have made more direct preparations for meeting the power of Spain. But such proceedings would have involved the infraction of Elizabeth's rule of well-considered policy. Her love of splendour and pleasure, even her love of dress were gratified at the expense of rich noble, gentleman and citizen. The 365 hogsheads of beer consumed at the entertainment at Kenilworth cost her nothing; the two or three thousand pounds expended in each of those twelve (from three to four weeks) visits to Burghley

Elizabeth's fiscal policy.

To make the rich pay for splendour,

at Theobalds did not come out of the royal exchequer. 'When it pleaseth her,' writes Harrison, 'in the summer season to recreate herself abroad, and view the estate of the country and hear the complaints of her poor commons, injured by her unjust officers or their substitutes, every nobleman's house is her palace, where she continueth during pleasure.' And the gifts received by her include not only the New Year's gifts expected from the nobility and leading gentry, but miscellaneous gifts, from the memorable present of silk stockings to purses filled with gold pieces. The value of these and the produce of grants of monopolies brought the total average annual receipts to a considerable sum. Moreover, she borrowed freely from the rich, in anticipation of revenue, but repaid quickly.[1] And for the rest her precept was, as before stated, to apply to Parliament for grants as rarely as possible, and by economical administration to manage with the very moderate ordinary revenue of the Crown.

and to spare the people.

If, before entering on the period of struggle regarding the Divine Right of Kings, we return, and, recommencing the Tudor period, sweep the eye rapidly along the course of the agricultural, industrial, and commercial history of the country, we find that:—

Agriculture, trade, and commerce during the Tudor period.

The history of agriculture during the times of the Tudors appears at first sight to resolve itself into the history of cattle, and wool the product of sheep, both—the product of grass. As Camden's Welshman puts it of cheese—'ap curds, ap milk, ap cow, ap

1. Agriculture.

---

[1] On this subject see Hallam, Constit. Hist., i. 244–5.

grass, ap earth.' But let us look more closely into the matter, fixing for starting point—say the last quarter of the fifteenth century.

A.D. 1485–1602.

After the cessation of the Wars of the Roses and the dispersion of military establishments by strict enforcement of the Statutes of Liveries, the English landowner, to a certain extent turned, so to put it, the sword, not indeed into the usual metaphorical ploughshare, but rather into a shepherd's crook. 'Not long after the commencement of the reign of Henry VII. inclosures became more frequent in England, whereby quantities of arable land which could not be manured[1] without much people and families, were turned into pasture, being thereby easily managed by a few herdsmen; and tenancies for years, lives, and at will—whereon much of the yeomanry lived—were turned into demesnes.'[2]

Inclosures and conversion of tilled lands into pasture.

Annexation of the smaller holdings to domains.

This conversion of arable land into pasture and annexation of the smaller holdings prevailed as regards lands let to farm, as well as lands held in hand. The greater began to swallow up the lesser farms, and were turned into pasture for cattle and sheep.

Enormous sheep farms are created.

In 1487, 'the Isle of Wight, in the County of South,' has, in the terms of the statute—'become desolate and not inhabited, but occupied with beast and cattle, so

---

[1] Cultivated by hand labour. This use of the term is frequent in enactments of this date. Thus also Milton uses the word—'They mock our scant manuring, and require more hands than ours to lop their wanton growth.'

[2] Bacon, Hist. Hen. VII.

that if hasty remedy be not provided, it will be open, and ready to the hands of the king's enemies, which God forbid.'—And accordingly, an Act is passed, prohibiting the holding in that island more farms than one exceeding altogether ten marks rent.[1] Endeavour is also made to check the process of absorption on the mainland, by penal enactment against 'the decaying of houses of husbandry, or not laying of convenient land for the maintenance of the same.'[2] And further provision to the same effect is made, in 1515, by enactment[3] that :—'If any person shall decay a town, a hamlet, or house of husbandry, or convert tillage into pasture, the immediate lord of the fee shall have the moiety of the offender's land, until the offence be reformed.' State of the Isle of Wight in 1487.
Statutes of Tillage.

The principal reasons for this conversion of arable land into pasture, and this enlargement of farms in accumulation of previously distinct holdings, appear clearly from the recital to an Act of 1533 ;[4] which is sufficiently interesting to justify its insertion here in full :— Principal reasons for this conversion of tilled lands into pasture, as stated in an Act of 1533.

'Forasmuch as divers and sundry of the king's subjects of this realm, to whom God in his goodness

---

[1] 4 Hen. VII., 1487, c. 16. 'The penalty of taking more farms than one in the Isle of Wight.' This enactment has the desired effect: the island is re-peopled, and thus is enabled to repulse an attempt at invasion by the French. To this, allusion is made by Camden in his Britannia, sub tit. Isle of Wight, where an interesting account is given of the inhabitants, &c.

[2] 4 Hen. VII., 1487, c. 19.   [3] 7 Hen. VIII., 1515, c. 1.

[4] 25 Hen. VIII., 1533, c. 13. 'Concerning the number of sheep one should keep.'

Rise of a monied trader class, and increased demand for farms, hath disposed great plenty and abundance of moveable substance, now of late within few years have daily studied, practised, and invented ways and means how they might accumulate and gather together into few hands, as well great multitude of farms as great plenty of cattle, and in especial sheep, putting such lands as they can get to pasture, and not to tillage; Whereby they have not only pulled down churches and towns, and enhanced the old rates of the rents of the possessions of this realm, or else brought it to such excessive fines that no poor man is able to meddle with it, but also have raised and enhanced the prices of all manner of corn, cattle, wool, pigs, geese, hens, chickens, eggs, and such other, almost double above the prices which have been accustomed; By reason whereof a marvellous multitude and number of the people of this realm be not able to provide meat, drink and clothes necessary for themselves, their wives and children, but be so discouraged with misery and poverty, that they fall daily to theft, robbery, and other inconveniences, or pitifully die for hunger and cold; And as it is thought by the king's most humble and loving subjects, that one of the greatest occasions that moveth and provoketh those greedy and covetous people so to accumulate and keep in their hands such great portions and parts of the grounds and lands of this realm from the occupying of the poor husbandmen, and so to use it in pasture, *and 'the great profit that cometh of sheep.'* and not in tillage, is only the great profit that cometh of sheep, which now be come to a few persons hands of this realm, in respect of the whole number of the king's subjects, that some have 24,000, some 20,000, some

GENERAL REMARKS. 301

10,000, some 6,000, some 5,000, and some more, and some less; By the which a good sheep for victual, that was accustomed to be sold for 2*s.* 4*d.*, or 3*s.* at the most, is now sold for 6*s.*, or 5*s.*, or 4*s.* at the least; a stone of clothing wool, that in some shires of this realm was accustomed to be sold for 1*s.* 6*d.*, or 1*s.* 8*d.*, is now sold for 4*s.*, or 3*s.* 4*d.* at the least; and in some countries where it hath been sold for 2*s.* 4*d.*, or 2*s.* 8*d.*, or 3*s.* at the most, it is now sold for 5*s.*, or 4*s.* 8*d.* the least, and so are raised in every part of this realm; Which things, thus used, be principally to the high displeasure of Almighty God, to the decay of the hospitality of this realm, to the diminishing of the king's people, and to the let of the cloth-making,[1] whereby many poor people have been accustomed to be set on work; and in conclusion, if remedy be not found, it may turn to the utter destruction and desolation of this realm, which God defend.'

'The several enormities that do ensue by the greedy desire of having many sheep.'

The remedy for these evils provided by the statute is—a limitation of the number of sheep in farmers' hands; 'none shall keep above 2,000[2] sheep, exclusive of lambs, at any one time.' But this restriction is not to extend to sheep kept on any man's own lands of inheritance—his 'demesne lands in hand' in England or Wales, or to spiritual persons keeping sheep on their own lands.[3] Secondly, no man is to hold more than two farm-

Attempt to diminish the evil. 1. By limitation of the number of sheep to be kept by any one farmer.

---

[1] This must be taken to refer to home labour in cottages. The manufacture in the aggregate was rapidly increasing.

[2] The number of the hundred of sheep is not the same in every county. In some counties 'the great hundred of six score' prevails; it is, therefore, enacted that, for the purposes of the Act, six score sheep are to be accounted an hundred.

[3] See ss. 7, 16.

2. By prohibition of holding more than two farms, and enforcement of the Statutes of Tillage.

houses with lands belonging; and if two such 'holds' are taken he is required to reside in the parishes where they be, upon penalty of 3s. 4d. for every week of absence. And lastly, the statutes of 1487 and 1515, before mentioned, concerning the decay of towns and the maintenance of husbandry, are continued in force.

These enactments prove no more than so many sticks stuck up to stop a tide. Riches increase; the demand for land continues, and the demand for wool. 'Shepe in myne opynyon,' writes the author of the Book of Husbandry, published in the following year, 1534, ' is the most profytablest cattell that man can have;' and such was the universal opinion at that time. After the passing of the Act, as before, ' quycksettynge dychynge and hedgeyng' continued on the increase; farms as well as domains enlarged their boundaries day by day, and tilled lands were still converted into pasture for cattle and sheep.

Tax imposed on wool and sheep, in 1548.

The importance sheep had acquired in times of Edward VI. may be illustrated, appropriately, in a volume treating of fiscal subjects, by reference to the subsidy Act of 1548,[1]—a proposal, in effect, to place the burden of taxation on the sheep's back; by which, after a curious and lengthy recital, touching 'the present state of the world, what great troubles be in all places;' . . . . ' perils from the enemies of the king the realm and the protestant religion;' personal preparations made to meet any foreign power; and con-

---

[1] 2 & 3 Edw. VI. c 36. 'An Act for the reliefe granted to the king's Majesty, out of sheep, clothes, goods, debts, &c., to be paid in three years.'

fidence that God will 'have special regard and eye to this little realm, and us his poor servants and little flock, taking to his charge and defence our little shepherd till years and strength make him better able to bicker with his enemies'—grants, for the purpose of 'making a mass of money to relieve and maintain the great and inestimable charges, &c., &c.':—A subsidy charged, (1) on all cloth made for sale in England, at the rate of 8$d.$ in the £ of the value; and (2) on sheep, at the rate of: for every ewe, 3$d.$; for every wether, 2$d.$; and for every sheep kept on a common, 1½$d.$

These taxes are granted for three years; but difficulties in collection lead to their abandonment in the following year, when 'the relief granted to the king out of sheep and clothes' is released, in consideration of the grant of an additional subsidy on goods.[1]

How wide spread was the demand for land, extending not only to those merchants and townsmen 'to whom God in his goodness had disposed great plenty and abundance of moveable substance,' but also to the well-to-do but less rich of the industrial population, is evidenced by the terms of an Act of Queen Mary's reign, one of the many Acts in Tudor times relating to the decay of towns.[2] This class, enriched by industry under the strong rule of the Tudors, and secure from rapacious hands outside the town wall since termination of the reign of men in armour, hastened to indulge the propensity to rural life to this day a marked characteristic

The decay of towns.

[1] 3 & 4 Edw. VI. 1549, c. 23.
[2] 1 Phil. & Mar. 1554, c. 7. 'An Act that persons dwelling in the country shall not sell divers wares in cities or towns corporate, by retail.'

of our countrymen; and began to live in the country frequenting the town only for purposes of business. The Act recites that :—' Before this time the ancient cities, boroughs, towns corporate and market towns within the realm of England have been very populous, and chiefly inhabited with merchants, artificers and handicraftsmen. . . . . . by reason whereof, the said cities, boroughs and towns corporate did then prosper in riches and great wealth, and were as then not only able to serve and furnish the King and Queen's Majesties, and other their noble progenitors Kings of this realm, as well with great numbers of good able persons, and well furnished, meet for the wars, as also then charged, and yet chargeable with great fee-farms, quindismes, taxes, and divers other payments to the King and Queen's Majesties, which at this present they be not able to pay and bear, but to their utter undoing, being few in number to pay and bear the same; but also the same cities, boroughs and towns corporate are likely to come very shortly to utter destruction, ruin and decay.' And the cause of decay is stated to be: that ' linen-drapers, woollen-drapers, haberdashers and grocers dwelling in the countries out of the said cities, boroughs, towns corporate and market towns, do not only occupy the art and mystery of the said sciences in the places where they dwell and inhabit, but also come unto the said cities, boroughs, towns corporate and market towns, and there sell their wares.' . . . . . .
' For remedy whereof, and for the better amendment of the said cities, boroughs, towns corporate and market towns, and to the end the same cities, boroughs and

The cause being the exodus of traders.

towns corporate may be better able to pay the said fee-farms, and also to bear the other ordinary charges within the same, and to furnish the King's and Queen's Majesties with number of able persons, like as they heretofore have done in times past in times of war,' the retail sale (except in open fairs) of any woollen cloth, linen cloth, haberdashery wares, grocery wares, or mercery wares in towns by persons inhabiting and dwelling in the country any where, is henceforth prohibited: unless they become free of a guild or liberty of the town, and there ' dwell or inhabit.'

The exodus from town to country cannot indeed be prevented; but as regards the class to which the statute refers, the burst of townsman into the open country is retarded till he is sufficiently rich to maintain both 'country box' and 'place of business' in town. In the main, therefore, the land history of the period undoubtedly is: Landowner increasing pasture for cattle and sheep; farmer with demand for larger farms and increased pasture for cattle and sheep; successful merchant and adventurer and successful tradesman or other townsman turning, whenever possible, into landowner or farmer, and following the practices of existing landowners and farmers. And this continues down to times of the civil war, involving of course inclosures and depopulation. 'Churches and houses go down together,' as it is strongly put—' Churches and towns are demolished,[1] and the people eaten up like

[1] The Catholics of the Middle Ages left us an inheritance of churches more than doubly sufficient for the wants of the Reformed communities which succeeded them; and it is only now, when the demand for church accommodation has overtaken the supply, that we should be glad if many

bread, to satisfy the greedy desires of a few, who do waste profusely as they do gather together unconscionably, and bring on their posterity that Wo which is pronounced to those that lay house to house and field to field, to dwell alone in the midst of the earth.'[1]

Agriculture in certain particulars.

But do not from this hastily infer no progress made in other directions. The first and leading Georgic has, certainly, for subject the care of cattle and wool-producing sheep; but Abel, the herdsman, does not wholly put an end to Cain, the tiller of land, as a quaint author puts it. For, in the first place, that considerable allowance must be made for exaggerated statement is clear, from information we have that, on suspension of the provisions of the Acts prohibiting the export of grain, by royal licence, under power conferred by the Acts, 'the country people began to ply their husbandry more diligently than formerly, by breaking up grounds that had remained untilled since all memory of man.'[2] And in the next place, we know that, as wealth increased in the hands of the new landholders, more care was taken, more capital was expended, and more hands were employed, in the cultivation of lands under tillage.

Wheat, barley and oats.

Nevertheless, undoubtedly, during the whole period, the cultivation of wheat is, except perhaps in those parts of Hertfordshire and Bedfordshire which produce the best wheat and barley, if not at a standstill, remarkably slow in advance. Long subsequently to this, the usual bread of the poorer sort of people is still

---

of those which, in Elizabeth's time, were deserted and left to fall to ruin, could be reappropriated to their original purposes. Fergusson, Hist. Mod. Architect. 273.

[1] Speech of Lord Keeper Coventry, June 17, 1635. Rushworth, ii. 205.
[2] Camden, quoted Anderson, Commerce, ii. 117.

made of barley,'[1] and 'hearty and wholesome bread for men' made of oats is consumed in some parts of England, Lancashire producing the best oat crop.[2]

Before the middle of the sixteenth century, however, treatises are written on agriculture; and, ere its close, we find that buckwheat is sown after barley; beans (specially a Leicestershire crop) and peas are mentioned as common crops; and lime and marl as common manures. *[Treatises on Agriculture. Buckwheat, beans, and peas.]*

Saffron, a plant brought into England, according to Camden, in the time of Edward III., and considered to possess such special virtue that Fuller attributes to its use his recovery from the small-pox, continues to be cultivated chiefly in Essex and Cambridgeshire, particularly in Essex near Saffron Walden, which, as the same author observes, it may be said to have coloured with its name. *[Saffron.]*

Hemp is also a common crop, and flax,[3] though not a tenth part of the flax spent in the kingdom is of native growth; the rest is imported. *[Hemp and Flax.]*

Hops, introduced from Artois in the Netherlands early in the reign of Henry VIII., though, even subsequently to this, considered by the citizens of London calculated 'to spoyle the taste of drynk and endanger the people,' and therefore ranked with coals, which 'in regard to their stench,' they considered another nuisance,[4] are also cultivated to a limited extent, and *[Hops.]*

---

[1] See Proclamation concerning malt and hops. Foedera, xx. 157.
[2] Fuller, Worthies, i. 537.
[3] See 24 Hen. VIII. 1532, c. 4; 33 Hen. VIII. 1541, c. 17, s. 2; 5 Eliz. 1562, c. 5, ss. 28, 29.
[4] Petition of the City of London to Parliament in 1649.

indeed have legislative sanction in the provisions of the Statutes of Tillage [1] which exempt land set with saffron or hops, or sown with hemp, flax, woad or madder, from the lands required to be reduced again to tillage for corn. In 1547, a treatise is written concerning the cultivation of hops. In 1562, they are mentioned in the 'Five Hundred Points of Husbandry' by Tusser, as a well known crop. And their use, henceforth, is confirmed by increase in frequency of long sea voyages, augmenting the demand for beer that will keep, and consequently the demand for hops, as the best if not the only known preservative. At first, however, the native producer encounters considerable competition from abroad: for the quantity of foreign hops imported annually must have been considerable, when an Act of Parliament estimates the loss to the subjects of the realm by 'late great frauds and deceits in the false packing of foreign hops with leaves, stalks, powder, sand, straw, loggets of wood, dross, and other soil, for increase of the weight thereof' at 'the value of £20,000 yearly at the least, besides the danger of the subjects healths.' [2]

The kitchen-garden.
Carrots, cabbages, turnips, and the potato.
Fruit trees. The Cherry

Turn into the kitchen garden. You will find abundant produce of carrots, cabbages, turnips and rape, and the 'batata,' imported from Virginia, and which Raleigh, as we know, was the first to plant in Ireland. You may gather from the tree the finer sort of cherry, another Flanders importation of royal Henry, first planted in Kent, where during his reign it spread

---

[1] See 5 & 6 Edw. VI. 1552, c. 5, &c.
[2] 1 Jac. i. 1604, c. 18. 'An Act for avoiding of deceit in selling, buying or spending corrupt or unwholsom hops.'

to 32 parishes, welcome addition to sorts previously known, and here existing since Roman times,[1] or the 'large fine pale gooseberry,' which we also owe, according to Anderson, to the same royal introduction; the pippin, said to have been first planted here in Leicestershire, prior to Kent, about 1583 ;[2] and a more delicious fruit—the Armenian apple—the lesser peach, which now endeavoured, with such sun as may pierce through our cloudy skies, to keep up that reputation for early ripening to which it owed the name of praecoqua, praecocia, or, as we termed it first, 'apricock.' *Gooseberry.* *Pippin and* *Apricot.*

For ages the Hive had supplied to us in this country what was wanting from lack of sugar. Bees form a favourite subject for every writer on the agriculture of this period; and the utility of their labour has statutory recognition in the Act of 1581, which states that :—' By the goodness of God this land doth yield great plenty of honey and wax, so as not only to suffice the necessary uses of the Queen's Majesty and her subjects, to be spent within the realm, but also great quantity to be spared, to be transported unto the realms and countries beyond the seas, by way of merchandize, to the great benefit of Her Majesty and the realm.'[3] *Honey.*

Lastly may be mentioned, an illustrious stranger *Turkeys.*

---

[1] See Wright, Dom. Manners, Loudon, Anderson Comm., and Fuller, Worthies. It is difficult to reconcile Mr. Wright's observations regarding the abundance of cherries in preceding times with the proverb quoted by Fuller; according to which ' to eat cherries with a nobleman ' was a proverbial expression for extravagant expenditure on luxuries. As to kitchen garden produce in the Middle Ages, see Turner, Dom. Architecture; and, as to gardens (royal) and their produce in his time, the chapter in Bacon's works.

[2] Anderson, Commerce, ii. 157.

[3] See 23 Eliz. c 8. ' An Act touching the true making, melting, and working of wax.'

lately welcome from America to Europe. In the sitting room of the duchesse d'Étampes at Fontainebleau, for amusement of Francis I. in his long illness, were portrayed, in Rosso's handiwork, the results of recent discoveries, new animals and birds, intermixed with those previously known or fabulous, all things monstrous, all things strange, ancients and moderns in confused harum-scarum of Rabelais, and it is said that of these none was more bizarre in appearance than the bird that stood conspicuously strutting next the Elephant, a recent arrival from the new Indies, and therefore termed in France le D'Inde. We, however, appear to have first made his acquaintance at Aleppo, or to have first imported him from thence; wherefore he is termed to this day 'the Turkey.'

Increase in the vagrant and pauper classes.

In postscript to the foregoing observations on agriculture during Tudor times, a few lines may be added regarding a subject connected therewith, interesting in itself, and of no mean importance to anyone who would grasp the subject of taxation in this country in all its bearings, *i.e.* that condition of the rural population, which dating its effective origin from the dispersion of the great military establishments and the application of the economic, as opposed to the feudal principle in cultivation and management of estates, became, after the dissolution of the great monastic establishments and on continuance of the practice of converting tilled lands to pasture, a subject of grave importance to the rulers of this kingdom:—the increase in the vagrant class and the rise of the pauper class during Tudor

Origin of local taxation.

times; which led to Vagrant laws, Poor Laws, Local Administration, and Local Taxation.

ORIGIN OF LOCAL TAXATION. 311

In following up this subject we have to deal with four classes of persons:—1. The aged and impotent poor in their own parish—the local poor. 2. The aged and impotent poor wandering begging out of their own parish—the vagrant. 3. The idle and able-bodied in their own parish; and 4. The idle and able-bodied vagabond. Let us endeavour to treat the four classes, as far as possible, separately.

The original provision for the local poor by fourfold division of the tithes of parishes, for (1) bishop, (2) church, (3) poor, and (4) parson, was changed subsequently, on ample endowment of bishoprics from other sources, to threefold—for (1) church, (2) poor, and (3) parson. This is what is intended by reference to the 'oold custome, that thryd parte of the goodes of holy Chirche, shuld be spendyd within the parache, opon the pore and the nedy of the parache,'[1] rather than any strictly legal obligation: for if (as has been stated) at common law the parson and parishioners were bound to maintain the poor 'so that none of them die for want of sustenance,' it is difficult to see how the obligation could be enforced. In short, the obligation was religious, or customary, rather than strictly legal. But whatever its origin or its character, an existing obligation of the tithe owner to local charity appears to have been generally recognized in earlier times. It is referred to in petitions of the commons to the king regarding neglect of duty by aliens holding benefice, and parsons non-resident, as pluralists, or from other cause.[2] It

Original provision for the local poor out of the tithes.

---
[1] Par. Rolls, iv. 290. A.D. 1425.
[2] See Par. Rolls, ii. 173, 337; iv. 290.

passed with the tithes to those who subsequently, by purchase or by gift, acquired the benefices of parishes. And when these 'appropriations' of benefices, as the transfer was termed, were found in practice to cause 'divers damages and hindrances to the parishoners of divers places,' the legislature interfered, and required, on every appropriation of benefice subsequent to 1391, a specific provision for the poor parishioners, in a stated sum, according to the value of the church, 'to be distributed yearly to them in aid of their living and sustenance for ever.'[1] And this statutory recognition of a claim in the local poor was repeated, when subsequently certain of the Religious Houses, who were by far the largest impropriators, attempted to appropriate the vicar's share of tithe by nomination of one of their own order to perform the office of vicar: for thereupon it is enacted that the vicar shall be a secular man and not a religious, and shall be 'covenably endowed by the discretion of the ordinary,' not only for performance of divine service, and to inform the people, but also 'to keep hospitality,'—that is, assist the poor.[2]

Maintenance of the poor during the middle ages.

During the middle ages the poor were maintained by those liable to such obligation as aforesaid and by supplementary private benevolence; including, under one or the other head, the dole from the buttery hatch of abbey and monastery, establishments, be it remembered, that in many cases were under additional obligation to maintenance of the poor under directions of a

---

[1] 15 Rich. II., 1391, c. 6; 4 Hen. IV., 1402, c. 12.
[2] 4 Hen. IV. 1402, c. 12. 'In appropriations of benefices provision shall be made for the poor and the vicar.'

founder who had borne in mind the poor as well as the church.

The rise of free labour, the extinction of villeinage, and the commencement of movement in an agricultural population hitherto chained, as it were, to the land, have been mentioned previously in this volume; and it is at the date of the Statute of Labourers of 1388, made in attempt to restrain the movement and still localize labour, that we must in proceeding take up the aged and impotent wanderer—with one melancholy retrospect at that saddening spectacle during the middle ages, the blind, maimed and mutilated remnant of man left by his enemy impotent; who could hardly have been denied some share in the crumbs that fell from the table, wherever he might roam. Henceforth we may trace a tripartite system of: (1) Compulsion to work, for able-bodied poor under 60 years of age; (2) Punishment of able-bodied vagabonds, after which they are to be sent to the parish to which they belong; (provisions that have reference to classes 3 and 4 of the present subject) and, what is more immediately to the purpose, (3) Provision for aged and impotent persons wandering begging. And the plan of the first Act on the subject in dealing with the last mentioned class is to localize them, *i.e.* require them to remain where found at the date of the Act, and thus incorporate them, as it were, with the local poor: ' but if the people there be unwilling or unable to provide for them, they shall, within forty days, remove them to other towns within the hundred, rape or wapentake, or to the towns where they were born; where they shall

First movement in the agricultural poor. Statutes of Labourers.

Aged and impotent vagrants,

remain for the rest of their lives.'[1] The same principle governs the subsequent legislation on the subject. 'Every beggar not able to work,' provides an Act of 1494,[2] 'shall resort to the hundred where he last dwelled, is best known, or was born, and there remain,' upon pain of punishment, as in the case of the able-bodied vagabond.

are to be returned to their parishes.

To pass over an Act of 1503;[3] and take the next subsequent Act on the subject, viz., that passed in 1530.[4] The numbers of vagabonds and beggars had 'increased into great routs and companies, as evidently and manifestly it doeth and may appear;' and now it is found necessary to relieve the pressure of pauperism in particular parishes, by establishment of a system of licensed begging, 'by such poor, aged, and impotent persons as the justices think to have most need,' and may license to beg within a certain defined precinct; with whipping and the stocks for all unlicensed beggars. This is the first symptom of the break down of the old system. Five years after this, 'voluntary and charitable alms' are required by Act of Parliament, on which 'the aged and impotent poor are to be kept in the towns or parishes where they were born or have dwelt for three years, so as none of them shall be compelled to go openly in begging.' And all open or common dole and gifts of alms in money except to the common boxes and common gatherings to be established in every parish are prohibited.[5]

Origin of licensed begging.

Breakdown of the old system.

---

[1] 12 Rich. II. 1388, c. 7. 'The punishment of beggars able to serve and a provision for impotent beggars.'
[2] 11 Hen. VII. c. 2. [3] 19 Hen. VII. c. 12.
[4] 22 Hen. VIII. c. 12. [5] 27 Hen. VIII. 1535, c. 25.

ORIGIN OF LOCAL TAXATION. 315

After this comes the dissolution of the monasteries, and the grant by the king of their lands to persons who, if equally disposed to charity, naturally regard the subject from a different and more business-like point of view. It is necessary therefore to strengthen a second invocation of 'the charitable devotion of the good people' of the town or parish to the work of relieving the local poor,[1] by prescribed exhortation of the minister, backed up by exhortation of the bishop, in the case of unwilling contributors. The next step is to establish weekly collections of alms of the charitable devotion of the inhabitants of the parish; extending the area of collection in relief of 'places surcharged with poor.'[2]

The dissolution of the monasteries.

The minister and the bishop,

In 1562, the appointment of collectors, for weekly collection and distribution of alms in each parish, is made compulsory, and the inhabitants are enforced to charity, by providing that if any parishioner 'obstinately refuses to pay reasonably towards the relief of the poor, or discourages others,' the justices may tax him to a reasonable weekly sum, and, on any refusal to pay, may commit him to prison. In case of parishes surcharged with poor, power is given to the justices to license begging in one or more hundreds of the same county.[3] And by a subsequent Act, in 1572, is introduced a system of assessments to be made on the parishioners of every parish, for relief of the poor of the parish.[4]

and the justices are required to enforce the 'voluntary' system.

Assessments introduced.

[1] 3 and 4 Edw. VI. 1549, c. 16. 5 and 6 Edw. VI. 1552, c. 2.
[2] 2 and 3 Phil. and Mar. 1555, c. 5.   [3] 5 Eliz. 1562, c. 3.
[4] 14 Eliz. 1572, c. 5. 'How vagabonds shall be punished, and the poor relieved.'

Thus gradually, step by step, the legislature approaches the final conclusion. Before the close of the reign of Elizabeth, all name of mere benevolence is discarded. After rejection of a Bill introduced in the House of Commons for the relief of the poor out of impropriations and church livings,[1] the burden is laid on the inhabitants and occupiers of property in every parish; and now is definitely established a compulsory system:—Overseers of the poor, consisting of the churchwardens and four, three, or two substantial householders in every parish appointed by the justices. Provision for parish apprentices. Provision for stock of materials (flax, hemp, wool, thread, iron and other ware and stuff) for compulsory work of the able-bodied idle. Provision for sums of money for necessary relief of the aged and impotent poor; and, A compulsory poor's rate to cover all. This system continued till recent times to form the basis of our pauper administration.[2]

The Act for the relief of the poor, 1601.

Class 3:—the idle and able-bodied in his own parish may briefly be dismissed with the observation that the same principle governs the legislation regarding him during the whole period: he is to be compelled to work; and, as stated immediately above, the cost of stock of material for that purpose is charged on the parish.

Compulsory work for the idle and able-bodied.

Lastly, as regards class 4:—the idle and able-bodied vagabond. The minstrel, jouglour, trouvere, palmer, pilgrim, and soldier 'home from the war,' of the middle ages, all had their song to sing or tale to tell in return for the hospitality that enabled a vagabond

The enactments against vagabonds.

---

[1] D'Ewes, Journals, p. 561, A.D. 1597.
[2] 39 Eliz. 1597, c. 3; and 43 Eliz. 1601, c. 2. 'An Act for the relief of the poor.'

life, and were probably welcome in those days of stagnation and dullness. Subsequently when, so to put it, those parts were played out, it was observed that the hospitality, which may entertain angels unawares, did, as far as was known, entertain a considerable number of ragamuffins, rogues, and robbers. The able-bodied vagabond always, as experience had proved, a willing thief to say the least, had now become a nuisance without any redeeming feature; and when the first outpour (as de Quincey puts it) of sturdy vagrants on break up of the old feudal households augmented the foul stream, and the character of establishments in the country changed from houses more or less fortified to less protected residences—when the gentry no longer 'slept in fortresses of security,' and smaller households became the rule, the vagabond class threatened to become dangerous. Henceforth the enactments on the subject are frequent and severe. By the Act of 1530[1] (which established the system of licensed begging) the able-bodied vagabond taken begging is to be whipped, and then sworn to return to his place of birth or where he last dwelt for three years, and there put himself to labour. To which is added, in 1535, a provision that if he 'continue his roguish life, he shall have the upper part of the gristle, or his right ear cut off; and if after that he be taken wandering in idleness, or doth not apply his labour, or is not in service with any master, he shall be adjudged and executed as a felon.'[2]

After the first outpour on break up of the military establishments.

These provisions, however, are lenient in comparison with succeeding legislation, when by a second outpour, from the broken up monastic establishments, of

After the second outpour on dissolution of the monasteries.

[1] 22 Henry VIII. 1530, c. 12.   [2] 27 Henry VIII. 1535, c. 25.

many a stout, idle and lazy brother, the able-bodied vagabond class has increased to alarming proportions. In 1547 the legislature, after reciting that 'idleness and vagabondrie is the mother and root of all thefts, robberies, and all evil acts and other mischiefs, and that the multitude of people given thereto had always been here within this realm very great, and more in number (as it may appear) than in other regions . . . . that the laws made for repression thereof had not had success partly by foolish pity and mercy of them that should have seen them executed,' and much more in the same strain—clears the ground, by repeal of all previous enactments concerning vagabonds, and then falls on the lazy crew tooth and nail: The 'idle and loitering servant or vagabond shall be marked with a hot iron on the breast, with the mark of V., and adjudged to be slave to the same person that brought him, to have to him, his executors or assigns, for two years after; who shall take the said slave, and give him bread, water or small drink, and refuse meat, and cause him to work, by beating, chaining, or otherwise, in such work and labour as he shall put him unto, be it never so vile.' If he run away, 'he shall be marked on the forehead, or the ball of the cheek, with an hot iron, with the sign of an S., and further shall be adjudged to be slave to his master for ever. And if the said slave run away a second time, he shall be adjudged a felon.' Some leniency is shown towards clerks attainted and convict: for they are not to be burnt in the breast. But they are included in the general provision that follows, rendering it lawful for 'every person to whom any shall be

Extreme severity. The Slave Act of 1547.

adjudged a slave, to put a ring of iron about his neck, arm, or leg.'[1]

Severity has now reached the apogee.[2] These provisions, 'the extreamite thereof having been occasion that they had not been put in force,' are repealed in 1549; and the old system of licenses, whipping, stocks, &c. is re-established.[3] *Return to the old system of whipping and the stocks.*

In the reign of Elizabeth, attempts are at first made to check the increasing evil in the old heroic manner. The vagabond is to be 'greviously whipped, and burned through the gristle of the right ear, with a hot iron of the compass of an inch, and if he after do fall again into a roguish life, he shall suffer death as a felon,' and power is given to the justices of the shire to rate and tax every parish in the shire towards the relief of the prisoners in the common gaol.[4] Subsequently, in 1576, provision is made for conveying the rogue from constable to constable, till he come to gaol; and Houses of Correction are to be assigned in every county.[5] *Legislation during the reign of Elizabeth.*

But our manufacturing industry is now developing rapidly; commerce is on the increase; wealth accumulates, and more capital is expended and more labour employed in cultivation of land; and all these combine to mitigate the evil of vagabondage and to prompt the legislature to more calm and humane treatment of the subject. The 'gaoling, boreing through the ear, and death in the second degree' previously in force had been

---
[1] 1 Edward VI. 1547, c. 3.
[2] An apology may be due for use of the term at a date when already it has been whispered about that the earth moves and not the sun.
[3] 3 & 4 Edwd. VI. 1549, c. 16.
[4] 14 Eliz. 1572, c. 5.
[5] 18 Eliz. 1576, c. 3.

The Act of 1597.

repealed, and the old plan of whipping, &c., of the Statute of Henry VIII.[1] revived, some years before[2] the passing of the Act which closes our subject—the Act of 1597, for 'the punishment of rogues, vagabonds, and sturdy beggars.'[3] This Act, making another clean sweep of all previous statutes, gives power to the justices in quarter sessions to order the erection of Houses of Correction, and provide stocks of money and all things necessary for the same; and, after describing in lengthy roll those who are to be accounted 'rogues, vagabonds, and sturdy beggars,' enacts more humane provisions for their restraint and punishment. The vagabond is to be 'stripped naked from the middle upward, openly whipt until his body be bloody,' and then conveyed back to his parish and set to labour. A dangerous rogue may be transported to parts beyond seas, or judged perpetually to the galleys. Only in case of return from transportation without license, is the rogue to be punished with death as a felon.

The Rogue Roll of the Act.

The Rogue Roll of the Act is interesting not only as containing a particular description of the various forms of vagrancy existing at that date, but as including some special forms that have a previous statutory history of their own, and also not a few (to look down instead of up the current of time) reproduced almost verbatim in Mr. Mayhew's London Labour and London Poor.[4]

[1] 22 Henry VIII. c. 12. See above, p. 317.
[2] By 35 Eliz. 1593, c. 7, ss. 24, 25.
[3] 39 Eliz. 1597, c. 4.
[4] Vol. iii. 22. Compare item 1, 'Persons calling themselves scholars,' with C, 'Respectable Beggars,' 2, pretended ushers, &c.; item 2, 'Seafaring men pretending losses of ships and goods,' with D, 'Disaster

Lastly, it may be observed that this severity of the legislature in dealing with the able-bodied vagabond, or 'sturdy rogue,' (it matters not how we name him) during Tudor times, was but the expression of the prevailing or rather the general feeling of detestation with which he was regarded; and was in places supplemented by a sort of Jedwood justice or Lynch Law. For instance, the 'Beggars Litany' of that day mentions three places as special objects of hatred:—'Hell, Hull, and Halifax.' Hull was said to be terrible to them as a town of good government where they were certain to meet with 'punitive charity.' But why Halifax? and the answer is, that in Halifax a member of this lazy creed, caught in the act of stealing cloth, was, without legal proceedings, on th' instant cut short: for which purpose an engine was kept there, in form perhaps the nearest recorded approach to the subsequent Guillotine.[1]

General hatred of idleness at this date.

After the foregoing brief, and it may be somewhat imperfect statement of the course of legislation which ended in establishment of rates—a term generally used in regard to local as opposed to imperial taxation —for maintenance of the poor, the expenses of prisoners in gaol, and maintenance of houses of correction, let us pass on, as originally proposed, from country to town, from agriculture to trade and manufactures.

2. Internal trade and industry.

Not on the trader did the storm fall during the Wars of the Roses. He flourished on lower ground whilst the tempest raged above; and acquisitions by

Beggars,' 1, 'Shipwrecked mariners;' and so on. The Rogue Roll of 1597 is too long for insertion in these pages in extenso, and is incapable of succinct abridgment without mutilation.

[1] See Fuller, Worthies, ii. 494.

industry during those times, augmented subsequently under protection of the strong government of the Tudors, enable him, as we have seen, after practical removal, by the legislation of Henry VII. and Henry VIII., of the bars that had impeded access to landed estate, to enter the market as purchaser of land. Subsequently in those days of Elizabeth, when, as Shakspeare puts it: 'Every man eats in safety, under his own vine, what he plants; and sings the merry songs of peace to all his neighbours,' increasing in wealth, and in investments in landed estate, and quitting town and business for country life and pursuits, the trader supplies from the richer members of the class one for that quartet of figures—of which the others are, (1) younger brother, wedded perhaps to the daughter of lord mayor, alderman, or other city magnate; (2) successful merchant or adventurer; and (3) crown grantee of the lesser sort—who form that new gentry henceforth so important an element in our social system.

Enrichment of the trader class.

To come to particulars. From what industries, either previously existing, or newly introduced during the period, was this increase of wealth during Tudor times mainly derived?

The woollen manufacture.

At top of the industrial ladder, with none other for many rungs below, stood the manufacturer of wool. The woollen manufacture introduced practically, as before observed, by Edward III., developed with remarkable rapidity, and is prominent through the whole Tudor period. The effect produced on agriculture by the increased demand for wool has before been noticed. The wool interest is supreme at home, and on many occasions even directs our foreign policy: for 'Upon every stop of the vent of cloth, there cometh'—as subsequently remarked by Lord Keeper Coventry—[1] 'such outcries by the weaver, fuller, spinner, and wool grower himself' that they cannot be disregarded. Turn to the Statute Book. It is thick set, page after page, with enactments relating directly or indirectly to wool and the woollen manufacture. It reads like a farce of Patelin: 'Ba,' 'Ba,' Act after Act; and the reader is no less constantly recalled to this as the really important and governing subject, than the draper by the judge:—'Revenons à nos moutons. Revenons à nos moutons.' It will be sufficient for present purposes to draw, from this abounding source, enough to show the principal seats of the manufacture.

The Act of 1552 [2] is the leading Act on the subject, and was passed 'after great deliberation and advice of men of experience and discrete and sage knights and burgesses.' It regulates the length, breadth and weight of every cloth, kersie, piece of frize and cotton thenceforth to be manufactured; and mentions particularly: The broadcloth of Kent and Sussex and the town of Reading. Long Worcesters and Coventrys (both of which were of white cloth), and the coloured clothes of the said cities; and white clothes called short Worcesters. The coloured long clothes, coloured

Principal seats of the manufacture.

Kent and Sussex and Reading. Worcester and Coventry.

---

[1] Speech to the Judges in the Star Chamber 14th February, 1636. Rushworth, ii. 353.

[2] 5 & 6 Edward VI. c. 6. 'An Act for the true making of woollen cloth.' See also 4 and 5 Phil. and Mar. 1557, c. 5; 1 Eliz. 1558, c. 14; 8 Eliz. 1565, c. 7; 14 Eliz. 1572, cc. 10, 12; 18 Eliz. 1576, c. 16; 27 Eliz. 1585, cc. 17, 23; 35 Eliz. 1593, cc. 9, 10; 39 Eliz. 1597, c. 20, relating to northern cloth; and 43 Eliz. 1601, c. 10.

short clothes, and coloured clothes commonly called *Suffolk, Norfolk and Essex.* handy-warps and whites being handi-warps, of Suffolk, Norfolk and Essex. The whites and reds, broad plunkets,[1] azures, blues and other coloured cloth of *Wiltshire, Gloucester and Somerset.* Wiltshire, Gloucester and Somerset. Ordinary kersies and sorting kersies (made in any part of England). *Devonshire. Taunton and Bridgewater. Wales. The Northern Counties. Manchester, Lancashire and Cheshire. Tavistock.* Devonshire kersies called dozens. Broad clothes called Taunton clothes and Bridgewaters. Check-kersie and straits, (to which no locality is assigned), Welsh cottons and Welsh frizes, made within the shires of Cardigan, Caermarthen and Pembroke. Northern clothes. Dozens, and penistones or forest whites (to which no special locality is assigned). Manchester, Lancashire and Cheshire cottons. Manchester rugs, otherwise called Manchester frizes. And cloth made at Tavistock or elsewhere in Devonshire, commonly called Tavistock clothes.[2]

The places thus mentioned were the principal seats of the manufacture of cloth; and subsequent Acts on the same subject mention more particularly Godalming, in Surrey; Bocking, Westbarfold, Dedham and Cockshall (Coggershall), in Essex; the towns and villages near adjoining to the water of Strowd, in Gloucestershire; and Oxfordshire in connexion with the manufacture. Towards the close of the century, the industry of the north makes rapid advance; and a *Special Act concerning northern cloth.* special Act is passed for regulating the trade of cloth-making in the counties of York, Lancaster, and other counties north of the Trent, 'whereupon so many

[1] A kind of blue.
[2] The provisions of the Act are not to extend to Tavistock clothes; which are to be made and sealed as before accustomed.

thousands of the Queen's subjects do now live and are maintained.'[1]

On the Welsh border, the drapers, cottoners and frizers of Shrewsbury are engaged in an extensive trade in Welsh cottons and linings, commonly called cottons, frizes and plains; and, in the east, in the county of Norfolk, long famous for the worsted [2] trade, the woollen manufacture of Norwich raised that city to a position of special importance. Indeed, after that 'the Netherlanders, weary of the duke of Alva's cruelty, and hating the bloody Inquisition, had repaired thither in great numbers' introducing ' the manufacture of saies, baies and other stuffs subsequently in great request,' Norwich attained such eminence, that it is written of her:— *Shrewsbury.* *Greatness of Norwich.*

'So sufficient in all herself and so complete is she,
'That, if need be, of all the realm the mistress she might be.'[3]

'The trade and faculty of woollen card making and drawing of card wire' maintains thousands in London, Bristol, Gloucester, Norwich, Coventry and other cities *Woollen card making and card wire drawing.*

[1] See 39 Eliz. 1597, c. 20.
[2] Deriving name from Worsted, in Norfolk. As arras, from Arras, in Artois; cambric, from Cambray; calico, from Calicut; muslin, from Moussul in Mesopotamia, &c. &c.
[3] Camden's translation of:—

    Omnia sic adeo sola haec sibi sufficit, ut si
    Fors regno desit, haec caput esse queat.

The following short statement of the deceits by which the statutes for the true making and working of woollen cloth were frustrated is not without interest. It appears that 'straining, stretching, want of weight, flocks, sollace, chalk, flour, deceitful things, subtil sleights and untruths' were used in the manufacture; so that cloth 'being put in water was found to shrink, be rewey, pursey, squally, cockling, bandy, light and notably faulty, to the great dislike of foreign princes, and to the hindrance and loss of the buyer and wearer.' 43 Eliz. 1601, c. 10, s. 1. See also 4 Jac. I. 1606, c. 2.

and towns. And, when the home manufacture suffers from foreign competition from France, it is protected by a prohibition of further importation of foreign cards for wool for sale.[1]

<small>Cap and Hat Manufacture.</small>

The art of making woollen caps (which, indeed, has a legislative history of its own[2]) is used in the times of Elizabeth by great multitudes of Her Majesty's true subjects.[3] In 1570 about eight thousand people are maintained by the manufacture in London alone, and probably twice as many elsewhere in England: for 'capping sets fifteen distinct callings at work.' But the manufacture declines before the steady advance of the felt hat, notwithstanding an attempt made to stay the hand of fate, by enactments, in force from 1571 to 1597, requiring every one above the age of seven years, with certain exceptions—'some of worship and quality except,' as Fuller puts it—to wear, upon every sabbath and holyday, a cap of wool knit thicked and dressed in England.[4]

<small>Stockings.</small>

To take in detail all the other trades connected with wool would be tedious. Let us conclude with a word concerning stockings. When the nether stocks first parted from the upper stocks remains to this day a doubtful question; but there is no difficulty in fixing a date for the first introduction in this country of the manufacture of woollen stockings. It commenced in

---

[1] 39 Eliz. 1597. c. 14.
[2] See 22 Edw. IV. c. 5; 4 Hen. VII. c. 9; 3 Hen. VIII. c. 15; 21 Hen. VIII. c. 9; 7 Edw. VI. c. 8; 8 Eliz. c. 11; 13 Eliz. c. 19; &c. &c.
[3] 8 Eliz. 1565, c. 11. An Act for uttering of caps, and for true making of hats and caps.
[4] 13 Eliz. 1570. 19; repealed by 39 Eliz. 1597, c. 18, s. 45.

the times of Queen Elizabeth. That tall, beautiful and stately form, before mentioned,[1] was supported right royally. In a word, Elizabeth had a handsome leg, and, according to historians who deal with such subjects, knew it. And we are told that, careful of her charms, on receiving from Mrs. Montague a pair of stockings particularly well fitting, she expressed an intention of wearing no more cloth stockings, but only such as those then given her. But this well-known story does not help us; for these stockings, probably of Italian or Spanish make, were silk stockings, such as in the preceding reign Sir T. Gresham had, on a certain occasion, presented to Edward VI., a present which, according to Dr. Howell, 'was then much taken notice of.' Worsted stockings of native manufacture first adorned the English leg in 1564: when William Rider, 'an apprentice living against St. Magnus Church at the foot of London bridge,' chanced to see a pair of knit worsted stockings brought from Mantua in the lodging of an Italian merchant, and borrowing them, made a pair by the pattern, and presented them to William, Earl of Pembroke, the first wearer of such stockings in England.[2] The introduction of the method of knitting by wires and needles was followed by the invention by Mr. Lee of the stocking frame, in the last decade of the century.[3]

Invention of the stocking frame.

---

[1] See above, p. 291.
[2] Stow. Chronicle.
[3] See Commerce, ii. 172. Long after this, however, stockings were only worn by the richer classes. In Steele's 'Mock Funeral, or Grief à la Mode,' Sable, in reference to a search for a coat of arms for the deceased Alderman Gathergrease, says:—'Let him bear A pair of stockings, for he is the first of his family that ever wore one.'

Leather. After wool in importance comes leather; and the high price of the leather, and increase in all the branches of industry connected with the manufacture, had no small share in prompting that conversion of arable lands into pasture of which so much has previously been stated. One of the first Acts of the reign of Elizabeth has for object the reformation of the mystery of tanning of leather;[1] and several other Acts are passed subsequently in relation not only to tanners, but also to curriers, shoemakers, and other artificers occupying the cutting of leather; in hopes of 'remedying the goodness of leather and the excess prices thereof.'[2] Whilst abundance of raw material is secured to shoemakers and other artificers of the realm working in leather, by prohibition of exportation of leather, tanned or untanned, or any hides for sale abroad,[3] or any sheepskins, woolfells, shorlings, morelings or skins of any stag, hind, buck, doe, goat, fawn or kid:[4] though, in 1565, 'forasmuch as great multitudes of Her Majesty's liege people have been set on work by converting of sheepskins and lambskins into tawed leather and parchment,' the prohibition is removed as regards tawed leather of sheepskins and lambskins.[5] The girdlers also, and the saddlers, glovers, point-makers and such like handicraftsmen in London and other cities, towns, and

Tanners, curriers, and shoemakers.

Girdlers, saddlers, &c.

---

[1] 1 Eliz. 1558, cc. 9, 10. As to tanners, see also 2 & 3 Edw. VI. 1548, c. 11.

[2] Forming part of the long series of Acts termed Statutes of Cordwainers, *i.e.* Shoemakers, from Cordwain, Cordovan, leather from Cordova, in Spain—Spanish leather.

[3] 1 Eliz. 1558, c. 10; 5 Eliz. 1562, c. 8; 14 Eliz. 1572, c. 4; 18 Eliz. 1576, c. 9.

[4] 5 Eliz. 1562, c. 22.   [5] 8 Eliz. 1565, c. 14.

boroughs are 'in their said faculties greatly wrought and greatly set on work'; especially after the Act of 1562, which protects their crafts (and that of the cutler[1]) from foreign competition, by revival of the prohibition on the importation from parts beyond the seas of any 'girdles, harness for girdles, rapiers, daggers, knives, hilts, pummels, lockets, chapes, dagger-blades, handles, scabbards and sheaths for knives, saddles, horse-harness, stirrups, bits, gloves, points, leather-laces or pins ready made, for sale.[2]

Previously to 1524, when the manufacture of soap was first introduced in London, the white soap used there was imported from beyond sea, principally from Castile; the 'grey soap speckled with white, very sweet and good, from Bristol, sold in London for a penny the pound, and never above a penny farthing, also black soap for a halfpenny the pound.'[3] But notwithstanding the competition, Bristol still continued a considerable manufacture, principally of grey soap. For many years subsequent to this period there existed in the west of England few better businesses than that of a Bristol ' sope boiler.'

Soap.

The trades of the maltster and brewer continued to flourish: for ale was the national beverage, and to its potent effects was ascribed the strength of arm that drew the bow at Crécy and Poitiers, of the continued existence of which King Henry himself afforded evidence at the Field of the Cloth of Gold. Hops began

Maltster and brewer.

[1] See below, p. 331.
[2] 5 Eliz. 1562, c. 7, and see 3 Edw. IV. 1463, c. 4; 1 Rich. III. 1483, c. 12.
[3] Howell, Londinopolis, p. 208.

to be used in brewing; and the term 'beer', to designate the stronger sort of malt liquor.[1] The old saw ;—

> 'Hops, Reformation, carp and beer
> came into England in one year'[2]

serving to mark their practically simultaneous origin. Beer soon began to be brewed in considerable quantities for ships' stores and for exportation; and the remote predecessors of Bass and Alsopp are to be discovered in those brewers who, on export of their beer were required, by the statute of Elizabeth,[3] to bring into the kingdom, 'with a view to the preservation of our timber of late years greatly decayed and consumed within the realm,' a certain quantity of clap-board fit to make casks of, or else to return the barrels in which the beer was exported, or 'so much other good and sweet cask in quantity.'

Introduction of the manufacture of sail cloth.

Towards the close of the reign of Elizabeth, when our navy and shipping first became prominent, about 1590,[4] is introduced the manufacture of sail cloth—viz. the skill and art of making and weaving 'the clothes

---

[1] The license granted by Henry VII. to a Fleming to export fifty tuns of 'ale called beer' shows that the stronger form of malt liquor was known here before the reign of Henry VIII.; and Peter Vanet is mentioned as a 'beer brewer' of Greenwich in 1492. See Foedera, xii. 471, 485. It seems probable that in former times some other bitter than hops, as wormwood perhaps, was in use for preservation of malt liquor for land or sea service.

[2] The other readings are:—

1. Hops, Reformation, bays, and beer.
2. Turkeys, carp, hops, piccarel, and beer.

[3] 35 Eliz. 1593, c. 11. This exportation of beer was probably under royal license; for the prohibition of export of beer enacted by 1 & 2 Phil. and Mar. 1554, c. 5, appears not to have been removed till 1605 by 3 Jac. I. c. 11.

[4] 32 Eliz. See recital to 1 Jac. I. c. 24.

called mildernix and powle-davies, whereof sail-clothes and other furniture for the navy and shipping are made; heretofore altogether brought out of France and other parts beyond the seas.' And the 'perfect art and skill of this manufacture is subsequently practised and continued in the realm, to the great benefit and commodity thereof.' A considerable manufacture also exists of cables, halsors and other kinds of cordage for the navy and other ships;[1] and of ordnance—cannons, culverins, &c. *Cables, cordage and ordnance.*

Forks are as yet if not wholly unknown, certainly not in general use. They are an introduction from Italy in the reign of James the 1st.[2] But knives of the finer sort are now made in England. There are knives and knives, as the saying is; and of a coarse sort of knife the manufacture had long time existed at Sheffield. The typical miller of an earlier date 'wore a Sheffield whittle in his hose'; and this manufacture continued to flourish subsequently. But of the finer sort of knives the manufacture was commenced in England only as late as 1562, by one Thomas Mathews, on Fleet Bridge, in London.[3] *Knives.*

The manufacture of an inferior kind of glass existed in this country before the reign of Elizabeth; but in her reign 'glass makers were scant in the land,' as a writer of the period states, confirming the statement by adding: 'yet one there is as I do understand in *Glass.*

[1] Anderson, Commerce, ii. 174; 35 Eliz. 1593, c. 8.

[2] S.:—'Forks? what be they?' M.:—'The laudable use of forks, brought into custom here as they are in Italy, to th' sparing o' napkins.' Jonson, Devil is an Ass.

[3] Present state of England 1685, p. 77, quoted Anderson, Commerce, ii. 119.

Sussex, at Cheddingfold.' Moreover, what Camden says of 'the glasse made in Sussex' would probably apply to all glass made in the kingdom at this date;—that 'by reason of the matter or the making, I wot not whether, it is likewise nothing so pure and clean, and therefore used of the common sort only.' And this was probably the sort of glass sold by the 'glassmen'—the itinerant vendors licensed by the justices, who were specially exempted from the provisions of the Vagrant Acts. A manufacture of Venice-glasses appears to have been introduced about 1558, the finer sort made at a place called Crutched Friars in London, by an Italian; and fine flint glass little inferior to that of Venice is stated to have been made in the Savoy House in the Strand. But be this as it may, the fact is incontestable, that from the times of the first crusade in the 13th century down to the date of Colbert's successful establishment of the manufacture in France, Venice had practically a monopoly of good glass making. The price even of ordinary drinking glasses must have been considerable: for a courtier, who through Leicester, had begged of Elizabeth the plate of the Cambridge colleges as not required by such persons, when the Queen 'grants his asking with a smile' upon condition to find the scholars in drinking glasses, quickly drops the subject.

Plate. Of plate the manufacture must have been considerable. The possession of a quantity of plate was a fashion with the rich; and when Burghley leaves, at his death, no less than 14,000 or 15,000 pounds in weight of silver plate, this quantity is considered not large for a man of his rank. Moreover, the great amount of plate melted down, subsequently, for the purposes of the civil war, on both sides, is notorious. Butler more than once refers to the masses of plate brought to Guildhall on the Parliamentary side,

> 'They coined,' he writes, 'bowls and flagons
> 'into officers of horse and dragoons;
> 'and into pikes and musqueteers,
> 'stamped beakers cups and porringers,'[1]

and other articles are mentioned by him which it is surprising to find made of silver. There is, however, little legislation on the subject. Except an Act of 1487[2] relating to finers of gold and silver, and an Act of 1576[3] relating to the standards for plate; which it fixes at 22 carats for gold wares, and at 11 oz. 2 dwt. for silver wares. The standards having previously been for gold 18 carats;[4] and for silver, regulated by reference to the coinage—'of the sterling allay or better.'[5] The Act also limits the price to be paid for plate to 12d. the oz. besides the fashion, above the Queen's Exchange or mint price, in the case of gold plate; and 12d. the pound, besides the fashion, above the mint price, for silver plate.

The standard for gold and silver plate.

To proceed from inland industry to commerce, extending the scope of our survey to the countries we frequent, or indeed to the countries known to us.

3. Commerce.

[1] Hudibras. Part I.
[2] 4 Hen. VII. 1487, c. 2.
[3] 18 Eliz. 1576, c. 15. An Act for the reformation of abuses in goldsmiths.
[4] See 17 Edw. IV. 1477, c. 1.
[5] Except from 1542 to 1560, silver money had since the Conquest been regulated by a standard of 11 oz. 2 dwt. Between 1542–4 the standard was 10 oz.; between 1544–52 it was sometimes 6 oz., sometimes 4 oz., and once, in 1551, 3 oz. only.

During this period the world of ancient days changes into the world of modern days.

<small>The world on the map of the Christian Topography.</small>

The old world, according to the map of the Christian Topography—Τοπογραφία Χριστιανική,[1] on which Pope Alexander VI. draws subsequently his celebrated line of demarcation, giving westward for ever to Spain, eastward for ever to Portugal, is a vast oblong surrounded by Ocean. Let us watch the progress of the transformation scene, first as regards the extension of the limits of the known world, and next as regards any material changes that occur in the condition of important nations and cities previously known.

<small>Discoveries of the Portuguese.</small>

Look towards the south. Already land discovery from Portugal, first as in fear, step after step, has stolen along the African coast by the ocean highway, and has reached Cape Bojador in 1412. Madeira has been discovered, by chance, in 1419; Cape Blanco, in 1441; in 1446, the group of Cape Verd Islands; and in 1449, as by a backward side stroke, the Azores. In 1471, the Equator has been passed; and not long subsequently, the Portuguese were first established on the coast of Guinea.

Sailing along the coast of the continent, Bartholomew Dias reaches, in 1487, 'the Cape of Storms,' which name, as the prospect beyond appears bright, King John II. changes to the ' Cape of Good Hope'— Cabo de Boa Esperança. And about ten years after this, Vasco da Gama, having doubled the Cape and passed the extreme point of Dias' voyage, on Christmas day, 1497, sights land on the eastern coast, which he

---

[1] This work is attributed to Cosmas Indicopleustes. See Dyer, Mod. Eur. i. 314.

accordingly names 'Natal;' and, after touching at Mozambique, Kiloa, and Melinda, completes, in August in the following year, the discovery of the sea route to India, when he brings up his vessels at Calicut side by side with those of the Arabian 'Moors,' who for centuries past had monopolised the commerce of those parts, and 'with scarlet cloth, crimson velvet, yellow satin, handbasons and ewers chased and gilt, besides a splendid gilt mirror, fifty sheaths of knives of Flanders with ivory handles and glittering blades, and many other objects of curiosity and novelty, banishes, at least for a time, any doubts in the mind of the Malabar monarch with regard to the honest intentions of the strangers!'[1] *Discovery of the sea route to India.*

This voyage of Vasco da Gama changes the commerce of the world.

Look towards the west. Columbus, many preliminary difficulties overcome, sails, in 1492, in search of the route to India on that side, in endeavour also to discover whence come those canes of unknown growth, holding two gallons of water between each knot, found floating in western waters, and the trees such as never grow in the Azores and timber carved by human hands that wind and wave in stormy days waft against Madeira rocks. He has read (for knowledge is now no more a fountain sealed) what of ancient, what of modern learning or speculation bears on the subject.[2] *Discovery of the New World by Columbus.*

---

[1] Lindsay, Merchant Shipping, ii. 14. The passage is quoted as showing the kind of gifts presented. The effect on the Malabar monarch was not deep or lasting.

[2] According to Dyer (Mod. Eur. i. 316), Columbus appears to have derived much of his information from the treatise De Imagine Mundi of Pierre d'Ailly, Bishop of Cambray.

'It may be he shall touch the Happy Isles' of ancient days, and arrive 'where the western gales breathe round the island of the blest, and the golden flowers shine'—ἔνθα μακάρων νᾶσον ὠκεανίδες αὖραι περιπνέουσιν, ἄνθεμα δὲ χρυσοῦ φλέγει. He may realise the fabled Atlantis of Plato.[1] For him Tethys may open out new worlds, and Thule cease to be the last of things.[2] But chiefly he aims for the land of gold and of spices, by whatever name, of India or 'Cathay;' and, aided by compass and astrolabe, he reaches the outposts of the New World on the morning of Friday, October 12th, 1492. In 1500 Cabral is blown off the African coast across to Brazil, and claims it for the Portuguese.[3] In 1513, the Great South Sea is seen for the first time. In 1521 we follow Magellan down to the straits that are to immortalise his name, and, after his death, his surviving companions as they gain the Moluccas, and doubling the Cape of Good Hope return, the first to complete the circle on 'the broad wave that sweeps around the world.'

A glance to the north-west shows Cabot of Bristol in search of a north-western passage to India, and first discoverer of the parts about Labrador and Hudson's

Bahamas discovered Oct. 12, 1492.

Magellan and his companions put a girdle round about the earth.

Cabot's discoveries, 1407.

---

[1] Timaeus, p. 25, tom. vii.
[2] The following lines of Seneca (Medea, act ii. v. 375, et seq.) are stated to have produced a deep effect on the mind of Columbus :—

> Venient annis saecula seris,
> quibus Oceanus vincula rerum
> laxet, et ingens pateat tellus,
> Tethysque novos detegat orbes,
> nec sit terris ultima Thule.

[3] Under the arrangement effected by the Treaty of Tordesillas, 1494, which fixed the 'line of demarcation' at 370 leagues west of the Cape Verd islands.

Bay. By this time, therefore, English enterprise is abroad.

The conquest by Cortez, in 1519-21, of 'rich Mexico the land of Montezume,' followed, not long subsequently, in 1531-6, by Pizarro's conquest of Peru, change the spirit of the dream of the west, removing all obscurity or dimness from the prospect, which now becomes one unclouded blaze of golden light. Wheat, and wine, and oil, and silk, and sugar, and iron, and inventions to which wisdom may assign an altar in a New Atlantis[1] the Old World has ; the New, what for ages we have been seeking — alchemyst, magician, philosopher—one and all, gold and silver and pearl and diamonds ; and these, precious to us, appear ' of little or no use or estimation to the inhabitants.'[2] Moreover the inhabitants are heathen. To convert them to the Christian religion, their gold and silver to the

Conquest of Mexico and Peru.

The New Crusade.

---

[1] Those to whom Bacon assigns a statue in Salomon's House are:—Columbus, the inventor of Ships, the inventor of Ordnance and Gunpowder, of Music, of Letters, of Printing, of observations of Astronomy, of works in Metal, of Glass, of Silk of the worm, of Wine, and of Sugars. —New Atlantis.

[2] See subsequent Commission to Sir W. Rawleigh who 'intendeth to undertake a voyage by sea and shipping into the south parts of America or elsewhere within America possessed and inhabited by heathen and savage people, to the end to discover and find out some commodities and merchandises in those countries that be necessary and profitable for the subjects of our kingdoms and dominions, whereof the inhabitants there make little or no estimation. Whereupon also may ensue by trade and commerce some propagation of the Christian faith and reformed religion amongst those savage and idolatrous people. . . .' These commodities Sir Walter is commissioned thence to ' bring into this our kingdom or other our dominions, paying and answering to us the full fifth part of all such gold and silver and bullion or ore of gold and silver and pearl and precious stone as shall be imported, over and besides the customs on other goods wares and merchandises.' Foedera, xvi. 789-90.

use of Christians—the latter an easy task as against a people unprovided with guns, gunpowder or horses—this is the new crusade which now commences with courtier, merchant, and pirate, in curious crowd of adventurers, speeding towards the west.

War with Spain. Drake's raid on Chili and Peru. War with Spain breaks out. Drake returns from his raid on Chili and Peru with spoils half a million in value. Religion, invoked afresh, now against difference of opinion, speeds the work of 'the elect' of every class in maintaining the reformed faith and sacking the returning Spanish galleons. New crowds of adventurers sweep across the wave; and thus commences commerce, in a certain sense, with the New World.

This extension of the limits of the known world by discoveries in the west, leads to the publication in 1598 of the New Map of the World 'with the augmentation of the Indies.'[1]

Discoveries of Willoughby and Chancellor. To return to Europe and nations previously known to us. Look towards the north. Is there no way to 'Cathay' by north-eastern passage? To Sir H. Willoughby's attempt to find one we owe the discovery, in 1553, of the passage into the great northern sea, now the White Sea, to the port afterwards named, from the monastery of St. Michael, Archangel; first step to the whale fishery of Spitzbergen. Henceforth we are in communication with Muscovy; and, in 1569, become *Our commerce with Muscovy.* so intimately connected with the Czar, as to obtain from him the grant of the whole trade of Muscovy

---

[1] With, it will be remembered, as many lines thereon as on Malvolio's smiling countenance. See Twelfth Night.

by patent to the English;[1] and he, whether charmed by reports of island beauty, or desirous of safe refuge from expected insurrection, would have married an English lady; but Lady Anne Hastings, selected by the Queen for that honour, declines to wed, as his eighth wife, Ivan 'the Terrible.'

Look, next, towards the centre of the commercial world—the Mediterranean Sea. Genoa certainly has a history of her own, and is, as late as 1520, counted one of the richest cities in Europe; but a creeping paralysis, so to put it, is the result to her of the fall of the Greek Empire. Port after port in the Black Sea is taken by the Turk, and from these losses and the evil results of excessive duties, her history is a history of collapse, or rather, of decline from commercial greatness to mere usury. Fix the eye on the city of palaces, memorials to this day of those centuries of successful commerce during which, in communication with Aleppo and Alexandria, Venice was the principal mart for the spices, drugs, precious stones, and other rich merchandise of Syria, Egypt, Arabia, Persia, and India. About the commencement of the sixteenth century, the light of Venice is on the wane; her recovery after the League of Cambray, 1508, is incomplete. Henceforth the decline is more rapid; and her whole commercial prospect is darkened on the discovery by the Portuguese of the new sea route to India. To them passes the principal part of her trade; and 'fair

The Mediterranean.

Decline of Genoa.

Decline of Venice.

New sea route to India.

---

[1] Anderson, Commerce, ii. 95. The patent was revoked by his son. The charter of the Russia Company, granted 1, 2 Phil. and Mar. 1554, was confirmed by Act of Parliament (8 Eliz. c. 1.) in 1565.

Greatness of Lisbon.

Lisbon' now takes rank as one of the greatest cities of the western world ; maintaining that position till times past the scope of the present volume—times of the greatness of the Dutch at sea, with Batavia in Java, and other colonies in those parts ; when she yields to Amsterdam, as Venice had yielded place to her—times also when England has acquired place amongst great commercial nations. Before leaving the Mediterranean let us note the arrival of the English merchant on the scene as a direct trader with the East. About 1583 he is presented to and acknowledged by the Grand Seignior, who previously had supposed our island a dependent province of France.[1]

Commencement of our Turkey and Levant trade.

And now is opened a 'trade to Turkey not heretofore in the memory of man now living known to be commonly used and frequented by way of merchandise by any the merchants or any subjects of the Queen of England or her progenitors;'[2] in short, henceforth commences our Turkey and Levant trade.

Greatness of Spain and the Low Countries united.

To leave Italy, a country of small consideration in future European history, except as the battle-field of other nations, and pass to Spain. Here, by union of Castile and Aragon, 1479, conquest of Granada, 1492, and acquisition of Navarre within the Pyrenees, 1512, the whole peninsula becomes united, and passes to Charles I.—the Emperor Charles V., who has also, through his paternal grandmother, Marie of Burgundy, the Low Countries and the county of Burgundy, form-

---

[1] Birch, Memoirs of the reign of Queen Elizabeth, i. 36.
[2] Charter of Incorporation granted by Queen Elizabeth to Sir E. Osborn and others, 1581.

ing, when united to possessions in Italy and conquests in the New World, a power that threatens universal empire. To these dominions his son Philip II. succeeds in 1555. In these parts Seville and Cadiz become, after the discovery of America, the great storehouses for the new riches from the western world.

Pass hence northwards to France, but only to note the consolidation effected since the termination of the Hundred. Years' War. Duc de Bourgoyne, duc d'Anjou, comte de Provence, duc de Bretagne, where are they at the commencement of the sixteenth century? On the death of Charles The Bold, when, in 1477, 'Fortune turned her back on him at Nancy,'[1] the duchy of Burgundy falls to Louis XI. as fief of the crown; Marie his only child taking the Netherlands, and eventually the county of Burgundy, to her husband, Maximilian. In 1481 Anjou, Maine, and Provence fall to Louis by inheritance. The marriage of Anne de Bretagne to Charles VIII. in 1491, and to Louis XII. his successor, in 1499, secures Britany.[2] On the accession of the last-mentioned king the duchy of Orleans had merged in the Crown; and in 1526 the possessions of the House of Alençon are added, by reverter. Bourbon alone remains outstanding. This is the 'Constable,' of the Field of the Cloth of Gold scene;[3] whose well-known career (terminating at the sack of Rome, by the hand, as some relate, of Benvenuto

<small>Consolidation of the kingdom of France.</small>

[1] See inscription on his tomb at Bruges by Charles V. in 1550. Guizot, Hist. France, ii. 426.
[2] Anne's eldest daughter, Claude, married, in 1514, Francis duc d'Angoulême, afterwards Francis I. The duchy of Britanny was formally aunexed to France in 1532.
[3] See above, p. 284, Note 3.

Cellini) leads to confiscation of his possessions in 1527. Add to this the taking of the German bishoprics of Metz, Toul and Verdun in 1552, and the recovery of Calais in 1558, and you have briefly the history of the consolidation of the kingdom of France during this period. For the rest of the century she was engaged in 'the Wars of Religion.'

Bruges, the great emporium of commerce,

Now fix the eye on parts commercially more important to us, where Bruges stands, from situation entre-port between north and south; half-way house for the Hanseatic merchants with marine stores, iron, copper, corn, hemp, flax and timber of the north, and the Venetian, Genoese and other Italian merchants, with all the various products of the east; conveniently placed also for repair of the merchants with wine from France, and with wool, lead, and tin from England. Here, looking at the port of Sluys in 1468, you might have seen of a day one hundred and fifty merchant ships arriving. But Bruges has seen her greatest day; and at the very commencement of the period under consideration, this great emporium of northern commerce during the middle ages is in effect ruined by the combined effect of her contest with the Archduke Maximilian and the decrease of the Zwyn and retreat of the sea from the ancient port of Damme. Bruges

yields to Antwerp.

yields to Antwerp, which henceforth becomes the great northern mart for the merchandise of both the Indies, for naval stores, and other commodities of

Greatness of Antwerp.

northern Europe; but thriving especially on her great trade with Lisbon. Her 'Bourse' is the place of meeting of all the great merchants of the world;

and affords a prototype for Sir Thomas Gresham, on the foundation in 1567, of 'Britain's Bourse,' subsequently re-named by Elizabeth 'The Royal Exchange.' But religious persecutions and the cruelties of Alva, in a word, Spanish policy ruins the trade of the Netherlands; and after the sacking of Antwerp,[1] in 1585, and closing of the Scheldt, the best part of her fishing trade removes to Holland; of her linen trade, to Haerlem and Amsterdam, while about a third of the merchants and workmen who worked and dealt in silks, damasks, and taffeties, and in baies, saies and serges take refuge with us, in London and Norwich, in welcome reinforcement of our rapidly increasing manufacturing and commercial industry. *Ruin of the trade of the Netherlands.*

The greatness of the Dutch and particularly of Amsterdam is rather later in date; but already the Easterlings, who till the middle of the fifteenth century had practically a monopoly of the carrying trade of the north, are yielding place to the Hollanders; whose manufactures, fishery, and traffic have drawn the owners of freight from the Eastland towns to their country. *The Eastland towns superseded as carriers by Amsterdam.*

The foregoing rapid survey may suffice to recall the circumstances under which our intercourse with the New World, our trade with Russia, and our Turkey and Levant trade commenced, and our trade with Antwerp and Amsterdam developed during this period; and there remains but to mention the commencement of our trade with the East Indies, which dates effectively *First Charter of the East India Company.*

---

[1] By the Prince of Parma; in 1576 the city had been pillaged by the Spanish garrison.

from the grant to the East India Company of their first charter in 1600.

London. If we except Bristol, London was the only seat of commerce in England worthy of mention at this date. Our capital had not however yet attained place amongst cities of the first rank, such as (take date of 1590) Constantinople, Moscow, Paris, and Lisbon, the last-named by reason of her commerce with 'the Ethiop' (Africa) India and Brazil; but the cancellation

Abolition of the Steel Yard. of the privileges[1] of the Hanseatic merchants and abolition of the Steel Yard, the additions to our commercial and industrial population by the refugees from Antwerp, and the spirit of adventure and enterprise excited by the golden dreams of the west, had already produced extraordinary results. Moreover, England had now taken up a position of considerable importance in foreign politics, as champion of the Protestant religion in direct antagonism to the greatest continental power,

Ship building. Rise of the navy. Spain. Our navy was formidable; our merchant shipping, considerable. The former may be said to have commenced with the 'Regent' of Henry VIII.;[2] for before times of cannon little difference existed between anything worthy the name of a merchant ship and a ship of war. But Queen Elizabeth gave special attention to her navy; and in 1577 the Queen has one-and-twenty great ships, beside three notable galleys, ' with the sight whereof and the rest of the navy royal it is incredible how much her Grace is delighted.'

[1] Commenced in 1552, but not completed till 1578. The Steel Yard was finally shut up in 1597. Anderson, Commerce, ii. 90, 146, 192.
[2] Dyer, Mod. Eur. ii. 20.

About this time also 'great masses of treasure' are expended on shipping; the merchant navy is commonly estimated at 1,700 or 1,800; and there 'be few merchant ships of the first or second sort that, being apparelled and made ready to sail, are not worth one thousand pounds or three thousand ducats at the least, if they should be presently sold.'[1] *Increase in merchant shipping.*

It is now that the practice of Sea Insurance, though dating from ancient times, and mentioned so far back as in the sea laws of Oleron, first assumes important proportions. And in 1601 a statute is passed establishing a court of commissioners, to meet weekly at the office of Insurance on the west side of the Royal Exchange, to hear and determine all causes relating to policies of assurance in a summary way.[2] *Practice of Sea Insurance.*

Lastly, Tudor times, particularly towards their close, were brisk times for all employed in the building of houses. *The new building in Tudor times.*

The Wars of the Roses and the supreme power the king possessed in the command of artillery, effected a revolution in the old feudal system. The large military households were now broken up; and landowners turned their attention to making the most of their estates. The period of internal tranquillity that followed afforded the opportunity for a change in the style of country residences and the introduction of houses in which, for the first time, convenience of arrangement was consulted more than security from

---

[1] Harrison, Description of Britain. Hume, Hist. Eng. iv. 428. Anderson, i. 404.

[2] 43 Eliz. 1601, c. 12. 'An Act concerning matters of assurances used among merchants.'

hostile attack, and the requirements of the various members of the family, rather than those of a large military household. This is the period of the Tudor development of Gothic architecture.

The Tudor development of the Gothic.

Notwithstanding the interest that attaches to the subject, we can here only skim lightly over the surface of things. Richmond Palace and 'Nonesuch,'[1] the new palaces of our kings, afforded precedents which were followed in the altered character of building, though not perhaps precisely in form, by many of our nobility and gentry; who, dispensing with licenses to crenellate, henceforth began to build, in lieu of castle and stronghold, mansions more adapted to the altered circumstances of the times, in the form of the 'Hall' and the 'House.'

The 'Hall' and 'House.'

This New Building received an impulse on the dissolution of the monasteries and abbeys and chantries and religious guilds,[2] and the redistribution of their lands amongst a numerous class of resident landowners. During the reigns of Henry VIII., Edward VI., and Mary, the crown grantees of land and every wool-merchant, grazier, and sheep-farmer whom success had enabled to buy land, all were willing builders of houses.

The impetus was accelerated in the times of Elizabeth, when there appeared yet another class of purchasers of land in the successful merchants and 'adventurers.' And now the rapid increase of wealth

---

[1] For a view of Henry VII.'s Palace of Richmond, see Knight, Hist. Eng., ii. 239; and for a view of Henry VIII.'s Palace of Nonesuch, in Surrey, see Ibid., 431.

[2] The Acts relating to the dissolution of the chantries and religious guilds are:—37 Hen. VIII. 1545, c. 4, and 1 Edw. VI. 1547, c. 14.

in all classes and in the higher classes the love of display drove the whole nation into bricks and mortar; in other words, the New Building attained proportions which render it one of the most remarkable features in the history of the times.

Of the Elizabethan manor houses that sprang into existence throughout the land numerous specimens still exist; rendering the form of house—three sides of a square with a porch and room above forming the tongue of the E, the chimneys, the gables and the mullioned windows—familiar to all. In the higher classes during the latter part of the reign of Elizabeth, a fashion, it may be termed a rage, for building fine houses prevailed. Holdenby, Theobalds, Sir T. Gresham's Osterley—large enough to make into two—are some of the many historical houses of this date. At Wollaton, Sir Francis Willoughby 'at great expense builds a most magnificent and elegant house with a fine prospect,' in ruinous imitation of Longleat, the magnificent design of Giovanni di Padua just completed. Burghley House rises by 'Stamford town.'[1] The magnificent 'Bess of Hardwick,' Elizabeth, Countess of Shrewsbury, is busy with Hardwick Hall, only one of her many magnificent buildings: for she is to die, so it is foretold, when she ceases to build. Sir E. Phelips Master of the Rolls, raises what Fuller terms 'a most successful fabric,' in Montacute House. The Knole of Dorset is finished in 1605. And this 'great bravery of building that set in in the times of Elizabeth' concludes in final expression of magnificence when, in

Elizabethan Manor Houses.

Elizabethan Halls.

1580.

1567-70.

[1] Only completed by the elder son of the great statesman in 1605.

'Jacobean' times. Jacobean times, such palaces are reared as Holland House; Audley End (Inn) which Fuller terms 'the best subject's house in England'; Cecil's Hatfield, 'for situation, building, contrivance, prospect, air, and all accordants inferior to no house in England'; and Bramshill, intended for the residence of Prince Henry, and in no respect inferior to Hatfield.

The style of these magnificent palaces, each in arrangement and design the expression of the personal taste of the building owner, and arabesqued, pilastered, and porticoed up to his individual knowledge or conception of Roman art, applied as far as pleasing to his eye—for there are no precise rules for 'Elizabethan' building, there is no type for English 'Hall,' as there is a distinct type for French 'château'—the style of these magnificent palaces; their luxuriant abundance in internal decoration where, surely, 'fairy hands'

'Have raised the ceilings' fretted height,
The walls in rich achievements clothing;'

the richness and quaintness of their carved chairs, Italian cabinets and other furniture; the broad terraces with 'statuas,' and gardens with fountains with which they are surrounded; and the love of space and light, of rich colour and ornament, the prodigality of magnificence they display, all render them peculiarly characteristic of the times. They bear the mark of refinement introduced from the more advanced civilization of Italy. They denote the extravagance of the new growth of wealth and a time when visions of El Dorados to be sacked and Spanish galleons filled with gold made life one continual dream of enrichment by adventure. And they represent the burst into full enjoyment of life and all that makes life glad consequent on the removal of the incubus of feudalism, and as yet unrestrained —the times of the Renascence in England. In Italy and in France the 'Renaissance' was, mainly, a revival of the arts of ancient Greece and Rome; of which classic civilization the memorials and types were driven, on capture of Constantinople by the Turk, into admiring Italy, and passed thence into France (on 'the invasion of the barbarians,' as an Italian, or on 'the discovery of Italy,' as a Frenchman would put it) inspiring a desire of emulation in nations weary of the confusion and barbarous forms of the feudal age—a Renaissance of painters, sculptors, and classical architecture. In England the Renascence was rather the awakening of the mind and energy of man, in the world of Luther, Columbus and Copernicus, with extended sphere for thought, and extended sphere for movement. This is the feeling that animates the strain of Spenser and of Shakspeare, and finds expression in what the great poet of modern times describes as :—

> 'The melodious burst that fills
> The spacious times of great Elizabeth.'

The principal event of fiscal importance in the reign of the sovereign to whom 'king of England, Scotland, France, and Ireland,' in a time of 'admirable peace and quietness' (March 1603) the High Court of Parliament 'upon the knees of their hearts do agnize their constant faith, obedience, and loyalty,'[1] is the cele-

The Stuart period.
Union of the Crowns of England and Scotland.

---
[1] See Recital 1 Jac. I. c. 1.

brated decision in Bates' case. The king by royal commission has set a special impost on currants imported. Bates, a Turkey merchant, paying the ordinary duty of poundage, refuses to pay the new impost. An information, the usual form of revenue proceeding, even to this day in 'the High Court of Justice,' is laid against him for non-payment. The case is heard in the Court of Exchequer in Michaelmas term 1606, and the judges decide that Bates must pay the new impost.

The decision in Bates' case

That Bates has to pay is small matter; but the decision amounts to a declaration that the king can by prerogative impose duties at will on imports and exports. 'And there is fear,' as represented in a petition of the Commons to the king in 1610, that from such a commencement, ' impositions may be extended to commodities which, growing in this kingdom, are not transported, but uttered to the subjects of the same.' As indeed happened in the instance of the duty of 1s. a chaldron on sea-coals rising in Blyth and Sunderland, subsequently imposed under pretext of royal prerogative by this king. This decision of the judges in the Great Case of Impositions[1] appeared, therefore, to shatter to pieces the very foundations of liberty in England.

Purveyance and pre-emption.

The other fiscal features of the reign are: the extension to an extreme point of the fiscal prerogatives of purveyance and pre-emption; the royal grants of

---

[1] For particulars of the Great Case of Impositions, on an information in the Exchequer by the Attorney-General against Mr. John Bates, merchant, Michaelmas, 4 James I. A.D. 1606-1610, see Lane's Rep. p. 22, and Howell, State Trials, ii. 371-534, and the references there given, in the notes, to 'more learning relative to the question.'

monopolies in foreign trade to exclusive companies, by which means considerable sums are raised, till the practice is restrained by the Statute of Monopolies;[1] compulsory loans and benevolences; a freedom in infliction of fines on political offenders; and, lastly, the frequent sale of honors and dignities.

The Statute of Monopolies.

The following values are assigned to peerages: for a barony, 10,000*l*.; a viscounty, 15,000*l*.; and for an earldom, 20,000*l*. Whilst admission to the newly-created order of baronet is gained on payment of the price of 'the maintenance of 30 foot soldiers for 3 years, at eightpence a day each,' to assist the king's troops in the reduction of Ulster, in Ireland, that is, at a cost of 1,095*l*.

Sale of honors.

The first lottery of importance known in England, at least as drawn under sanction of public authority, dates in this reign; and the profit is dedicated principally to payment of expenses attending our Settlements in America.[2]

The first public lottery.

In administration of the government of countries it not unfrequently happens that two departments of office are guided, in treating a given subject, by different, if not conflicting, views. This is especially the case where the Minister of the Interior has for object restraint of drinking, and the Minister of Finance would derive the greatest possible revenue from licenses for sale of drink. Here two voices, speaking in affairs of state, say, one: 'drink not, drink not;' the other: 'drink,

Origin of the Laws in restraint of 'drinking.'

[1] 21 Jac. I. 1623, c. 3. 'An Act concerning monopolies and dispensations with penal laws, and the forfeitures thereof.'
[2] Sinclair, Hist. Rev. i. 245.

but pay.' The laws relating to the subject of 'drink' (to use a convenient and familiar term) are therefore necessarily governed by principles differing as they relate to the one or the other branch of the subject; but on our Statute Book the threads of legislation are interwoven in such a manner that it is difficult to separate them, and indeed a correct comprehension of the fiscal enactments cannot be attained without study of those relating to regulations of police. These precede in date of origin the revenue laws, and may be traced to statutes passed in the reign of James I., times when (to pass over royal excesses and pictures which historians give of ladies sprawling drunk about the presence chamber) more spare money at disposal than heretofore led 'lewd and idle people to spend their time in lewd and drunken manner in drinking and tippling in inns, ale-houses, and other victualling-houses.'

What kind of places were these inns, ale-houses, and victualling-houses? And to what, if any, restraints and regulations were such houses at this date subject, either in regard to commencement of business, or in regard to conduct of business when established?

The inn or hostel of former times.

The inn or hostel of the middle ages, not unfitly represented by the 'Tabard' of Chaucer, was both then and subsequently principally used as a place of entertainment 'for the receipt, relief and lodging of wayfaring people travelling from place to place.'[1] Neither by the common law nor by any statutory law was any restriction imposed on the establishment of inns, to any

[1] See recital to 1 Jac. I. 1603, c. 9.

number, but it was, in many places, regulated by local custom.

Ale-houses and victualling-houses belonged to a different class of places of entertainment. 'The ancient, true and principal use' of such houses was—'for supply of the wants of such people as are not able by greater quantities to make provision of victuals,' and the keepers of these local drinking and eating houses were subject at this date to enactments of which the history is as follows :— {The alehouse and the victuallinghouse.}

Under certain Acts of 1388, 1409, and 1477,[1] servants of husbandry, and labourers and servants of artificers and of victuallers were required to have bows and arrows, and use the same on Sundays and holidays, and to 'abstain from all playing of hand-ball or football, coits, dice, casting of the stone, kails, and other such importune games,' and 'the more recently imagined games called closh-kailes, half-bowl, hand-in-and-hand-out, and queck-board.' These were termed 'unlawful games;' and the premises of ale-house and victualling-house appear not unfrequently to have been used (as well might be) for such unlawful games. Hence it is that we find in the Act of 1494,[2] relating to vagrancy, idleness, and the suppression of unlawful games, power given to two justices of the peace to 'reject common selling of ale;' a power which is continued to them in a similar Act passed in 1503.[3] After this followed the Acts of Henry VIII.'s reign, enforcing the practice of {The statutes against 'unlawful games.'}

---

[1] 12 Rich. II. c. 6; 11 Hen. IV. c. 4; 17 Edw. IV. c. 3.
[2] 11 Hen. VII. 1494, c. 2.
[3] 19 Hen. VII. 1503, c. 12.

archery,[1] and more strictly prohibiting unlawful games (amongst which 'carding, loggats and shove-groat' now appear) as tending to decay of archery. And it was probably as an auxiliary measure, in order to back up, as it were, this prohibition, as much as with a view to the maintenance of good rule in other respects, that the Act of 1552 was passed, which recites that 'intolerable hurts and troubles to the common wealth of this realm do daily grow and increase through such abuses and disorders as are had and used in common ale-houses and other houses called tippling-houses;' re-enacts the power for the justices of the peace to 'remove and put away common selling of ale;' and requires all keepers of ale-houses and tippling-houses to be licensed by the justices in open sessions,[2] and to give security by recognizance against using of unlawful games, and for the maintenance of good order and rule in the house.[3]

First licenses for ale and tippling house.

Another sort of house of entertainment was the tavern, where wine was sold; and as about this date 'many taverns had been of late newly set up in very great numbers in back lanes, corners, and suspicious places,' the legislature 'for the avoiding of many inconveniences, much evil rule and common resort of misruled persons frequenting the same,' swept these also into the net, by limiting the sale of wine by retail to towns, and placing it, in cities, boroughs, and

The tavern.

---

[1] 3 Hen. VIII. 1511, c. 3; 33 Henry VIII. 1541, c. 9. 'An Act for maintaining archery and the debarring of unlawful games.'

[2] Or by two justices, one to be of the quorum.

[3] 5 & 6 Edw. VI. c. 25. 'For keepers of ale-houses and tippling-houses to be bound by recognizance.'

towns corporate, under the regulation of the mayor and local authorities, and in towns not corporate, under the justices of the shire.[1]

Hitherto the legislation on the subject of houses where drink was sold does not appear to have had for object any restriction of drinking; but during the wars in the Netherlands in the reign of Elizabeth, the habit of drinking revived; and before the close of the reign had so increased, that we were re-established in our pride of place of Anglo-Saxon times; and in drinking power, as Shakspeare puts it:—'Your Dane, your German, and your swag-bellied Hollander are nothing to your English.' The inn now appears as the scene of local carousal in company with the ale-house and the victualling-house; and an Act is passed including the trio, and imposing a penalty on any inn-keeper, victualler or ale house keeper permitting local residents to continue unlawful drinking or tippling in his house;[2] but persons invited by any traveller and lodgers are exempted, and an hour is allowed for dinner of labourers and handicraftsmen. This is the first of the Acts against tippling. In 1606, an attempt is made to repress unlicensed ale-houses— 'whereof the multitudes and abuses have been and are found intolerable, and still do and are like to increase'[3]—by stopping the supply; and a penalty is imposed on the sale or delivery of any ale or beer,

Revival of the habit of drinking during the wars in the Netherlands.

First Act against tippling in inns, ale-houses and victualling houses.

[1] 7 Edw. VI. 1553, c. 5.
[2] 1 Jac. I. 1604, c. 9. 'An Act to restrain the inordinate haunting and tippling in inns, ale-houses, and other victualling-houses.'
[3] 4 Jac. I. 1606, c. 4. 'An Act to restrain the utterance of beer and ale to ale-house keepers and tipplers not licensed.'

except for household use, to any person who sells it as a common tippler or ale-house keeper, unless he has a license in force. And in the same year is passed a second Act against tippling [1]—for repressing the odious and loathsome sin of drunkenness, described as ' of late grown into common use within the realm, being the root and foundation of many other enormous sins, as bloodshed, stabbing, murder, swearing, fornication, adultery, and such like, to the great dishonour of God, and of our nation, the overthrow of many good arts and manual trades, the disabling of divers workmen, and the general impoverishing of many good subjects, abusively wasting the good creatures of God'—which Act, aimed more particularly at the drunkard and the tippler, punishes the sin of drunkenness and the offence of ' continuing drinking or tippling in any inn, victualling-house, or ale-house in the place where the offender dwells,' by fine, followed, in case of non-payment, by the stocks.[2]

In vain all these enactments: the tide continues to swell; for, in the words of an Act of 1609, 'notwithstanding all former laws and provisions already made, the inordinate and extreme vice of excessive drinking and drunkenness doth more and more abound, to the great offence of Almighty God, and the wasteful destruction of God's good creatures.'[3] And therefore the penalty imposed upon the ale-house keeper

[1] 4 Jac. I. 1606, c. 5.
[2] The exceptions of the first Act against tippling are continued, but by a subsequent Act, 21 Jac. I. 1623, c. 7, the penalty is extended to all persons continuing tippling, wheresoever his habitation or abiding be.
[3] 7 Jac. I. 1609, c. 10, 'An Act for the reformation of ale-house keepers.'

(the principal offender) is strengthened by enactment that a conviction under the Acts against tippling shall carry with it disability to keep an ale-house for the space of three years next ensuing the conviction; and, subsequently to this, an Act of 1623 extends the penalty against tippling to all persons caught in the act, whether local residents or not.[1]

Hitherto the tavern keeper had been outside the provisions of the Acts against tippling; but in 1625 he also is brought within the net, by an enactment[2] which provides that 'all keepers of taverns and such as sell wine in their houses and do also keep inns, or victualling in their houses, shall be taken to be within the said statutes,'—the Acts against tippling.

The Acts against tippling extended to tavern keepers.

To the enactments contained in the Acts before mentioned may be traced the origin of our laws in restraint of drinking, and for regulation of houses where drink is sold, in the attempt to mitigate an evil which, in uninterrupted flow and increasing volume, has continued its course from those times to our own.[3] And now at last the legislature, as if angry at want of success, has thought fit to brand beer and wine, in their use the most wholesome of beverages, with an ill name by reference to their abuse; has chained John Barleycorn and Bacchus to the Gin Fiend; and has pilloried

---

[1] 21 Jac. I. 1623, c. 7.

[2] Car. I. 1625, c. 4, 'An Act for the further restraint of tippling in inns, ale-houses, and other victualling-houses,' s. 2.

[3] In the following reign the failure of the descent on Cadiz is attributed to inability of the troops to keep hands off a find of casks of Spanish wine.

the three as necessarily producers of 'Intoxicating Liquor.'[1]

Amount of the revenue in 1617.

According to 'an Abstract or Brief Declaration of His Majesty's Revenue as it stood in 1617,' the crown lands produced 80,000*l.* a year; the customs and new impositions, as hereinbefore stated, about 190,000*l.*; and wards and other various branches of revenue, besides purveyance, 180,000*l.*; forming a total of 450,000*l.*

Charles I. and his Parliaments.

The first struggles in the great contest which commences in the reign of Charles I. between the King and the nation as represented in the House of Commons—the contest regarding the Divine Right of Kings as it has been termed—have principally relation to the power of taxation: all the real fighting is on fiscal ground. The most important transaction in the first Parliament of King Charles is the grant by the Commons[2] of the port duties for a year only, in lieu of for life as in the case of preceding sovereigns; and in the second Parliament, the appointment of the committee of grievances and their report against the practice of impositions and the levy of port duties without authority of Parliament.[3] During the interval of time between the dissolution of this Parliament in June 1626 and the meeting of the third Parliament in March 1628, subsidies are levied by means of forced loans; the seaports are required to provide and maintain a fleet of ships for three months; illegal commissions

---

[1] See definition clause, s. 74, of 35 & 36 Vict. 1872, c. 94. 'An Act for regulating the Sale of Intoxicating Liquors.'

[2] The Bill did not pass in the House of Lords. It was read only once.

[3] For the king's order to levy port duties, see Rushworth, i. 669.

for levy of 173,411*l*, the amount of charge for the outfit of the intended expedition to retrieve affairs after Buckingham's failure at Rochelle, are issued, and then revoked; and additional imposts are laid on merchandise at the ports, and then are cancelled. The principal transaction in the third Parliament is the passing of the famous Petition of Right, and this petition is grounded mainly on complaints of false imprisonment of persons on account of the loan; and a further remonstrance against levy of port duties without consent of Parliament leads to the dissolution. After this, no Parliament is summoned for eleven years. Meanwhile the unauthorised levy of port duties is continued; fines for knighthood are revived, and so are monopolies, the list including wine, soap, salt, almost every article of domestic consumption. Speaking of the monopolists, subsequently, in the Long Parliament, Colepepper says: —'They sup in our cup, they dip in our dish, they sit by our fire; we find them in the dye vat, the washbowls and the powdering tub; they share with the cutler in his box; they have marked and sealed us from head to foot.' And be it remembered that in some cases, as in the famous instance of soap, the conditions on which the monopoly is granted amount to the imposition of a duty on the manufactured article.[1] Other attempts are made to recruit the revenue, which may fitly be classed under the general head of miscel-

[1] The corporation of soap boilers paid a duty of 8*l*. per ton on all soap manufactured, in addition to the 10,000*l*. for their patent. Foedera, xix. 92, 381. As to the attempts made to 'hinder the King's good intentions' in this matter of soap, and his rigorous measures for enforcing his intentions, see 'a proclamation for the well ordering of the making of soft soap, and for the settling the price thereof.' Foedera, xix. 566.

laneous extortions. And lastly, the famous ship-writs are issued. Notwithstanding all these attempts to bring revenue up to expenditure a necessity for extraordinary supplies arises, in order to meet the expenses of preparations for the Scotch campaign; the fourth Parliament is summoned, and meets in April 1640, but is dissolved in the following month, on probability of refusal to proceed at once to the question of supply. Then comes the Long Parliament, and the passing of the Acts granting port duties for limited periods, and the Act for the abolition of ship-money.

Nov. 1640.

After this victory of the House of Commons in maintaining the constitutional right of taxation, other questions come to the front. Such violent measures as the Solemn Remonstrance; the impeachment of the bishops; the arrest of the five members; and the issue of the royal commissions of array on the one side, and the passing of the ordinance for the appointment of Lieutenants of the militia on the other side, show that the time for parliamentary settlement of difficulties is past. And the sequel is the scene in a field at Nottingham on a dark and stormy day (Aug. 22, 1642), termed the raising of the Standard.[1]

During the forty years' interval between the 'setting of that bright occidental star, Queen Elizabeth, of happy memory,' and these unhappy times, our manufactures and our commerce had rapidly developed; as indeed is clearly shown by the increase observable in the revenue from port duties. To tax the reader's attention again with details is, however, unnecessary,

---

[1] See Rushworth, Part III. vol. i. 783.

except just to note the first appearance of certain special contributories to the revenue in times to come.

The first of these are coaches, private and public. As far back as 1580 coaches, in the sense of carriages for the nobility and gentry, had been introduced into this country by FitzAllen, Earl of Arundel; but it took a quarter of a century to bring them into anything like general use; and not till 1625, after the lapse of nearly half a century since the introduction of coaches, do we find hackney coaches plying in London, standing at inns ready for call when wanted. Ten years hence, their rapid increase in number has to be restrained by an order in council;[1] and in 1637 a limit is imposed on the number of hackney coachmen in London, and licenses are required for them from the King's Master of the Horse. But, before this, the danger to passengers and delay to cart traffic caused in the narrow 'streets and passages of London and Westminster, and the suburbs of the same, by the unnecessary multitude of coaches therein used,' has led to the introduction of the Sedan chair; for which Sir Saunders Duncombe, on representing that 'in many parts beyond the seas, the people there are much carried in streets in chairs that are covered, by which means very few coaches are used amongst them,' and that he is willing at his own costs to provide a proper supply of such chairs, has a grant of a special monopoly for fourteen years.[2]

Introduction of private coaches and hackney carriages.

The Sedan chair.

---

[1] Rushworth, ii. 316.

[2] 1634 Foedera, xix. 572. For a picture of the hackney coach-stand in Palace Yard and a Sedan chair of the time, see Knight, Hist. Eng., iii. 416, 417. Buckingham, in the reign of James I., had caused indig-

Clocks and watches. The next to be mentioned of these special contributories to the revenue in times to come are clocks and watches. The clock, the successor to the clepsydra and the sun-dial, is said to have derived its name from the cloche or time-bell of monastery and abbey. The first clocks or orologes, as they were also termed, made in England were probably the work of the 'three orlogists from Delft in Holland,' to whom Edward III. grants license in 1368 to come and practise their occupation in this country.[1] Chaucer's cock it will be remembered 'crowed as regularly as clock or abbey orloye.' These orologes were worked by means of weights; but at a subsequent date coiled springs were introduced as an improvement on the weights; and this is the interesting turning-point in the history of clock-making: for henceforth the small or table clock was a possibility. Next came watches; and the Emperor Charles V., whose interest in time-pieces is historical, is said to have been the first who possessed anything that could rightly be called a pocket-clock or watch. Oval and round watches were first made towards the close of the sixteenth century. And, at the date at which we have arrived in the narrative, probably most persons of property possessed a clock, and many of them a pocket-clock or 'watch,' either of home manufacture, as made by a member of the company of clockmakers established by charter of Charles in 1637, or imported from the Netherlands,

nation by being carried about in a chair borne by men. The unfortunate King, Charles I., was carried to his trial and back in a sedan; but they did not come into general use till about 1640.

[1] Foedera, vi. 500.

where resided at this date the principal clock, dial, and watch makers of Europe.[1]

Thirdly, playing cards and dice had already been enlisted as contributories to the King's revenue. In 1631 an office had been erected for sealing packs of playing cards, to which the master and wardens of the company of makers of playing cards sent, in pursuance of a contract made with the King, a certain number of packs of cards weekly. A similar contract was made with the company of dicemakers. The taxes—if such a term be applicable to illegal imposts—were farmed; and the packs of cards and the dice were required to be sealed and stamped.[2]

Cards and dice.

Lastly, of the great future contributories to our revenue from port duties we have now tobacco, in addition to wine and sugar; but the use of spirits as a beverage has hardly yet commenced, and the introduction of hot drinks—tea and coffee—is still later in date.

In conclusion of the volume may be added the following remarks of Michiel[3] the Venetian ambassador and Lord Bacon regarding taxation in England in their times, and, with a view to leaving as it were a hook on which to hang any future sketch in continuation of the subject, a few words on the subject of future taxation

---

[1] 'Timekeeper' is the word used to include clock and watch in the taxing Act of 1797, 37 Geo. iii. c. 108.

[2] See Rushworth, ii. 103; Foedera, xx. 145.

[3] In description of foreigners care should be taken to avoid 'filching from them their good name.' Some writers spell this name Michel, some Micheli, in reference to one or the other of the Doges or ambassadors the family supplied to Venice. In the text the name is printed as used by the present representative of the family.

Remarks of Michiel and Bacon regarding taxation in England.

Michiel in description of England in 1557 states: 'The liberty of this country is really singular and wonderful; indeed there is no other country, in my opinion, less burdened and more free. For they have not only no taxes of any kind, but they are not even thought of; no tax on salt, wine, beer, flour, meat, cloth, and other necessaries of life, which, in all parts of Italy especially, and in Flanders, are the more productive the greater is the number of inhabitants which consume them.'[1] Lord Bacon's remark is to the same effect: 'He that shall look into other countries and consider the taxes and tallages and impositions and assizes and the like, that are everywhere in use, will find that the Englishman is most master of his own valuation and the least bitten in purse of any nation in Europe.'[2]

List of taxes of the future.

A glance down the vista of the future shows a very different state of fiscal things. We see taxes on: —beer, malt, hops, wine, cider and perry, mead and metheglin, sweets and made wines, spirits, tea, coffee, chocolate, cocoa, sherbet, vinegar, sugar, pepper, salt, tobacco and snuff; glass (plate, window, broad, flint, bottle), bricks and tiles, timber, candles, soap, starch, stone bottles, wire, plate, paper, pamphlets, newspapers, almanacks, tobacco pipes, leather, hats, gloves and mittens, ribbons, printed goods, hair pomatum, hair powder, tooth powder, perfumes, cosmetics, medicine,

---

[1] Sir H. Ellis, Original Letters, 2 series, vol. ii.

[2] Observations on a recent libel. Spain, towards the close of the sixteenth century, was loaded with taxes, which were comparatively unproductive through sale of offices. And France was saved from the ruin that threatened Spain only by Sully.

cards, dice; the possession or use of watches and clocks, carriages, armorial bearings, servants, horses, race horses, dogs, and guns; locomotion by means of post-horses, stage carriages, hackney carriages, and railways; sporting licenses, auctions, advertisements, insurance—sea, fire, and life; births, deaths, and marriages; almost every document that can bear a stamp; almost every trade or profession that can bear a license—hawker, pedlar and petty chapman, pawnbroker, appraiser, house agent, banker, attorney— to say nothing of the thousands of articles included in the tariff; the duties on devolution of property on death—probate, legacy and succession duties; some capitation taxes; and taxes on every species of income that can arise from any description of property, office, or employment in life.

Most of these are special taxes, the separate head having a history of its own, and in some cases that history is a narrative of the strangling of industry by taxation, so that as regards the particular tax England has nothing to boast in any comparison with the worst specimens of Italian, French, or even Spanish taxation.

END OF VOLUME THE FIRST.

39 PATERNOSTER ROW, E.C.
LONDON, *August* 1875.

GENERAL LIST OF WORKS

PUBLISHED BY

MESSRS. LONGMANS, GREEN, AND CO.

	PAGE
ARTS, MANUFACTURES, &c.	26
ASTRONOMY & METEOROLOGY	16
BIOGRAPHICAL WORKS	7
CHEMISTRY & PHYSIOLOGY	24
DICTIONARIES & other BOOKS of REFERENCE	14
FINE ARTS & ILLUSTRATED EDITIONS	24
HISTORY, POLITICS, HISTORICAL MEMOIRS, &c.	1
INDEX	40 to 43
MENTAL & POLITICAL PHILOSOPHY	8
MISCELLANEOUS & CRITICAL WORKS	12
NATURAL HISTORY & PHYSICAL SCIENCE	18
POETRY & the DRAMA	35
RELIGIOUS & MORAL WORKS	28
RURAL SPORTS, HORSE & CATTLE MANAGEMENT, &c.	36
TRAVELS, VOYAGES, &c.	32
WORKS of FICTION	34
WORKS of UTILITY & GENERAL INFORMATION	37

HISTORY, POLITICS, HISTORICAL MEMOIRS, &c.

Journal of the Reigns of King George the Fourth and King William the Fourth.

By the late Charles Cavendish Fulke Greville, Esq.

Edited by *Henry Reeve*, Esq.

Fifth Edition. 3 vols. 8vo. price 36s.

The Life of Napoleon III. derived from State Records, Unpublished Family Correspondence, and Personal Testimony.

By *Blanchard Jerrold*.

Four Vols. 8vo. with numerous Portraits and Facsimiles. VOLS. I. and II. price 18s. each.

*** Vols. III. and IV. are in preparation.

A

Recollections and Suggestions, 1813-1873.
By *John Earl Russell, K.G.*
New Edition, revised and enlarged. 8vo. 16s.

Introductory Lectures on Modern History delivered in Lent Term 1842; with the Inaugural Lecture delivered in December 1841.
By the late Rev. *Thomas Arnold, D.D.*
8vo. price 7s. 6d.

On Parliamentary Government in England: its Origin, Development, and Practical Operation.
By *Alpheus Todd.*
2 vols. 8vo. £1. 17s.

The Constitutional History of England since the Accession of George III. 1760-1870.
By Sir *Thomas Erskine May, K.C.B.*
Fourth Edition. 3 vols. crown 8vo. 18s.

Democracy in Europe; a History.
By Sir *Thomas Erskine May, K.C.B.*
2 vols. 8vo. [*In the press.*]

The History of England from the Fall of Wolsey to the Defeat of the Spanish Armada.
By *J. A. Froude, M.A.*
CABINET EDITION, 12 vols. cr. 8vo. £3. 12s.
LIBRARY EDITION, 12 vols. 8vo. £8. 18s.

The English in Ireland in the Eighteenth Century.
By *J. A. Froude, M.A.*
3 vols. 8vo. £2. 8s.

The History of England from the Accession of James II.
By Lord Macaulay.
STUDENT'S EDITION, 2 vols. cr. 8vo. 12s.
PEOPLE'S EDITION, 4 vols. cr. 8vo. 16s.
CABINET EDITION, 8 vols. post 8vo. 48s.
LIBRARY EDITION, 5 vols. 8vo. £4.

Critical and Historical Essays contributed to the Edinburgh Review.
By the Right Hon. Lord Macaulay.
Cheap Edition, authorised and complete, crown 8vo. 3s. 6d.
STUDENT'S EDITION, crown 8vo. 6s.
PEOPLE'S EDITION, 2 vols. crown 8vo. 8s.
CABINET EDITION, 4 vols. 24s.
LIBRARY EDITION, 3 vols. 8vo. 36s.

Lord Macaulay's Works.
Complete and uniform Library Edition.
Edited by his Sister, Lady Trevelyan.
8 vols. 8vo. with Portrait, £5. 5s.

Lectures on the History of England from the Earliest Times to the Death of King Edward II.
By *W. Longman, F.S.A.*
Maps and Illustrations. 8vo. 15s.

The History of the Life and Times of Edward III.
By *W. Longman, F.S.A.*
With 9 Maps, 8 Plates, and 16 Woodcuts. 2 vols. 8vo. 28s.

NEW WORKS PUBLISHED BY LONGMANS & CO.

History of England under the Duke of Buckingham and Charles the First, 1624–1628.
By S. Rawson Gardiner, late Student of Ch. Ch.
2 vols. 8vo. with two Maps, 24s.

History of Civilization in England and France, Spain and Scotland.
By Henry Thomas Buckle.
3 vols. crown 8vo. 24s.

A Student's Manual of the History of India from the Earliest Period to the Present.
By Col. Meadows Taylor, M.R.A.S.
Second Thousand. Cr. 8vo. Maps, 7s. 6d.

Studies from Genoese History.
By Colonel G. B. Malleson, C.S.I. Guardian to His Highness the Maharájá of Mysore.
Crown 8vo. 10s. 6d.

The Native States of India in Subsidiary Alliance with the British Government; an Historical Sketch. With a Notice of the Mediatized and Minor States.
By Colonel G. B. Malleson, C.S.I. Guardian to His Highness the Maharájá of Mysore.
With 6 Coloured Maps, 8vo. price 15s.

The History of India from the Earliest Period to the close of Lord Dalhousie's Administration.
By John Clark Marshman.
3 vols. crown 8vo. 22s. 6d.

Indian Polity; a View of the System of Administration in India.
By Lieut.-Colonel George Chesney.
Second Edition, revised, with Map. 8vo. 21s.

Waterloo Lectures; a Study of the Campaign of 1815.
By Colonel Charles C. Chesney, R.E.
Third Edition. 8vo. with Map, 10s. 6d.

Essays in Modern Military Biography.
By Colonel Charles C. Chesney, R.E.
8vo. 12s. 6d.

The Imperial and Colonial Constitutions of the Britannic Empire, including Indian Institutions.
By Sir E. Creasy, M.A.
With 6 Maps. 8vo. 15s.

The Oxford Reformers—John Colet, Erasmus, and Thomas More; being a History of their Fellow-Work.
By Frederic Seebohm.
Second Edition. 8vo. 14s.

The New Reformation, a Narrative of the Old Catholic Movement, from 1870 to the Present Time; with an Historical Introduction. By Theodorus.
8vo. price 12s.

The Mythology of the Aryan Nations.
By Geo. W. Cox, M.A. late Scholar of Trinity College, Oxford.
2 vols. 8vo. 28s.

A History of Greece.
By the Rev. Geo. W. Cox, M.A. late Scholar of Trinity College, Oxford.
Vols. I. and II. 8vo. Maps, 36s.

A School History of Greece to the Death of Alexander the Great.
By the Rev. George W. Cox, M.A. late Scholar of Trinity College, Oxford; Author of 'The Aryan Mythology' &c.
1 vol. crown 8vo.   [*In the press.*

The History of the Peloponnesian War, by Thucydides.
Translated by Richd. Crawley, Fellow of Worcester College, Oxford.
8vo. 21s.

The Tale of the Great Persian War, from the Histories of Herodotus.
By Rev. G. W. Cox, M.A.
Fcp. 8vo. 3s. 6d.

Greek History from Themistocles to Alexander, in a Series of Lives from Plutarch.
Revised and arranged by A. H. Clough.
Fcp. 8vo. Woodcuts, 6s.

General History of Rome from the Foundation of the City to the Fall of Augustulus, B.C. 753—A.D. 476.
By the Very Rev. C. Merivale, D.D. Dean of Ely.
With 5 Maps, crown 8vo. 7s. 6d.

History of the Romans under the Empire.
By Dean Merivale, D.D.
8 vols. post 8vo. 48s.

The Fall of the Roman Republic; a Short History of the Last Century of the Commonwealth.
By Dean Merivale, D.D.
12mo. 7s. 6d.

The Sixth Oriental Monarchy; or the Geography, History, and Antiquities of Parthia. Collected and Illustrated from Ancient and Modern sources.
By Geo. Rawlinson, M.A.
With Maps and Illustrations. 8vo. 16s.

The Seventh Great Oriental Monarchy; or, a History of the Sassanians: with Notices Geographical and Antiquarian.
By Geo. Rawlinson, M.A.
8vo. with Maps and Illustrations. [*In the press.*]

Encyclopædia of Chronology, Historical and Biographical; comprising the Dates of all the Great Events of History, including Treaties, Alliances, Wars, Battles, &c. Incidents in the Lives of Eminent Men, Scientific and Geographical Discoveries, Mechanical Inventions, and Social, Domestic, and Economical Improvements.
By B. B. Woodward, B.A. and W. L. R. Cates.
8vo. 42s.

The History of Rome.
By Wilhelm Ihne.
Vols. I. and II. 8vo. 30s. Vols. III. and IV. in preparation.

History of European Morals from Augustus to Charlemagne.
By W. E. H. Lecky, M.A.
2 vols. 8vo. 28s.

History of the Rise and Influence of the Spirit of Rationalism in Europe.
By W. E. H. Lecky, M.A.
Cabinet Edition, 2 vols. crown 8vo. 16s.

Introduction to the Science of Religion: Four Lectures delivered at the Royal Institution; with two Essays on False Analogies and the Philosophy of Mythology.
By F. Max Müller, M.A.
Crown 8vo. 10s. 6d.

The Stoics, Epicureans, and Sceptics.
Translated from the German of Dr. E. Zeller, by Oswald J. Reichel, M.A.
Crown 8vo. 14s.

Socrates and the Socratic Schools.
Translated from the German of Dr. E. Zeller, by the Rev. O. J. Reichel, M.A.
Crown 8vo. 8s. 6d.

Sketch of the History of the Church of England to the Revolution of 1688. By T. V. Short, D.D. sometime Bishop of St. Asaph. New Edition. Crown 8vo. 7s. 6d.

The Historical Geography of Europe. By E. A. Freeman, D.C.L. 8vo. Maps. [*In the press.*

Essays on the History of the Christian Religion. By John Earl Russell, K.G. Fcp. 8vo. 3s. 6d.

The Student's Manual of Ancient History: containing the Political History, Geographical Position, and Social State of the Principal Nations of Antiquity. By W. Cooke Taylor, LL.D. Crown 8vo. 7s. 6d.

The Student's Manual of Modern History: containing the Rise and Progress of the Principal European Nations, their Political History, and the Changes in their Social Condition. By W. Cooke Taylor, LL.D. Crown 8vo. 7s. 6d.

The History of Philosophy, from Thales to Comte. By George Henry Lewes. Fourth Edition, 2 vols. 8vo. 32s.

The Crusades. By the Rev. G. W. Cox, M.A. Fcp. 8vo. with Map, 2s. 6d.

The Era of the Protestant Revolution. By F. Seebohm, Author of 'The Oxford Reformers.' With 4 Maps and 12 Diagrams. Fcp. 8vo. 2s. 6d.

The Thirty Years' War, 1618–1648. By Samuel Rawson Gardiner. Fcp. 8vo. with Maps, 2s. 6d.

The Houses of Lancaster and York; with the Conquest and Loss of France. By James Gairdner. Fcp. 8vo. with Map, 2s. 6d.

Edward the Third. By the Rev. W. Warburton, M.A. Fcp. 8vo. with Maps, 2s. 6d.

BIOGRAPHICAL WORKS.

Autobiography.
By *John Stuart Mill.*
8vo. 7s. 6d.

The Life and Letters of Lord Macaulay.
By his Nephew, G. Otto Trevelyan, M.P. for the Hawick District of Burghs.
2 vols. 8vo. [*In the press.*

Admiral Sir Edward Codrington, a Memoir of his Life; with Selections from his Private and Official Correspondence. Abridged from the larger work, and edited by his Daughter, Lady Bourchier.
With Portrait, Maps, &c. crown 8vo. price 7s. 6d.

Life and Letters of Gilbert Elliot, First Earl of Minto, from 1751 to 1806, when his Public Life in Europe was closed by his Appointment to the Vice-Royalty of India. Edited by the Countess of Minto.
3 vols. post 8vo. 31s. 6d.

Recollections of Past Life.
By Sir *Henry Holland,* Bart. M.D. F.R.S.
Third Edition. Post 8vo. 10s. 6d.

Isaac Casaubon, 1559-1614.
By *Mark Pattison,* Rector of Lincoln College, Oxford.
8vo. price 18s.

The Memoirs of Sir John Reresby, of Thrybergh, Bart. M.P. for York, &c. 1634-1689. Written by Himself. Edited from the Original Manuscript by *James J. Cartwright, M.A.* Cantab. of H.M. Public Record Office.
8vo. price 21s.

Biographical and Critical Essays, reprinted from Reviews, with Additions and Corrections.
By A. *Hayward,* Q.C.
Second Series, 2 vols. 8vo. 28s. Third Series, 1 vol. 8vo. 14s.

The Life of Isambard Kingdom Brunel, Civil Engineer.
By I. *Brunel,* B.C.L.
With Portrait, Plates, and Woodcuts. 8vo. 21s.

Lord George Bentinck; a Political Biography.
By the Right Hon. B. *Disraeli, M.P.*
New Edition. Crown 8vo. 6s.

The Life and Letters of the Rev. Sydney Smith. Edited by his Daughter, Lady Holland, and Mrs. Austin.
Crown 8vo. 2s. 6d. sewed; 3s. 6d. cloth.

Essays in Ecclesiastical Biography. By the Right Hon. Sir J. Stephen, LL.D.
Cabinet Edition. Crown 8vo. 7s. 6d.

Leaders of Public Opinion in Ireland; Swift, Flood, Grattan, O'Connell. By W. E. H. Lecky, M.A.
Crown 8vo. 7s. 6d.

Dictionary of General Biography; containing Concise Memoirs and Notices of the most Eminent Persons of all Ages and Countries. By W. L. R. Cates.
New Edition, 8vo. 25s. Supplement, 4s. 6d.

Life of the Duke of Wellington. By the Rev. G. R. Gleig, M.A.
Crown 8vo. with Portrait, 5s.

Felix Mendelssohn's Letters from Italy and Switzerland, and Letters from 1833 to 1847. Translated by Lady Wallace.
With Portrait. 2 vols. crown 8vo. 5s. each.

The Rise of Great Families; other Essays and Stories. By Sir Bernard Burke, C.B. LL.D.
Crown 8vo. 12s. 6d.

Memoirs of Sir Henry Havelock, K.C.B. By John Clark Marshman.
Crown 8vo. 3s. 6d.

Vicissitudes of Families. By Sir Bernard Burke, C.B.
2 vols. crown 8vo. 21s.

MENTAL and POLITICAL PHILOSOPHY.

Comte's System of Positive Polity, or Treatise upon Sociology. Translated from the Paris Edition of 1851-1854, and furnished with Analytical Tables of Contents. In Four Volumes, each forming in some degree an independent Treatise:—

Vol. I. *General View of Positivism and Introductory Principles.* Translated by J. H. Bridges, M.B. *formerly Fellow of Oriel College, Oxford.* 8vo. price 21s.

Vol. II. *The Social Statics, or the Abstract Laws of Human Order.* Translated by Frederic Harrison, M.A. [*In Oct.*

Vol. III. *The Social Dynamics, or the General Laws of Human Progress* (the *Philosophy of History*). Translated by E. S. Beesly, M.A. *Professor of History in University College, London.* 8vo. [*In Dec.*

Vol. IV. *The Synthesis of the Future of Mankind.* Translated by Richard Congreve, M.D., and an *Appendix*, containing the Author's *Minor Treatises*, translated by H. D. Hutton, M.A. *Barrister-at-Law.* 8vo. [*Early in* 1876.

Order and Progress:
Part I. Thoughts on Government; Part II. Studies of Political Crises.
By Frederic Harrison, M.A. of Lincoln's Inn.
8vo. 14s.

Essays, Political, Social, and Religious.
By Richd. Congreve, M.A.
8vo. 18s.

Essays, Critical and Biographical, contributed to the Edinburgh Review.
By Henry Rogers.
New Edition. 2 vols. crown 8vo. 12s.

Essays on some Theological Controversies of the Time, contributed chiefly to the Edinburgh Review.
By Henry Rogers.
New Edition. Crown 8vo. 6s.

Democracy in America.
By Alexis de Tocqueville. Translated by Henry Reeve, Esq.
New Edition. 2 vols. crown 8vo. 16s.

On Representative Government.
By John Stuart Mill.
Fourth Edition, crown 8vo. 2s.

On Liberty.
By John Stuart Mill.
Post 8vo. 7s. 6d. crown 8vo. 1s. 4d.

Principles of Political Economy.
By John Stuart Mill.
2 vols. 8vo. 30s. or 1 vol. crown 8vo. 5s.

Essays on some Unsettled Questions of Political Economy.
By John Stuart Mill.
Second Edition. 8vo. 6s. 6d.

Utilitarianism.
By John Stuart Mill.
Fourth Edition. 8vo. 5s.

A System of Logic, Ratiocinative and Inductive. By John Stuart Mill.
Eighth Edition. 2 vols. 8vo. 25s.

The Subjection of Women.
By John Stuart Mill.
New Edition. Post 8vo. 5s.

Examination of Sir William Hamilton's Philosophy, and of the principal Philosophical Questions discussed in his Writings.
By John Stuart Mill.
Fourth Edition. 8vo. 16s.

Dissertations and Discussions.
By John Stuart Mill.
Second Edition. 3 vols. 8vo. 36s. VOL. IV. (completion) price 10s. 6d.

Analysis of the Phenomena of the Human Mind. By JAMES MILL. New Edition, with Notes, Illustrative and Critical. 2 vols. 8vo. 28s.

A Systematic View of the Science of Jurisprudence. By SHELDON AMOS, M.A. 8vo. 18s.

A Primer of the English Constitution and Government. By SHELDON AMOS, M.A. Second Edition. Crown 8vo. 6s.

Principles of Economical Philosophy. By H. D. MACLEOD, M.A. Barrister-at-Law. Second Edition, in 2 vols. Vol. I. 8vo. 15s. Vol. II. Part I. price 12s.

The Institutes of Justinian; with English Introduction, Translation, and Notes. By T. C. SANDARS, M.A. Fifth Edition. 8vo. 18s.

Lord Bacon's Works, Collected and Edited by R. L. ELLIS, M.A. J. SPEDDING, M.A. and D. D. HEATH. New and Cheaper Edition. 7 vols. 8vo. £3. 13s. 6d.

Letters and Life of Francis Bacon, including all his Occasional Works. Collected and edited, with a Commentary, by J. SPEDDING. 7 vols. 8vo. £4. 4s.

The Nicomachean Ethics of Aristotle. Newly translated into English. By R. WILLIAMS, B.A. 8vo. 12s.

The Politics of Aristotle; Greek Text, with English Notes. By RICHARD CONGREVE, M.A. New Edition, revised. 8vo. 18s.

The Ethics of Aristotle; with Essays and Notes. By Sir A. GRANT, Bart. M.A. LL.D. Third Edition. 2 vols. 8vo. price 32s.

Bacon's Essays, with Annotations. By R. WHATELY, D.D. New Edition. 8vo. 10s. 6d.

Picture Logic; an Attempt to Popularise the Science of Reasoning by the combination of Humorous Pictures with Examples of Reasoning taken from Daily Life. By A. SWINBOURNE, B.A. With Woodcut Illustrations from Drawings by the Author. Fcp. 8vo. price 5s.

Elements of Logic.
By R. Whately, D.D.
New Edition. 8vo. 10s. 6d. cr. 8vo. 4s. 6d.

Elements of Rhetoric.
By R. Whately, D.D.
New Edition. 8vo. 10s. 6d. cr. 8vo. 4s. 6d.

An Outline of the Necessary Laws of Thought: a Treatise on Pure and Applied Logic.
By the Most Rev. W. Thomson, D.D. Archbishop of York.
Ninth Thousand. Crown 8vo. 5s. 6d.

An Introduction to Mental Philosophy, on the Inductive Method.
By J. D. Morell, LL.D.
8vo. 12s.

Elements of Psychology, containing the Analysis of the Intellectual Powers.
By J. D. Morell, LL.D.
Post 8vo. 7s. 6d.

The Secret of Hegel: being the Hegelian System in Origin, Principle, Form, and Matter.
By J. H. Stirling, LL.D.
2 vols. 8vo. 28s.

Sir William Hamilton; being the Philosophy of Perception: an Analysis.
By J. H. Stirling, LL.D.
8vo. 5s.

Ueberweg's System of Logic, and History of Logical Doctrines.
Translated, with Notes and Appendices, by T. M. Lindsay, M.A. F.R.S.E.
8vo. 16s.

The Senses and the Intellect.
By A. Bain, LL.D. Prof. of Logic, Univ. Aberdeen.
8vo. 15s.

Mental and Moral Science; a Compendium of Psychology and Ethics.
By A. Bain, LL.D.
Third Edition. Crown 8vo. 10s. 6d. Or separately: Part I. Mental Science, 6s. 6d. Part II. Moral Science, 4s. 6d.

The Philosophy of Necessity; or, Natural Law as applicable to Mental, Moral, and Social Science.
By Charles Bray.
Second Edition. 8vo. 9s.

Hume's Treatise on Human Nature.
Edited, with Notes, &c. by T. H. Green, M.A. and the Rev. T. H. Grose, M.A.
2 vols. 8vo. 28s.

Hume's Essays Moral, Political, and Literary.
By the same Editors.
2 vols. 8vo. 28s.

⁎⁎⁎ The above form a complete and uniform Edition of HUME'S Philosophical Works.

MISCELLANEOUS & CRITICAL WORKS.

Miscellaneous and Posthumous Works of the late Henry Thomas Buckle. Edited, with a Biographical Notice, by Helen Taylor.
3 vols. 8vo. £2. 12s. 6d.

Short Studies on Great Subjects.
By J. A. Froude, M.A. formerly Fellow of Exeter College, Oxford.
CABINET EDITION, 2 vols. crown 8vo. 12s.
LIBRARY EDITION, 2 vols. 8vo. 24s.

Lord Macaulay's Miscellaneous Writings.
LIBRARY EDITION, 2 vols. 8vo. Portrait, 21s.
PEOPLE'S EDITION, 1 vol. cr. 8vo. 4s. 6d.

Lord Macaulay's Miscellaneous Writings and Speeches.
Students' Edition. Crown 8vo. 6s.

Speeches of the Right Hon. Lord Macaulay, corrected by Himself.
People's Edition. Crown 8vo. 3s. 6d.

Lord Macaulay's Speeches on Parliamentary Reform in 1831 and 1832.
16mo. 1s.

Manual of English Literature, Historical and Critical.
By Thomas Arnold, M.A.
New Edition. Crown 8vo. 7s. 6d.

The Rev. Sydney Smith's Essays contributed to the Edinburgh Review.
Authorised Edition, complete in One Volume. Crown 8vo. 2s. 6d. sewed, or 3s. 6d. cloth.

The Rev. Sydney Smith's Miscellaneous Works.
Crown 8vo. 6s.

The Wit and Wisdom of the Rev. Sydney Smith.
Crown 8vo. 3s. 6d.

The Miscellaneous Works of Thomas Arnold, D.D. Late Head Master of Rugby School and Regius Professor of Modern History in the Univ. of Oxford.
8vo. 7s. 6d.

Realities of Irish Life.
By W. Steuart Trench.
Cr. 8vo. 2s. 6d. sewed, or 3s. 6d. cloth.

Lectures on the Science of Language.
By F. Max Müller, M.A. &c.
Eighth Edition. 2 vols. crown 8vo. 16s.

Chips from a German Workshop; being Essays on the Science of Religion, and on Mythology, Traditions, and Customs.
By F. Max Müller, M.A. &c.
3 vols. 8vo. £2.

Southey's Doctor, complete in One Volume.
Edited by Rev. J. W. Warter, B.D.
Square crown 8vo. 12s. 6d.

Families of Speech.
Four Lectures delivered at the Royal Institution.
By F. W. Farrar, D.D.
New Edition. Crown 8vo. 3s. 6d.

Chapters on Language.
By F. W. Farrar, D.D. F.R.S.
New Edition. Crown 8vo. 5s.

A Budget of Paradoxes.
By Augustus De Morgan, F.R.A.S.
Reprinted, with Author's Additions, from the Athenæum. 8vo. 15s.

Apparitions; a Narrative of Facts.
By the Rev. B. W. Savile, M.A. Author of 'The Truth of the Bible' &c.
Crown 8vo. price 4s. 6d.

Miscellaneous Writings of John Conington, M.A.
Edited by J. A. Symonds, M.A. With a Memoir by H. J. S. Smith, M.A.
2 vols. 8vo. 28s.

Recreations of a Country Parson.
By A. K. H. B.
Two Series, 3s. 6d. each.

Landscapes, Churches, and Moralities.
By A. K. H. B.
Crown 8vo. 3s. 6d.

Seaside Musings on Sundays and Weekdays.
By A. K. H. B.
Crown 8vo. 3s. 6d.

Changed Aspects of Unchanged Truths.
By A. K. H. B.
Crown 8vo. 3s. 6d.

Counsel and Comfort from a City Pulpit.
By A. K. H. B.
Crown 8vo. 3s. 6d.

Lessons of Middle Age.
By A. K. H. B.
Crown 8vo. 3s. 6d.

Leisure Hours in Town.
By A. K. H. B.
Crown 8vo. 3s. 6d.

The Autumn Holidays of a Country Parson.
By A. K. H. B.
Crown 8vo. 3s. 6d.

Sunday Afternoons at the Parish Church of a Scottish University City.
By A. K. H. B.
Crown 8vo. 3s. 6d.

The Commonplace Philosopher in Town and Country.
By A. K. H. B.
Crown 8vo. 3s. 6d.

Present-Day Thoughts.
By A. K. H. B.
Crown 8vo. 3s. 6d.

Critical Essays of a Country Parson.
By A. K. H. B.
Crown 8vo. 3s. 6d.

The Graver Thoughts of a Country Parson.
By A. K. H. B.
Two Series, 3s. 6d. each.

DICTIONARIES and OTHER BOOKS of REFERENCE.

A Dictionary of the English Language.
By R. G. Latham, M.A. M.D. Founded on the Dictionary of Dr. S. Johnson, as edited by the Rev. H. J. Todd, with numerous Emendations and Additions.
4 vols. 4to. £7.

Thesaurus of English Words and Phrases, classified and arranged so as to facilitate the expression of Ideas, and assist in Literary Composition.
By P. M. Roget, M.D.
Crown 8vo. 10s. 6d.

English Synonymes.
By E. J. Whately. Edited by Archbishop Whately.
Fifth Edition. Fcp. 8vo. 3s.

Handbook of the English Language. For the use of Students of the Universities and the Higher Classes in Schools.
By R. G. Latham, M.A. M.D. &c. late Fellow of King's College, Cambridge; late Professor of English in Univ. Coll. Lond.
The Ninth Edition. Crown 8vo. 6s.

A Practical Dictionary of the French and English Languages.
By Léon Contanseau, many years French Examiner for Military and Civil Appointments, &c.
Post 8vo. 10s. 6d.

Contanseau's Pocket Dictionary, French and English, abridged from the Practical Dictionary, by the Author.
Square 18mo. 3s. 6d.

New Practical Dictionary of the German Language; German-English and English-German.
By Rev. W. L. Blackley, M.A. and Dr. C. M. Friedländer.
Post 8vo. 7s. 6d.

A Dictionary of Roman and Greek Antiquities. With 2,000 Woodcuts from Ancient Originals, illustrative of the Arts and Life of the Greeks and Romans.
By Anthony Rich, B.A.
Third Edition. Crown 8vo. 7s. 6d.

The Mastery of Languages; or, the Art of Speaking Foreign Tongues Idiomatically.
By Thomas Prendergast.
Second Edition. 8vo. 6s.

A Practical English Dictionary.
By John T. White, D.D. Oxon. and T. C. Donkin, M.A.
1 vol. post 8vo. uniform with Contanseau's Practical French Dictionary.
[*In the press.*

A Latin-English Dictionary.
By John T. White, D.D. Oxon. and J. E. Riddle, M.A. Oxon.
Third Edition, revised. 2 vols. 4to. 42s.

White's College Latin-English Dictionary; abridged from the Parent Work for the use of University Students.
Medium 8vo. 18s.

A Latin-English Dictionary adapted for the use of Middle-Class Schools,
By John T. White, D.D. Oxon.
Square fcp. 8vo. 3s.

White's Junior Student's Complete Latin-English and English-Latin Dictionary.
Square 12mo. 12s.

Separately { ENGLISH-LATIN, 5s. 6d.
            { LATIN-ENGLISH, 7s. 6d.

A Greek-English Lexicon.
By H. G. Liddell, D.D. Dean of Christchurch, and R. Scott, D.D. Dean of Rochester.
Sixth Edition. Crown 4to. 36s.

A Lexicon, Greek and English, abridged for Schools from Liddell and Scott's Greek-English Lexicon.
Fourteenth Edition. Square 12mo. 7s. 6d.

An English-Greek Lexicon, containing all the Greek Words used by Writers of good authority.
By C. D. Yonge, B.A.
New Edition. 4to. 21s.

C. D. Yonge's New Lexicon, English and Greek, abridged from his larger Lexicon.
Square 12mo. 8s. 6d.

M'Culloch's Dictionary, Practical, Theoretical, and Historical, of Commerce and Commercial Navigation.
Edited by H. G. Reid.
8vo. 63s.

A General Dictionary of Geography, Descriptive, Physical, Statistical, and Historical; forming a complete Gazetteer of the World.
By A. Keith Johnston, F.R.S.E.
New Edition, thoroughly revised.
[*In the press.*

The Public Schools Manual of Modern Geography. Forming a Companion to 'The Public Schools Atlas of Modern Geography'
By Rev. G. Butler, M.A.
[*In the press.*

The Public Schools Atlas of Modern Geography. In 31 Maps, exhibiting clearly the more important Physical Features of the Countries delineated.
Edited, with Introduction, by Rev. G. Butler, M.A.
Imperial quarto, 3s. 6d. sewed; 5s. cloth.

The Public Schools Atlas of Ancient Geography. Edited, with an Introduction on the Study of Ancient Geography, by the Rev. G. Butler, M.A.
Imperial Quarto. [*In the press.*

ASTRONOMY and METEOROLOGY.

The Universe and the Coming Transits; Researches into and New Views respecting the Constitution of the Heavens.
By R. A. Proctor, B.A.
With 22 Charts and 22 Diagrams. 8vo. 16s.

Saturn and its System.
By R. A. Proctor, B.A.
8vo. with 14 Plates, 14s.

The Transits of Venus; A Popular Account of Past and Coming Transits, from the first observed by Horrocks A.D. 1639 to the Transit of A.D. 2012.

By R. A. Proctor, B.A.

With 20 Plates (12 Coloured) and 27 Woodcuts. Crown 8vo. 8s. 6d.

Essays on Astronomy.
A Series of Papers on Planets and Meteors, the Sun and Sun-surrounding Space, Stars and Star Cloudlets.
By R. A. Proctor, B.A.
With 10 Plates and 24 Woodcuts. 8vo. 12s.

The Moon; her Motions, Aspect, Scenery, and Physical Condition.
By R. A. Proctor, B.A.
With Plates, Charts, Woodcuts, and Lunar Photographs. Crown 8vo. 15s.

The Sun; Ruler, Light, Fire, and Life of the Planetary System.
By R. A. Proctor, B.A.
Second Edition. Plates and Woodcuts. Cr. 8vo. 14s.

The Orbs Around Us; a Series of Familiar Essays on the Moon and Planets, Meteors and Comets, the Sun and Coloured Pairs of Suns.
By R. A. Proctor, B.A.
Second Edition, with Chart and 4 Diagrams. Crown 8vo. 7s. 6d.

Other Worlds than Ours; The Plurality of Worlds Studied under the Light of Recent Scientific Researches.
By R. A. Proctor, B.A.
Third Edition, with 14 Illustrations. Cr. 8vo. 10s. 6d.

Brinkley's Astronomy. Revised and partly re-written, with Additional Chapters, and an Appendix of Questions for Examination.
By. John W. Stubbs, D.D. and F. Brünnow, Ph.D.
With 49 Diagrams. Crown 8vo. 6s.

Outlines of Astronomy.
By Sir J. F. W. Herschel, Bart. M.A.
Latest Edition, with Plates and Diagrams. Square crown 8vo. 12s.

A New Star Atlas, for the Library, the School, and the Observatory, in 12 Circular Maps (with 2 Index Plates).
By R. A. Proctor, B.A.
Crown 8vo. 5s.

Celestial Objects for Common Telescopes.
By T. W. Webb, M.A. F.R.A.S.
New Edition, with Map of the Moon and Woodcuts. Crown 8vo. 7s. 6d.

Larger Star Atlas, for the Library, in Twelve Circular Maps, photolithographed by A. Brothers, F.R.A.S. With 2 Index Plates and a Letterpress Introduction.
By R. A. Proctor, BA.
Second Edition. Small folio, 25s.

Dove's Law of Storms, considered in connexion with the ordinary Movements of the Atmosphere. Translated by R. H. Scott, M.A.
8vo. 10s. 6d.

Air and Rain; the Beginnings of a Chemical Climatology.
By R. A. Smith, F.R.S.
8vo. 24s.

Air and its Relations to Life, 1774–1874. Being, with some Additions, a Course of Lectures delivered at the Royal Institution of Great Britain in the Summer of 1874.
By Walter Noel Hartley, F.C.S. Demonstrator of Chemistry at King's College, London.
1 vol. small 8vo. with Illustratrations. [Nearly ready.

Magnetism and Deviation of the Compass. For the use of Students in Navigation and Science Schools.
By J. Merrifield, LL.D.
18mo. 1s. 6d.

Nautical Surveying, an Introduction to the Practical and Theoretical Study of.
By J. K. Laughton, M.A.
Small 8vo. 6s.

Schellen's Spectrum Analysis, in its Application to Terrestrial Substances and the Physical Constitution of the Heavenly Bodies.
Translated by Jane and C. Lassell; edited, with Notes, by W. Huggins, LL.D. F.R.S.
With 13 Plates and 223 Woodcuts. 8vo. 28s.

NATURAL HISTORY and PHYSICAL SCIENCE.

The Correlation of Physical Forces.
By the Hon. Sir W. R. Grove, F.R.S. &c.
Sixth Edition, with other Contributions to Science. 8vo. 15s.

Professor Helmholtz' Popular Lectures on Scientific Subjects.
Translated by E. Atkinson, F.C.S.
With many Illustrative Wood Engravings. 8vo. 12s. 6d.

Ganot's Natural Philosophy for General Readers and Young Persons; a Course of Physics divested of Mathematical Formulæ and expressed in the language of daily life.
Translated by E. Atkinson, F.C.S.
Second Edition, with 2 Plates and 429 Woodcuts. Crown 8vo. 7s. 6d.

Ganot's Elementary Treatise on Physics, Experimental and Applied, for the use of Colleges and Schools.
Translated and edited by E. Atkinson, F.C.S.
New Edition, with a Coloured Plate and 726 Woodcuts. Post 8vo. 15s.

Weinhold's Introduction to Experimental Physics, Theoretical and Practical; including Directions for Constructing Physical Apparatus and for Making Experiments.
Translated by B. Loewy, F.R.A.S. With a Preface by G. C. Foster, F.R.S.
With 3 Coloured Plates and 404 Woodcuts. 8vo. price 31s. 6d.

Principles of Animal Mechanics.
By the Rev. S. Haughton, F.R.S.
Second Edition. 8vo. 21s.

Text-Books of Science, Mechanical and Physical, adapted for the use of Artisans and of Students in Public and other Schools. (The first Ten edited by T. M. Goodeve, M.A. Lecturer on Applied Science at the Royal School of Mines; the remainder edited by C. W. Merrifield, F.R.S. an Examiner in the Department of Public Education.)
Small 8vo. Woodcuts.

Edited by T. M. Goodeve, M.A.
Anderson's *Strength of Materials*, 3s. 6d.
Bloxam's *Metals*, 3s. 6d.
Goodeve's *Mechanics*, 3s. 6d.
—— *Mechanism*, 3s. 6d.
Griffin's *Algebra & Trigonometry*, 3s. 6d.
  Notes on the same, with Solutions, 3s. 6d.
Jenkin's *Electricity & Magnetism*, 3s. 6d.
Maxwell's *Theory of Heat*, 3s. 6d.
Merrifield's *Technical Arithmetic*, 3s. 6d.
  Key, 3s. 6d.
Miller's *Inorganic Chemistry*, 3s. 6d.
Shelley's *Workshop Appliances*, 3s. 6d.
Watson's *Plane & Solid Geometry*, 3s. 6d.

Edited by C. W. Merrifield, F.R.S.
Armstrong's *Organic Chemistry*, 3s. 6d.
Thorpe's *Quantitative Analysis*, 4s. 6d.
Thorpe and Muir's *Qualitative Analysis*, 3s. 6d.

Fragments of Science.
By John Tyndall, F.R.S.
New Edition, in the press.

Address delivered before the British Association assembled at Belfast.
By John Tyndall, F.R.S. President.
8th Thousand, with New Preface and the Manchester Address. 8vo. price 4s. 6d.

Heat a Mode of Motion.
By *John Tyndall*, F.R.S.
Fifth Edition, Plate and Woodcuts.
Crown 8vo. 10s. 6d.

Sound.
By *John Tyndall*, F.R.S.
Third Edition, including Recent Researches on Fog-Signalling; Portrait and Woodcuts. Crown 8vo. 10s. 6d.

Researches on Diamagnetism and Magne-Crystallic Action; including Diamagnetic Polarity.
By *John Tyndall*, F.R.S.
With 6 Plates and many Woodcuts. 8vo. 14s.

Contributions to Molecular Physics in the domain of Radiant Heat.
By *John Tyndall*, F.R.S.
With 2 Plates and 31 Woodcuts. 8vo. 16s.

Six Lectures on Light, delivered in America in 1872 and 1873.
By *John Tyndall*, F.R.S.
Second Edition, with Portrait, Plate, and 59 Diagrams. Crown 8vo. 7s. 6d.

Notes of a Course of Nine Lectures on Light, delivered at the Royal Institution.
By *John Tyndall*, F.R.S.
Crown 8vo. 1s. sewed, or 1s. 6d. cloth.

Notes of a Course of Seven Lectures on Electrical Phenomena and Theories, delivered at the Royal Institution.
By *John Tyndall*, F.R.S.
Crown 8vo. 1s. sewed, or 1s. 6d. cloth.

A Treatise on Magnetism, General and Terrestrial.
By *H. Lloyd*, D.D. D.C.L.
8vo. price 10s. 6d.

Elementary Treatise on the Wave-Theory of Light.
By *H. Lloyd*, D.D. D.C.L.
Third Edition. 8vo. 10s. 6d.

An Elementary Exposition of the Doctrine of Energy.
By *D. D. Heath*, M.A.
Post 8vo. 4s. 6d.

The Comparative Anatomy and Physiology of the Vertebrate Animals.
By *Richard Owen*, F.R.S.
With 1,472 Woodcuts. 3 vols. 8vo. £3. 13s. 6d.

Sir H. Holland's Fragmentary Papers on Science and other subjects.
Edited by the Rev. J. Holland.
8vo. price 14s.

Light Science for Leisure Hours; Familiar Essays on Scientific Subjects, Natural Phenomena, &c.
By *R. A. Proctor*, B.A.
First and Second Series. 2 vols. crown 8vo. 7s. 6d. each.

Kirby and Spence's Introduction to Entomology, or Elements of the Natural History of Insects.
Crown 8vo. 5s.

NEW WORKS PUBLISHED BY LONGMANS & CO.

Strange Dwellings; a Description of the Habitations of Animals, abridged from 'Homes without Hands.'
By Rev. J. G. Wood, M.A.
With Frontispiece and 60 Woodcuts. Crown 8vo. 7s. 6d.

Homes without Hands; a Description of the Habitations of Animals, classed according to their Principle of Construction.
By Rev. J. G. Wood, M.A.
With about 140 Vignettes on Wood. 8vo. 14s.

Out of Doors; a Selection of Original Articles on Practical Natural History.
By Rev. J. G. Wood, M.A.
With 6 Illustrations from Original Designs engraved on Wood. Crown 8vo. 7s. 6d.

The Polar World: a Popular Description of Man and Nature in the Arctic and Antarctic Regions of the Globe.
By Dr. G. Hartwig.
With Chromoxylographs, Maps, and Woodcuts. 8vo. 10s. 6d.

The Sea and its Living Wonders.
By Dr. G. Hartwig.
Fourth Edition, enlarged. 8vo. with many Illustrations, 10s. 6d.

The Tropical World.
By Dr. G. Hartwig.
With about 200 Illustrations. 8vo. 10s. 6d.

The Subterranean World.
By Dr. G. Hartwig.
With Maps and Woodcuts. 8vo. 10s. 6d.

The Aerial World; a Popular Account of the Phenomena and Life of the Atmosphere.
By Dr. George Hartwig.
With Map, 8 Chromoxylographs, and 60 Woodcuts. 8vo. price 21s.

Game Preservers and Bird Preservers, or 'Which are our Friends?'
By George Francis Morant, late Captain 12th Royal Lancers & Major Cape Mounted Riflemen.
Crown 8vo. price 5s.

A Familiar History of Birds.
By E. Stanley, D.D. late Ld. Bishop of Norwich.
Fcp. 8vo. with Woodcuts, 3s. 6d.

Insects at Home; a Popular Account of British Insects, their Structure Habits, and Transformations.
By Rev. J. G. Wood, M.A.
With upwards of 700 Woodcuts. 8vo. 21s.

Insects Abroad; being a Popular Account of Foreign Insects, their Structure, Habits, and Transformations.
By Rev. J. G. Wood, M.A.
With upwards of 700 Woodcuts. 8vo. 21s.

Rocks Classified and Described.
By B. Von Cotta.
English Edition, by P. H. LAWRENCE (with English, German, and French Synonymes), revised by the Author. Post 8vo. 14s.

Heer's Primæval World of Switzerland.
Translated by W. S. Dallas, F.L.S. and edited by James Heywood, M.A. F.R.S.
2 vols. 8vo. with numerous Illustrations. [*In the press.*

The Origin of Civilisation, and the Primitive Condition of Man; Mental and Social Condition of Savages.
By Sir J. Lubbock, Bart. M.P. F.R.S.
Third Edition, with 25 Woodcuts. 8vo. 18s.

The Native Races of the Pacific States of North America.
By Hubert Howe Bancroft.
Vol. I. Wild Tribes, their Manners and Customs; with 6 Maps. 8vo. 25s.
Vol. II. Native Races of the Pacific States. 25s.
⁎ To be completed early in the year 1876, in Three more Volumes—
Vol. III. Mythology and Languages of both Savage and Civilized Nations.
Vol. IV. Antiquities and Architectural Remains.
Vol. V. Aboriginal History and Migrations; Index to the Entire Work.

The Ancient Stone Implements, Weapons, and Ornaments of Great Britain.
By John Evans, F.R.S.
With 2 Plates and 476 Woodcuts. 8vo. 28s.

The Elements of Botany for Families and Schools.
Eleventh Edition, revised by Thomas Moore, F.L.S.
Fcp. 8vo. with 154 Woodcuts, 2s. 6d.

Bible Animals; a Description of every Living Creature mentioned in the Scriptures, from the Ape to the Coral.
By Rev. J. G. Wood, M.A.
With about 100 Vignettes on Wood. 8vo. 21s.

The Rose Amateur's Guide.
By Thomas Rivers.
Tenth Edition. Fcp. 8vo. 4s.

A Dictionary of Science, Literature, and Art.
Re-edited by the late W. T. Brande (the Author) and Rev. G. W. Cox, M.A.
New Edition, revised. 3 vols. medium 8vo. 63s.

On the Sensations o Tone, as a Physiological Basis for the Theory of Music.
By H. Helmholtz, Professor of Physiology in the University of Berlin. Translated by A. J. Ellis, F.R.S.
8vo. 36s.

The History of Modern Music, a Course of Lectures delivered at the Royal Institution of Great Britain.
By *John Hullah*, Professor of Vocal Music in Queen's College and Bedford College, and Organist of Charterhouse.

New Edition, 1 vol. post 8vo. [*In the press.*

The Treasury of Botany,
or Popular Dictionary of the Vegetable Kingdom; with which is incorporated a Glossary of Botanical Terms.
Edited by *J. Lindley*, F.R.S. and *T. Moore*, F.L.S.

With 274 *Woodcuts* and 20 *Steel Plates*. Two Parts, fcp. 8vo. 12s.

A General System of Descriptive and Analytical Botany.
Translated from the French of *Le Maout* and *Decaisne*, by Mrs. *Hooker*. Edited and arranged according to the English Botanical System, by *J. D. Hooker*, M.D. &c. Director of the Royal Botanic Gardens, Kew.

With 5,500 *Woodcuts*. *Imperial* 8vo. 52s. 6d.

Loudon's Encyclopædia of Plants;
comprising the Specific Character, Description, Culture, History, &c. of all the Plants found in Great Britain.

With upwards of 12,000 *Woodcuts*. 8vo. 42s.

Handbook of Hardy Trees, Shrubs, and Herbaceous Plants;
containing Descriptions &c. of the Best Species in Cultivation; with Cultural Details, Comparative Hardiness, suitability for particular positions, &c. Based on the French Work of *Decaisne* and *Naudin*, and including the 720 Original Woodcut Illustrations.
By *W. B. Hemsley*.

Medium 8vo. 21s.

Forest Trees and Woodland Scenery, as described in Ancient and Modern Poets.
By *William Menzies*, Deputy Surveyor of Windsor Forest and Parks, &c.

In One Volume, *imperial* 4to. with Twenty Plates, Coloured in facsimile of the original drawings, price £5. 5s.
[*Preparing for publication.*

CHEMISTRY and PHYSIOLOGY.

Miller's Elements of Chemistry, Theoretical and Practical.
Re-edited, with Additions, by H. Macleod, F.C.S.

3 vols. 8vo. £3.

PART I. CHEMICAL PHYSICS, 15s.
PART II. INORGANIC CHEMISTRY, 21s.
PART III. ORGANIC CHEMISTRY, New Edition in the press.

A Dictionary of Chemistry and the Allied Branches of other Sciences.
By Henry Watts, F.C.S. assisted by eminent Scientific and Practical Chemists.

6 vols. medium 8vo. £8. 14s. 6d.

Second Supplement to Watts's Dictionary of Chemistry, completing the Record of Discovery to the year 1873.

8vo. price 42s.

Select Methods in Chemical Analysis, chiefly Inorganic.
By Wm. Crookes, F.R.S.
With 22 Woodcuts. Crown 8vo. 12s. 6d.

Todd and Bowman's Physiological Anatomy, and Physiology of Man.
Vol. II. with numerous Illustrations, 25s.
Vol. I. New Edition by Dr. LIONEL S. BEALE, F.R.S. Parts I. and II. in 8vo. price 7s. 6d. each.

Health in the House, Twenty-five Lectures on Elementary Physiology in its Application to the Daily Wants of Man and Animals.
By Mrs. C. M. Buckton.
Crown 8vo. Woodcuts, 5s.

Outlines of Physiology, Human and Comparative.
By J. Marshall, F.R.C.S. Surgeon to the University College Hospital.
2 vols. cr. 8vo. with 122 Woodcuts, 32s.

The FINE ARTS and ILLUSTRATED EDITIONS.

Poems.
By William B. Scott.
I. Ballads and Tales. II. Studies from Nature. III. Sonnets &c.
Illustrated by Seventeen Etchings by L. Alma Tadema *and* William B. Scott.
Crown 8vo. 15s.

Half-hour Lectures on the History and Practice of the Fine and Ornamental Arts.
By W. B. Scott.
Third Edition, with 50 Woodcuts. Crown 8vo. 8s. 6d.

NEW WORKS PUBLISHED BY LONGMANS & CO. 25

In Fairyland; Pictures from the Elf-World. By Richard Doyle. With a Poem by W. Allingham.

With 16 coloured Plates, containing 36 Designs. Second Edition, folio, 15s.

A Dictionary of Artists of the English School: Painters, Sculptors, Architects, Engravers, and Ornamentists; with Notices of their Lives and Works. By Samuel Redgrave.

8vo. 16s.

The New Testament, illustrated with Wood Engravings after the Early Masters, chiefly of the Italian School.

Crown 4to. 63s.

Lord Macaulay's Lays of Ancient Rome. With 90 Illustrations on Wood from Drawings by G. Scharf.

Fcp. 4to. 21s.

Miniature Edition, with Scharf's 90 Illustrations reduced in Lithography.

Imp. 16mo. 10s. 6d.

Moore's Lalla Rookh, Tenniel's Edition, with 68 Wood Engravings.

Fcp. 4to. 21s.

Moore's Irish Melodies, Maclise's Edition, with 161 Steel Plates.

Super royal 8vo. 31s. 6d.

Sacred and Legendary Art. By Mrs. Jameson.

6 vols. square crown 8vo. price £5. 15s. 6d. as follows:—

Legends of the Saints and Martyrs.

New Edition, with 19 Etchings and 187 Woodcuts. 2 vols. 31s. 6d.

Legends of the Monastic Orders.

New Edition, with 11 Etchings and 88 Woodcuts. 1 vol. 21s.

Legends of the Madonna.

New Edition, with 27 Etchings and 165 Woodcuts. 1 vol. 21s.

The History of Our Lord, with that of his Types and Precursors. Completed by Lady Eastlake.

Revised Edition, with 13 Etchings and 281 Woodcuts. 2 vols. 42s.

D

The USEFUL ARTS, MANUFACTURES, &c.

Industrial Chemistry; a Manual for Manufacturers and for Colleges or Technical Schools. Being a Translation of Professors Stohmann and Engler's German Edition of Payen's 'Précis de Chimie Industrielle,' by Dr. J. D. Barry. Edited, and supplemented with Chapters on the Chemistry of the Metals, by B. H. Paul, Ph.D.
8vo. with Plates and Woodcuts. [*In the press.*

Gwilt's Encyclopædia of Architecture, with above 1,600 Woodcuts.
Fifth Edition, with Alterations and Additions, by Wyatt Papworth.
8vo. 52s. 6d.

The Three Cathedrals dedicated to St. Paul in London; their History from the Foundation of the First Building in the Sixth Century to the Proposals for the Adornment of the Present Cathedral. By W. Longman, F.S.A.
With numerous Illustrations. Square crown 8vo. 21s.

Lathes and Turning, Simple, Mechanical, and Ornamental.
By W. Henry Northcott.
With 240 Illustrations. 8vo. 18s.

Hints on Household Taste in Furniture, Upholstery, and other Details. By Charles L. Eastlake, Architect.
New Edition, with about 90 Illustrations. Square crown 8vo. 14s.

Handbook of Practical Telegraphy.
By R. S. Culley, Memb. Inst. C.E. Engineer-in-Chief of Telegraphs to the Post-Office.
Sixth Edition, Plates & Woodcuts. 8vo. 16s.

Principles of Mechanism, for the use of Students in the Universities, and for Engineering Students.
By R. Willis, M.A. F.R.S. Professor in the University of Cambridge.
Second Edition, with 374 Woodcuts. 8vo. 18s.

Perspective; or, the Art of Drawing what one Sees: for the Use of those Sketching from Nature.
By Lieut. W. H. Collins, R.E. F.R.A.S.
With 37 Woodcuts. Crown 8vo. 5s.

Encyclopædia of Civil Engineering, Historical, Theoretical, and Practical. By E. Cresy, C.E.
With above 3,000 Woodcuts. 8vo. 42s.

A Treatise on the Steam Engine, in its various applications to Mines, Mills, Steam Navigation, Railways and Agriculture.

By *J. Bourne, C.E.*

With *Portrait*, 37 *Plates, and* 546 *Woodcuts.* 4*to.* 42*s.*

Catechism of the Steam Engine, in its various Applications.

By *John Bourne, C.E.*

New Edition, with 89 *Woodcuts. Fcp.* 8*vo.* 6*s.*

Handbook of the Steam Engine.

By *J. Bourne, C.E. forming a* KEY *to the Author's Catechism of the Steam Engine.*

With 67 *Woodcuts. Fcp.* 8*vo.* 9*s.*

Recent Improvements in the Steam Engine.

By *J. Bourne, C.E.*

With 124 *Woodcuts. Fcp.* 8*vo.* 6*s.*

Lowndes's Engineer's Handbook; explaining the Principles which should guide the Young Engineer in the Construction of Machinery.

Post 8*vo.* 5*s.*

Ure's Dictionary of Arts, Manufactures, and Mines. Seventh Edition, re-written and greatly enlarged by R. Hunt, F.R.S. assisted by numerous Contributors.

With 2,100 *Woodcuts.* 3 *vols. medium* 8*vo. price* £5. 5*s.*

Practical Treatise on Metallurgy,

Adapted from the last German Edition of Professor Kerl's Metallurgy by W. Crookes, F.R.S. &c. and E. Röhrig, Ph.D.

3 *vols.* 8*vo. with* 625 *Woodcuts.* £4. 19*s.*

Treatise on Mills and Millwork.

By *Sir W. Fairbairn, Bt.*

With 18 *Plates and* 322 *Woodcuts.* 2 *vols.* 8*vo.* 32*s.*

Useful Information for Engineers.

By *Sir W. Fairbairn, Bt.*

With many Plates and Woodcuts. 3 *vols. crown* 8*vo.* 31*s.* 6*d.*

The Application of Cast and Wrought Iron to Building Purposes.

By *Sir W. Fairbairn, Bt.*

With 6 *Plates and* 118 *Woodcuts.* 8*vo.* 16*s.*

Practical Handbook of Dyeing and Calico-Printing.

By *W. Crookes, F.R.S. &c.*

With numerous Illustrations and Specimen of Dyed Textile Fabrics. 8*vo.* 42*s.*

Occasional Papers on Subjects connected with Civil Engineering, Gunnery, and Naval Architecture.
By Michael Scott, Memb. Inst. C.E. & of Inst. N.A.
2 vols. 8vo. with Plates, 42s.

Mitchell's Manual of Practical Assaying.
Fourth Edition, revised, with the Recent Discoveries incorporated, by W. Crookes, F.R.S.
8vo. Woodcuts, 31s. 6d.

Loudon's Encyclopædia of Gardening; comprising the Theory and Practice of Horticulture, Floriculture, Arboriculture, and Landscape Gardening.
With 1,000 Woodcuts. 8vo. 21s.

Loudon's Encyclopædia of Agriculture; comprising the Laying-out, Improvement, and Management of Landed Property, and the Cultivation and Economy of the Productions of Agriculture.
With 1,100 Woodcuts. 8vo. 21s.

RELIGIOUS and MORAL WORKS.

An Exposition of the 39 Articles, Historical and Doctrinal.
By E. H. Browne, D.D. Bishop of Winchester.
New Edition. 8vo. 16s.

Historical Lectures on the Life of Our Lord Jesus Christ.
By C. J. Ellicott, D.D.
Fifth Edition. 8vo. 12s.

An Introduction to the Theology of the Church of England, in an Exposition of the 39 Articles. By Rev. T. P. Boultbee, LL.D.
Fcp. 8vo. 6s.

Three Essays on Religion: Nature; the Utility of Religion; Theism.
By John Stuart Mill.
Second Edition. 8vo. price 10s. 6d.

Sermons Chiefly on the Interpretation of Scripture.
By the late Rev. Thomas Arnold, D.D.
8vo. price 7s. 6d.

Sermons preached in the Chapel of Rugby School; with an Address before Confirmation.
By the late Rev. Thomas Arnold, D.D.
Fcp. 8vo. price 3s. 6d.

Christian Life, its Course, its Hindrances, and its Helps; Sermons preached mostly in the Chapel of Rugby School. By the late Rev. Thomas Arnold, D.D.
8vo. 7s. 6d.

Christian Life, its Hopes, its Fears, and its Close; Sermons preached mostly in the Chapel of Rugby School. By the late Rev. Thomas Arnold, D.D.
8vo. 7s. 6d.

Synonyms of the Old Testament, their Bearing on Christian Faith and Practice. By Rev. R. B. Girdlestone.
8vo. 15s.

The Primitive and Catholic Faith in Relation to the Church of England. By the Rev. B. W. Savile, M.A. Rector of Shillingford, Exeter; Author of 'The Truth of the Bible' &c.
8vo. price 7s.

Reasons of Faith; or, the Order of the Christian Argument Developed and Explained. By Rev. G. S. Drew, M.A.
Second Edition Fcp. 8vo. 6s.

The Eclipse of Faith; or a Visit to a Religious Sceptic. By Henry Rogers.
Latest Edition. Fcp. 8vo. 5s.

Defence of the Eclipse of Faith. By Henry Rogers.
Latest Edition. Fcp. 8vo. 3s. 6d.

A Critical and Grammatical Commentary on St. Paul's Epistles. By C. J. Ellicott, D.D.

8vo. Galatians, 8s. 6d. Ephesians, 8s. 6d. Pastoral Epistles, 10s. 6d. Philippians, Colossians, & Philemon, 10s. 6d. Thessalonians, 7s. 6d.

The Life and Epistles of St. Paul. By Rev. W. J. Conybeare, M.A. and Very Rev. J. S. Howson, D.D.

LIBRARY EDITION, with all the Original Illustrations, Maps, Landscapes on Steel, Woodcuts, &c. 2 vols. 4to. 42s.

INTERMEDIATE EDITION, with a Selection of Maps, Plates, and Woodcuts. 2 vols. square crown 8vo, 21s.

STUDENT'S EDITION, revised and condensed, with 46 Illustrations and Maps. 1 vol. crown 8vo. 9s.

An Examination into the Doctrine and Practice of Confession. By the Rev. W. E. Jelf, B.D.
8vo. price 7s. 6d.

Fasting Communion, how Binding in England by the Canons. With the testimony of the Early Fathers. An Historical Essay.

By the Rev. H. T. Kingdon, M.A.

Second Edition. 8vo. 10s. 6d.

Evidence of the Truth of the Christian Religion derived from the Literal Fulfilment of Prophecy.

By Alexander Keith, D.D.

40th Edition, with numerous Plates. Square 8vo. 12s. 6d. or in post 8vo. with 5 Plates, 6s.

Historical and Critical Commentary on the Old Testament; with a New Translation.

By M. M. Kalisch, Ph.D.

Vol. I. Genesis, 8vo. 18s. or adapted for the General Reader, 12s. Vol. II. Exodus, 15s. or adapted for the General Reader, 12s. Vol. III. Leviticus, Part I. 15s. or adapted for the General Reader, 8s. Vol. IV. Leviticus, Part II. 15s. or adapted for the General Reader, 8s.

The History and Literature of the Israelites, according to the Old Testament and the Apocrypha.

By C. De Rothschild and A. De Rothschild.

Second Edition. 2 vols. crown 8vo. 12s. 6d.
Abridged Edition, in 1 vol. fcp. 8vo. 3s. 6d.

Ewald's History of Israel.
Translated from the German by J. E. Carpenter, M.A. with Preface by R. Martineau, M.A.

5 vols. 8vo. 63s.

The Types of Genesis, briefly considered as revealing the Development of Human Nature.
By Andrew Jukes.

Third Edition. Crown 8vo. 7s. 6d.

The Second Death and the Restitution of all Things; with some Preliminary Remarks on the Nature and Inspiration of Holy Scripture. (A Letter to a Friend.)
By Andrew Jukes.

Fourth Edition. Crown 8vo. 3s. 6d.

Commentary on Epistle to the Romans.
By Rev. W. A. O'Conor.

Crown 8vo. 3s. 6d.

A Commentary on the Gospel of St. John.
By Rev. W. A. O'Conor.

Crown 8vo. 10s. 6d.

The Epistle to the Hebrews; with Analytical Introduction and Notes.
By Rev. W. A. O'Conor.

Crown 8vo. 4s. 6d.

Thoughts for the Age.
By Elizabeth M. Sewell.
New Edition. Fcp. 8vo. 3s. 6d.

Passing Thoughts on Religion.
By Elizabeth M. Sewell.
Fcp. 8vo. 3s. 6d.

Preparation for the Holy Communion; the Devotions chiefly from the works of Jeremy Taylor.
By Elizabeth M. Sewell.
32mo. 3s.

Bishop Jeremy Taylor's Entire Works; with Life by Bishop Heber.
Revised and corrected by the Rev. C. P. Eden.
10 vols. £5. 5s.

Hymns of Praise and Prayer.
Collected and edited by Rev. J. Martineau, LL.D.
Crown 8vo. 4s. 6d. 32mo. 1s. 6d.

Spiritual Songs for the Sundays and Holidays throughout the Year.
By J. S. B. Monsell, LL.D.
9th Thousand. Fcp. 8vo. 5s. 18mo. 2s.

Lyra Germanica; Hymns translated from the German by Miss C. Winkworth.
Fcp. 8vo. 5s.

Endeavours after the Christian Life; Discourses.
By Rev. J. Martineau, LL.D.
Fifth Edition. Crown 8vo. 7s. 6d.

Lectures on the Pentateuch & the Moabite Stone; with Appendices.
By J. W. Colenso, D.D. Bishop of Natal.
8vo. 12s.

Supernatural Religion; an Inquiry into the Reality of Divine Revelation.
Fifth Edition. 2 vols. 8vo. 24s.

The Pentateuch and Book of Joshua Critically Examined.
By J. W. Colenso, D.D. Bishop of Natal.
Crown 8vo. 6s.

The New Bible Commentary, by Bishops and other Clergy of the Anglican Church, critically examined by the Rt. Rev. J. W. Colenso, D.D. Bishop of Natal.
8vo. 25s.

TRAVELS, VOYAGES, &c.

Italian Alps; Sketches in the Mountains of Ticino, Lombardy, the Trentino, and Venetia. By Douglas W. Freshfield, Editor of 'The Alpine Journal.'
Square crown 8vo. Illustrations. 15s.

Here and There in the Alps. By the Hon. Frederica Plunket.
With Vignette-title. Post 8vo. 6s. 6d.

The Valleys of Tirol; their Traditions and Customs, and How to Visit them. By Miss R. H. Busk.
With Frontispiece and 3 Maps. Crown 8vo. 12s. 6d.

Two Years in Fiji, a Descriptive Narrative of a Residence in the Fijian Group of Islands; with some Account of the Fortunes of Foreign Settlers and Colonists up to the time of British Annexation. By Litton Forbes, M.D. L.R.C.P. F.R.G.S. late Medical Officer to the German Consulate, Apia, Navigator Islands.
Crown 8vo. 8s. 6d.

Eight Years in Ceylon. By Sir Samuel W. Baker, M.A. F.R.G.S.
·New Edition, with Illustrations engraved on Wood by G. Pearson. Crown 8vo: Price 7s. 6d.

The Rifle and the Hound in Ceylon. By Sir Samuel W. Baker, M.A. F.R.G.S.
New Edition, with Illustrations engraved on Wood by G. Pearson. Crown 8vo. Price 7s. 6d.

Meeting the Sun; a Journey all round the World through Egypt, China, Japan, and California. By William Simpson, F.R.G.S.
With Heliotypes and Woodcuts. 8vo. 24s.

The Dolomite Mountains. Excursions through Tyrol, Carinthia, Carniola, and Friuli. By J. Gilbert and G. C. Churchill, F.R.G.S.
With Illustrations. Sq. cr. 8vo. 21s.

The Alpine Club Map of the Chain of Mont Blanc, from an actual Survey in 1863-1864. By A. Adams-Reilly, F.R.G.S. M.A.C.
In Chromolithography, on extra stout drawing paper 10s. or mounted on canvas in a folding case, 12s. 6d.

NEW WORKS PUBLISHED BY LONGMANS & CO.

The Alpine Club Map of the Valpelline, the Val Tournanche, and the Southern Valleys of the Chain of Monte Rosa, from actual Survey. By A. Adams-Reilly, F.R.G.S. M.A.C.

Price 6s. on extra Stout Drawing Paper, or 7s. 6d. mounted in a Folding Case.

Untrodden Peaks and Unfrequented Valleys; a Midsummer Ramble among the Dolomites. By Amelia B. Edwards.

With numerous Illustrations. 8vo. 21s.

The Alpine Club Map of Switzerland, with parts of the Neighbouring Countries, on the scale of Four Miles to an Inch. Edited by R. C. Nichols, F.S.A. F.R.G.S.

In Four Sheets, in Portfolio, price 42s. coloured, or 34s. uncoloured.

The Alpine Guide. By John Ball, M.R.I.A. late President of the Alpine Club.

Post 8vo. with Maps and other Illustrations.

Eastern Alps.
Price 10s. 6d.

Central Alps, including all the Oberland District.
Price 7s. 6d.

Western Alps, including Mont Blanc, Monte Rosa, Zermatt, &c.
Price 6s. 6d.

Introduction on Alpine Travelling in general, and on the Geology of the Alps.
Price 1s. Either of the Three Volumes or Parts of the 'Alpine Guide' may be had with this Introduction prefixed, 1s. extra. The 'Alpine Guide' may also be had in Ten separate Parts, or districts, price 2s. 6d. each.

Guide to the Pyrenees, for the use of Mountaineers. By Charles Packe.

Second Edition, with Maps &c. and Appendix. Crown 8vo. 7s. 6d.

How to See Norway; embodying the Experience of Six Summer Tours in that Country. By J. R. Campbell.

With Map and 5 Woodcuts, fcp. 8vo. 5s.

Visits to Remarkable Places, and Scenes illustrative of striking Passages in English History and Poetry. By William Howitt.

2 vols. 8vo. Woodcuts, 25s.

WORKS of FICTION.

Whispers from Fairyland.
By the Rt. Hon. E. H. Knatchbull-Hugessen, M.P. Author of 'Stories for my Children,' &c.

With 9 Illustrations from Original Designs engraved on Wood by G. Pearson. Crown 8vo. price 6s.

Lady Willoughby's Diary during the Reign of Charles the First, the Protectorate, and the Restoration.

Crown 8vo. 7s. 6d.

The Folk-Lore of Rome, collected by Word of Mouth from the People.
By Miss R. H. Busk.

Crown 8vo. 12s. 6d.

Becker's Gallus; or Roman Scenes of the Time of Augustus.

Post 8vo. 7s. 6d.

Becker's Charicles: Illustrative of Private Life of the Ancient Greeks.

Post 8vo. 7s. 6d.

Tales of the Teutonic Lands.
By Rev. G. W. Cox, M.A. and E. H. Jones.

Crown 8vo. 10s. 6d.

Tales of Ancient Greece.
By the Rev. G. W. Cox, M.A.

Crown 8vo. 6s. 6d.

The Modern Novelist's Library.

Atherstone Priory, 2s. boards; 2s. 6d. cloth.
Mlle. Mori, 2s. boards; 2s. 6d. cloth.
The Burgomaster's Family, 2s. and 2s. 6d.
MELVILLE'S Digby Grand, 2s. and 2s. 6d.
———— Gladiators, 2s. and 2s. 6d.
———— Good for Nothing, 2s. & 2s. 6d.
———— Holmby House, 2s. and 2s. 6d.
———— Interpreter, 2s. and 2s. 6d.
———— Kate Coventry, 2s. and 2s. 6d.
———— Queen's Maries, 2s. and 2s. 6d.
———— General Bounce, 2s. and 2s. 6d.
TROLLOPE'S Warden, 1s. 6d. and 2s.
———— Barchester Towers, 2s. & 2s. 6d.
BRAMLEY-MOORE'S Six Sisters of the Valleys, 2s. boards; 2s. 6d. cloth.

Novels and Tales.
By the Right Hon. Benjamin Disraeli, M.P.

Cabinet Editions, complete in Ten Volumes, crown 8vo. 6s. each, as follows:—

Lothair, 6s.	Venetia, 6s.
Coningsby, 6s.	Alroy, Ixion, &c. 6s.
Sybil, 6s.	Young Duke, &c. 6s.
Tancred, 6s.	Vivian Grey, 6s.
Henrietta Temple, 6s.	
Contarini Fleming, &c. 6s.	

Stories and Tales.
By Elizabeth M. Sewell, Author of 'The Child's First History of Rome,' 'Principles of Education,' &c. Cabinet Edition, in Ten Volumes:—

Amy Herbert, 2s. 6d.	Ivors, 2s. 6d.
Gertrude, 2s. 6d.	Katharine Ashton, 2s. 6d.
Earl's Daughter, 2s. 6d.	Margaret Percival, 3s. 6d.
Experience of Life, 2s. 6d.	Laneton Parsonage, 3s. 6d.
Cleve Hall, 2s. 6d.	Ursula, 3s. 6d.

POETRY and THE DRAMA.

Ballads and Lyrics of Old France; with other Poems. By A. Lang.
Square fcp. 8vo. 5s.

Moore's Lalla Rookh, Tenniel's Edition, with 68 Wood Engravings.
Fcp. 4to. 21s.

Moore's Irish Melodies, Maclise's Edition, with 161 Steel Plates.
Super-royal 8vo. 31s. 6d.

Miniature Edition of Moore's Irish Melodies, with Maclise's 161 Illustrations reduced in Lithography.
Imp. 16mo. 10s. 6d.

Milton's Lycidas and Epitaphium Damonis. Edited, with Notes and Introduction, by C. S. Jerram, M.A.
Crown 8vo. 2s. 6d.

Lays of Ancient Rome; with Ivry and the Armada. By the Right Hon. Lord Macaulay.
16mo. 3s. 6d.

Lord Macaulay's Lays of Ancient Rome. With 90 Illustrations on Wood from Drawings by G. Scharf.
Fcp. 4to. 21s.

Miniature Edition of Lord Macaulay's Lays of Ancient Rome, with Scharf's 90 Illustrations reduced in Lithography.
Imp. 16mo. 10s. 6d.

Horatii Opera, Library Edition, with English Notes, Marginal References and various Readings. Edited by Rev. J. E. Yonge.
8vo. 21s.

Southey's Poetical Works with the Author's last Corrections and Additions.
Medium 8vo. with Portrait, 14s.

Poems by Jean Ingelow.
2 vols. Fcp. 8vo. 10s.
FIRST SERIES, containing 'Divided,' 'The Star's Monument,' &c. 16th Thousand. *Fcp. 8vo. 5s.*
SECOND SERIES, 'A Story of Doom,' 'Gladys and her Island,' &c. 5th Thousand. *Fcp. 8vo. 5s.*

Poems by Jean Ingelow. First Series, with nearly 100 Woodcut Illustrations.
Fcp. 4to. 21s.

Bowdler's Family Shakspeare, cheaper Genuine Edition.
Complete in 1 vol. medium 8vo. large type, with 36 Woodcut Illustrations, 14s. or in 6 vols. fcp. 8vo. price 21s.

The Æneid of Virgil Translated into English Verse.
By J. Conington, M.A.
Crown 8vo. 9s.

RURAL SPORTS, HORSE and CATTLE MANAGEMENT, &c.

Down the Road; or, Reminiscences of a Gentleman Coachman.
By C. T. S. Birch Reynardson.
Second Edition, with 12 Coloured Illustrations from Paintings by H. Alken. Medium 8vo. price 21s.

Blaine's Encyclopædia of Rural Sports; Complete Accounts, Historical, Practical, and Descriptive, of Hunting, Shooting, Fishing, Racing, &c.
With above 600 Woodcuts (20 from Designs by JOHN LEECH). 8vo. 21s.

A Book on Angling: a Treatise on the Art of Angling in every branch, including full Illustrated Lists of Salmon Flies.
By Francis Francis.
Post 8vo. Portrait and Plates, 15s.

Wilcocks's Sea-Fisherman: comprising the Chief Methods of Hook and Line Fishing, a glance at Nets, and remarks on Boats and Boating.
New Edition, with 80 Woodcuts. Post 8vo. 12s. 6d.

The Ox, his Diseases and their Treatment; with an Essay on Parturition in the Cow.
By J. R. Dobson, Memb. R.C.V.S.
Crown 8vo. with Illustrations 7s. 6d.

Youatt on the Horse.
Revised and enlarged by W. Watson, M.R.C.V.S.
8vo. Woodcuts, 12s. 6d.

Youatt's Work on the Dog, revised and enlarged.
8vo. Woodcuts, 6s.

Horses and Stables.
By Colonel F. Fitzwygram, XV. the King's Hussars.
With 24 Plates of Illustrations. 8vo. 10s. 6d.

The Dog in Health and Disease.
By Stonehenge.
With 73 Wood Engravings. Square crown 8vo. 7s. 6d.

The Greyhound.
By Stonehenge.
Revised Edition, with 25 Portraits of Greyhounds, &c. Square crown 8vo. 15s.

Stables and Stable Fittings.
By W. Miles, Esq.
Imp. 8vo. with 13 Plates, 15s.

The Horse's Foot, and how to keep it Sound.
By W. Miles, Esq.
Ninth Edition. Imp. 8vo. Woodcuts, 12s. 6d.

A Plain Treatise on Horse-shoeing.
By W. Miles, Esq.
Sixth Edition. Post 8vo. Woodcuts, 2s. 6d.

Remarks on Horses' Teeth, addressed to Purchasers.
By W. Miles, Esq.
Post 8vo. 1s. 6d.

The Fly-Fisher's Entomology.
By Alfred Ronalds.
With 20 coloured Plates. 8vo. 14s.

The Dead Shot, or Sportsman's Complete Guide.
By Marksman.
Fcp. 8vo. with Plates, 5s.

WORKS of UTILITY and GENERAL INFORMATION.

Maunder's Treasury of Knowledge and Library of Reference; comprising an English Dictionary and Grammar, Universal Gazetteer, Classical Dictionary, Chronology, Law Dictionary, Synopsis of the Peerage, Useful Tables,&c.
Fcp. 8vo. 6s.

Maunder's Biographical Treasury.
Latest Edition, reconstructed and partly rewritten, with about 1,000 additional Memoirs, by W. L. R. Cates.
Fcp. 8vo. 6s.

Maunder's Scientific and Literary Treasury; a Popular Encyclopædia of Science, Literature, and Art.
New Edition, in part rewritten, with above 1,000 new articles, by J. Y. Johnson.
Fcp. 8vo. 6s.

Maunder's Treasury of Geography, Physical, Historical, Descriptive, and Political.
Edited by W. Hughes, F.R.G.S.
With 7 Maps and 16 Plates. Fcp. 8vo. 6s.

Maunder's Historical Treasury; General Introductory Outlines of Universal History, and a Series of Separate Histories. Revised by the Rev. G. W. Cox, M.A.
Fcp. 8vo. 6s.

Maunder's Treasury of Natural History; or Popular Dictionary of Zoology.
Revised and corrected Edition. Fcp. 8vo. with 900 Woodcuts, 6s.

The Treasury of Bible Knowledge; being a Dictionary of the Books, Persons, Places, Events, and other Matters of which mention is made in Holy Scripture. By Rev. J. Ayre, M.A.
With Maps, 15 Plates, and numerous Woodcuts. Fcp. 8vo. 6s.

Collieries and Colliers: a Handbook of the Law and Leading Cases relating thereto. By J. C. Fowler.
Third Edition. Fcp. 8vo. 7s. 6d.

The Theory and Practice of Banking. By H. D. Macleod, M.A.
Second Edition. 2 vols. 8vo. 30s.

Modern Cookery for Private Families, reduced to a System of Easy Practice in a Series of carefully-tested Receipts. By Eliza Acton.
With 8 Plates & 150 Woodcuts. Fcp. 8vo. 6s.

A Practical Treatise on Brewing; with Formulæ for Public Brewers, and Instructions for Private Families. By W. Black.
Fifth Edition. 8vo. 10s. 6d.

Three Hundred Original Chess Problems and Studies. By Jas. Pierce, M.A. and W. T. Pierce.
With many Diagrams. Sq. fcp. 8vo. 7s. 6d. Supplement, price 3s.

The Theory of the Modern Scientific Game of Whist. By W. Pole, F.R.S.
Seventh Edition. Fcp. 8vo. 2s. 6d.

The Cabinet Lawyer; a Popular Digest of the Laws of England, Civil, Criminal, and Constitutional.
Twenty-fourth Edition, corrected and extended. Fcp. 8vo. 9s.

Pewtner's Comprehensive Specifier; a Guide to the Practical Specification of every kind of Building-Artificer's Work. Edited by W. Young.

Crown 8vo. 6s.

Protection from Fire and Thieves. Including the Construction of Locks, Safes, Strong-Room, and Fireproof Buildings; Burglary, and the Means of Preventing it; Fire, its Detection, Prevention, and Extinction; &c. By G. H. Chubb, Assoc. Inst. C.E.

With 32 Woodcuts. Cr. 8vo. 5s.

Chess Openings. By F. W. Longman, Balliol College, Oxford.

Second Edition, revised. Fcp. 8vo. 2s. 6d.

Hints to Mothers on the Management of their Health during the Period of Pregnancy and in the Lying-in Room. By Thomas Bull, M.D.

Fcp. 8vo. 5s.

The Maternal Management of Children in Health and Disease. By Thomas Bull, M.D.

Fcp. 8vo. 5s.

INDEX.

Acton's Modern Cookery 38
Aird's Blackstone Economised 39
Alpine Club Map of Switzerland 33
Alpine Guide (The) 33
Amos's Jurisprudence 10
———— Primer of the Constitution........... 10
Anderson's Strength of Materials 19
Armstrong's Organic Chemistry 19
Arnold's (Dr.) Christian Life 29
———————— Lectures on Modern History 2
———————— Miscellaneous Works 12
———————— School Sermons 28
———————— (T.) Manual of English Literature 12
Atherstone Priory...................................... 34
Autumn Holidays of a Country Parson ... 13
Ayre's Treasury of Bible Knowledge 38

Bacon's Essays, by *Whately* 10
———— Life and Letters, by *Spedding* ... 10
———— Works 10
Bain's Mental and Moral Science............. 11
———— on the Senses and Intellect 11
Baker's Two Works on Ceylon 33
Ball's Guide to the Central Alps 33
———— Guide to the Western Alps............ 33
———— Guide to the Eastern Alps 33
Bancroft's Native Races of the Pacific...... 22
Becker's Charicles and Gallus................... 34
Black's Treatise on Brewing 38
Blackley's German-English Dictionary...... 15
Blaine's Rural Sports 36
Bloxam's Metals 19
Boultbee on 39 Articles............................ 28
Bourne's Catechism of the Steam Engine . 27
———— Handbook of Steam Engine....... 27
———— Treatise on the Steam Engine ... 27
———— Improvements in the same.......... 27
Bowdler's Family *Shakspeare*................... 36
Bramley-Moore's Six Sisters of the Valley . 36
Brande's Dictionary of Science, Literature,
and Art 22
Bray's Philosophy of Necessity 11
Brinkley's Astronomy 18
Browne's Exposition of the 39 Articles...... 28
Brunel's Life of *Brunel* 7
Buckle's History of Civilisation 3
———— Posthumous Remains 12
Buckton's Health in the House 24
Bull's Hints to Mothers 39
———— Maternal Management of Children . 39
Burgomaster's Family (The) 34
Burke's Rise of Great Families 8

Burke's Vicissitudes of Families 8
Busk's Folk-lore of Rome 34
———— Valleys of Tirol 32

Cabinet Lawyer...................................... 38
Campbell's Norway 33
Cates's Biographical Dictionary................ 8
———— and *Woodward's* Encyclopædia ... 5
Changed Aspects of Unchanged Truths ... 13
Chesney's Indian Polity 3
———— Modern Military Biography...... 3
———— Waterloo Campaign 3
Chubb on Protection 39
Clough's Lives from Plutarch.................... 4
Codrington's Life and Letters 7
Colenso on Moabite Stone &c. 31
———— 's Pentateuch and Book of Joshua. 31
———— Speaker's Bible Commentary ... 31
Collins's Perspective................................ 26
Commonplace Philosopher in Town and
Country, by A. K. H. B. 14
Comte's Positive Polity 8
Congreve's Essays 9
———— Politics of Aristotle 10
Conington's Translation of Virgil's Æneid 36
———— Miscellaneous Writings.......... 13
Contanseau's Two French Dictionaries ... 14
Conybeare and *Howson's* Life and Epistles
of St. Paul.. 29
Counsel and Comfort from a City Pulpit... 13
Cox's (G. W.) Aryan Mythology 4
———— Crusades 6
———— History of Greece 4
———— School ditto 4
———— Tale of the Great Persian
War.. 4
———— Tales of Ancient Greece ... 34
———— and *Jones's* Teutonic Tales 34
Crawley's Thucydides 4
Creasy on British Constitution 3
Cresy's Encyclopædia of Civil Engineering 26
Critical Essays of a Country Parson......... 14
Crookes's Chemical Analysis 24
———— Dyeing and Calico-printing......... 27
Culley's Handbook of Telegraphy............. 26

Dead Shot (The), by *Marksman* 37
De Caisne and *Le Maout's* Botany 23
De Morgan's Paradoxes 13
De Tocqueville's Democracy in America... 9
Disraeli's Lord George Bentinck 7

NEW WORKS PUBLISHED BY LONGMANS & CO.

Disraeli's Novels and Tales 34
Dobson on the Ox 36
Dove's Law of Storms 18
Doyle's Fairyland 25
Drew's Reasons of Faith 29

Eastlake's Hints on Household Taste 26
Edwards's Rambles among the Dolomites 33
Elements of Botany 22
Ellicott's Commentary on Ephesians 29
——————————————— Galatians 29
——————————————— Pastoral Epist. . 29
——————————————— Philippians, &c. . 29
——————————————— Thessalonians . . 29
—————— Lectures on Life of Christ 28
Evans's Ancient Stone Implements 22
Ewald's History of Israel 30

Fairbairn's Application of Cast and Wrought Iron to Building ... 27
—————— Information for Engineers 27
—————— Treatise on Mills and Millwork . 27
Farrar's Chapters on Language 13
—————— Families of Speech 13
Fitzwygram on Horses and Stables 36
Forbes's Two Years in Fiji 32
Fowler's Collieries and Colliers 38
Francis's Fishing Book 36
Freeman's Historical Geography of Europe 6
Freshfield's Italian Alps 32
Froude's English in Ireland 2
—————— History of England 2
—————— Short Studies 12

Gairdner's Houses of Lancaster and York 6
Ganot's Elementary Physics 19
—————— Natural Philosophy 19
Gardiner's Buckingham and Charles 3
—————— Thirty Years' War 6
Gilbert and Churchill's Dolomites 32
Girdlestone's Bible Synonyms 29
Goodeve's Mechanics 19
—————— Mechanism 19
Grant's Ethics of Aristotle 10
Graver Thoughts of a Country Parson 14
Greville's Journal 1
Griffin's Algebra and Trigonometry 20
Grove on Correlation of Physical Forces 18
Gwilt's Encyclopædia of Architecture ... 26

Harrison's Order and Progress 9
Hartley on the Air 18
Hartwig's Aerial World 21
—————— Polar World 21
—————— Sea and its Living Wonders 21
—————— Subterranean World 21
—————— Tropical World 21
Haughton's Animal Mechanics 19
Hayward's Biographical and Critical Essays 7
Heath on Energy 20
Heer's Switzerland 22
Helmholtz on Tone 22

Helmholtz's Scientific Lectures 18
Helmsley's Trees, Shrubs, and Herbaceous Plants 23
Herschel's Outlines of Astronomy 18
Holland's Fragmentary Papers 20
—————— Recollections 7
Howitt's Visits to Remarkable Places ... 32
Hullah's History of Modern Music 23
Hume's Essays 11
—————— Treatise on Human Nature 11

Ihne's History of Rome 5
Ingelow's Poems 35

Jameson's Legends of Saints and Martyrs 25
—————— Legends of the Madonna 25
—————— Legends of the Monastic Orders . 25
—————— Legends of the Saviour 25
Jelf on Confession 29
Jenkin's Electricity and Magnetism 19
Jerram's Lycidas of Milton 35
Jerrold's Life of Napoleon 1
Johnston's Geographical Dictionary 16
Jukes's Types of Genesis 30
—————— on Second Death 30

Kalisch's Commentary on the Bible 30
Keith's Evidence of Prophecy 30
Kerl's Metallurgy, by Crookes and Röhrig 27
Kingdon on Communion 30
Kirby and Spence's Entomology 20
Knatchbull-Hugessen's Whispers from Fairy-Land 34

Landscapes, Churches, &c. by A. K. H. B. 13
Lang's Ballads and Lyrics 35
Latham's English Dictionary 14
—————— Handbook of the English Language 14
Laughton's Nautical Surveying 18
Lawrence on Rocks 22
Lecky's History of European Morals 5
—————— Rationalism 5
—————— Leaders of Public Opinion 8
Leisure Hours in Town, by A. K. H. B. .. 13
Lessons of Middle Age, by A. K. H. B. .. 13
Lewes's Biographical History of Philosophy 6
Liddell and Scott's Greek-English Lexicons 15
Lindley and Moore's Treasury of Botany 23
Lloyd's Magnetism 20
—————— Wave-Theory of Light 20
Longman's Chess Openings 39
—————— Edward the Third 2
—————— Lectures on History of England . 2
—————— Old and New St. Paul's 26
Loudon's Encyclopædia of Agriculture ... 28
—————— Gardening 28
—————— Plants 23
Lowndes's Engineer's Handbook 27
Lubbock's Origin of Civilisation 22
Lyra Germanica 31

F

NEW WORKS published by LONGMANS & CO.

Macaulay's (Lord) Essays 2
——— History of England .. 2
——— Lays of Ancient Rome 25, 35
——— Life and Letters......... 7
——— Miscellaneous Writings 12
——— Speeches 12
——— Works 2
McCulloch's Dictionary of Commerce 16
Macleod's Principles of Economical Philosophy 10
——— Theory and Practice of Banking 38
Mademoiselle Mori 34
Malleson's Genoese Studies 3
——— Native States of India............ 3
Marshall's Physiology 24
Marshman's History of India............... 3
——— Life of Havelock 8
Martineau's Christian Life................. 31
——— Hymns....................... 31
Maunder's Biographical Treasury.......... 37
——— Geographical Treasury 37
——— Historical Treasury 38
——— Scientific and Literary Treasury 37
——— Treasury of Knowledge 37
——— Treasury of Natural History ... 38
Maxwell's Theory of Heat 19
May's History of Democracy............... 2
——— History of England 2
Melville's Digby Grand 34
——— General Bounce 34
——— Gladiators 34
——— Good for Nothing 34
——— Holmby House 34
——— Interpreter 34
——— Kate Coventry 34
——— Queen's Maries 34
Mendelssohn's Letters 8
Menzies' Forest Trees and Woodland Scenery 23
Merivale's Fall of the Roman Republic ... 4
——— General History of Rome ... 4
——— Romans under the Empire 4
Merrifield's Arithmetic and Mensuration... 19
——— Magnetism 18
Miles on Horse's Foot and Horse Shoeing 37
——— on Horse's Teeth and Stables......... 37
Mill (J.) on the Mind 10
——— (J. S.) on Liberty............... 9
——— Subjection of Women........... 9
——— on Representative Government 9
——— Utilitarianism........... 9
———'s Autobiography 7
——— Dissertations and Discussions 9
——— Essays on Religion &c. 28
——— Hamilton's Philosophy 9
——— System of Logic 9
——— Political Economy 9
——— Unsettled Questions 9
Miller's Elements of Chemistry 24
——— Inorganic Chemistry................ 19
Minto's (Lord) Life and Letters........... 7
Mitchell's Manual of Assaying 28
Modern Novelist's Library.................. 34
Monsell's 'Spiritual Songs' 31
Moore's Irish Melodies, illustrated 25, 35
——— Lalla Rookh, illustrated 25, 35
Morant's Game Preservers.................. 21
Morell's Elements of Psychology 11
——— Mental Philosophy 11
Müller's Chips from a German Workshop. 12

Müller's Science of Language 12
——— Science of Religion 5

New Reformation, by *Theodorus* 4
New Testament, Illustrated Edition......... 25
Northcott's Lathes and Turning 26

O'Conor's Commentary on Hebrews 30
——— Romans 30
——— St. John 30
Owen's Comparative Anatomy and Physiology of Vertebrate Animals 20

Packe's Guide to the Pyrenees 33
Pattison's Casaubon......................... 7
Payen's Industrial Chemistry............... 26
Pewtner's Comprehensive Specifier 39
Pierce's Chess Problems 38
Plunket's Travels in the Alps............... 32
Pole's Game of Whist 38
Prendergast's Mastery of Languages 15
Present-Day Thoughts, by A. K. H. B. ... 14
Proctor's Astronomical Essays 17
——— Moon 17
——— Orbs around Us 17
——— Other Worlds than Ours 17
——— Saturn 17
——— Scientific Essays (New Series) ... 20
——— Sun 17
——— Transits of Venus 16
——— Two Star Atlases.............. 17
——— Universe 16
Public Schools Atlas 16
——— Modern Geography 16
——— Ancient Geography 16

Rawlinson's Parthia......................... 5
——— Sassanians 5
Recreations of a Country Parson 13
Redgrave's Dictionary of Artists 25
Reilly's Map of Mont Blanc 32
——— Monte Rosa................ 33
Reresby's Memoirs 7
Reynardson's Down the Road 36
Rich's Dictionary of Antiquities 15
River's Rose Amateur's Guide 22
Rogers's Eclipse of Faith................... 29
——— Defence of Eclipse of Faith 29
——— Essays...................... 9
Roget's Thesaurus of English Words and Phrases 14
Ronald's Fly-Fisher's Entomology 37
Rothschild's Israelites 30
Russell on the Christian Religion............ 6
———'s Recollections and Suggestions ... 2

Sandars's Justinian's Institutes 10
Savile on Apparitions....................... 13
——— on Primitive Faith 29

NEW WORKS PUBLISHED BY LONGMANS & CO. 43

Schellen's Spectrum Analysis 18
Scott's Lectures on the Fine Arts 24
——— Poems 24
——— Papers on Civil Engineering 28
Seaside Musing, by A. K. H. B. 13
Seebohm's Oxford Reformers of 1498......... 3
——— Protestant Revolution 6
Sewell's Passing Thoughts on Religion...... 31
——— Preparation for Communion 31
——— Stories and Tales 34
——— Thoughts for the Age 31
Shelley's Workshop Appliances 19
Short's Church History 6
Simpson's Meeting the Sun..................... 32
Smith's (Sydney) Essays 12
——— ——— Life and Letters............ 8
——— ——— ——— Miscellaneous Works ... 12
——— ——— Wit and Wisdom 12
——— (Dr. R. A.) Air and Rain 18
Southey's Doctor 13
——— Poetical Works.................... 35
Stanley's History of British Birds 26
Stephen's Ecclesiastical Biography........... 8
Stirling's Secret of Hegel 11
——— Sir *William Hamilton* 11
Stonehenge on the Dog......................... 36
——— on the Greyhound 36
Sunday Afternoons at the Parish Church of a University City, by A. K. H. B. 13
Supernatural Religion 31
Swinbourne's Picture Logic 10

Taylor's History of India 3
——— Manual of Ancient History 6
——— Manual of Modern History 6
——— *(Jeremy)* Works, edited by *Eden*. 31
Text-Books of Science........................... 20
Thomson's Laws of Thought 11
Thorpe's Quantitative Analysis 19
——— and *Muir's* Qualitative Analysis ... 19
Todd (A.) on Parliamentary Government... 2
——— and *Bowman's* Anatomy and Physiology of Man 24
Trench's Realities of Irish Life ..:............. 12
Trollope's Barchester Towers................... 36
——— Warden 36

Tyndall's American Lectures on Light 20
——— Belfast Address ,................... 19
——— Diamagnetism....;................ 20
——— Fragments of Science............. 19
——— Lectures on Electricity 20
——— Lectures on Light 20
——— Lectures on Sound* 20
——— Heat a Mode of Motion 20
——— Molecular Physics..:\.............. 20

Ueberweg's System of Logic 11
Ure's Dictionary of Arts, Manufactures, and Mines 27

Warburton's Edward the Third 6
Watson's Geometry 19
Watts's Dictionary of Chemistry 24
Webb's Objects for Common Telescopes ... 18
Weinhold's Experimental Physics............. 19
Wellington's Life, by *Gleig* 8
Whately's English Synonymes 14
——— Logic 11
——— Rhetoric 11
White and *Donkin's* English Dictionary... 15
——— and *Riddle's* Latin Dictionaries ... 15
Wilcocks's Sea-Fisherman 36
Williams's Aristotle's Ethics................... 10
Willis's Principles of Mechanism............. 26
Willoughby's (Lady) Diary..................... 34
Wood's Bible Animals 22
——— Homes without Hands 21
——— Insects at Home 21
——— Insects Abroad 21
——— Out of Doors 21
——— Strange Dwellings 21

Yonge's English-Greek Lexicons 15,16
——— Horace......................,............ 35
Youatt on the Dog 36
——— on the Horse 36

Zeller's Socrates 5
——— Stoics, Epicureans, and Sceptics... 5

Spottiswoode & Co., Printers, New-street Square, London.

www.ingramcontent.com/pod-product-compliance
Lightning Source LLC
Chambersburg PA
CBHW051735300426
44115CB00007B/573